THE NEW VIRGINIA ONE-DAY TRIP BOOK

For my delightful daughter
Alexis Ashley Smith!

THE NEW VIRGINIA ONE-DAY TRIP BOOK

*From the mountains
to the sea, six geographical
regions offer 375 scenic,
historic and recreational
delights*

JANE OCKERSHAUSEN

EPM Publications, Inc.
McLean, Virginia

Library of Congress Cataloging-in-Publication Data

Ockershausen, Jane.
  The new Virginia one-day trip book / Jane Ockershausen.
    p.   cm.
  Includes index.
  ISBN 1-889324-00-0
  1. Virginia—Tours.
  F224.3.028   1996
  91735504 ' 43—dc20 —dc20
  [917.5504 ' 43]   96-26634
                                                          CIP

EPM Publications, Inc., 1003 Turkey Run Road
  McLean, VA 22101
Printed in the United States of America

Cover and book design by Tom Huestis
Cover photographs courtesy of Virginia Division of Tourism:
  Mabry Mill, Meadows of Dan (p. 271)
  Tomb of the Unknowns, Arlington National Cemetery (p. 29)
  Godspeed, Jamestown Settlement (p. 162)

Contents

THE VIRGINIA ONE-DAY TRIP BOOK

EASTERN SHORE

CENTRAL VIRGINIA

LYNCHBURG

NELSON COUNTY

ORANGE COUNTY

PETERSBURG COUNTY

RICHMOND

SMITH MOUNTAIN LAKE

NEED A GOOD VIRGINIA ROAD MAP?

To obtain a free state road map call (800) 932-5827 or write Virginia Division of Tourism, 901 East Byrd Street, Richmond Virginia 23219. Maps are also available at the 10 Highway Welcome Centers and the local/regional information centers listed below. You can also receive information on Virginia travel by visiting the state's web site, HTT://www.virginia.org.

ABINGDON
ABINGDON VISITORS CENTER
335 Cummings Street
Abingdon, VA 24210
(800) 435-3446

ALEXANDRIA
RAMSAY HOUSE VISITOR CENTER
221 King Street
Alexandria, VA 22314
(703) 838-4200

ARLINGTON
ARLINGTON VISITOR CENTER
735 South 18th Street
Arlington, VA 22202
(800) 677-6267

CHARLOTTESVILLE
CHARLOTTESVILLE/ALBEMARLE
CONVENTION & VISITORS
BUREAU
P.O. Box 161, Route 20 South
Charlottesville, VA 22902
(804) 293-6789

CHINCOTEAGUE
CHINCOTEAGUE CHAMBER OF
COMMERCE
P.O. Box 258
Chincoteague, VA 23336
(804) 336-6161

EASTERN SHORE
EASTERN SHORE TOURISM
COMMISSION
P.O. Box R
Melfa, VA 23410
(804) 786-2460

FAIRFAX CITY
FAIRFAX MUSEUM/VISITOR
CENTER
10209 Main Street
Fairfax, VA 22030
(800) 545-7950

FREDERICKSBURG
FREDERICKSBURG VISITORS
CENTER
706 Caroline Street
Fredericksburg, VA 22401
(800) 678-4748

HAMPTON
HAMPTON VISITOR CENTER
710 Settlers Landing Road
Hampton, VA 23669
(800) 800-2202

LEXINGTON
LEXINGTON VISITORS CENTER
106 E. Washington Street
Lexington, VA 24450
(540) 463-3777

LOUDOUN COUNTY
LOUDOUN TOURISM COUNCIL
108-D South Street, S.E.
Leesburg, VA 22075
(800) 752-6118

LYNCHBURG
LYNCHBURG VISITORS
INFORMATION CENTER
216 12th Street at Church
Lynchburg, VA 25404
(804) 847-1811

NEWPORT NEWS
NEWPORT NEWS TOURIST
INFORMATION CENTER
13560 Jefferson Avenue
Newport News, VA 23606
(800) 333-7787

NORFOLK
NORFOLK VISITOR
INFORMATION CENTER
4th View Street
Norfolk, VA 23503
(800) 368-3097

PETERSBURG
PETERSBURG VISITOR CENTER
425 Cockade Alley
Petersburg, VA 23803
(804) 733-2400

RICHMOND
METRO RICHMOND VISITORS
CENTER
1710 Robin Hood Road
Richmond, VA 23220
(804) 358-5511

SHENANDOAH VALLEY
SHENANDOAH VALLEY TRAVEL
ASSOCIATION
P.O. Box 1040
New Market, VA 22844
(540) 740-3132

SOUTHWEST HIGHLANDS
SOUTHWEST HIGHLANDS
GATEWAY VISITORS CENTER
Factory Merchants of Fort Chiswell
Drawer B-12
Max Meadows, VA 24360
(800) 446-9670

STAUNTON
STAUNTON/AUGUSTA VISITOR
CENTER
1303 Richmond Avenue
Staunton, VA 24401
(800) 332-5219

VIRGINIA BEACH
VIRGINIA BEACH VISITORS
INFORMATION CENTER
2100 Parks Avenue
Virginia Beach, VA 23451
(800) VA-BEACH

WAYNESBORO
WAYNESBORO REGIONAL
VISITOR CENTER
Route 1, Box 446
Afton Mountain, VA 22920
(540) 943-5187

WESTERN HIGHLANDS
WESTERN HIGHLANDS TRAVEL
COUNCIL
241 West Main Street
Covington, VA 24426
(540) 962-2178

WILLIAMSBURG
WILLIAMSBURG VISITOR CENTER
Colonial Williamsburg Foundation
Williamsburg, VA 23185
(800) HISTORY

WINCHESTER
WINCHESTER-FREDERICK
COUNTY VISITORS CENTER
1360 S. Pleasant Valley Road
Winchester, VA 22601
(540) 662-4135

——Discover Virginia!——

Ten years ago when I wrote the first edition of *The Virginia One-Day Trip Book*, I said that life-long residents, newcomers and visitors alike will discover daytrips they never expected to find in or near their own backyards. That still holds true, this edition updates old favorites and adds new destinations to explore. The selections reveal little-known facts and stories often omitted in guidebooks and overlooked on brief visits. This edition expands the scope of the first book to include Virginia's magnificent western mountains and her coastal villages. The book is organized according to the state's six travel regions and there are new attractions in each region.

In revisiting personal favorites throughout the state, I've found that many attractions have made changes. Museums are bigger, new programs added and new information uncovered that change the historical thrust. Carter's Grove, Mariners' Museum and the Yorktown Victory Center are greatly expanded and provide a more enriching experience. I encourage you to visit spots you toured years ago; even if the sites remain the same, your experience of them changes because you see them from a different perspective.

My two decades of travel in Virginia have taken me to hundreds of historic homes, museums, parks and other sites. I find that at each spot visitors learn or see something new. Day trips take only a few hours, so you can pursue new challenges, revive old hobbies, or just concentrate on and expand your current interests. Trips highlight history, horticulture, viticulture, agriculture, astronomy, and a host of other academic disciplines. When you pick a destination, read about the other options in the area. It is often possible to combine several nearby attractions for a diverse day's fun. You can easily plan a weekend or week-long vacation in any of the six regions.

A calendar of events is provided to help you plan outings that include festivals and fairs. Some daytrippers prefer to avoid crowds and for them these popular annual events are occasions to avoid.

When I wrote the first One-Day Trip Book in 1975 most families took an annual two-week vacation. Nowadays more fami-

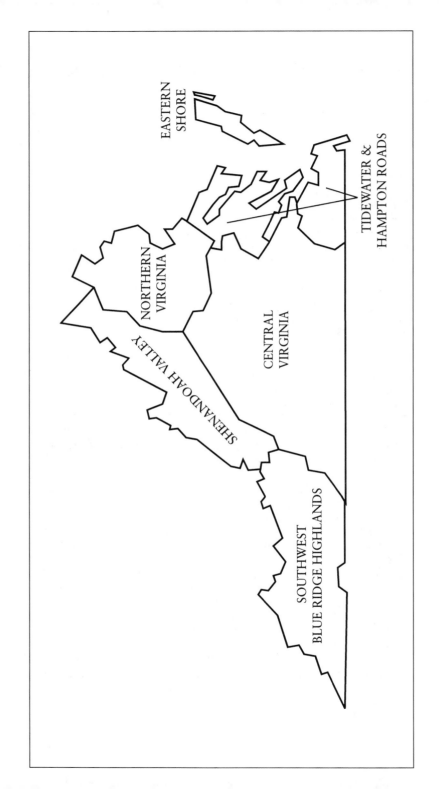

lies opt for short mini-vacations. The nine One-Day Trip Books are written for these travelers. They realize that short excursions spaced weekly or monthly throughout the year offer a fall fling, an escape from the winter doldrums, a jump on spring and a wide array of outdoor summer recreation. One-day trips provide enrichment for the whole family and create shared experiences that children will long remember.

Timing is important, so before beginning your trip read the entire selection. Nothing is worse than arriving to discover the attraction is closed for the day. Hours of operation are given at the end of each selection but these can change, so it's best to double check.

Just remember that yes, Santa Claus, there is a Virginia!

ACKNOWLEDGMENTS

A special thanks to Martha Steger, Director of Promotion and Media Development at the Virginia Department of Economic Development. Her assistance made my journeys through Virginia easier and more productive. I would also like to thank Diann Stutz of the Hampton Department of Convention & Tourism and Catherine Fox with The Roanoke Valley Convention & Visitors Bureau.

——Northern Virginia——

This more than any other, is a region full of contrasts—bustling cities and bucolic countryside. Even within the cities there is contrast, the past has been preserved within the context of vibrant living communities: Alexandria, Fredericksburg and Leesburg.

Names from the pages of history, trod this region. George Washington's beloved home, Mount Vernon, still offers a commanding view of the Potomac River. The gristmill he owned is adjacent to his plantation. Nearby, on land Washington gave as a wedding gift, is Woodlawn, the home of his foster daughter Nellie Parke Custis and Lawrence Lewis, the son of his sister Betty. Kenmore, Betty's home can be visited in Fredericksburg. It is just a few steps away from the Mary Washington House, home of George and Betty's mother. Their brother Charles's Rising Sun Tavern is also nearby. In Alexandria, Washington worshiped at Christ Church and shopped at the Stabler-Leadbeater Apothecary Shop. His step-grandson's home Arlington House, serves as a connection between the Washington and Lee families. Alexandria has several Lee homes—the Boyhood Home of Robert E. Lee and the Lee-Fendall House. After visiting Mount Vernon and Gunston Hall, owned by Washington's friend George Mason, it is quite a contrast to see the Claude Moore Colonial Farm, a simple home typical of the vast majority of farmers.

The quiet rolling fields are repopulated with warring armies in the videos and displays at significant Civil War battlefield parks in this region. Manassas, Fredericksburg, Wilderness, Spotsylvania and Fort Ward all bring back the tumultuous days of this great internecine conflict. More recent history is recalled at the Iwo Jima Memorial and Arlington National Cemetery where the eternal flame burns at the grave of John F. Kennedy.

History is only one aspect of the region, Prince William Forest Park provides trails that lead deep into the woods, the Flying Circus present a barnstorming show guaranteed to keep you on the edge of your seat and shoppers can make a day of it at Occoquan or Potomac Mills.

ALEXANDRIA

Alexandria Archaeology Museum and Torpedo Factory Art Center

On the Waterfront

Alexandria is one of the few cities in America attempting to pre-serve archeological sites within an urban environment. The city operates a lab and the **Alexandria Archaeology Museum** at the **Torpedo Factory Art Center**, where visitors can gain an appre-ciation of the scope of the archeological work. The mere fact that such a program exists prompts developers to be sensitive to the significance of artifacts uncovered by their bulldozers. Many builders in Alexandria have given archeologists the opportunity to examine promising discoveries before they are lost to 20th-century progress.

The museum's laboratory displays the latest finds, but this is more of a spot to observe conservators and archeologists at work. Visitors can check out photographs of current field activity and watch videos of recent digs.

Alexandria's history as a city goes back to the mid-1700s. George Washington, who considered Alexandria his home town, surveyed the city's waterfront as early as 1748, just one year be-fore the city was founded. At that time the banks of the Potomac River rose just over Lee Street, then called Water Street. When larger ships began plying the river, residents filled in the land to deeper water, extending the riverbank by 100 yards.

The city's maritime heritage is preserved at the Trans Potomac Canal Center. Like so much of the South, Alexandria was figu-ratively and literally drained by the Civil War. The city built the canal after Congress granted the necessary charter in 1830. Alexandria was then linked with the Chesapeake and Ohio Canal at Georgetown. When Federal troops occupied Alexandria dur-ing the Civil War, they drained the Alexandria Canal. Although it was refilled after the war, it never regained its prewar pros-perity. The canal is commemorated by the restoration of Lift Lock and Pool No. 1.

Although there is plenty of action on the Potomac River, it also serves as artistic inspiration to some 175 artists who have studios at the Torpedo Factory Art Center. An unimposing struc-ture used during both world wars to manufacture torpedoes and later as a storehouse for captured war records, the factory has been renovated into a bright and busy art center. Navy Seabees

The city of Alexandria claims its Scottish origins throughout the year but never more colorfully nor loudly than when the clans gather for the Virginia Scottish Games in July.

ALEXANDRIA TOURIST COUNCIL

presented a talisman from the past when the center opened. The Seabees' housewarming present was a sickly green 3,000-pound Mark 14 torpedo case made at this factory in 1944. Now the once-drab factory has a central atrium surrounded by classrooms and studios. A ceiling skylight provides natural light for some of the area's most talented artists.

More than three-quarters of a million visitors each year enjoy the open door policy practiced by most of these working artists. You can watch them at work and make purchases at prices lower than those at downtown galleries. You'll see a wide diversity of painters, sculptors, potters, fiber artists, printers, stained-glass workers, jewelers, batik designers, musical instrument makers and other artists and craftspeople.

The Torpedo Factory Art Center is open daily 10:00 A.M. to 5:00 P.M. It's located on the river in Old Town historic district just north of the intersection of King and Union streets at 105 N. Union Street.

Docked behind the Torpedo Art Factory are **Potomac Riverboat Company** excursion boats that take visitors on 40-minute tours of Alexandria's waterfront and 90-minute tours past Washington's imposing monuments; call (703) 548-9000 for schedules and rates. Docked at the foot of Prince Street just down from the center is the **Dandy Restaurant Cruise Ship**. Brunch, lunch, dinner cruises and specialty trips are scheduled year-round; call (703) 683-6976 for details.

Directions: From I-495/95 take Exit 1, U.S. 1 north into Alexandria. Turn right at King Street and head down to the river where you turn left for the Torpedo Factory Art Center.

Gadsby's Tavern and Stabler-Leadbeater Apothecary Shop

Bottled Remedies

Even the patronage of such illustrious colonial gentlemen as George Washington, George Mason and the Lees did not preclude an evening that would, by today's standards, be considered unruly. At 18th-century dinner parties, such as those held at **Gadsby's Tavern** in Alexandria, breakage was typically figured in the cost of the evening.

A tavern bill from a 1778 party for 270 gentlemen included a charge for breakage of 96 wine glasses, 29 jelly glasses, 9 glass dessert plates, 11 china plates, 3 china dishes, 5 decanters and a large inkstand! This excessive damage is perhaps explained by reading the listing of alcoholic beverages consumed by yet another party of 55 at a 1787 dinner party. The 55 revelers were charged for 22 bottles of Porter, 54 of Madeira, 60 of claret, 8 of Old Stock, 8 of cider, 8 of beer and 7 large bowls of punch.

They don't have parties like that any more. They do, however, still serve lunch, dinner and Sunday brunch at Gadsby's Tavern, the "finest publick house in America." The 18th century is evoked by the menu, service and surroundings in the three restored tavern rooms.

Even if you don't stop by for a taste of the past, you should stop for a tour of Gadsby's Tavern Museum. The tavern consists of two buildings: the 1770 tavern and the 1792 City Hotel acquired by John Gadsby in 1796. Gadsby's Tavern was the center of Alexandria's political, social and cultural life. Here the colonial leaders met both before and after the Revolution. One of the grand events of the year was George Washington's birthnight ball, first held in 1789 and still a popular Alexandria event. The tavern tour includes the restored ballroom where Washington enjoyed dancing. There are also restored bedrooms to give you an idea of tavern accommodations. Guided tours of Gadsby's Tavern are given daily at quarter of and quarter after the hour from 10:00 A.M. to 4:15 P.M. and on Sunday 1:00 to 5:00 P.M. from April through September. Winter hours are Tuesday through Saturday 11:00 A.M. to 4:00 P.M. and on Sunday 1:00 to 4:00 P.M. For lunch and dinner reservations call (703) 548-1288.

In the same year that City Hotel was built, 1792, a new shop opened in Alexandria, the **Stabler-Leadbeater Apothecary Shop**. It is the second oldest drugstore in the United States, predated only by a shop in Bethlehem, Pennsylvania.

Although it is often called George Washington's drugstore there is no documentation of any personal visits from him. A note from Martha dated April 22, 1802, reads: "Mrs. Washington desires Mr. Stabler will send by the bearer a quart bottle of his best castor oil."

The Alexandria lot on which the store stands was originally purchased in 1752 by Washington's neighbor, George Mason of Gunston Hall. It was purchased later in 1774 for $17.00 by Philip Dawe, who built the three-story brick building that still stands. He leased it to Edward Stabler who ran an apothecary shop until 1852. At that time his son-in-law, John Leadbeater, took over the shop. This drugstore served the community for 141 years until it closed in 1933, a victim of the Depression.

The shop has the largest and most valuable collection of medicinal glass in North America. Long wooden shelves border the narrow store. Since many customers were unable to read, color was used to convey warnings. Poison was always put in blue bottles deliberately roughened so that even in the dark their message could be read by touch. Another warning was conveyed by the large apothecary jars in the shop window; when they were filled with red liquid it meant danger—an epidemic in town. Green liquid meant "all clear." Many of the containers of this repository of the past still hold their original potions.

According to local lore, Robert E. Lee was making a purchase at the Stabler-Leadbeater Shop on October 17, 1859, when Lieutenant Jeb Stuart hurried in to bring orders that would take both him and Lee, two young Marines, to Harpers Ferry to quell John Brown. The two southerners ultimately resigned their commissions to fight in the Confederate army. You can visit this shop at 105 S. Fairfax Street from 10:00 A.M. to 4:00 P.M. Monday through Saturday, 1:00 to 5:00 P.M. on Sunday. Entrance is through the adjoining antique shop. Admission is charged.

Directions: From the Washington Beltway, I-495/95 take Exit 1, U.S. 1. Take U.S. 1, north into Alexandria. Turn right on Franklin Street, left on Washington Street, then right onto King Street to Royal. Gadsby's Tavern is one block to the left at 134 North Royal Street. For the Stabler-Leadbeater Apothecary Shop continue down King Street one more block and then turn right onto South Fairfax Street.

Fort Ward Park

Capital Defense

On May 23, 1861, Virginia seceded from the United States, creating panic in the capital. Washington, D.C. found itself on the front lines of a divided country, without any defenses. The realization of the city's peril brought quick action. On the very day that Virginia's secession became effective, Union troops crossed the Potomac River and seized Alexandria and Arlington Heights with the intention of building defensive forts on these sites. Troops also began working on forts at three sites south of the river.

When the South won the first major battle of the war on July 21, 1861 at Bull Run (Manassas), the work to defend Washington intensified. Forts were begun that would encircle Alexandria, Washington and Georgetown. These fortifications were modeled on 17th-century fieldworks designed by the French military genius Sebastien Le Prestre Vauban. By the end of 1862 more than 40 forts had been built.

With this degree of protection, Federal confidence was restored until August 1862 when the South won the Second Battle of Bull Run. After this setback, some of the forts were enlarged, more guns were added and new forts built. By the end of 1863, Washington was the most heavily defended location in the Western Hemisphere. There were 68 forts and 93 batteries bristling with over 900 guns, linked by over 30 miles of trenches and roads.

Fort Ward was the fifth largest of the forts surrounding Washington. It was begun in September 1861 and named for Commander James Harmon Ward, the first Union naval officer killed in the Civil War. Major General John G. Barnard, Chief Engineer of the Defenses of Washington, considered Fort Ward to be ". . . one of the major forts in the defense system." After the Battle of Second Manassas in August 1862 the fort's fire power was strengthened. A 100-pound Parrott rifled siege gun was positioned in the fort's southwest bastion on a center pintle carriage that permitted it to fire in any direction. A south and northwest bastion were added. When completed, Fort Ward had 36 guns mounted in five bastions. Work continued on the star-shaped fort throughout the war and finishing touches were added after General Lee surrendered the Army of Northern Virginia at Appomattox on April 9, 1865. Work on the ceremonial entrance gate, crowned by the turreted castle and symbolizing the Army Corp of Engineers, was completed in May 1865. However, by the end of 1865, Fort Ward was dismantled.

Today visitors can see much of Fort Ward as it was over 100 years ago during the Civil War. There is a replica of the fort's 1865 Ceremonial Gate. The Northwest Bastion has been carefully restored, complete with exact duplicates of the cannons that once stood here. Using original Corps of Engineers drawings, an Officer's Hut and Civil War Headquarters building (the latter serves as a museum) have also been reconstructed.

Fort Ward Museum contains a large collection of Civil War items. The museum hosts frequent special exhibits relating to the Civil War period. Before exploring the fort take the time to watch the 12-minute video "Fort Ward, Silent Guardian of the Capital City."

Fort Ward Park is open daily at no charge from 9:00 A.M. to sunset. The museum is open 9:00 A.M. to 5:00 P.M. and Sunday NOON to 5:00 P.M. Closed on Mondays, Thanksgiving, Christmas and New Years Day.

Directions: From I-95/495, the Capital Beltway, take Exit 2N, Telegraph Road. Follow the signs, and take Route 236 west. Turn right on Quaker Lane and proceed to the second traffic light. Turn left on West Braddock Road and travel approximately one-half mile to Ford Ward entrance. From I-395, take Seminary Road exit east and proceed to the fourth traffic light. Turn left on North Howard Street and follow the signs to Fort Ward.

Lee-Fendall House and Boyhood Home of Robert E. Lee

Certain-Lee

Nothing succeeds like excess—Philip Richard Fendall was not content with one Lee wife, he had three! Philip, himself the grandson of Philip Lee of Blenheim, first married a cousin, Sarah Lettice Lee. He next wed Elizabeth Steptoe Lee, widow of Philip Ludwell Lee and the mother of Matilda, who grew up to marry Henry "Lighthorse Harry" Lee. To further complicate the matter Philip's third wife was Harry Lee's sister, Mary.

Visitors will be thoroughly confused if they try to keep track of the 37 Lees who lived at the **Lee-Fendall House** from 1785 to 1903. (As a historical footnote, the last resident-owner of the house, from 1937 to 1969, was labor leader John L. Lewis.)

Philip Fendall built this rambling frame house in 1785. Both George Washington and Harry Lee were frequent visitors. In March 1789, the mayor of Alexandria interrupted dinner at the Fendall House and asked Harry Lee to write a farewell address from the citizens of Alexandria to their favorite son. George Washington was to ride through town on his way to his inauguration in New York. Lee moved from the table to a nearby desk and wrote the requested farewell message. He would write another and final farewell to his old friend ten years later expressing the esteem in which he was held throughout the nation: "First in war, first in peace, and first in the hearts of his countrymen."

Though the Lee-Fendall House is furnished with family heirlooms spanning the 118 years of Lee occupancy, it is the way the house appeared in the 1850s, as a grand mansion, that you see on your tour. Lees were born in this home up until 1892. Favorite toys down through the years can be seen in the children's room. There is Traveller, the rocking horse, and Minerva, a doll ordered from the first Sears and Roebuck catalog. An antique dollhouse collection is also displayed.

Tours are given at the Lee-Fendall House, 614 Oronoco Street, from 10:00 A.M. until 4:00 P.M. Tuesday through Saturday and NOON to 4:00 P.M. on Sunday. Admission is charged.

Across the street is the **Boyhood Home of Robert E. Lee**. As if the Lee family tree wasn't complicated enough, there is a link between the Lee and Washington families. Martha Washington's grandson, George Washington Parke Custis, married Mary Fitzhugh on July 7, 1804 at this Oronoco Street house. Twenty-seven years later their daughter, Mary Anne Randolph Custis, married Robert E. Lee. He had spend part of his boyhood growing up in the house where his bride's parents had married.

William Fitzhugh, formerly the owner of Chatham (see selection), purchased this Alexandria house two years after it was built in 1795 by businessmen, John Potts. In 1811 another hero of the war, "Lighthorse Harry" Lee rented the house and moved here with his wife and five children. It was just prior to the War of 1812 and at that time Alexandria was part of the District of Columbia. When the British burned the Capitol in 1814 they sacked the warehouses of Alexandria. It was a tense time for all the citizens including seven-year-old Robert E. Lee, who perhaps felt it more keenly because his father had left his family and traveled to the West Indies in a fruitless attempt to improve his health. In the upstairs bedroom you can imagine young Robert anxiously watching the Potomac both in hopes of his father's return and in fear of the British. Robert lived here until 1825.

When Robert E. Lee was preparing for West Point, his father's famous friend, the Marquis de Lafayette, paid a courtesy visit on Ann Hill Carter Lee, the widow of his comrade-in-arms, General "Lighthorse Harry" Lee. The downstairs parlor, or sitting room is called the "Lafayette Room" in honor of his October 1824 visit. This short call was followed by a dinner visit in December of the same year.

The Boyhood Home of Robert E. Lee at 607 Oronoco Street is open Monday through Saturday 10:00 A.M. to 4:00 P.M. and Sunday 1:00 to 4:00 P.M. Admission is charged.

Directions: From I-495/95, the Washington Beltway, take Exit 1, U.S. 1 north into Alexandria. Turn right on Oronoco Street which is 10 blocks past Franklin Street.

Ramsay House, Carlyle House and Christ Church

Historical Triumvirate

Both the **Ramsay House** and Carlyle House, just five doors apart on Fairfax Street, reveal Scottish influences. The Ramsay House was built about 24 years before Alexandria was founded. Its gambrel roof makes it an unusual structure on the city's skyline. Historians believe that in 1749 William Ramsay's house was barged up the Potomac River from the Scottish settlement at Dumfries. It was the first residence placed on the newly auctioned Alexandria lots.

Over the years the house has been substantially altered, and little of the original structure remains.

Scottish merchant John Carlyle built his grand mansion three years later, in 1752. It was inspired by an elaborate Scottish country house in a popular architectural pattern book. Its manor house design, like the Ramsay House design, was unique to Alexandria.

William Ramsay and John Carlyle made more than architectural history in the newly developing town. Ramsay served his community as town trustee, census taker, postmaster, member of the Committee of Safety, Colonel of the Militia Regiment and honorary Lord Mayor. One of his eight children would later be elected Mayor of Alexandria. His wife, Anne, raised over $75,000 for the cause of American independence. At William Ramsay's funeral in 1785 George Washington, his close friend, joined the funeral procession.

The **Carlyle House** found its place in history just three years after it was built when General Edward Braddock chose it as his headquarters. Braddock summoned five colonial governors to a meeting that John Carlyle called ". . . the Grandest Congress . . . ever known on the Continent." The idea of taxing the colonies to support British expenditures in the New World was first proposed at this meeting as a means of financing the French and Indian War. This concept of taxation without representation was one that the colonists would bitterly reject. When it was imposed ten years later by the Stamp Act, it became a leading cause of the American Revolution.

John Carlyle, like William Ramsay, was a merchant. His marriage to Sarah Fairfax linked him with one of the most powerful families in Virginia. He was a partner in two merchant firms and acquired great wealth.

The Carlyle House is furnished to suggest the elegant life style of the Carlyles. One room, however, has been left unfurnished and serves as an architectural exhibit room. It clearly reveals even to the untrained eye how the 18th-century work was changed in the 19th century, then returned to its original appearance in the 20th century. Carlyle House at 121 North Fairfax Street can be visited from 10:00 A.M. to 4:30 P.M. Tuesday through Saturday and NOON to 4:40 P.M. on Sunday. Admission is charged.

Although the Ramsay tartan hangs on the front door, the Ramsay House is not interpreted as a private residence, but as a visitor center. It is the ideal first stop for anyone exploring Alexandria. You can obtain maps, brochures and up-to-date information on special events, museums, shops, restaurants and hotels—plus parking passes for non-residents. There is a free orientation video and a gift shop. Ramsay House is open daily 9:00 A.M. to 5:00 P.M. It is closed Thanksgiving, Christmas and New Year's Day.

If time permits walk five blocks west along Cameron Street up to **Christ Church** at Cameron and Washington streets. James Wren, descendant of the noted British architect Sir Christopher Wren, helped design the interior of Christ Church. Some authorities hold that he also contributed to the exterior design. George Washington was the first member of the congregation to purchase a pew. A silver plate marks the pew he bought for 36 pounds and 20 shillings (approximately $20).

When the widowed Martha Washington died, her grandson, George Washington Parke Custis, gave the Washington family bible to Christ Church. Another prominent American family, the Lees, considered this their family church. Robert E. Lee and two of his daughters were confirmed at Christ Church.

Christ Church is open daily until 4:00 P.M. and there is a regularly scheduled service every Sunday. Nearly all of America's presidents have attended service here on the Sunday closest to George Washington's birthday.

Directions: From I-495/95 take Exit 1, U.S. 1 north into Alexandria. Continue down U.S. 1 to King Street and turn right. The Ramsay House is at the corner of King and Fairfax streets.

ARLINGTON

Arlington House and Arlington National Cemetery

A Place to Remember

The story of George Washington throwing a silver dollar across the Potomac River has become an accepted part of American folklore. As in the children's game "Rumor," each retelling of the original incident brought changes: the Rappahannock became the Potomac, the Spanish doubloon became a dollar, and the story became suspect. But it was included in the book *Young Washington* that George Washington Parke Custis wrote about his step-grandfather after Washington's death.

George Washington raised Custis after his father, Washington's step-son John Parke Custis, died of fever following the Battle of Yorktown at the end of the American Revolution. After George Washington's death, as the principal male heir, Custis inherited the Mount Vernon portraits, china, silver and many other valuable pieces. He began building **Arlington House** in 1802 with the idea of making it a "treasury of Washington heirlooms." It was designed by British architect George Hadfield, who had come to the Washington area to help design the U.S. Capitol.

In 1804 Custis married Mary Lee Fitzhugh. Many of the notable figures of the time came to Arlington House to pay tribute to the Washington legend. A frequent guest was the young Robert E. Lee. After graduating from West Point, Lee married Mary Anna Randolph Custis, the only surviving Custis child. The marriage on June 30, 1831 was celebrated in the family parlor at Arlington House.

Mary Anna stayed in her girlhood home and raised their seven children. Lee's military career left him little time to spend with her. When Lee left to serve in the war, he never saw Arlington House again. Mrs. Lee and the children moved to Richmond and the house was occupied by Federal troops. The grounds became part of the capital defenses. After the Civil War, the 1,100-acre estate was confiscated by the federal government, and the Washington family possessions scattered. A Supreme Court decision in 1882 returned the house to Robert E. Lee's son, but in 1883 he sold it back to the federal government for $150,000. In 1925, the house was restored to its appearance during the Lee years. George Washington Parke Custis links two great American families, the Washingtons and the Lees, and through them two epic periods of United States history. Arlington House symbolizes that link.

The house, part of **Arlington National Cemetery**, is open to the public without charge from 9:30 A.M. to 4:00 P.M. during the winter months and until 6:00 P.M. the rest of the year. Maps of the house with details of the rooms and furnishings permit visitors to explore at their own pace. Many of the pieces exhibited are copies of original work, though others are Lee family pieces and a few Custis furnishings. The grand Greek Revival exterior with its eight massive pillars is in counterpoint with the simple and hospitable interior. The view from the portico of the Lincoln Memorial across the river is riveting.

The use of Arlington land to bury slain soldiers was initiated by happenstance. In May 1864, President Lincoln and General Meigs were visiting the wounded in the tent hospital on the Arlington grounds. They realized that with the number of Civil War fatalities mounting daily a new burial site would be needed, so they decided to bury the dead at Arlington. Meigs' intention was to punish Lee for joining the Confederate army. Thousands would rest there before the end of the Civil War.

Buried at Arlington are the known and unknown, the famous and the ordinary citizen soldier. All of our country's wars are represented, including the American Revolution, the War of 1812 and the Mexican War. Since Arlington officially began during the Civil War, veterans of these earlier conflicts were disinterred and reburied. Subsequent military deaths in the Indian campaigns, Spanish-American War, the Philippine Insurrection, World Wars I and II, the Korean Conflict, Vietnam and the Persian Gulf all are represented by soldiers who lie at Arlington National Cemetery.

There are special memorials to soldiers who died in battle and could never be identified, but the most famous is the Tomb of the Unknowns. On October 22, 1921, four unknown American soldiers were exhumed from separate military cemeteries in France where slain soldiers from World War I were buried. A highly-decorated soldier, Army Sergeant Edward F. Younger, placed a spray of white roses on one casket on October 24, 1921 and this became the unknown soldier of World War I. The following month on Armistice Day, November 11, President Warren G. Harding headed the dignitaries on hand to officially inter the soldier at the plaza of the Arlington National Cemetery Memorial Amphitheater.

During the Eisenhower administration unknown soldiers from World War II and Korea were interred at Arlington on Memorial Day, 1958. Americans from all across the country come to Arlington to pay tribute to these valorous soldiers guarded around the clock by the Tomb Guards from the U.S. Army 3rd U.S. Infantry (The Old Guard). The impressive changing of the guard ceremony takes place every 30 minutes during summer hours, every hour during the winter.

This was not the earliest monument honoring unknown soldiers at Arlington. The first unidentified battle dead came from Northern Virginia battlefields, most from the fields of Bull Run. There are about 2,111 unknown soldiers from the Civil War in a vault beneath a massive sarcophagus south of Arlington House. The mast of the battleship *U.S.S. Maine* is adjacent to the burial spot of 167 unidentified who went down with the ship in Havana Harbor during the Spanish-American War.

Names from the pages of American history are found throughout Arlington National Cemetery: Pierre Charles L'Enfant, Oliver Wendell Holmes, Philip H. Sheridan, William Jennings Bryan, Robert Todd Lincoln, John J. Pershing, George C. Marshall, Walter Reed, Robert E. Peary, Richard E. Byrd, James V. Forestal, John Foster Dulles, Virgil Grissom, Roger B. Chaffee and two presidents of the United States.

William Howard Taft, Chief Justice of the U.S. and the 27th president, is buried at Arlington. There is also a special memorial with an eternal flame marking the spot where John Fitzgerald Kennedy, the 35th president, is buried. The walls of the plaza are inscribed with excerpts from President Kennedy's Inaugural

Address including his moving words, "Now the trumpet summons us again. . ." Two children who pre-deceased their father are also buried at the Kennedy gravesite. Jacqueline Lee Bouvier Kennedy Onassis was buried next to the president in 1994. Robert Kennedy's nearby grave is marked by a small white cross and the sound of water flowing over a fountain spillway.

Arlington National Cemetery is open October through March from 8:00 A.M. to 5:00 P.M. and April through September until 7:00 P.M. Maps at the visitor center orient visitors and indicate specific burial sites. The cemetery is not open to vehicular traffic. Cars must be parked at the visitor center parking lot, but tour buses are available (for a fee) for those who do not want to walk.

North of the Arlington National Cemetery on Arlington Boulevard is the often photographed **U.S. Marine Corps Memorial**. It was carved to duplicate the photo of the Marines raising the U.S. flag on Mount Suribachi during World War II. The 78-foot sculpture is imposing, the largest ever cast in bronze. On Tuesday evenings during the summer months the Marines have a dress parade and color ceremony at this memorial. Near the memorial is the Netherlands Carillon. The carillon tower and bells were a gift from the people of the Netherlands in gratitude for American assistance during and after World War II. The bells are played every Saturday from April to September, starting at 2:00 P.M.

Traveling still farther north you'll reach **Freedom Park** at 1101 Wilson Boulevard in Arlington. The park includes The Freedom Forum Journalists Memorial with the names of approximately 1,000 journalists who died while reporting the news. The park's grassy plazas display icons of freedom including pieces of the Berlin Wall, a toppled, headless statue of Lenin and a bronze casting of a cell door from the Birmingham, Alabama jail where Dr. Martin Luther King was held in 1963 during the civil rights protests. Opening in 1997 is the **Newseum**, the world's only museum dedicated exclusively to news. Multi-media presentations and exhibits will examine the past, present and future of news. A video news will present more news feeds than any other single place in the world, including front pages from every state and broadcast news as it happens through fiber optics and satellite feeds. The museum will include an operating news broadcast studio and a high definition video theater.

Directions: Take I-95 to the perimeter of Washington. At the intersection with the Beltway (I-495/95) and I-395, take the latter and head toward the city. Then exit at Memorial Bridge/Rosslyn exit onto Route 110 north. From Route 110 exit at Memorial Bridge/Washington. At the top of the exit turn left onto Memorial Drive which goes directly to the entrance of Arlington National Cemetery and Arlington House.

FAIRFAX

Colvin Run Mill and Sully Historic Site

Down by the Old Mill Stream

Just past the commercial bustle of northern Virginia's Tysons Corner is a bucolic reminder of the past—**Colvin Run Mill**. The mill was built circa 1810 along Difficult Run which ran beside the Leesburg Turnpike. Even in the 19th century this turnpike was a major artery from Shenandoah Valley farms to the bustling port in Alexandria.

Local businessmen Philip Carper designed Colvin Run according to the recommendations of Oliver Evans, whose book *The Young Millwright and Miller's Guide,* suggested substituting waterpower for manpower in all steps of milling grain except weighing.

Water from Difficult Run was drained into a pond and millrace; then it flowed over the waterwheel to power the milling process. On each floor of the mill a different process was performed. Grain moved by elevators, chutes and sifters from floor to floor and process to process. This smooth, efficient operation was necessary for large merchant mills like Colvin Run that produced flour for foreign markets: Europe, Canada and the West Indies.

Colvin Run Mill Historic Site includes several additional restorations. The Miller's House, built about the same time as the mill, now serves as a museum with an exhibit on "The Millers and the Mill" detailing the lives and times of the families who milled at Colvin Run. The barn, representing a 19th century dairy barn, is used for interpretative exhibits and demonstrations. The General Store, an original structure, served the local community during the early 20th century. When the mill is grinding you can purchase flour products as well as candy and handicrafts.

Throughout the year Colvin Run Mill sponsors special events, including Civil War encampments, an autumn celebration and a traditional Christmas event which features Santa in the Mill. Colvin Run is open daily 11:00 A.M. to 5:00 P.M. March through December and weekends only in January and February. It is closed Tuesdays, Thanksgiving and Christmas. Admission is charged.

While in the area you should plan to visit nearby **Sully Historic Site**. Like the mill, it is operated by the Fairfax County Park Authority. This Virginia country house was built by Richard Bland Lee in 1794. Lee combined two architectural styles he had

Historic Sully in Chantilly looks almost as it did in 1794 when it was built by Richard Bland Lee, the first Congressman from Northern Virginia. Fairfax County Park Authority

grown to love: the Georgian colonial of his native state and the Philadelphia frame exterior he had admired while serving as northern Virginia's first congressman.

The Philadelphia influence helped make his wife feel at home. Elizabeth Collins was the daughter of a prominent Quaker merchant in Philadelphia. The Haights, later owners of Sully, were also Quakers from the north. Their pacifist beliefs did not protect them during the Civil War. The men were forced to leave their southern farm and retreat behind the Union lines. The women of the Haight family stayed at Sully and protected their home from the foraging armies of both North and South.

Today Sully is restored and decorated with Federal furnishings. After touring the main house you can see the dependencies: the kitchen-laundry, smokehouse and stone dairy.

Historic Sully hosts special events. Perennial favorites are the Quilt Show in September, Antique Car Show in June and World War II: The Home Front in October. Sully Historic Site is open daily from March through December from 11:00 A.M. to 5:00 P.M. and on weekends in January and February. It is closed on Tuesdays, Thanksgiving and Christmas. Admission is charged.

Directions: From the Washington, D.C. Beltway, I- 95/495 in Virginia take Exit 10B, Route 7, west for five miles. Colvin Run is on the right. For Sully take Beltway Exit 9, Route 66 west. Continue on Route 66 to Route 50 west and proceed for 5.5 miles to Route 28. Turn right on Route 28 and go $^3/_4$ of a mile to Sully. An alternative route for Sully from I-495/95 is Route 267, the toll road, to Route 28, turn left and take Route 28 four miles to the entrance.

George Washington's Gristmill Historical State Park and Pohick Church

In George's Footsteps

For three decades George Washington hired a miller to run the gristmill on his Mount Vernon estate. The first miller he hired became so fond of the liquor made at the mill distillery that, despite his family of seven children, Washington was compelled to dismiss him.

The gristmill at Mount Vernon was the second mill Washington owned. There was a mill at Mount Vernon when Washington acquired the estate from his sister-in-law, but it was not operating efficiently. In 1770, Washington had the three-and-half story stone millhouse you see today constructed. Associated with the mill was the distillery that so tempted the first miller, a cooper's shop and a stable.

All of these activities are represented at **George Washington's Gristmill Historical State Park**. There is much to see and the displays offer an insightful look at the ingenuity of our forebears. A taped message from the miller's wife explains what happened when grain was brought by customers to be ground. The "merchant trade" had wheat ground into flour, while the "country trade" relied more on ground corn. Each customer's grain was tagged and ground separately, for each wanted to be sure he received his own batch. You can see the machinery used for this colonial operation.

An intriguing feature of the mill is that the three floors above the ground level permit a number of perspectives from which to view the large waterwheel. On the ground floor there is a "cog pit" where the wheel can be seen head on, while on the upper levels you look down on the massive wheel.

The cooper's art is represented in exhibits and diagrams. Once wheat was ground into flour, it was stored in barrels. This is why coopers were so often found operating in the vicinity of mills. On the top floor of the mill there is a display of early American tools: a mallet, axe, froe club, sashsaw and hand adze.

In 1799, George Washington rented his mill to his nephew Lawrence Lewis, but he still kept an eye on its operation. This mill was the last place Washington visited before his death. It was a snowy day and he caught a cold from which he never recovered.

The George Washington Gristmill Historical State Park is open weekends only Memorial Day to Labor Day from 10:00 A.M. to 6:00 P.M. There is a nominal admission.

If you've visited Christ Church in Alexandria (see selection) you will easily recognize **Pohick Church**. They were both designed by Colonel James Wren. Pohick, a Native American word for hickory, was built between 1769 and 1774. George Washington and neighbor George Mason (see Gunston Hall selection) were on the building committee; Mason supervised the construction. Unlike Christ Church, this church had no steeple because the congregation did not live close enough to hear church bells. The interior was badly damaged during the Civil War. It has been restored and you can see the box pews belonging to Washington and Mason.

Directions: From I-495/95, the Capital Beltway, take Exit 1, U.S. 1 south seven miles. Near the Woodlawn Plantation entrance (see selection) turn left on the Mount Vernon Memorial Parkway, Route 235. The mill is about ¹/₄ mile on the left. For Pohick Church, continue south on Route 1 and the church will be on your right.

Gunston Hall Plantation and Mason Neck National Wildlife Refuge

Eagle Eye

George Mason built for the future; both his words and his house endure. With his words, in the 1776 Virginia Declaration of Rights, he built a framework of freedom. "That all men are by nature equally free and independent and have certain inherent rights . . . namely, the enjoyment of life and liberty, with the means of acquiring and possessing property, and pursuing and obtaining happiness and safety." His immortal document served as the inspiration for the U.S. Declaration of Independence, Federal Bill of Rights and the French Declaration of Rights of Man. After being copied in many emerging democracies, it also served as a model for the United Nations' Declaration of Human Rights.

Mason's concern for detail, so evident in the careful choice of the right words in his documents, reveals itself again and again in his plantation home, **Gunston Hall**, in northern Virginia. His keen powers of concentration, you'll learn, sometimes caused him to lose track of some very important details, however, such as the whereabouts of his nine children. His son, John, said, "I have frequently known his mind, tho' always kind and affectionate to his children, so diverted from the objects around him that he would not for days together miss one of the family who may have been absent, and would sometimes at table enquire for one of my sisters who had perhaps been gone a week on a visit to some friend, of which he had known but forgotten."

George Mason suffered from gout and therefore served the cause of the Revolution primarily with his pen from the confines of his study at Gunston Hall. He did, in spite of his handicap, attend every session of the Constitutional Convention in Philadelphia during the long hot summer of 1787. He made dozens of speeches and helped draft the Constitution, but when he lost the battle to include a Bill of Rights and a ban on the slave trade he refused to sign the finished document.

For the most part he did not travel great distances, content to travel instead in his mind. John Mason recalled, "The small dining room was devoted to (my Father's) service when he used to write, and he absented himself as it were from his family sometimes for weeks together, and often until very late at night during the Revolutionary War . . ." Mason's walnut writing table was salvaged from a fire in July 1880, and has been returned to the study at Gunston Hall.

It is the interior woodwork that places Gunston Hall among the most attractive of Virginia's colonial plantations. The house, unassuming from the outside, is unrivaled in its exquisitely carved interior woodwork. This work was designed by William Buckland, a 21-year-old indentured carpenter whom George Mason's brother engaged in England. He chose well, for Buckland went on to achieve distinction in the roughly five buildings he designed before his early death. He was one of the first to use chinoiserie in America. He used the new style in the dining room at Gunston Hall, designing scalloped frames over the windows and doors, each with intricate fretwork, or designs. This is the only room with a chinoiserie woodwork scheme to survive from the colonial era.

Buckland's delightfully designed drawing room combines the strong classicism typical of mid-century English design, reflecting the influence of Andrea Palladio, with rococo elements which were a popular part of the "modern" or French-influenced style that was fashionable in Mason's day. On the wall is a portrait of Ann Eilbeck Mason, of whom her devoted husband, George, said, "She never met me without a smile."

If you think you've seen a representative sampling of Virginia colonial houses, you haven't until you see Gunston Hall. It is not only beautifully built and decorated; it also features a picturesque Colonial Revival garden. From the main house you gaze down a 230-foot boxwood allée, planted by George Mason, to the Potomac River overlook. This allée is the only truly original feature of the garden. Flanking the garden on raised knolls are twin gazebos. On either side of the allée on both upper and lower terraces are networks of flower beds (parterres) which, though balanced, are not similarly designed or planted. The garden design was based on the remembrances of John Mason combined with current understanding of colonial garden design.

The gazebos offer a view of the house, garden, river and Deer Park, which was once stocked with white-tailed deer. You can take the two-mile Barn Wharf Nature Trail which begins at the front of the house. The trail offers the chance to enjoy spring wildflowers and nesting bluebirds. Hours at Gunston Hall are 9:30 A.M. to 5:00 P.M. daily except Thanksgiving, Christmas and New Year's Day. An orientation film about George Mason is shown at the visitor center. Admission is charged.

Bird fanciers may want to extend their day by visiting the nearby **Mason Neck National Wildlife Refuge**. The wildlife refuge is open year-round. This is the first sanctuary established for the protection of the American bald eagle. Here on this 2,272-acre refuge a wide variety of wildlife make their home. Much of the marshlands, forests and wooded swamps are inaccessible to visitors, but the peaceful protection they offer serves both wildlife and man. More than 226 species of birds have been spotted at Mason Neck. When you visit bring binculars and a field guide for bird identification, as you will undoubtedly spot some unfamiliar varieties. There are two hiking trails: Great Marsh Trail is $3/4$ of a mile long and handicap accessible; Woodmarsh Trail is three miles long with mild hills and contours.

Directions: From I-95 northbound, take the Fort Belvoir exit. The sign reads "Mt. Vernon-Ft. Belvoir." Travel north on Route 1, then turn right on Route 242, Gunston Road, for Gunston Hall and Mason Neck National Wildlife Refuge. From I-95 southbound, take the Lorton exit and turn left on Lorton Road. You will then make a right on Armistead Road, then right (southbound) on Route 1, Richmond Highway, Route 242. Proceed four miles to the entrance for Gunston Hall or $4^3/4$ miles for Mason Neck National Wildlife Refuge.

Mount Vernon

There's No Place Like Home!

George Washington's great-grandfather acquired the land on which Mount Vernon stands in 1674. George Washington's father obtained Little Hunting Creek Plantation, as it was first called, in 1726. At his death George's elder half-brother, Lawrence, inherited it. Lawrence renamed the estate Mount Vernon in honor of his commanding officer Admiral Vernon.

At Lawrence's death, George first leased Mount Vernon from his brother's widow, then inherited the family estate. On January 6, 1759, George married the wealthy widow, Martha Dandridge Custis, whose worth by today's standards has been calculated by some historians (who may exaggerate) as approaching six million dollars, not counting the vast acres of land she owned. Before he moved his bride and her two children to Mount Vernon, Washington enlarged the main house to $2^1/2$ stories.

George Washington continued to enlarge, ornament and plan the grounds of his Virginia plantation throughout the long years of his military and political service. He took an interest in the day-to-day activities of his estate amid the turmoil of war and the travail of establishing a new government. Take, for example, his letter in 1776 to his cousin, Lund Washington, Mount Vernon's wartime manager. The letter mixes disturbing wartime news with directions for the building of the two-story dining room addition. Washington advises: "The chimney of the new room should be exactly in the middle of it—the doors and everything else to be exactly answerable and uniform—in short I would have the whole executed in a masterly manner."

Or consider the letter he wrote on June 6, 1796: "Tell the Gar-

37

dener I shall expect everything that a Garden ought to produce, in the most ample manner." Washington also wrote: "My agricultural pursuits and rural amusements . . . (have) been the most pleasing occupation of my life, and the most congenial to my temper."

No detail was too small for him. There are 37 volumes of Washington's writings, plus letters and weekly garden reports. These precise records helped the Mount Vernon Ladies' Association in restoring Washington's home to its appearance at the time of his death, on December 14, 1799, as did a room-by-room inventory.

Bushrod Washington and John Augustine Washington, inheritors of Mount Vernon, worked hard to keep up the estate, but because it was no longer agriculturally productive it was difficult to maintain. Their concern that it be preserved as a shrine led them to approach the federal government and the Commonwealth of Virginia about purchasing Mount Vernon; neither accepted the offer.

Mount Vernon's journey back to its days of glory began on a moonlit night in 1853 when Mrs. Robert Cunningham, cruising the Potomac, saw the rundown house on the hilltop. She wrote her daughter, "I was painfully distressed at the ruin and desolation of the home of Washington." She further related, "The thought passed through my mind: why was it that the women of his country did not try to keep it in repair, if the men could not do it? It does seem such a blot on our country."

The recipient of this letter, Ann Pamela Cunningham, realized her mother's hopes by founding the Mount Vernon Ladies' Association. After both state and federal governments had refused to purchase Washington's home, her group bought the estate in 1858 for $200,000. Nineteenth-century additions were removed, furniture was restored and the atmosphere of the original plantation that Washington so enjoyed was recaptured. Visitors can imagine the great man strolling the home he once called "a well resorted tavern." It was never a glittering environment of power but always the home of a gentlemen farmer. The presence of George Washington can be sensed at Mount Vernon, and this is perhaps the greatest legacy the Mount Vernon Ladies' Association offers to succeeding generations.

Mount Vernon now provides a glimpse of the 316 former residents that have until recently been ignored on most tours. "Slave Life at Mount Vernon" a half-hour walking tour focuses on the slaves who built and operated the estate. The tours, led by historical interpreters, are offered at no extra charge; call (703) 780-2000 for a current schedule. George Washington inherited slaves from his father when he was 11. Although slavery was considered a necessity in colonial Virginia, after the American

Colonial Weekends at Mount Vernon, scheduled from Memorial Day through Labor Day, illustrate life on this busy plantation with demonstrations of spinning and weaving, military reenactments and 18th-century music and dance.

Revolution, Washington resolved never to buy or sell another slave. By 1797 his view was even more extreme, he wrote, "I wish from my soul that the Legislature of this State could see the policy of a gradual Abolition of Slavery." Washington freed his slaves in his will.

Visitors who take this tour discover that the operation of the plantation depended on slave labor not only for field and house work. Slaves were also blacksmiths, gardeners, carpenters, spinners and animal caretakers. The work day began at sunrise and lasted until dark, which meant up to 14 hours in the summer. Women did much of the field work—they plowed, hoed and planted. The tour encompasses both living and work space. Many of the details presented on this tour come from Washington's diaries though family histories of former slaves also provided information.

Mount Vernon is open 9:00 A.M. to 4:00 P.M. November through February , 9:00 A.M. to 5:00 P.M. March, September and October and 8:00 A.M. to 5:00 P.M. April to August. Admission is charged. During the summer months special children's programs offer hands- on-history lessons and theme weekends that re-create the atmosphere of a busy plantation.

Directions: From I-95 south of Alexandria take Exit 54, U.S. 1. Take U.S. 1 north to Route 235, the Old Mount Vernon Highway. Make a right turn on Route 235 which will take you directly to the traffic circle in front of Mount Vernon. You can also take the Mount Vernon Parkway from Alexandria to the estate.

Woodlawn Plantation and Frank Lloyd Wright's Pope-Leighey House

By George!

George Washington's last birthday, February 22, 1799, was a happy one. There was a family wedding at Mount Vernon on that date, uniting his foster daughter, Eleanor (Nelly) Parke Custis, and his sister Betty's son, Major Lawrence Lewis. The delighted Washington, noted for buying land, rather than giving it away, made the newlyweds a present of a portion of his beloved Mount Vernon estate. He said the 2,000 acres would be a "most beautiful site for a gentleman's seat."

The architect, Dr. William Thronton, who did the first work on the U.S. Capitol, designed a stately Georgian mansion for the crest of the highest hill on the Lewises' property. While their house was being built they lived at Mount Vernon, comforting the grief-stricken Martha Washington who was widowed on December 14, 1799. In 1802, at Martha's death, the Lewises and their two young children moved into the completed wing areas of **Woodlawn**. The center portion wasn't finished until 1805.

Visiting Woodlawn gives you a sense of the deep grief Nelly felt at the death of the only father she ever knew. She placed his bust on a pedestal as high as Washington's own considerable height. A swath was cut through the trees so that she could see Mount Vernon, her girlhood home, from Woodlawn's river entrance.

In the music room you see Nelly's music on a pianoforte similar to one she once played. Her husband was more interested in hunting than harmonics. He imported thoroughbred horses and the first merino sheep in North America. When Lawrence Lewis died in 1839, his widow moved to Clarke County to live with her son and his family at Audley Plantation.

The Garden Club of Virginia has re-created the formal gardens. An unexpected addition to this 19th-century plantation is the 20th-century Usonian **Pope-Leighey House**. It is the second home of this type designed by Frank Lloyd Wright, built of cypress and not of concrete like his later models.

The house, named after its two owners, was in Falls Church, Virginia in the early 1940s and moved to the current Woodlawn site to avoid destruction by the impending path of Route 66. The Usonian Houses were designed and built to "meet the housing needs of Middle Class America." Pope-Leighey embodies a simple lifestyle. In keeping with the projected owners, the architectural design does not call attention to itself, but rather becomes an integral part of its surroundings. Complete with its original furnishings, also Wright-designed, it was ahead of its time. It was seen as "futuristic," with its radiant-heated floors, carport and recessed lighting. It fits beautifully into the world of today.

The unique opportunity exists at this site to allow the visitor to compare two different time periods, houses, lifestyles and famous architects. Woodlawn Plantation and the Pope-Leighey House are museum properties of the National Trust for Historic Preservation. They are open daily from 9:30 A.M. to 4:30 P.M. from March through December and on weekends in January and February from 9:30 A.M. to 4:30 P.M. The houses are closed on Thanksgiving, Christmas and New Year's Day. Many special events are scheduled throughout the year.

Directions: From I-495/95 take Exit 1, U.S. 1 south to Fort Belvoir. Woodlawn is located on Route 1 and Virginia Route 235 in Mount Vernon.

FREDERICKSBURG

Belmont

Artistic Environs

Expectation can tax the creative. Consider the chef who wants to have friends over for a potluck supper, the novelist who wants to dash-off a quick note or the artist who wants to create a comfortable home. All must cope with the busman's holiday syndrome that never permits them to be off duty.

It's nice to report that **Belmont**, the home of American artist Gari Melchers, does not disappoint. Belmont combines the beauty of nature with the beauty of the artist's creations. A long promenade of boxwoods and century-old trees leads down to the banks of the Rappahannock River from a lovely old white frame house, with colonnaded porches on the first and second floors. Built sometime between 1790 and 1800, the house was enlarged in 1843. Gari Melchers lived here from 1916 to 1932, the last 16 years of his life. Melchers filled his home with his own work and art that he and his wife collected while in Europe. His one structural addition was a cheerful sun porch.

Gari Melchers's father was a sculptor who came to America from Germany. He is remembered today primarily for his wooden cigar-store Indians. Young Gari studied in his father's drawing classes, then traveled to Dusseldorf, Germany and Paris, France to continue his art education. Before moving to Belmont Melchers and his wife, Corinne, spent a great deal of time in Europe. He had studios in Paris, France; Egmond, Holland and Weimar, Germany.

At Belmont, old family pieces mix with European antiques to form a stylish but comfortable home. An 18th-century desk from Holland has four secret compartments so well hidden that the guides have trouble remembering their locations. Oriental carpets, English Regency slipper chairs and Victorian bedroom furniture vie for attention with American antiques acquired in Fredericksburg.

Both Gari and his wife painted. There are many family portraits. Gari painted his mother when he was 24 and his father ten years later. Melchers also did a self-portrait. In the dining room there is a portrait of Mrs. Melchers and her brother. The work of both Melcherses and European artists like Frans Synders and Berthe Morisot mix harmoniously at Belmont.

After a guided tour of the house you're invited to walk down the path to Melchers's stone studio. More than 50 of his paintings fill the studio walls. The brush, paint and palettes create the illusion that the artist is only momentarily missing. Belmont has the largest repository of Melchers's paintings in the world. The collection includes 1,600 items.

Belmont is open March through November from 10:00 A.M. to 5:00 P.M. Monday through Saturday and 1:00 to 5:00 P.M. on Sunday. From December through February hours are 10:00 A.M. to 4:00 P.M. Monday through Saturday and 1:00 to 4:00 P.M. on Sunday.

Art lovers will want to include a stop at **The Silversmith House** located on the banks of the Rappahannock River at the foot of George Street in Fredericksburg. The house, built around 1785 by silversmith and jeweler James Brown, is architecturally little-altered. It is now used as exhibition and studio space by the Fredericksburg Center for the Creative Arts. There is free admission Tuesday through Sunday from NOON to 4:00 P.M. For information on exhibits call (540) 373- 5646.

Directions: From I-95 near Fredericksburg, take the Falmouth-Warrenton exit. Follow Route 17 east toward Falmouth for $1^1/_4$ mile to Washington Street and turn right to Belmont.

Chancellorsville, Wilderness and Spotsylvania Battlefields

Unacceptable Losses

Since colonial times Fredericksburg was one of the chief river ports for the Shenandoah Valley, along with Alexandria and Richmond. The Rappahannock River made this an irresistible military target during the Civil War and the town changed hands seven times (see Fredericksburg National Military Park selection). The town was also a target because of the presence of the railroad and the various wagon roads that crossed through Fredericksburg. Within 15 miles of this transportation hub, you will find the greatest concentration of preserved battlefields in the state: Chancellorsville, Wilderness and Spotsylvania. In a two year period, the Union and Confederate armies, together totaling nearly 200,000 men, battled four times near Fredericksburg.

West of Fredericksburg, at the **Battle of Chancellorsville** in May 1863, General Lee won a great victory but lost an irreplaceable officer when General "Stonewall" Jackson was accidently shot by his own men during a lull in the fighting.

Lee's victory was a triumph of boldness over numbers, determination over vacillation; he had the courage to take enormous risks based on his information regarding the enemy's position and intentions. It wasn't that General Joseph Hooker didn't come up with a good plan. He did; he had to, as he was very much aware that he was replacing General Burnside, who made such a poor showing at Fredericksburg. So Hooker was determined to beat Lee. After reorganizing the 120,000 Union troops during the winter camp he was ready. "My plans are perfect," said Hooker. "May God have mercy on General Lee, for I will have none."

Hooker attempted to hold Lee's force at Fredericksburg while simultaneously moving around Lee's left side with a large segment of his army. He succeeded, but Lee didn't do the expected and withdraw or surrender, instead he attacked.

As Hooker moved to attack Lee's left flank with 75,000 men, Lee left only 10,000 men under General Jubal Early's command in Fredericksburg and moved the larger 45,000 man force toward Chancellorsville. When Hooker met the advance troops he fell back to Chancellorsville and dug in rather than attacking the inferior force. In so doing he buried his hopes of victory over Lee.

Lee arrived and met with General Jackson at what is now Auto Stop 7 on the battlefield tour to devise a bold and daring maneuver. The plan was to divide Lee's already vastly outnumbered force in two, one segment would hold the line where Hooker was dug in, while Jackson with 30,000 men would march around the Union force and envelope its right flank. This surprise move was enormously effective, and $1^1/_2$ miles of the federal line caved in. It was at this time that the fates ceased smiling on the Confederates. Jackson, who had ridden out in front of his own line to reconnoiter the federal position in order to plan that night's offensive, was hit three times—fired on by his own men as he returned.

Devastated, the southern troops could not even stop to mourn their commander. Intelligence was received regarding an attack that forced General Early to evacuate the heights behind Fredericksburg. Lee left J.E.B. Stuart in command of Jackson's corps and took 20,000 men east to defeat Sedgwick, who threatened his rear.

The entire story of this tragic Confederate victory is told at the Chancellorsville Visitor Center. A short film covers the May 1–4, 1863 battle. Maps available at the center highlight stops on the auto route. At the onset of the battle, Hooker lost his nerve and he dug in, abandoning the offensive to Lee. One stop is the Chancellorsville Inn where Hooker made his headquarters. While Hooker was leaning against one of the inn's porch pillars on May 3, he was wounded during a shelling by falling masonry. Part of this tour is the 12-mile route Jackson followed as he encircled Hooker's flank.

As a footnote to the battle stop at the small frame office building at Guinea Station. After being shot, Jackson was taken to Wilderness Tavern where his arm was amputated. He was then moved to the white clapboard office building of Fairfield, the Chandler Plantation. He contracted pneumonia and died on Sunday, May 10, 1863. His last words were, "Let us cross over the river and rest under the shade of the trees." The building where he died is now part of the **Stonewall Jackson Shrine**.

In May 1864 the Army of the Potomac under General-in-Chief Ulysses S. Grant started south again. He adopted an approach similar to Hooker's, attempting to turn Lee's right flank. On May 4, the Union army entered the **Wilderness**. Here the opposing armies engaged in "bushwhacking on a grand scale," to quote one old veteran.

In this overgrown terrain armies could not maintain regular lines and some soldiers either were shot by their own men or discovered, to their eternal regret, that they were completely surrounded by the enemy. A further problem produced by the heavy but dry vegetation was fire—muzzle flashes set the tinder ablaze and it raged out of control impartially killing wounded Union and Confederate who could not escape the deadly inferno.

Losses in the two-day Wilderness fighting were 18,000 Union men shot or burned and an estimated 8,000 to 12,000 Confederates. Lee could no longer accept that many casualties, as he had only half as many men as General Grant. So this marked the end of the aggressive Confederate charges that had turned the tide at numerous battles before this, including the previous year's encounter at Chancellorsville.

The Battle of the Wilderness ended when General Grant began pulling out his men on May 7. The Army of the Potomac had withdrawn from every encounter with Lee. As the lead column reached the intersection that would indicate either retreat or a continued battle, the men raised a cheer to Grant when they realized they were heading farther south to engage Lee's force once again. The Wilderness Battlefield has a self-guided auto route with interpretive road signs. Only a portion of the battlefield survives, but some trenches are visible from the road.

When Grant's soldiers cheered as they left the overgrown Wilderness to engage Lee farther south, they did not envision the encounter at **Spotsylvania Court House**. For orientation to this brutal two-week stalemate that cost approximately 30,000 lives, stop at the Spotsylvania Exhibit Center. A walking tour takes in the ground over which the heaviest fighting took place at the center of Lee's line where it jutted into the Union position. At this point, called the "Bloody Angle," assault after assault was launched. Fighting was hand-to-hand, with soldiers firing at point blank range, clubbing and bayoneting each other in savage frenzy. Spotsylvania's tragic distinction is that the Bloody Angle climax was the single most terrible 24 hours of the war. One marker on the trail indicates where a 22-inch oak tree was cut down by a barrage of rifle bullets. Along the auto route, houses are indicated that were used as headquarters by the opposing sides. After almost two weeks, Grant decided to shift to a more southern position. On May 21 he started in the direction of Richmond and another deadly conflict ten days later at Cold Harbor.

There are two additional points of interest at Spotsylvania. The present courthouse stands on the location of the earlier structure that was badly damaged during the war. In the small brick Old Berea Church, also badly damaged during the fighting, and now the Spotsylvania County Museum, you can see relics from the battlefield. Nearby is a Confederate cemetery.

Directions: From I-95 in the Fredericksburg area take Route 3 west to Chancellorsville. For the Jackson Shrine take the Thornburg exit off I-95 and proceed east on Route 606. For the Wilderness Battlefield auto-route, take Route 3 off I-95 at Fredericksburg, and turn left on Route 20 for the beginning of the auto route. For Spotsylvania, from Route 3, turn left and head south on Route 613, Brock Road and travel just over 13 miles to the exhibit shelter at the battlefield area.

Fredericksburg National Military Park

Ministering Angels

Civil War buffs who visit **Fredericksburg National Military Park** are fascinated by battle strategy, but most travelers are held enthralled by individual stories of heroism and tragedy. Fredericksburg is rich in stories about individuals who transcended the ordinary, it was a place "where uncommon valor was commonplace." The Confederates on Marye's Heights mowed down the Union troops as they advanced column after column in a futile attempt to take the hill. By the end of the Battle of Fredericksburg more than 12,000 Union men lay dead or wounded. The plight of the wounded so moved Sergeant Richard Kirkland, a Confederate from South Carolina, that he asked his commanding officer, General Joseph Kershaw, for permission to carry water to the Union wounded lying in agony near his position. Permission was granted, but he was not allowed to carry a flag of truce and he was warned that Federal troops were apt to fire at him as soon as he climbed over the wall. Although bullets started flying, cheers soon filled the air as Kirkland ministered to the wounded. Today you can see the Kirkland Monument honoring the soldier who became known as the "Angel of Marye's Heights."

Four major battles were fought around Fredericksburg because

The Richard Kirkland Monument, on the Fredericksburg Battle-field, pays tribute to the South Carolina soldier, known as the "Angel of Marye's Heights," who risked his life to give water to wounded Union soldiers.

of its strategic position between Washington and Richmond. In December 1862, the Battle of Fredericksburg resulted in a Union debacle. In May 1863, Lee's great victory at Chancellorsville was marred by a volley fired by his own men that eventually cost Stonewall Jackson his life. In May 1864, the Battle of the Wilderness proved costly to both sides, and it was followed by the fearsome two-week battle of Spotsylvania Court House which encompassed the single most terrible 24 hours of the war.

Fredericksburg was first drawn into the war in April 1862 when the town was occupied for four months by Union troops. Betty Maury recorded in her diary: "Their flags are everywhere, over foundry, bank, bridges, stores, stretched in lines across the streets, tacked on trees, stuck on soldier's guns, tied to horns of oxen." When Federal troops arrived they conducted a house-by-house search for weapons and confiscated five swords at the Maury house. The Federal troops left a path of destruction in their wake: bayoneted paintings, wrecked furniture and broken china and crystal.

Residents were almost entirely Confederate supporters, and so in December 1862 when sentries were anxiously watching the Rappahannock River for signs of an imminent Union attack, they weren't surprised to hear a woman's voice calling a warning across the river. "Yankees cooking big ration! March tomorrow!" The Confederates had retreated just a short distance outside the town and entrenched themselves in a seven-mile line. The crucial half-mile of their line was behind a protective stone wall.

To gain an overview of the battle, stop at the Fredericksburg National Park Service Visitor Center. It provides a slide show, exhibits and a self-guided battlefield tour map for Fredericksburg, Chancellorsville, Wilderness and Spotsylvania. There is also a visitor center at Chancellorsville.

Before leaving Fredericksburg be sure to visit **Chatham**. This gracious 18th-century Georgian mansion paid a high price for its choice location overlooking the Rappahannock River. The house was a front-line headquarters for Union General Edwin V. Sumner and others. Chatham was also a field hospital, served by Clara Barton, known as the "Angel of the Battlefield." Walt Whitman, one of America's most revered poets, also worked in the hospital.

Chatham is also noteworthy because it is the only home still standing where both George Washington and Abraham Lincoln are known to have been entertained. Local enthusiasts claim that George Washington wrote in a letter to William Fitzhugh, "I have put my legs oftener under your mahogany at Chatham than anywhere else in the world, and have enjoyed your good dinners, good wine and good company more than any other." The builder of Chatham, William Fitzhugh, achieved such a reputation for hospitality he was exhausted by a steady stream of guests. He finally sold Chatham and moved to a smaller house in Alexandria, now known as the Boyhood Home of Robert E. Lee (see selection), where he could more readily restrict his social calendar.

You can tour Chatham and see several rooms of museum exhibits. The gardens have been restored and from the river overlook there is a panoramic view of Fredericksburg. Chatham and the Fredericksburg Visitor Center are open at no charge daily from 9:00 A.M. to 5:00 P.M.

Directions: From I-95 take the Fredericksburg exit. Take Route 3 east into town. Turn right on Littepage Street and right again on Lafayette Boulevard to reach the Fredericksburg Visitor Center. Chatham is two miles from the visitor center, off Route 218, east of the Rappahannock River.

Hugh Mercer Apothecary Shop and Rising Sun Tavern

Both Mixed a Mean Brew

Combine business and pleasure 18th-century style when you visit Fredericksburg. On Caroline Street, you will find the **Hugh Mercer Apothecary Shop** and the Rising Sun Tavern, social centers of town during the colonial period.

The apothecary shop looks as it did the day in 1776 when Mercer left Fredericksburg to serve in the Continental army. Mercer, a brigadier general, was killed at the Battle of Princeton. His shop, though filled with few original items, does authentically reflect the colonial practice of both diagnosing ailments and preparing medications. (Of note: General George S. Patton of World War II fame was Huge Mercer's great, great, great grandson.)

Dr. Mercer obtained his medical degree in Scotland at the University of Aberdeen. He served as assistant surgeon to the Army of the Pretender, Charles Edward Stuart, and provided medical assistance at the Battle of Culloden. Mercer's support for a losing cause forced his emigration to Philadelphia in 1746. Later when he moved to Fredericksburg, he entered into practice with Dr. Ewen Clements. They placed the following ad in an issue of the *Virginia Gazette* in 1771: ". . . This day became Partners in the Practice of Physick and Surgery, and have opened Shop on Main Street, furnished with a large assortment of Drugs and Medicines just imported from London."

Dr. Mercer had become friends with several Virginians while serving in the French and Indian War. One of his closest friends was George Washington. Since Washington's mother, sister and brother lived in Fredericksburg (see Kenmore Plantation and Mary Washington House selection), the two men were able to maintain close ties. It is likely that many Virginia patriots gathered with these two experienced soldiers in the candle-lit office library to discuss British intransigence.

The Hugh Mercer Apothecary Shop at 1020 Caroline Street is open daily 9:00 A.M. to 5:00 P.M. A nominal admission is charged.

Just down the street at 1304 Caroline Street is another popular meeting spot, the **Rising Sun Tavern**. Built in 1760 for Charles Washington, George's younger brother, it was his home and not a tavern. Later in the century it became a tavern, where entertainment was provided by traveling players. Balls and many meetings took place as well. The tavern also served as the stage coach stop and Post Office.

Visitors to Rising Sun Tavern see the original tavern; although it has been extensively restored and refurnished, it has never been structurally altered. It is a simple colonial story-and-a-half-frame house that looks more residential than commercial. The hand-beveled clapboard, steep gabled roof and narrow dormer windows look quite homey.

During renovations the original bar railing was found. This has made it possible to rebuild the bar to its 18th-century specifications. The tap room has an impressive collection of English and American pewter. There are also gaming tables reflecting the sporting nature of the tavern.

Guided tours of the Rising Sun Tavern are given daily April through November from 9:00 A.M. to 5:00 P.M. From December through March hours are 10:00 A.M. to 4:00 P.M. The tavern is closed on major holidays. Admission is charged.

James Mercer, a lawyer who moved to Fredericksburg in 1768, was also a friend of the Washington family. He wrote the will of Mary Ball Washington (George's mother) in 1788. Mercer purchased ten lots in a new part of Fredericksburg created by Fielding Lewis (the husband of George Washington's sister, see Kenmore selection).

Mercer called his small gambrel-roofed house, **St. James House**, in rememberance of the Dublin, Ireland street where his family's home was located. Mercer was politically active, serving in 1779 as one of Virginia's delegates to the Continental Congress and ending his career by serving as a judge on the Virginia Court of Appeals.

The house, filled with elegant English and American antiques as well as outstanding 18th-century porcelain and glass, is now owned by the Association for the Preservation of Virginia Antiquities. It is open during Historic Garden Week and the first week in October, and other times by appointment; call (540) 373-0776.

Directions: From I-95 take the Fredericksburg exit, Route 3. Take Route 3 to William Street, then follow the blue visitor signs and turn right on Princess Ann Street. Then turn left on Caroline Street. Continue following blue signs to the Fredericksburg Visitor Center on Caroline Street. You can obtain maps and brochures on all the city attractions. St. James House is at 1300 Charles Street.

The Rising Sun Tavern was built in 1760 as a home for Charles Washington, George's younger brother. It became a tavern later in the century and served as a stage coach stop.

Kenmore Plantation and Gardens and Mary Washington House

All in the Family

Like mother, like daughter. If Mary Ball Washington and her daughter Betty Washington Lewis were not completely alike, they were at least very similar. Both were widowed, both lived in Fredericksburg and both had households supported in part, if not entirely, by George Washington.

Betty's husband Fielding Lewis was a wealthy landowner, businessman, court justice and member of the House of Burgesses. Lewis spared no expense building a luxurious Georgian mansion shortly after marrying Betty in 1750. **Kenmore** was one of the earliest colonial mansions to have plastered rather than paneled walls. The ornate plasterwork on walls and ceilings is considered the finest example of the art in the United States. The drawing room ceiling is a masterpiece and deservedly was included in Helen Comstock's *100 Most Beautiful Rooms in America* (now unfortunately out of print).

It is good that Fielding Lewis did not wait to build his bride a home; his efforts to support the Continental army bankrupted him. He used his substantial fortune to found the Fredericksburg Gunnery, which manufactured and repaired munitions for the army. He also outfitted ships. His death just two months after Yorktown gave him no opportunity to recoup his losses, thus it fell to Betty's brother George to help support her household.

The furnishings you see on your tour match the inventory taken after Colonel Lewis's death in December 1781, with additional items reflecting the belongings sold after Betty's death in 1797. One family piece is Betty's portrait in the dining room. She looked like her brother. According to one account, "It was a matter of frolic to throw a cloak around her and, placing a military hat on her head, such was her amazing resemblance that battalions would have presented arms. . ."

The path to the kitchen leads through the 18th-century formal boxwood gardens; spend some time exploring this recreated haven with its flanking gazeboes. The brick path once led to **Mary Washington's House** just two blocks away. It is said that when Lafayette visited Fredericksburg he, too, used this garden path, and came upon the commander-in-chief's mother working in her boxwood garden in her apron.

George purchased this town house for his mother on September 18, 1772. As he explained to his friend Benjamin Harrison, "Before I left Virginia (to make her more comfortable and free from care) I did at her request, but at my own expense, purchase a commodious house, garden and Lotts (of her own choosing) in Fredericksburg that she might be near my sister Lewis, her own daughter. . ." Although she suggested the move Mary Washington often complained of the city noises and water. According to local legend, she sent a slave back to Ferry Farm, her former rural residence, each day for fresh well water.

This was not the only complaint she made. She repeatedly upbraided George for his neglect. While Washington was struggling with Congress to obtain funds for the Continental Army, his mother was petitioning the Virginia Legislature for a pension to offset the stinginess of her son. Embarrassed at this news, he responded that she "had an ample income of her own" and that further he had provided funds for her whenever they were requested. He was careful, however, to note them in the debit side of his detailed ledgers. In the midst of the staggering deprivations of the Valley Forge winter encampment, Washington's mother wrote to him, "I would be much obliged to you to send me four pounds cash for corn . . . I have never lived so poor in my life. . . ."

Like Kenmore, the town house is furnished to reflect items in the wills of Augustine and Mary Washington. Eighteenth-century pieces fill the rooms; only a few, like the looking glass, engravings and *Book of Meditations,* belonged to Mary Washington.

Mary Ball Washington lived for the last 17 years of her life in this house. She died four months after George Washington's inauguration on August 25, 1789. At her request she is buried on land that was once part of Kenmore near Mediation Rock.

Kenmore Plantation and Gardens is open March through December 10:00 A.M. to 5:00 P.M.; on Sunday it opens at NOON. In January and February it is open Monday through Friday by reservation only, Saturday and President's Day 10:00 A.M. to 4:00 P.M. and Sunday NOON to 4:00 P.M. It is closed on major holidays. Tickets are purchased in Kenmore's Museum Shop. Hours at the Mary Washington House are 9:00 A.M. to 5:00 P.M. March through November and 10:00 A.M. to 4:00 P.M. December through February. Both charge admission.

Directions: From I-95 take the Fredericksburg exit and follow Route 3 east. It becomes William Street. Make a left on Washington Avenue for Kenmore. For the Mary Washington House continue down William Street to Charles and turn left. The house is at 1200 Charles Street.

The Monroe Presidential Center

Man for All Seasons—Statesman for All Occasions

In the famous painting, *Washington Crossing the Delaware,* James Monroe is depicted as the young man behind George Washington holding the flag. Monroe did not stay in the background for long. (He wasn't actually in the background on that icy crossing. Still a very young lieutenant, Monroe wasn't with Washington when the general crossed the river. Monroe and Washington's nephew, Captain William Washington, crossed the river the day before to scout for British troops. The two young men spent the night depicted in the painting spying on Hessian

53

troops in the town of Trenton.) Monroe had an illustrious career: he went on to become U.S. Senator, American Ambassador to France, England and Spain, four-term Governor of Virginia, Secretary of State, Secretary of War and two-term President of the United States.

It is the young James Monroe who is remembered in Fredericksburg. It was here that he began his legal practice after reading law with Thomas Jefferson in Williamsburg. **The Monroe Presidential Center** is in a brick building on the site where Monroe practiced law from 1786 to 1789. For many years it was thought that Monroe actually practiced law in this building, but studies have shown it was not here prior to 1815. Monroe probably worked in a wooden structure on this town lot which he sold for a nice profit in 1792–93.

Inside the center you'll see reminders of Monroe's long career of public service. Perhaps the most significant is his Louis XVI desk. It was at this desk in 1823 that Monroe signed the message to Congress containing the section that has become known as the Monroe Doctrine. The desk has three secret compartments that were not discovered until 1906. They held 200 letters Monroe received from Alexander Hamilton, Benjamin Franklin and other statesmen of his day.

James Monroe, fifth president, was the first to occupy the White House after it was burned by the British in 1814. Since all the furniture had been destroyed, the Monroes had to fill the house with their own pieces. While in France representing the United States they had acquired a great many Louis XVI pieces of mahogany and brass. Today you see the originals in this Fredericksburg museum. (The White House has copies, made at Mrs. Hoover's direction in 1932.)

Among the museum's most popular exhibits are selections of Mrs. Monroe's gowns. There is a stunning Empire-styled velvet gown and citrine jewels that she wore to the Court of Napoleon and a green velvet suit worn by Mr. Monroe.

For scholars the museum has an extensive library about James Monroe and his pivotal foreign policy doctrine. A reconstruction of a 19th-century Virginia gentleman's library is also housed here. You'll leave the museum through an old-fashioned walled garden with a bronze bust of James Monroe. The bust was by Margaret French Cresson, daughter of Daniel Chester French, who created the "sitting Lincoln" in marble at the Lincoln Memorial in Washington, D.C.

The Monroe Presidential Center is open 9:00 A.M. to 5:00 P.M. from March through November. From December through February it is open 10:00 A.M. to 4:00 P.M. It is closed on Thanksgiving, Christmas Eve and Day and New Year's Eve and Day. Admission is charged.

Directions: From I-95 take the Fredericksburg exit and follow Route 3 east to the heart of town. Turn right on Charles Street and you will see The Monroe Presidential Center at 908 Charles Street.

NORTHERN VIRGINIA

Claude Moore Colonial Farm at Turkey Run

A History Lesson Kids Gobble Up

Most agricultural recreations portray the plantations of the prosperous, a few represent the freeholders' farms but far too few let you see the far more common dirt farmer's homestead. This gives 20th-century visitors a distorted view of life in colonial times—we don't see how the majority of people actually lived. This oversight is corrected at **The Claude Moore Colonial Farm at Turkey Run** which provides a glimpse of just such a low-income farm of the 18th century.

This living history farm is run the way it would have been more than two centuries ago in the 1770s. It is easy to believe that you have stepped back in time when the guide, dressed in appropriate colonial work clothes, explains that his work in the fields prevented him from putting in the board floor. The woman of the house sweeps the dirt floor with a hand-bound straw broom and says she hopes to get the board floor in soon. She is also likely to complain that the cabin was built in such a hurry the logs were not stripped and the mud mortar is crumbling where the logs meet so it doesn't provide enough protection from the elements.

The one-room cabin is surrounded by fields of tobacco and corn, which the farmer plants, hoes and harvests. Tobacco is grown in hopes of raising a little money. Subsistence crops like beans, pumpkins, squash, corn and melons feed the family. Various foods are dried, smoked or salted to make the lean wintertime a little easier. The farm has livestock appropriate to the period: chickens, hogs and horses.

You can watch the never-ending tasks that made up life on a colonial farm. Soap had to be made from tallow and cloth from sheep's wool. Animal skins were tanned to make shoes; buttons were made from bone or deer antlers. Water was fetched daily from a nearby stream and gourds hollowed out for serving bowls and utensils. Although the farmer and his wife only come in by

A worker demonstrates how tobacco was harvested in the 18th-century on a low-income farm at Claude Moore Colonial Farm at Turkey Run.

the day, they present a masterful illusion that they actually live here and that you have stepped into a time machine and have been transported back to colonial Virginia.

Just inside the entrance to the Claude Moore Colonial Farm several picnic tables invite you to sylvan spots. The farm is open April through mid-December, Wednesday through Sunday from 10:00 A.M. to 4:30 P.M. Admission is charged. During the farm season, staff present seven "Food Preservation" programs focusing on such topics as: salting fish, making cheese and butter, herbs, pickling produce, drying vegetables, smoking meat and others. They also host three 18th-century Market Fairs on the third full weekend of May, July and October. There are several other special farm family events; for a schedule call (703) 442-7557.

Directions: From I-495/95, the Capital Beltway, take Exit 13, Route 193, Georgetown Pike east toward Langley for 2$^1/_3$ miles. Turn left at the sign for the Claude Moore Colonial Farm.

The Flying Circus

Old Stuff Still the Right Stuff

The Flying Circus is an old-fashioned barnstorming extravaganza that has re-created the halcyon days of aviation for more than 25 years. It proudly claims to have "the authenticity of a museum with amusement park thrills."

All across America small towns used to look forward to the excitement of the visiting barnstorming show. Town folk would run out into yards and fields when the new-fangled flying wonders buzzed their community. The Flying Circus near Bealeton is one of the last examples of this highly popular form of entertainment.

Shows are given at 2:30 P.M. on Sunday afternoons from May through October by an enthusiastic group of aviation buffs, including broadcasters, military and airline pilots. As one airline pilot said, "The Circus gives you freedom to enjoy what you're doing. At 200 feet, you can feel your speed, see the ground go rushing by under you. At 35,000, you feel like you're standing still."

Many of the flyers at the Circus have rebuilt their own biplanes, planes with double wings. Among the vintage planes flying here (and seen elsewhere only in museums) are a 1940 Stearman, a Waco and a 1929 Fleet. Like the barnstormers of old, the pilots take them through all kinds of aerobatics (stunt flying). The audience gasps seeing these biplanes made of cloth, wood and wire turn somersaults, fly upside down and plummet dangerously close to the ground.

Young and old are impressed when a pilot breaks a series of balloons with his plane's propeller blades. As a stunt flyer explains, "First impression is that all you have to do is hit the balloons with the airplane, which is no big deal, but if you don't slice it with the last four to six inches of the propeller, it won't pop." Another popular stunt is slicing a falling ribbon three times before it hits the ground, an incredible demonstration of the maneuverability of biplanes.

The Flying Circus parachutist can land on a dime; or at least an airshow equivalent, the tiny platform directly in front of the cheering crowd. The top crowd pleaser is the wing walker. Exactly like less sophisticated audiences of the 1920s and 30s, today's visitors hold their breaths when the daredevils climb out of the cockpit. Without parachutes they stand on the wing while the plane loops and barrel rolls. The biggest applause comes when the wing walker hangs by his heels as the plane makes a low pass across the field. The tension is relieved by watching the clowns and the tethered hot air balloons.

The Roaring '20s Barnstorming show with 15 acts lasts about 90 minutes, but visitors (picnickers included) may come as early as 11:00 A.M. when the field opens. After the show you can view the biplanes up close and talk to the pilots.

For an experience you'll never forget, try a ride in one of the vintage planes. It's worth the fee, especially if you're willing to indulge in a bit of aerobatics. Passengers ride in the front cockpit and once you put on the helmet and goggles you'll feel like a flying ace. There are also hot air balloon rides.

Plane models can be purchased in the wooden hanger that serves as a small museum. A stand sells snacks and cold drinks. Admission is charged. Special events, include model airplane competitions, antique car meets and the annual Hot Air Balloon Festival in mid-August. For additional information call (540) 439-8661.

Directions: From I-95 at Fredericksburg take Route 17 north for 22 miles. The Flying Circus is just off Route 17 on Route 644 near Bealeton, watch for signs.

Manassas

War and Peace

Soldiers from the Union and Confederate armies met on the battlefield at Manassas more than twice. Of course, the First and Second Battles of Manassas are the occasions you read about in history books. The opening salvos on July 21, 1861, were the first of the many major battles that would be fought by the Blue and the Gray. The Confederate victory at Second Manassas gave the South the momentum to carry the struggle into the North. **Manassas National Battlefield Park** has an audiovisual presentation, electric map program and battlefield maps that provide details of the two pivotal battles. You can rent an automobile tour tape for the Second Battle of Manassas.

The less well-known meetings are also filled with human interest and historical significance. In the years after the great struggle soldiers from both armies often visited this battlefield. They came to remember fallen comrades, reflect on the battles they survived and perhaps relive the times they could not forget. In the 1920s, before the Manassas battlefield came under the jurisdiction of the federal government, Mr. Adoniram Powell was caretaker.

Mr. Powell conducted tours of the battlefield and there were occasions when veterans from both sides joined forces to help him retrace the action. Imagine the difficulty of guiding those who had fought one another and had quite different memories. During one such awkward tour Mr. Powell pointed out the land where, he said, Jeb Stuart had led his First Virginia Cavalry in a sudden and violent attack that broke through the ranks of the New York Fire Zouaves. "T'ain't so!" snorted a grizzled Union veteran. "That ain't the way it was. I was there, and I know." With trepidation because the mood of his mixed audience was unpredictable, Mr. Powell explained that according to the stories he had heard, the resplendent Zouaves retreated. The old warrior proclaimed, "We didn't retreat. We ran like hell."

Mr. Powell is long gone, as are the veterans of this bitter struggle, but rangers still provide walking tours of First Manassas on the hilly ground surrounding the visitor center. During the summer months there are special programs highlighting key action during both battles.

The Manassas National Battlefield Park Visitor Center is open daily, except Christmas Day. Hours are 8:30 A.M. to 5:00 P.M., extended to 6:00 P.M. in the summer months. A park entrance fee, payable at the visitor center, allows for park use and activities for seven days.

The story of the first peaceful meeting between Union and Confederate soldiers at Manassas is one that is all too frequently overlooked. It was called the National Jubilee of Peace and took place on July 21, 1911, 50 years after the first confrontation. The day began with soldiers of the Blue and the Gray once again lined up facing each other. This time, instead of responding to the order to fire, they slowly closed the gap between the lines and solemnly clasped hands in friendship.

The Peace Jubilee continued in town with a speech by President William Howard Taft which, according to a letter by his

59

aide Major Archie Butt, was "a flubdub speech about the Blue and the Gray which brought tears to the eyes of veterans of both sides and smiles to the faces of politicians." At the base of the stone monument, in front of the former Prince William County Courthouse, are cannons and naval anchors (contributed by Assistant Secretary of Navy Franklin Delano Roosevelt) to commemorate the Jubilee.

The Peace Jubilee Monument is one of the points of interest on the tours (either walking or driving) of **Old Town Manassas**. There are two museums: the Manassas Museum and Rohr's Museum, adjacent to the late Mayor Edgar Rohr's old-fashioned variety store. The latter houses a collection of antique cars including a custom-made 1933 Rohr sedan, as well as a rare 1905 Paragon. Other cars are a 1917 Detroit Electric and a 1957 Thunderbird. The second floor of **Rohr's Museum** has everything from toys and dolls to light bulbs and license plates. Rohr's Museum is open 2:00 to 5:00 P.M. on summer Sundays and by appointment at other times. To arrange a visit call (703) 368-3000.

The **Manassas Museum** interprets the history of the Northern Virginia Piedmont region with Manassas as the focal point. Exhibits feature prehistoric stone tools, Civil War weapons and uniforms, Victorian furnishings, railroad items and textiles. Two video programs, "A Place of Passages" and the award-winning "A Community at War" tell the story of the region's development and the effects of the Civil War. Annual events include a series of outdoor living history programs in the summer and a holiday open house in early December.

The Manassas Museum, at 9191 Prince William Street, is open 10:00 A.M. to 5:00 P.M. Tuesday through Sunday. The museum is closed on Mondays, except federal holidays, and Thanksgiving, Christmas Eve and Day and New Year's Day. For information on special events call (703) 368-1873.

Directions: From the Washington Beltway in Virginia take I-66 west to Manassas, Exit 47B. The Manassas National Park Visitor Center is one mile north of exit at 6511 Sudley Road, Route 234. From I-95 south of Alexandria, take Exit 152 to Route 234 into Manassas. This will take you through Old Town Manassas. You can stop at Manassas Visitor Center at 9025 Center Street for additional information and walking and driving tour brochures.

Morven Park and Oatlands

Band Box Perfection

The two lavish country estates, **Morven Park** and Oatlands, on either side of Leesburg, would appear at first glance to create a problem of choice. These grand houses are white and have columned entrance ways, but their differences are far greater than their similarities, making it worth a visit to each.

Although from the outside Morven Park may suggest Scarlet O'Hara's Tara, the opulent interior is more reminiscent of William Randolph Hearst's San Simeon. The mixture of architectural styles—the Renaissance grand hall, French drawing room and Jacobean dining room—is matched by furnishings collected from around the world by the 20th-century owners, Governor Westmoreland Davis and his wife.

The house the Davises purchased in 1903 has changed dramatically over the years. Originally the land was farmed by Pennsylvanians who settled in the area in the late 1700s. An unpretentious stone house was built here around 1781. In 1808 Thomas Swann acquired the land and built a Federal-style home which he enlarged after he retired. It was Swann who added the Greek Revival four-columned entrance portico. Swann named his estate after the Princeton, New Jersey home of Commodore Robert F. Stockton, who was flattered by his gesture but suggested that he add "Park" to the name because of the vast acreage (roughly 2,562 acres at that time).

After inheriting his father's estate, Thomas Swann, Jr. was too involved in business and politics to spend much time at this Leesburg estate. His position as president of the Baltimore & Ohio Railroad made it necessary for him to spend time in Baltimore. He maintained Morven Park as a summer residence while living in Annapolis as governor of Maryland and in the Washington area as a five-term congressman. Despite the claims on his schedule, he still exerted a great deal of influence on Morven Park. It was Thomas Swann, Jr., who embarked on the last major building program, integrating the three separate buildings into the one imposing mansion you see today.

If the exterior reflects Governor Swann, the interior reflects the taste of Governor and Mrs. Davis. They filled the house with treasures from Europe, including the 1550 Brabant tapestries that line the great hall. Their grandeur is matched by the red velvet thrones from the Pitti Palace that sit beneath them. The ornately carved dining room furniture is reflected in huge rococo mirrors.

The house tour at Morven Park is just the beginning. There is a great deal more to see. The Museum of Hounds and Hunting traces fox hunting in America from George Washington's day to the present. The Winmill Carriage Collection was bequeathed to the estate. It provides a mini-history of transportation in the 18th century. Names you may only have encountered in books take on fascinating form, as you examine landaus, sulkies, breaks and phaetons as well as the more easily recognized carriages, sleighs, carts, coaches and buggies in the 70-vehicle collection, which rotates exhibits.

Nature lovers will find an extensive garden. The Marguerite G. Davis Boxwood Garden has the largest living stand of boxwoods in the United States. Spring bushes and bulbs add color and in the summer months roses, dahlias and crepe myrtle bloom.

Morven Park is open April through October from NOON to 5:00 P.M. weekdays and 10:00 A.M. to 5:00 P.M. on weekends. It is open weekends only in November. There are special December hours; call (703) 777-2414 for details. Admission is charged.

Oatlands traces its lineage back to Virginia's early days. The land was purchased by the Carter family from Lord Fairfax as part of the 11,357-acre Goose Creek Tract. George Carter, drew close to 5,000 acres in a lottery held by his father for his ten surviving children. In 1804, Carter built a post-colonial country house on his estate. George Carter married a 39-year old widow, Elizabeth Grayson Lewis, when he was 60. He died after only nine short years of wedded life.

Elizabeth and their two sons briefly abandoned Oatlands at the start of the Civil War. The boys served in the Confederate army and the house served as a billet for Confederate troops. After the war the Carter family had difficulty maintaining the house. They took in boarders for a time but eventually were forced to sell the family home and 60 acres.

The Greek Classical Revival house has a three-story pavilion flanked by two-story wings. In a break with tradition, it has a staircase on each end of the house rather than one in the center. Oatlands, like Morven Park, did undergo some remodeling over the first 20 years, 1804–1829. When the vogue for octagonal rooms caught on, a square-shaped room was converted to an eight-sided drawing room. One of the most distinctive features of the interior design is the elaborate plasterwork done in the 1820s.

The house and garden you see today were reclaimed by Mr. and Mrs. William Corcoran Eustis after years of neglect. He was the grandson of the founder of the Corcoran Gallery in Washington, D.C. They furnished the house with American, English and French pieces. The dessert plates you'll see on the dining table once belonged to George Washington.

The Eustises restored the boxwood garden laid out by George Carter, reclaiming and expanding to create what is now considered one of Virginia's finest gardens. Mrs. Eustis, in describing the garden, said it was noted for "mystery, variety and the unexpected." It is the only garden in the country to use boxwood for the pleached, or tunnel, walk. The wisteria walk is a springtime delight. Specialty areas include a rosarium and an herb garden.

Oatlands is open April through late December, Tuesday through Saturday and federal holiday Mondays from 10:00 A.M. to 4:30 P.M. and Sunday from 1:00 to 4:30 P.M. Admission is charged.

Directions: From I-95 in the Fredericksburg area, take Route 17 northwest until it merges with Route 29/15. Turn right on Route 29/15 and continue north. Once you are beyond Warrenton, Route 29/15 divides. Take Route 15 north toward Leesburg. Oatlands is off Route 15 on the right just before Leesburg; Morven Park is off Route 15 on the left just past Leesburg. From the Washington Beltway I-495/95, take Route 7 west to Leesburg, then Route 15 south toward Warrenton. Oatlands is on Route 15, six miles south of Leesburg.

Occoquan

A Trail of Mills

One explanation for the country saying "mean as an old dog" is that it derives from the irascible temperament of the Dogue Indians who once lived in Virginia. The name **Occoquan** comes from a Dogue word meaning "at the end of the waters."

Occoquan, at the head of the Tidewater and the foot of the Piedmont region, was established as a milling community in the early 18th century. In 1734 the Virginia Assembly chose Occoquan as the location for a public tobacco warehouse.

Though its early existence was industrial, it is now a picturesque artisans' community. Ninety-seven retail shops sit within a four block square, designated a Virginia Historic District and included on the National Register of Historic Places. Many of the artist-owners teach their craft as well as sell their work. For example, at the Country Shop on Mill Street, Milly Lehto teaches quilting, sells a wide selection of fabrics and quilting supplies and advises the White House on the quilts they acquire.

At the Basket Case, you can learn to weave baskets or purchase locally made, creatively designed baskets. Classes are given at the Occoquan Gallery and The Undertaking Artists' Coop. The latter, originally a funeral home, is just one of several shops that, according to local lore, is haunted. In the late evening brisk steps echo through deserted corridors. Artists-in-residence call their unseen companion the conscientious undertaker.

The last Native American in Occoquan is said to haunt the Occoquan Inn, one of several dining spots. A reflection of the tall Brave with long black hair is reported to have been seen in an upstairs mirror. The Dogue Indians lived in harmony with the European settlers and this shadowy reminder is said to be a peaceful presence.

Most shops in Occoquan are open daily, but some do close on Monday. For more town history stop at the historic **Occoquan Museum** on Mill Street, open June through September. Hours are Tuesday through Saturday, 11:00 A.M. to 4:00 P.M. and Sunday 1:00 to 5:00 P.M. The museum is also open on weekends during April, May and October.

While in Occoquan, also plan on visiting Prince William County's attractive Visitor Information Center, located across from the riverfront at 200 Mill Street. The center's staff will help with directions and information on attractions throughout the county and advise on accommodations and restaurants. Hours are 9:00 A.M. to 5:00 P.M.

Heading south on I-95 you will come to **Potomac Mills** (Exit 156 Dale City), billed as one of the world's largest value/outlet centers. More than 220 manufacturer's outlets, retail outlets and traditional discounters are found inside a 1.7 million-square-foot enclosed shopping center. With prices 20% to 60% below retail and hardwood floors for easy walking through nine neighborhoods of discounts, Potomac Mills is the number one shopping magnet of Virginia. Stores included are Nordstrom Rack, JC Penney Outlet, Spiegel Outlet, Macy's, Waccamaw, The Clearinghouse, Saks Fifth Avenue, Ann Taylor Factory Store, Eddie Bauer Outlet, Zales Jewelry Outlet, Barneys New York Outlet and IKEA of Sweden which claims to be the world's largest home furnishings retailer. A food court with 15 eateries and movie theaters provide respite for shoppers. Potomac Mills Mall is open Monday through Saturday 10:00 A.M. to 9:30 P.M. and Sunday from 11:00 A.M. to 6:00 P.M. For information call (800) VA-MILLS.

Leaving Potomac Mills, trade the excitement of bargain-hunting for a few hours of extraordinary beauty and soul-restoring quiet as you visit **Leesylvania State Park**, arguably the finest waterfront access point on the Potomac. Here, at one of the state's newest parks, you'll find well-designed nature and hiking trails, excellent recreational facilities and provisions for all types of boating and fishing. Here too, history buffs will discover the ruins of "Light Horse" Harry Lee's plantation home. Lee, a renowned colonial soldier and Virginia statesmen, was also the forbearer of Robert E. Lee.

Directions: From I-95 north, for Potomac Mills take Exit 156 toward Dale City. Then follow Route 784 west to Gideon Road (the first stoplight). Make a right on Gideon, then cross Smoketown Road and turn into the Potomac Mills parking lot. For Occoquan continue north on I-95 toward Washington. Take Exit 160, Route 123, which will take you into the historic town.

Prince William Forest Park

Plus Marines and Weems-Botts Museums

If the idea of hiking all day through a woodland watershed, passing only a few fellow nature lovers, appeals to you, then visit **Prince William Forest Park**, managed by the National Park Service.

The park's 37 miles of trails and fire roads crisscross the north and south branches of the Quantico Creek. The land now reclaimed by the forest was once farm land. Settlement in the area goes back to 1756 when Scottish settlers established a port in Dumfries that rivaled any in the New World. It is from Dumfries that historians believe William Ramsay barged his home up the Potomac River to his lot in the new town of Alexandria (see selection). Poor farming practices led to soil erosion and the harbor at Quantico Creek became silted. It eventually became an unpenetrable marsh. Now whistling swans winter over along Quantico Creek at Dumfries.

The land on which Prince William Forest Park stands was originally acquired by the federal government as the Chopawamsic Recreation Demonstration Area in 1934. The Civilian Conservation Corps began the process of restoring this land to its natural state. As you follow the forest trails you'll see old orchards, building foundations, overgrown cemeteries and an old pyrite mine site.

Today songbirds, raptors, white-tail deer, foxes, ruffed grouse, flying squirrels, wild turkeys and beavers populate the woods. You are more likely to see signs of the beavers' presence than any of these shy animals. Throughout the woods beaver dams are under construction across meandering streams. If you have a fishing license you can try your luck catching the bass, bluegill, perch and catfish found in the park's streams. Park rangers will direct you where you can go to get a fishing license.

The Pine Grove Forest Trail, at the Pine Grove Picnic Area, is paved to provide access for strollers and wheelchairs. Taped messages at audio stations tell about the animals found here. At the Oak Ridge campground, the Farms to Forest Trail shows the process of reclamation from cleared land to forest land. For park information and trail maps, stop at the park's visitor center, approximately one mile past the main entrance.

While in the area be sure to stop at the **Marine Corps Air-Ground Museum** across Route 1 from the park. You need no advance reservations. The Marine guard at the sentry booth will check your driver's license when you enter the base and issue you a Visitor's Pass.

For many years the museum was limited primarily to Marine aviation but now the scope is broader and includes ground equipment and weapons. Currently there are three hangars open to the public: the first covering the "Early Years" of the air-ground team (1900–1941), the second covering World War II, and a third hangar on the Korean War.

Quantico's association with aviation goes back to the Civil War when hot air balloons were used for reconnaissance over the Potomac River near Quantico. Dr. Samuel Pierpont Langley launched a 25-pound, 13-foot flying model from the roof of a wooden houseboat moored in the river. He believed the water would make recovery of the craft more likely. Langley models were the forerunner of the Wright brothers' airplane. Langley did try two unsuccessful manned flights before the Wright brothers succeeded at Kitty Hawk.

Langley's flying machine is on display in the main lobby of the National Air and Space Museum in Washington, but the Marine Corps Air-Ground Museum exhibits some of his early models in the first hangar. Included in this exhibit are a Curtiss airplane "Pusher" and World War I vintage aircraft: a Thomas-Morse "Scout" advance trainer and a DeHaviland D.H. 4B fighter bomber of the type flown by Marine pilots in France. There are also two Boeing fighter planes from the late 1920s and 1930s as well as a Stearman N25-3 primary trainer. A Wright J-5 "Whirlwind" engine on display is the same type that powered Lucky Lindy's "Spirit of St. Louis."

In addition to the airplanes, there are track and wheeled vehicles, artillery, small arms, uniforms, personal equipment, photographs and art—all part of the story of the Marine Corps' air-ground attack and defense.

The museum is open April through the third Sunday in November from 10:00 A.M. to 5:00 P.M. Tuesday through Saturday and NOON to 5:00 P.M. on Sunday. It is closed on Mondays and Easter Sunday. Guided tours are provided for groups by prior arrangement; call (703) 784-2606. No guided tours begin after 4:00 P.M.

One other museum in the area is the **Weems-Botts Museum** just up Route 1 in Dumfries. Parson Weems was a physician, preacher and traveling bookseller. In the early 1800s, Parson Mason Locke Weems wrote the first biography of George Washington. His apocryphal anecdotes, including the cherry-tree story, have become part of American folklore.

Weems purchased this story-and-a-half house in 1798 to use as a bookstore. In 1802 Benjamin Botts purchased the house to use as his law office. Benjamin Botts was the youngest lawyer on Aaron Burr's defense team during Burr's 1807 trial for treason. It is good that Botts achieved early fame for he met a tragic death along with his wife, the governor of Virginia and 162 other patrons who perished in the Richmond Theater fire of 1811. An addition to the Weems-Botts house built in the mid-1800s by the Merchant family, now houses artifacts from the Dumfries area. The museum hours are 10:00 A.M. to 4:00 P.M. Tuesday through Saturday.

Directions: From I-95 south of Alexandria take Exit 150, the Quantico-Triangle exit. The exit sign will also indicate the turns for Prince William Forest Park (Exit 150-B) just off the interstate about $^1/_4$ mile west. For the Marine Corps Air-Ground Museum take Route 619 east for about a mile. For the Weems-Botts Museum take Exit 151 off I-95 and follow signs to the museum.

Warrenton, Marshall and Sky Meadows State Park

Village Vignettes

A trading post at the juncture of two rural Virginia roads was the earliest community gathering spot at what would become Warrenton, the county seat of Fauquier County. When the county was apportioned in 1759, it was the frontier of English civilization in the colony. Richard Henry Lee, who proposed the adoption of a Declaration of Independence, donated 71 acres of land for the county seat. Construction on the courthouse, the first genuine public building, did not begin until after independence in 1790.

The **Old Court House** you see today was built in 1893. The white-columned, clock-spired building is a replica of the 1841 courthouse that was adapted from the one finished in 1791. Before walking into this historic old building, be sure to take in the view from the portico of the distant Bull Run Mountains. A roster of distinguished lawyers are associated with this courthouse. The painting of John Marshall is significant because this courthouse is where he was first licensed to practice law. Another lawyer who argued cases here was Samuel Chilton, who defended John Brown.

Flanking the courthouse are monuments to John Marshall and Col. John Singleton Mosby (the partisan leader is buried in the nearby Warrenton Cemetery, adjacent to a memorial marking the graves of 600 Confederate casualties). To the right you'll also see The **Old Jail Museum** (open Tuesday through Sunday 10:00 A.M. to 4:00 P.M.), now the headquarters of the Fauquier Historical Society with exhibits on Warrenton and the county. Displays include memorabilia associated with John Marshall and military artifacts with special emphasis on the Civil War. Another exhibit focuses on canals, there is a bateau found in the Rappahannock River and an array of personal items from local residents dating from the 1700s and 1800s. Harkening to the building's history you can see the original kitchen of the 1808 jail, an 1823 cell room and a maximum security cell room (in use until 1966) complete with prisoner graffiti. You'll also see the exercise yard where once a three-person gallows was located. Prisoners were required to observe executions from the jail's second story windows.

There are other spots of interest to be seen on a self-guided walking tour. Be sure to allocate enough time to browse through the enticing shops along Warrenton's Main Street. On Wednesday (7:30 A.M. to 11:00 P.M.) and Saturday (7:30 A.M. to 1:00 P.M.) there is a farmer's market off Main Street on Fifth Street.

Just seven miles south of Warrenton off Route 643 is the 100-acre **C.M. Crockett Park** with its 109-acre lake. You can enjoy it by land on the extensive nature trails or by water either by bringing your own boat or by renting a rowboat, paddle boat or canoe.

If you head north of Warrenton on Route 17, you will reach the charming village of Marshall. Here, too, you can pick up a self-guided Heritage Map that pinpoints 38 points of interest in the second oldest town in the county, founded as Salem in 1797. The name was changed in 1882 to avoid confusion with another Virginia town that had the same name. The name Marshall honored the fourth chief justice of the Supreme Court, whose home, Oak Hill, is just three miles west of town on Route 55. Two churches in Marshall are of interest: the 1771 Baptist meeting house, the county's oldest surviving colonial church and Salem Baptist Church, organized in 1872 by former enslaved African Americans.

Continuing north on Route 17 leads to Paris and **Sky Meadows State Park**; here nature trails link up with the Appalachian Trail. The 1,862-acre park is a felicitous blend of pasture and woodlands. The Mt. Bleak farmhouse, now the visitor center, has stood here for over 150 years. The park has six hiking trails, two bridle trails, a fishing pond, picnic tables and 12 primitive hike-in camping areas. If you want to explore the rural back roads and villages of Fauquier County, pick up a copy of the *Sampler* which has a northern and southern driving tour. You can obtain a copy by calling the visitor center at (800) 820-1021.

Directions: From I-95 take Route 17 north, then pick up Routes 15/29 north to Warrenton. Or from I-66, take Route 29 south to Warrenton.

Waterford

A Fair-ly Long Run

Waterford has for diverse reasons—philosophic, economic and geographic—remained isolated over the centuries. This distancing has enabled Waterford to survive. The houses, shops, churches, schools, barns and fields all evoke a simpler way of life and preserve the unspoiled image of a 19th-century village.

Waterford was settled in 1733 by Quakers from Bucks County, Pennsylvania, who established a community of small farms. They were soon joined by Scotch-Irish craftsmen, also from the Pennsylvania colony, whose skills were responsible for the elaborately carved interiors of many of the Waterford homes. The community remained largely Quaker, however, and few took part in the American Revolution. Those who did fight were read out of meeting (see South River Meeting House selection). After the war and on through the early part of the 19th-century Waterford prospered. Many of the homes and shops you'll see date from this period.

It is interesting to discover that during the Civil War years the only organized troops in Virginia to fight for the North were the independent Loudoun Rangers, a group formed by Samuel Means, a miller from Waterford. After continued Confederate harassment, Mr. Means abandoned the Quaker principle of nonviolence. He organized the fighting brigade. The town came under Union fire because of its southern location. This crossfire resulted in numerous farms being torched by both sides.

Its geographical isolation left Waterford behind when the railroad brought new business to the nearby town of Leesburg. Many commercial establishments in Waterford failed because customers could buy cheaper machine-made goods "from outside." The arrival of the railroad was a boon to the farmers, most of whom were able to expand their markets. Many of those fields are still being farmed today, and form the setting for the village.

Restoration of the houses in the village was attempted on a small scale in the 1930s, but the real impetus to improvement came in 1943 with the establishment of the Waterford Foundation. For more than 50 years the foundation has been sponsoring an annual fair held the first weekend in October. It started small with the villagers gathering together to sell their handicrafts. Now it's called "the fairest of fairs." It's the oldest juried craft fair in Virginia and the three-day event is one of the best on the East Coast. More than 140 craft demonstrators take part. There is also entertainment as well as tours of 18th-and 19th-century private homes in the village. Fair time is one of the few

69

The Quaker village of Waterford, which began its restoration with a weekend fair some four decades ago, now offers house tours and 250 craftspeople annually at the state's "fairest of fairs."

times during the year that residents open their doors to visitors. During the fair 10 to 12 private homes can be explored. The fair admission is used to continue the foundation's renovation and restoration work and many educational programs. Efforts thus far have been successful, as you will discover.

The foundation has been rewarded by having Waterford included on the Virginia Historic Landmark Register and the National Register of Historic Places. The entire village and surrounding farmland is listed as a National Historic Landmark.

Although fair week in October is the best time to visit, there is one home in Waterford that operates as a bed and breakfast inn. The Pink House in the center of town was once used to billet troops during the Civil War; it now offers art, antiques and a pretty garden. To arrange a visit call (540) 882- 3453.

Waterford's tree-shaded streets are ideal for an old-fashioned walk. This town is not commercial, nor a museum; it's a community and visitors get a warm welcome. It's nice to know towns like this still exist.

Directions: From I-95 in the Fredericksburg area take Route 17B north to the intersection with Routes 29/15. Follow this around Warrenton toward Manassas and when the road splits take Route 15 to Leesburg. At the Route 7 Bypass around Leesburg, take Route 7 north four miles to Route 9. Take Route 9 for $1/4$ mile to Route 662 and turn right on Route 662 for Waterford. From the Washington Beltway take Route 7, Tyson's Corner exit and head west past Leesburg to Route 9. Turn right on Route 9 and follow above directions.

Begin exploring Hampton at the Visitor Center right beside the picturesque Hampton Harbor, embarkation point for excursion boats to Fort Wool.

Tidewater &
———Hampton Roads———

The historical triangle of Jamestown, Williamsburg and York-town is a window on the settlement, development and revolutionary zeal that fired the first years of American history.

America's first permanent English settlement was established in 1607 on Jamestown Island, now a national historical park. Replicas of the ships on which they arrived, a rebuilt fort and Native American village at Jamestown Settlement offer an expanded glimpse. This in-depth look at the first settlement is matched by the detail to be found at Colonial Williamsburg, the world's largest and most extensively restored 18th-century town. The colonists won their war for independence at Yorktown and the national battlefield and Yorktown Victory Center tell that story. More of the country's early history is revealed at the plantations along the James River. Berkeley is home to the first Thanksgiving in 1619 and the home of a Declaration signer and two presidents. Neighboring Sherwood Forest was the home of John Tyler, the 10th president. This region boasts the homes where George Washington and Robert E. Lee were born.

The 1,280 miles along the Atlantic Ocean and Cheasapeake Bay offer a wide array of recreational opportunities. A series of outstanding state-of-the-art facilities provide a fascinating look at the sea from diverse aspects: Nauticus, Virginia Living Museum, Virginia Marine Science Museum and The Mariners' Museum. The Norfolk Naval Base, the world's largest naval base, displays the might of the United States naval force. NASA's might and accomplishments can be explored at Hampton's Virginia Air and Space Center.

HAMPTON

The Casemate Museum

Roommates and Casemates

Edgar Allan Poe, tired of army life after spending the dark winter months of 1828–29 at Fort Monroe, sold his enlistment for $75, ending his career as an army artilleryman. After wandering through the gloomy chambers of **The Casemate Museum** you may wonder if he hadn't just decided that he had enough inspiration for his tales of horror. Casemates, the damp, dungeonlike artillery vaults within the fort's mammoth stone walls, make a perfect setting for a Poe story. They also make a good setting for exhibits on the people and events in the history of Fort Monroe.

If Poe found the casemates inspirational, Robert E. Lee more than likely found them educational. Lee, an army engineer, worked from 1831 to 1834 on the construction of Fort Monroe. During the Civil War he was careful not to attack the "Gibralter of Chesapeake Bay." The name was well deserved. Fort Monroe was the largest stone fort built in North America. At the time it was completed, it was also the largest enclosed fortification in the United States. The designer, General Simon Bernard, had been trained to think big as aide-de-camp to Napoleon Bonaparte.

The fort's impenetrable stone walls imprisoned Jefferson Davis at the conclusion of the Civil War. He was charged with plotting to assassinate Lincoln, mistreating Union prisoners and treason. After his capture on May 22, 1865, the former president of the Confederacy spent five months in casemate cell 2. For the first five days he was kept manacled in leg irons, but even after these were removed his dank, spartan cell was a bitter home for a man who had just led the Confederacy, albeit to defeat. After five months Davis was transferred to better accommodations in Carroll Hall; its location is marked on the Fort Monroe Walking Tour. Davis was released on $100,000 bail May 13, 1867. Two years later all charges were dropped.

Though Davis was a most reluctant resident, some Federal officers made comfortable homes in the casemates. Photographs from the 1900s show four such living quarters. You wonder as you look at the piano in the re-created casemate parlor if the fort kept a tuner on the payroll.

Another exhibit focuses on the four-hour Civil War battle that occurred just off Fort Monroe in Hampton Roads between the ironclads *Monitor* and *Merrimack* (the traditional spelling is

Robert E. Lee helped construct Fort Monroe, Edgar Allan Poe ended his military enlistment after being stationed at the fort, and Jefferson Davis was imprisoned within Fort Monroe's stone casemates.

without a "k," but naval historians prefer Merrimack, after the New England river for which it was named).

Scale models of weapons from the army's Coast Artillery branch are also exhibited here. The Coast Artillery School was located at Fort Monroe, which served as the headquarters for the defenses of the Chesapeake Bay during World War II. Fort Monroe has an extensive collection of artillery pieces. On the walking tour you'll see a 15-inch Rodman gun, called the Lincoln gun in the President's honor and used to bombard Confederate batteries on Sewell's Point. You can also drive along Fenwick Road on the Chesapeake Bay and see Fort Monroe's seacoast batteries.

The Casemate Museum is open at no charge 10:30 A.M. to 4:30 P.M. daily, and closed Thanksgiving, Christmas and New Year's Day.

Directions: From I-95 in the Richmond area, take I-64 east to Exit 268 for Hampton. The entrance to Fort Monroe is immediately before the Hampton Roads Bridge Tunnel.

Fort Wool

They Never Pull the Wool Over Your Eyes Here

Fort Wool, strategically located at the mouth of Hampton Roads Harbor directly across from Fort Monroe, is the only moat-enclosed active duty military installation in the country. This is one historic site where getting there is definitely part of the fun, as the fort is accessible only by boat.

The 65-foot *Miss Hampton II* is moored at the picturesque Hampton Harbor right beside the visitor center, where tickets are purchased. The $2^1/_2$ to 3-hour cruise sails out on the Hampton River, past Blackbeard's Point, where legend claims the pirate's head was displayed on a post after his violent death in November 1718, off Ocracoke Island, North Carolina. Ocracoke legend claims that after the decapitation Blackbeard's body swam around his adversary's boat seven times looking for its head.

The cruise takes passengers along the coast of Old Point Comfort, named by Capt. John Smith because of the "great comfort" it brought his crew to discover a safe navigable channel for the passage of their ships. The point was the site of one of the earliest forts in America, built in 1609.

It was decided that companion forts would be built to guard the entrance to Hampton Roads. The War of 1812 and the British burning of the White House in Washington reinforced the idea that fortifications were needed to protect the East Coast and Gulf Coast. A panel in 1818 suggested building 26 forts from Maine to Florida and along the Gulf. Among them was a fort across from Point Comfort, to create crossfire to guard this significant harbor.

In 1819 construction was begun on Fort Monroe and Fort Wool. Lieut. Robert E. Lee, an Army engineer, was involved in supervising construction of both forts. Fort Monroe, completed

76

in 1834, was the largest stone fort ever built in the United States. Before beginning work on Fort Wool, an island had to be created on which to build. Workers needed to haul 40,000 to 50,000 perch (a cubic measure for stone) of stone to the mouth of the harbor before they could begin building Fort Wool. Stones were brought in from river beds and quarries. Cranes and rails were used to dump the stone into the water to create an island. Between 1819 to 1823, the workers managed to raise the island six feet above high water and construction work began. The plan for Fort Wool consisted of three tiers of casemates and a barbette tier (4 tiers designed to mount 232 guns). About half of the second casemate as well as one tier and a part of the second tier was completed before work stopped in 1830. The island was sinking at a rate of eight inches a year. Originally the fort was named Fort Calhoun (although informally it was called Castle Calhoun) after the Secretary of War, John C. Calhoun.

Although incomplete, President Andrew Jackson was so taken with the island's seclusion, he brought family and friends to the fort for a summer getaway in 1829, 1831, 1833 and 1835. Guests were housed in the officers' quarters. Jackson entertained dignitaries here including the Prussian Ambassador. In 1842, President John Tyler sought the seclusion of the island to mourn the death of his wife.

Thousands of pounds of additional stones were added to the island and work resumed on the casemates in 1858. The onset of the Civil War halted construction. The fortification remained in Union hands throughout the conflict. The fort finally got 10 cannons in 1861, a small part of the 232 planned for the completed facility. The Union troops at Fort Wool fired on the Georgia battery occupying Sewell's Point across the harbor in June 1861. The shots landed past the southerners' position, but it was clear that the cannon would reach across the water. The following March, two new-fangled ships, the ironclads *Monitor* and *Merrimack*, met in Hampton Roads Harbor.

The *Monitor* was launched from a New York City shipyard on January 30, 1862. Six weeks later, on March 9, it encountered the *CSS Virginia*, formerly the *USS Merrimack*. The Union had scuttled their wooden steam frigate to prevent it falling into Confederate hands, but the South was able to salvage the vessel and convert her into an ironclad. For four hours the ironclads lobbed cannon balls at each other's hulls at point-blank range. When a Confederate shell exploded in the sight-hole of the *Monitor,* it temporarily blinded Capt. John Worden. The *Monitor* withdrew and so the South claimed victory. Neither side was a clear victor; the only decisive winner was the metal ship.

Lincoln visited Fort Wool in 1862. From this vantage point he supervised the unsuccessful invasion of Norfolk. (Later, Gen.

Wool successfully captured Norfolk and Portsmouth but Lincoln was not on hand.) Secretary of War Stanton ordered Fort Calhoun's name changed in order to honor Wool, rather than a southern secessionist.

In the early 1900s, the fort entered a new phase of construction. The walls were torn down and replaced with concrete fortifications to defend against new weapons. Eight of the casemates remained and the outside stone wall was incorporated into the new concrete structure. Six 3" rapid fire guns and six 6" disappearing guns were added. A third stage of construction took place in World War II, when battery No. 229 was added. On December 7, 1941 troops reoccupied the island but the fort never came under fire and the men never saw combat. Park rangers provide guided tours to all visitors, beginning with the pre-Civil War section of the fort, then moving through the World War II portion.

Cruises are given aboard the *Miss Hampton II* from April through October. While aboard the *Miss Hampton* you'll be able to see the behemoths of modern warfare when you cruise past Norfolk Naval Base's two-mile waterfront. This is the world's largest naval installation (see selection). Onboard narrators will provide information on the aircraft carriers, guided missile cruisers, destroyers and nuclear powered submarines that you will see moored at the base.

Time and fees vary. Reservations are recommended, so be sure and call ahead at (800) 244-1040 or (804) 727-1102. Tickets are sold at the Hampton Visitor Center.

Directions: From I-64 take Exit 267, Hampton University and follow Routes 60/143 west-bound to old downtown Hampton. The excursion boat to Fort Wool departs from Hampton's main dock near the visitor center. There is a parking garage at the dock.

Hampton University Museum

African American Heritage

On January 1, 1863 during the dark days of the War Between the States, President Abraham Lincoln issued the Emancipation Proclamation, freeing the enslaved people of the Confederacy. Under an oak on what is now the Hampton University campus, Lincoln's Proclamation was read to the people of Hampton. Classes had been conducted near the oak tree since September 17, 1861. The teacher was Mary Peake, a free-born woman of color, who for years ignored statues forbidding the education of blacks. She started some of the first organized programs to teach both free and enslaved African Americans to read and write. The Emancipation Oak is a significant African American landmark. Five years after the Proclamation was issued, Hampton Normal and Agricultural Institute (later University) was established to educate the newly freed African Americans.

Established the same year as the school, the **Hampton University Museum** is one of the oldest museums in the state. The African art collection, exhibited in the museum, is one of the first collections gathered by an African American, missionary-explorer, Dr. William H. Sheppard. There is also an extensive and historic Native American collection. Currently located on the waterfront overlooking the Hampton River and Hampton Roads Harbor, the museum is in the 1881 Academy Building, a National Historic Landmark (there are plans for a new, state-of-the-art museum building).

The African collection has about 3,500 objects from nearly 100 ethnic groups and cultures. Between 1890 and 1910, Sheppard, a Hampton alumnus, gathered 400 objects that became the nucleus of the museum's collection. The material on display deserves close scrutiny since much of the work is exquisitely detailed with intricate bead patterns or carvings. Included are a battle-ax from Zaire, a Kuba royal belt, a Zulu bride costume, a Kenya headdress and an impressive hunter's shirt that is from West Africa.

The Native American galleries offer a fascinating look at the artistic handiwork from more than 93 Native American tribes. It encompasses over 1,600 pieces that the museum has collected since 1878. That was the year the federal government began sending Native American students from the western reservations to Hampton. A significant number of Native Americans attended the school until 1923, when the federal government ended its support of this educational program. The museum's outstanding collection resulted from this association with Native Americans from these diverse tribes.

In 1967, the Harmon Foundation presented a noted fine arts collection to the museum. Much of the museum's 1,500-piece collection of paintings, graphics and sculpture was part of this gift. Harlem Renaissance-inspired artists are well-represented, including two of Jacob Lawrence's earliest series. The museum also has nine paintings by Henry O. Tanner, perhaps the most renowned African American artist. His evocative canvas, *The Banjo Lesson*, done in 1893, is a favorite with visitors.

The Oceanic collection includes 18 cultures: Melanesian, Micronesian, Polynesian and Australian work. There is also a significant Asian collection as well as a growing Hampton University history collection.

Hampton University's African art collection has objects from nearly 100 ethnic groups and cultures. Congolese artifacts include an intricately carved cup used for drinking poison, a fierce witch doctor's mask and a king's ceremonial knife.

The Hampton University Museum is open Monday through Friday 8:00 A.M. to 5:00 P.M. and weekends NOON to 4:00 P.M. While on the campus be sure to stop at the **Booker T. Washington Memorial Garden** with its imposing statue of Hampton's most famous graduate as well as the William R. and Norma B. Harvey Library which has two imposing murals by Dr. John Biggers.

In 1879, a few miles from Hampton's campus, university students built a tiny African American missionary chapel, the only one in Virginia. Now a National Historic Landmark, the **Little England Chapel** has a permanent exhibit and video on the religious lives of post-Civil War African Americans. The chapel, at the corner of Kecoughton and Ivy Home roads, is open Tuesday through Saturday from 10:00 A.M. to 4:00 P.M.

Directions: Take I-64 east to Exit 267 (Hampton University, Downtown Hampton, Phoebus). Proceed straight on Tyler Street through the intersection to the second stop light. Turn left onto Emancipation Drive; go one block, turn right on Marshall Avenue and travel across campus to the waterfront. The museum is located at Marshall Avenue and Shore Road. There are signs for the museum once you exit I-64. From campus to reach the chapel, take Tyler Street to County Street. At the intersection turn left and travel over the Booker T. Washington Bridge. Continue straight on Settler's Landing Road to the fifth stop light. Turn left onto Kecoughtan Road and travel approximately one mile to Ivy Home Road. The chapel is on the left on the corner of Ivy Home Road.

Virginia Air and Space Center and Hampton Roads History Center

Looking Forward, Looking Back

Since opening in April 1992 the **Virginia Air and Space Center** has been informing and entertaining visitors. The facility on the Hampton waterfront, the official visitor center for NASA Langley Research Center, is visually striking with its immense glassed exhibit space soaring skyward. It is a highly successful design that conveys a sense of space so appropriate for the museum's themes.

To get the most out of your visit, start by watching the short video at the Orientation Theater. You'll get a brief summary of the museum's history and an overview of the exhibits. The self-guided tour begins in a large open space where an array of small

81

models traces the evolution of the airplane from its earliest days. Full-size airplanes hang suspended from the ceiling. Many of the planes hanging in the enclosed space had to be brought in before the final walls were put in place.

The suspended planes include a prototype YF-16 Fighting Falcon like the Air Force precision Thunderbirds fly and a Chance Vought F4U-ID Corsair, a huge aircraft with a 38-foot wing span. Another exhibited aircraft is a F-4E Phantom II that saw combat in Vietnam. There is also a Langley Aerodrome, Schleiche ASW-12 Glider, the world's largest paper airplane, and an applications technology Satellite 6 as well as eight other planes. These can be seen from several levels; you can even look down on them from a gantry that crosses high above the museum's ground floor. The gantry also provides a birds-eye view of the Apollo 12 Command Module that has pride of place on the main floor.

On the ground floor is the **Hampton Roads History Center** and a 300-seat IMAX theater, with a giant five-story projection screen and 16,000 watts of wrap-around sound—both are entertaining and educational.

Hampton was an official Royal Port for the Virginia colony. A wharf exhibit focuses on the importance of trade and tobacco to the area. In colonial times, the Bunch of Grapes Tavern stood on the site of this museum. It was in this tavern that irate patriots gathered to discuss their unhappiness with English rule. An audiovisual program brings the statuary-customers to life so that you can hear a conversation that might have occurred in this tavern. Shipbuilding was significant in this area, so you'll see exhibits detailing the struggle to create a navy and defend the shores against the British in the American Revolution and War of 1812. Hampton Roads is forever associated with the dueling ironclads and there is a full-size replica of the casement of the *Merrimack* (also called the *Virginia*). There is also a large scale portion of the *Monitor*. It surprises many visitors to discover that the *Merrimack*, at 275 feet in length, was more than twice the size of the space shuttle. Continuing the Hampton story, there are exhibits on the local watermen and on the influence of the navy in the area including replicas of carriers and models of aircraft carriers. This museum is hands-on and with a push of a button you can experience the sights and sounds of U.S. naval aviation.

The space gallery is on the second floor; at the exhibit entrance is a cradle with an infant dressed, not in traditional bunting, but in a space suit. Over the cradle there is a quote from the "Father of Soviet Rocketry," Konstantin Tsiolovsky: "Earth is the cradle of mankind, but we cannot live in the cradle forever." Space research has been conducted at NASA Langley Research Center since 1917—early strides and future goals are encompassed in the gallery. Achievements are recognized with

At the Virginia Air and Space Center's Astronaut-for-a-Minute display visitors discover how they would look as an astronaut. The center houses a dozen full-size aircraft, space capsules, a moon rock and an IMAX theater.

items like the moon rock, the Viking orbiter and lander and the space shuttle exhibit. Interactive displays let you play at being an "astronaut for a minute." There is also a simulated space launch. Other topics covered include rockets, satellites, aerospace research exhibits and the role of space in science fiction.

Level three has an observation gantry for an overview of the hanging exhibits and an observation deck for a panoramic view of the Hampton Harbor.

The center is open during the summer from Monday through Wednesday 10:00 A.M. to 5:00 P.M., Thursday through Sunday until 7:00 P.M. Winter hours are Monday through Sunday 10:00 A.M. to 5:00 P.M. Admission is charged to the exhibits and the IMAX performances. There are usually two IMAX movies shown on a five story-high screen; for additional information call (800) 296-0800. You should allow at least an hour to explore the museum and 45 minutes for an IMAX movie.

Directly across the street from the museum is the 1920 **Hampton Carousel**. This antique merry-go-round delights young and old with its colorfully painted horses and chariots. The 48 hand-carved horses are fine examples of a vanishing American folk art. The pavilion still has the original mirrors it had when it was delivered in 1921 to Hampton's Buckroe Beach Amusement Park. When the park closed in 1985, the city purchased and restored the carousel. The carousel operates on a regular schedule from April through October.

Directions: Take I-64 east from the Richmond area to Exit 267, Settlers Landing Road. This will take you to downtown Hampton. The Virginia Air and Space Center is on the left. Parking is available across from the center.

NORFOLK

The Chrysler Museum of Art

Art is the Driving Force

Though the *Wall Street Journal* considers **The Chrysler Museum of Art** "one of the 20 top museums in the country," its origins were humble. Its roots go back to the years after the Civil War when two Norfolk teachers founded the Leache-Wood Female Seminary.

Irene Leache and Anne Cogswell Wood traveled to Europe each summer, returning with paintings and sculpture. Most travelers end up with their mementos stored in the attic, but in 1901 seminary alumni took steps to find a permanent home for their teachers' collection. This led to the establishment of the Norfolk Society of Arts in 1917. Through the group's efforts, the city was persuaded to build a museum that opened in 1933 and was enlarged in 1967 and 1976.

In 1971 Walter P. Chrysler, Jr., son of the founder of Chrysler Corporation, donated a large portion of his extensive and significant art collection to the Norfolk Museum thrusting it upon the world stage. Mr. Chrysler, who began collecting art when he was quite young, purchased a Renoir landscape when he was 13. His collection spans the continents and the centuries from classical antiquities to modern art. A major $10 million expansion of The Chrysler Museum of Art, begun in 1985, doubled the museum's space and allowed many works heretofore in storage to be exhibited.

Art is subjective and visitors have their personal favorites, but certain pieces in the museum's collection merit mentioning. Gauguin's *The Loss of Innocence* has been singled out for attention by John Russell of *The New York Times* who also said the museum's *Bust of the Savior* by Bernini was "one of the greatest single works of art in the country." Bernini was considered by his contemporaries to be Michelangelo's successor. This bust has an interesting history. It disappeared during the 18th century and wasn't identified as being Bernini's long-lost masterpiece until 1971.

Another museum masterpiece is the painting of *Saint Philip* by Georges de La Tour. It is one of only 30 works by this artist whose rediscovery in the 1930s has been called "the triumph of art history." The museum has Renoir's 1882 *The Daughters of Durand-Ruel*, which critics call "one of the painter's most impressive" works. Another crowd pleaser is itself a crowd scene, *The Artists' Wives* by Tissot.

The Chrysler Museum of Art has amassed one of the world's finest glass collections. The museum has nearly 7,000 pieces that provide a comprehensive survey of the history of glass. One of the early pieces, an Ennion bowl, dates from the 1st century A.D. But it is the Tiffany lamps and vases that leave visitors exclaiming. These are but a part of the museum's 400-piece Tiffany collection. There is also a comprehensive 2,500-piece collection of American Sandwich glass. The Worcester porcelain display is also outstanding.

The Chrysler has a rapidly expanding photographic collection, a decorative arts department and three galleries devoted to exhibits on loan. Visitors with an academic or general interest in art may want to use the 50,000-volume Jean Outland Chrysler Library.

The Chrysler Museum is open 10:00 A.M. to 4:00 P.M. Tuesday through Saturday and 1:00 to 5:00 P.M. on Sunday. It is closed Monday and major holidays. There is no admission, but donations are encouraged.

A scant 300 feet from the front entrance of the Chrysler Museum is a charming bed & breakfast, The **Page House Inn** at 33

Fairfax Avenue. The rooms of this Georgian Revival in-town mansion are filled with antiques and several offer gas fireplaces and whirlpool tubs. Innkeepers Stephanie and Ezio DiBelardino create a hospitable spot for you to stay overnight. Call (804)625-5033 for more information.

Directions: From I-95 in the Richmond area take I-64 east and exit at I-264. Continue on I-264 to the final exit, Waterside Drive. Stay on Waterside Drive as it turns into Boush Street. Take a left at Brambleton, then an immediate right on Duke Street. The museum is on your left $2^1/_2$ blocks down Duke Street in the picturesque Ghent district of Norfolk.

Douglas MacArthur Memorial

Some Soldiers Never Fade Away

When Douglas MacArthur was born January 26, 1880, in Little Rock, Arkansas, the Norfolk, Virginia paper reported, "Douglas MacArthur was born . . . while his parents were away." This was not a medical first, simply a hometown paper commenting on a local personality. His mother, Mary Pinkney Hardy MacArthur, had been born in Norfolk and since his father, Arthur MacArthur, was a peripatetic military officer, Norfolk was always their "home by choice."

Although General Douglas MacArthur never actually lived in Norfolk, he nevertheless acceded to the city's suggestion of a memorial in 1960 and helped plan the complex you'll see. Norfolk redesigned the 1850 city hall done by Thomas Walter, who is noted for his work on the U.S. Capitol dome and its House and Senate wings. The **MacArthur Memorial** opened in 1964 on the general's 84th birthday. When MacArthur died on April 5, 1964, he was buried in the rotunda he helped design. Not for him Washington, D.C., where he said he had never won a battle.

Begin your visit at the MacArthur Memorial theater where you'll see a 22-minute newsreel compilation of footage that captures significant events in American history in which the general played a pivotal role. The film gives added life to the still photographs and memorabilia in the nine galleries surrounding the rotunda.

The first gallery contains exhibits that depict MacArthur's family, his youth and his four years at West Point. You'll see reminders of the young MacArthur, who had the highest entrance marks to West Point and graduated with one of the highest averages in the academy's history.

Galleries two through seven cover MacArthur's service in the

The General Douglas MacArthur Memorial in Norfolk houses MacArthur's tomb and such historic memorabilia as the surrender papers signed by the Japanese aboard the USS Missouri.

Philippines, World War I and II and the Korean War. Photographs, uniforms, weapons, medals and maps help tell the story. Large murals show MacArthur's return to the Philippines, his attendance at the Japanese surrender and his address to Congress in 1951 after President Truman relieved him of command. Gallery eight reflects on MacArthur's twilight years of retirement where his achievements in business, writing and other pursuits are fully recorded.

Gallery nine contains the well-remembered corn-cob pipe, sunglasses and visored cap identified with MacArthur. There are also two large cases of medals presented by countries around the world and by the U.S. government. His Congressional Medal of Honor is prominent among the latter; his receipt of it made the MacArthurs the only father and son in American history to receive the award. This very dramatic display also contains the general's desk and chair, plus a special video presentation that highlights MacArthur's career and his impact on world history.

Be sure to see the changing exhibit galleries in the theater and the large gift shop where the general's sedan is on display.

The MacArthur Memorial is open at no charge 10:00 A.M. to 5:00 P.M. Monday through Saturday and 11:00 A.M. to 5:00 P.M. on Sunday. It is closed Thanksgiving, Christmas and New Year's Day.

Directions: From I-95 in the Richmond area, take I-64 to Norfolk; then take I-264 and exit on City Hall Avenue. Proceed three blocks west. Parking is available on the north side of City Hall Avenue.

Hermitage Foundation Museum

Little Russia

The Hermitage is a house museum with an art collection to be savored. The dark-visaged witches supporting the ceiling, satyrs over the library door, drunken winemakers on the ivory netsuke, multiple secret panels and a thundering organ all combine to delight the visitor who takes the time to look and listen to the tales of the guides who bring this astounding collection to life.

It's hard to imagine a better setting than the Sloanes' English Tudor house. Although it began as a five-room summer cottage for textile manufacturer William Sloane, it was expanded into a 42-room mansion. Three master carvers worked 22 years on its elaborate paneling, mantles, beams and custom-designed furniture.

The mood is firmly and loudly established when the guide inserts a roll in the 1935 Moller organ and music on a grand scale fills the air. It's the perfect accompaniment to the Old World Gothic drawing room. Separating the organ from the drawing room is a rood screen, used in churches to divide the choir from the congregation. Unlike most museums, the Hermitage allows photography, which is fortunate because the details of this ornately carved wooden screen are well worth capturing. The drawing room is filled with art from around the world: a 16th-century Flemish tapestry, 16th- and 17th-century Spanish religious art and one of two massive limestone fireplaces from Bath, England.

The Sloanes amassed one of the largest privately owned oriental art collections on the East Coast including a linden wood statue of Kuan Yin, goddess of mercy, which is more than 1,000 years old. Other rarities are the T'ang Dynasty clay carved horses which were buried with the deceased to help carry their possessions into the next world and a 6th-century Chinese marble Buddha.

The dining room faces the Lafayette River, but it did not always do so. To change the view the Sloanes hired a contractor who had a crane lift and move two rooms, exchanging the location of the dining room with that of the parlor.

This house, like most Tudor mansions, has a great hall. It is here that four witches support the ceiling to ward off evil spirits. Two Tiffany lamps provide muted light. The carpet has the five-toed dragon design, symbol of the Chinese Imperial family. If you want to learn how 15th-century Spanish merchants smuggled, have a look at one of their intricately carved sample boxes (vagueno) displayed here.

In the morning room, perhaps the most intriguing items of all are displayed: the lily shoes worn by women to keep their feet from growing. Some feet were bound to lengths of no more than five inches. The upstairs has additional exhibits not to be missed, including Faberge creations.

The Hermitage Foundation Museum is open daily from 10:00 A.M. to 5:00 P.M. On Sunday it opens at 1:00 P.M. It is closed on Thanksgiving, Christmas and New Year's Day. Admission is charged, but those under six and U.S. military service personnel are admitted free.

Directions: From I-95 in the Richmond area, take I-64 east to Route 165 and turn right on Little Creek Road. At the intersection of Little Creek Road and Hampton Boulevard (Route 337), turn left onto Hampton Boulevard. Continue to North Shore Road and turn right. The Hermitage Foundation Museum is one-half mile on the left. Norfolk Tour signs indicate the route.

Hunter House Victorian Museum and Freemason Historic District

Sense an Opulent Era

In 1894, Boston architect W. D. Wentworth designed and built an elegant Richardsonian Romanesque home on cobblestoned Freemason Street in Norfolk. His client was James Wilson Hunter, a prosperous merchant and banker. Hunter and his wife Lizzie moved in with their three children, James Wilson Jr., Harriet Cornelia and Eloise Dexter. The children never married and this was their family home until 1965.

The original design details of the **Hunter House Victorian Museum** still delight the senses. Family furnishings fill the rooms, but a sense of the individual personalities who lived here is elusive. No diaries reveal intimate details of their lives, no anecdotes provide colorful glimpses of events in their lives; the family is reflected by their time and the popular taste of their era. The parlor, supposedly a mirror of their world, is a microcosm of their travels, their taste and their heritage. The room has an elliptical design with a bow window in the front and a curved door in the back. The paintings by artists of the Hudson River School were modern when purchased by the Hunters. Their home reflects the latest in styles in art and in conveniences; they installed steam-heat radiators, indoor plumbing, hot and cold water and gas lighting. Intriguing architectural details include coffered ceilings, frosted and bottled glass, an inglenook, or chimney corner on the stair landing and spindle work on the stair banister.

Evenings at home were spent in the library, with its built-in bookshelves and scrapbooks of embossed flowers. The flowers were purchased in sheets at stationery stores, then cut-out. This was a popular pastime of the Victorian era.

The dining room looks surprisingly masculine; the medieval tapestries lend a baronial look. It is thought that the wooden-tapestry chairs may have been designed for the room by the architect. The tilting water pitcher was used to serve ice water at the table, showing off the fact that the family had one of the new-fangled ice boxes. Adjacent to the dining room is a china room with a sink to wash the dishes and cutlery. The kitchen is not included on the tour.

The family's living quarters were on the second floor where all the rooms are connected in a horseshoe pattern. The master bedroom at the front of the house has a bow window overlooking the street. Here you'll see Mrs. Hunter's desk with her fan and dance cards as well as her mourning calling cards used when she visited the bereaved. In another bedroom there is a crazy quilt, a family memento made in 1887 perhaps to commemorate the Hunter's 20th wedding anniversary. A nearby nursery is filled with toys, although the Hunter children were all too old for toys when the family moved here. The three children would have taken their meals in this schoolroom rather than joining the adults in the formal dining room. A bathroom in the back of the house features a state-of-the-art flush toilet.

One of the pieces in the exhibit of early 20th-century medical memorabilia is Dr. Hunter's 1930s battery-operated electrocardiograph machine. James Wilson Hunter, Jr. died in Hot Springs, Arkansas of heart trouble. The third floor, which once had guest bedrooms, is now used for storage and there is an unfinished attic space.

Before ending your visit, stop at the gift shop which carries delightful period items like Victorian cards and paper dolls, children's toys, books, Christmas ornaments and activity books for children. Be sure to also notice the cutting garden along the fence and the benches beneath the trees. Take the time to observe the exterior architectural details like the arched windows and doors and the stone balconies.

Hunter House Victorian Museum is open April through December Wednesday through Saturday from 10:00 A.M. to 4:00 P.M. and Sunday NOON to 4:00 P.M. Admission is charged. The museum hosts special events including theme teas, patriotic picnics and a Memorial Day cemetery decoration at nearby Elmwood Cemetery. Before leaving the Hunter House pick up a walking tour map, the **Freemason Historic District** is one of three Walking Tours of Historic Norfolk. There are 23 points of interest on this tour including private homes and public buildings. Norfolk's oldest house, the 1790 Allmand-Archer House is located in this district. The stone paving on Freemason and Botetourt streets was originally used as ship ballast. One of the neighborhood's old churches, the **Freemason Abbey**, has been converted into a delightful restaurant and tavern. Norfolk's Second Presbyterian Church congregation built the church in 1873. In 1902 it was sold to First Church of Christ Scientists and from 1948 to 1987 it was used as a meeting hall for the Independent Order of Odd Fellows. It was converted into a restaurant in 1988, while maintaining the architectural integrity of this old historic landmark. It is not only details like the cathedral roof trusses that make this a noteworthy spot; the restaurant is renowned for its lobsters and serves over 1000 whole fresh lobsters each month. For reservations call (804) 622-3966.

Directions: From I-64 take Granby Street Exit 276, make a right turn on Freemason Street for the Hunter House Victorian Museum at 240 W. Freemason St. The Freemason Abbey is at the

The elegant Hunter House Victorian Museum was designed for the Hunters in 1894 and remained in the family until 1965.

corner of Freemason and Boush streets. To obtain a free guide to Norfolk with attraction, lodging and restaurant information call (800) 843-8030.

Moses Myers House

Jewish Merchant Prince

When Eliza Abraham and Moses Myers were married in 1787 they chartered a boat and moved from New York to Norfolk. Myers was the first Jewish settler in Norfolk. Within four years, he had established a five-vessel fleet for his import-export business and built a classic Georgian townhouse.

The oldest four-square portion of the house was constructed of 18th-century English ballast bricks. In 1796 the **Moses Myers House** was expanded from 10 to 13 rooms. From the outside you can clearly see the difference between the English and American bricks. Five generations of Myerses lived here and 70 percent of the furniture is original. Moses Myers was a community leader and his home reflects his successful life style.

Myers was president of the common council, a major in the Virginia militia, consul from the United States to France, the Netherlands and Denmark, president of the Assembly Ball, superintendent of the Bank of Richmond and collector of customs.

From the moment you pull the old English bell to gain entrance, you'll be intrigued by this remarkably well-preserved old city mansion. The Myerses did not carry door keys; servants were always on hand with a massive one pound key to unfasten the English triple box lock. The entrance hall still has the original four-inch native heart pine floor boards and a decorative snowflake pattern plaster ceiling.

In the formal parlor you'll see Gilbert Stuart's portraits of Moses Myers, painted when he was in his early fifties, and of Mrs. Myers when she was in her early forties. The parlor's Portuguese tole chandelier is a curiosity—the light prongs surrounding the eternal flame bear the supposed likeness of Christopher Columbus. The mantle decoration around the parlor fireplace also reveals the visage of an important historical figure. George Washington gazes out from the rosettes flanking the fireplace on this unique mantle.

The dining room is regarded as one of the most beautiful in the South. Here the Myerses entertained the Marquis de Lafayette, President James Monroe, Daniel Webster, Stephen Decatur, Henry Clay and General Winfield Scott. In the china cabinet you'll see Mrs. Myers' apricot Spode tea and coffee set. The white, grey and silver decor combines with the black and white patterned canvas matting on the floor to create a surprisingly modern look.

The Myerses were all musical and their music room has a pianoforte and harp. The family reputedly had the largest collection of musical books in early American, with George Washington a distant second. The three Myers daughters copied musical scores in quite a number of books.

Displayed in the upstairs hallways are the dueling pistol possibly used in the 1820 Barron-Decatur duel. Another room has a seven-lock iron money chest that Myers anchored to the floor with iron bolts. There is also a grand harmonicon. Only five of the 25 glasses have survived, but it is enough to give visitors a look at an instrument for which both Beethoven and Mozart composed.

Over the Myers's bed is a carved acorn, symbol of fertility. It obviously was effective; they had 12 children. In Mrs. Myers's bedroom you'll see her oriental sewing worktable. The back bedroom had a six-foot modified sleigh bed. Before ending your tour be sure to visit the outside kitchen and the garden.

The mansion is open from April through December, 10:00 A.M. to 5:00 P.M. Tuesday through Saturday. On Sunday it opens at NOON. From January through March the house is open NOON to 5:00 P.M. Tuesday through Saturday and closed on Sundays, Mondays and major holidays. This is one of the few historic homes in which Hanukkah, the Jewish Festival of Lights, which occurs in December, is celebrated. Candles are lit in a brass menorah for each of the festival's eight days. Admission is charged.

Directions: From I-95 in the Richmond area, take I-64 east to Norfolk, then follow I-264 east to the Waterside Drive Exit. Take Waterside Drive to St. Paul's Boulevard, then turn left on Market Street and right onto Bank Street. The Moses Myers House is at the corner of Freemason and Bank streets.

Nauticus, The National Maritime Center

National Maritime Center

Adults work on computers, children play on them—this perhaps explains the enthusiasm younger visitors express for **Nauticus**, the ultimate marriage of computer and museum. Almost all the maritime exhibits have some interactive components: banks of monitors present menus of mini-movies, documentaries, animation and first-person interviews—all focusing on the power of the sea.

For real state-of-the-arts battle action enter the AEGIS Theater, where you sit amid the action in the Combat Information Center on the world's most sophisticated destroyer. When the ship comes under enemy aircraft attack, you help the officers (they're convincing actors) make battle choices. The AEGIS system is not a dramatic creation, it's the actual early warning system used by the navy to detect and destroy enemy submarines, aircraft and ships. Taking part in the drama at the AEGIS Theater will give you an appreciation for the speed needed in formulating command decisions. The sense of reality is heightened by the actors and reinforced by actual screen footage of attacking aircraft complete with realistic sound effects. The dramatic scenario creates the illusion that you are on board an AEGIS destroyer. On three sides of the stage-like bridge, panels simulate advanced radar and sonar screens; you push buttons indicating whether you want to send a warning, use a gatling gun or send a Tomahawk missile. You'll discover it isn't enough to make the right decision, you also have to make it within the correct time frame—it's seconds that separate the great commanders from the competent. The battle scenario was prepared with the help of a former commander of an AEGIS ship and was reviewed by the navy—it's an exciting experience available only at Nauticus.

If you are lucky you may even be able to board an AEGIS equipped navy ship docked at the Nauticus International Pier. A variety of ships dock here as part of the virtually year-round Ships Visitation Program (it runs in all but the dead of winter).

If being part of the decision-making process whets your appetite for command, your next stop should be the interactive Virtual Adventures, another one-of-a-kind adventure that combines features of a ride, a movie and a game. It is the ultimate computer game, where you actually become part of the action as you don polarized 3-D glasses and enter a compact submersible. Via virtual reality you travel to the depths of Scotland's Loch Ness, navigating the undersea terrain in search of the infamous Loch Ness Monster. Each member of the six-man submersible crew has a task, either as commander, pilot, periscope operator or as one of two operators of the robotic arms used to retrieve the eggs of the Loch Ness Monster. There are five other subs plus sea monsters who pose a threat to your craft; so again, speedy command decisions are necessary. This is the only group networked virtual reality attraction currently operating. Exit polls and other visitor monitoring has indicated this is youngsters' favorite spot in the museum.

For the computer-phobic, Nauticus offers the hauntingly beautiful giant-screen film "The Living Sea" with a stirring score composed and performed by Sting. Commissioned by Nauticus, the movie was filmed on location around the world. It celebrates the sea, as seen from a myriad of perspectives. Although there is not a bad seat in the house, the best perspective is in the center toward the back. Undersea footage is breathtaking, with never-before-seen views of deep water denizens. The sight of millions of jellyfish in the waters off the Central Pacific islands of Palua is sure to make you shiver. The dramatic finale focusing on the Norfolk waterfront always garners spontaneous applause from the audience.

If you wished you could reach out and touch some of the delicate underwater creatures, then the nearby hands-on shark tank should be your next stop. On busy afternoons, visitors wait in line for the chance to pet a nurse shark. There are other touch tanks that provide tactile contact with sea urchins, sea stars and a wide variety of undersea life.

Nauticus has six themed exhibit areas: Exploratorium, Navigation, Commerce, Modern Navy, Research and Aquaria and Environment. Youngsters' creativity is encouraged in the "Grandma and Me" computer storyboards in the Exploratorium. Colorful computer games allow children to tell a story by selecting from a menu of options. This exhibit also includes a ship's bridge and a 1944 periscope and telescopes that afford a good look at the port of Hampton Roads. In Navigation you can engage in interactive shipbuilding, making choices regarding the hull, buoyancy, stability and other practical considerations. After you learn the principles of navigation, you can use a computer to take a ship into San Francisco Harbor. Commerce is a fitting topic since Hampton Roads Harbor is one of the world's largest commercial ports. More than 75 shipping lines stop at this port bringing $28 billion annually in imports and exports. This harbor also has the largest dry dock in the world. The Commerce exhibits reveal how man has crossed the oceans to exchange the world's resources. There are two films dealing with international maritime trade. The Modern Navy lets you meet, through videos, many of the people who make up today's navy. Working laboratories and environmental exhibits on maintaining the quality of water in the Chesapeake Bay are part of the Research and Aquaria area. Finally, you can videotape your own weather report after learning about climatic conditions in the Environment section of the museum.

This futuristic museum doesn't neglect the past, it provides space for the **Hampton Roads Naval Museum**, one of 11 museums officially operated by the U.S. Navy. Now located at Nauticus, it's a separate identity and the only part of the complex for which there is no charge. The museum provides an overview of naval action off Virginia's Capes during the American Revolution, the decisive Civil War action in Hampton Roads and the efforts to keep open the Atlantic Ocean shipping lanes during

Nauticus, The National Maritime Center, is a multi-level educational and entertainment showplace in downtown Norfolk along the Elizabeth River waterside. This Bio-Accumulation Machine shows how toxins travel through the food chain.

both World Wars. Even when looking back in time, high-tech methods are used. A fiber optic map combines electronics and graphics to dramatically explain the battle between the *Monitor* and the *Merrimack*.

Nauticus is open daily May through September from 10:00 A.M. to 7:00 P.M.; the rest of the year it closes at 5:00 P.M. Tuesday through Sundays, and is closed on Mondays. Nauticus is closed on Thanksgiving, Christmas and New Year's Day. General admission is charged, plus tickets must be purchased for specific times for the three premium attractions: AEGIS Theater, Virtual Adventures and The Living Sea. There is a well-stocked gift shop, cafe and visitor information center for the Virginia waterfront on the museum's ground floor.

After this exposure to the majesty and mystery of the sea, a perfect end to your day's adventure would be a sunset sail aboard the *American Rover* docked at Norfolk's Waterside. This 135-foot three-masted topsail schooner is the largest passenger schooner sailing under U.S. flag. It is a stirring sight to watch the crew set the sails. The ship's design was inspired by 19th-century cargo schooners, modified for the comfort of today's passengers. Seats line the ship's railings on the topside deck and there is a below deck cocktail lounge and ship's store where you can purchase souvenirs and sandwiches.

Day and evening two and three-hour sailings take you past historic spots on the Elizabeth River and along the Norfolk Naval Base where you will see the huge aircraft carriers, submarines and other naval vessels. On the return voyage there is often live entertainment. It is an ideal way to cap off a day in Norfolk. For sailing schedule and rates call (804) 627-7245.

Directions: From the Richmond area take I-64 east to I-264 west, Waterside Drive exit. Nauticus is at One Waterside Drive. Parking is available at city garages within two blocks of the museum.

The *American Rover* is docked in front of the blue-roofed Waterside Festival Marketplace.

Norfolk Botanical Garden

Gardens-By-The-Sea

Glide on a trackless train along meandering wooded paths brightened by colorful azaleas, rhododendrons and bright annuals, or float along the wandering canals for a different view—both options are available at the **Norfolk Botanical Garden**. Either 30-minute ride provides a perfect introduction to the 20 focal spots

98

at this 155-acre garden. Once you gain an overview you can enjoy a closer look along the 12 miles of walkways.

Norfolk Botanical Garden claims "there is something always in bloom," but undoubtedly the best time to visit is in the spring. During April and May the more than 200,000 azaleas begin the floral extravaganza. What began as a WPA project in 1938 has grown into one of the best azalea gardens on the East Coast.

Blooming concurrently with the azaleas in May are the more than 150 varieties of rhododendron. Banks of these lovely spring bushes line the canals, train paths and walkways. Tulips, daffodils and spring bulbs add to the seasonal show.

The end of May is highlighted by the emergence of $1/4$ million rose blooms in one of the top ten rose collections in the country. The award-winning Bicentennial Rose Garden continues to bloom through October with almost 300 varieties of roses and roughly 3,000 bushes. The fragrant blossoms, enhanced by sculpture and fountains, can be enjoyed from the pedestrian terrace, overlooks and garden walkways.

Camellias begin to bloom in November and continue through March. Over 700 varieties of camellias make this one of the largest collections in the country. In January and February, many cold-loving plants such as witch hazel, wintersweet and pyracantha, provide color for visitors to enjoy. This is particularly true since the more northern collections have suffered severe damage from sub-zero winters.

More than 20 theme gardens include the Fragrance, Colonial Herb, Renaissance, Conifer, Holly, English Border, Healing Gardens as well as the 17-acre Flowering Arboretum and The Tropical Pavilion. In addition, there are the renovated Japanese and Perennial Gardens and a three-acre Wildflower Meadow.

Visitors can coordinate their trip to view horticultural displays with one of the many annual events held at the garden. Every April since 1954, Norfolk Botanical Garden has been the site of the International Azalea Festival, which honors the North Atlantic Treaty Organization. The Spring Plant Sale in April and the Fall Plant Sale in October are excellent ways to gather bits of the Norfolk Botanical Garden for your own home. Music lovers can enjoy The Virginia Symphony and local bands throughout the spring, summer and fall. During the holidays, the garden is aglow with a spectacular display during the Garden of Lights from Thanksgiving through to the new year. Detailed information on these events is available by calling (804) 441-5830.

Norfolk Botanical Garden is open daily 8:30 A.M. to sunset, but closes for some holidays and special events. Narrated train tours, March through October, and narrated boat tours, April through September, both run daily from 10:00 A.M. to 4:00 P.M. Admission is charged, plus there is a fee for the train and boat tours. There is a Garden House Cafe and the Baker Hall Visitor Center. The latter includes a visitor orientation room, information center, exhibit area and a short video introduction to the garden. There is also a well-stocked Garden Gift Shop.

During the summer, you can extend your stay by heading over to Norfolk's **Ocean View Beaches** which paradoxically overlook the Chesapeake Bay. Both visitors and natives enjoy the calm waters and uncrowded beaches. Beach parking, often a problem, is solved here by large free public lots at both 9th Street and Ocean View Avenue and 6th Street and Ocean View Avenue. Boardwalks provide beach access. Other pluses at Norfolk beaches are the gently sloping sandbars, free of undertow, where youngsters can swim and play in safety. Deeper water is free of buffeting waves. Only occasionally will a northeast wind churn up the waves and currents. In late July and August you do get an influx of jellyfish but no more than you'll find at nearby ocean beaches. Lifeguards are on duty from 11:00 A.M. to 7:00 P.M. There are restrooms and shaded picnic areas. Two commercial fishing piers with bait shops and tackle rentals are popular with fishermen and crabbers. For boaters there is a ramp at 13th and Ocean View Avenue which is open at no charge year-round. If you plan to bring your boat to Norfolk call (804) 441- 2222 for docking information.

Directions: From I-95 in the Richmond area, take I-64 east to Norfolk. For the Norfolk Botanical Garden take Exit 279 onto Norview Avenue heading east. Make a left turn onto Azalea Garden Road just before Norfolk International Airport; the garden is located on the right side. For Ocean View Beaches take Bay View Boulevard off I-64, which will intersect with Ocean View Avenue, Route 60.

Norfolk Naval Base

Nautical but Nice!

The **Norfolk Naval Base**—the world's largest naval base— certainly demonstrates the magnitude of America's military strength. The long line of destroyers, aircraft carriers, submarines and support ships tied up at Norfolk is truly an impressive sight.

Norfolk's naval significance dates from the Civil War when the famous battle of the ironclads, the *Monitor* and the *Merrimack*, occurred in Hampton Roads harbor. Today there are 100 ships, 32 aircraft squadrons and 35 shore based activities in the South Hampton Roads command. The Norfolk Naval Base extends over 3,400 acres and provides a great deal of interesting information and sights.

Tours leave daily between 9:00 A.M. and 2:00 P.M. from the Naval Base Tour Office at 9809 Hampton Boulevard. They leave on the half-hour during the summer months and take about 45 minutes. The schedule changes in the off-season, so be sure to call (804) 444-7637 in advance for current times. There is a fee, but no reservations are required.

It seems everything is bigger at the Norfolk Naval Base! Fleet Industrial Supply Center boasts that it is the "World's Largest Store." It is open daily year-round and employs 1,605 civilians and 53 military personnel. It's easy to see why this Norfolk facility has a $48 million federal payroll.

Near the top of the military payroll are the Flag Officers. Along "Admiral's Row" you'll see replicas of famous homes from various states built in 1907 for the Jamestown Exposition and all now used as officers' homes. For example, the Georgia House is a copy of the summer home of Franklin Delano Roosevelt's mother, known for a time as the Little White House. A typical colonial homestead represents Delaware. A lovely porticoed Virginia plantation house is the quarters of the Supreme Allied Commander of NATO. Along this fascinating drive there is also a scaled-down replica of Independence Hall.

Based at Norfolk are Sea King, Sea Knight and Sea Sprite helicopters. All weather early warnings, surveillance coordination, search and rescue missions and numerous other functions are carried out by the Eighth Carrier Airborne Early Warning Squadrons home based at Norfolk. You are sure to see some of the Hawkeye planes they fly.

What's a military installation without confusing shorthand? On the tour you pass both the FASOTRAGRULANT and the NCTAMSLANT. The former is a sophisticated flight simulator facility. The latter is the largest and most complex communication station in the world.

All of the above is just icing on the cake as far as most visitors are concerned. They come to see the ships and there are plenty to see! As you enter the two-mile waterfront area the first you see, berthed along Pier 12, are the world's largest warships. You'll learn how to tell the difference between the nuclear-powered and conventional-powered ships. (Just a hint: it has to do with the color of the antennas.) You may see a nuclear-powered aircraft carrier such as the *America* or the *Eisenhower*. These massive ships are 18 stories high and as long as three football fields plus an extra 100 feet at both ends. The size comes into focus when you learn that each link in the anchor chain weighs 350 pounds. The warships carry more than 6,200 men each. Due to recent changes in the laws, women can now serve in combat onboard aircraft carriers. The *USS George Washington* already has a contingent of women.

Next, at the Cargo Ship Pier, you'll see 23 types of boats and ships: destroyers, cruisers, amphibious ships, helicopter ships, fleet oilers and tugs. On weekends from 1:00 to 4:30 P.M. there are usually two ships that you can board although these rarely include aircraft carriers and submarines. The final part of the harbor portion of the tour takes you past the workhorses of the Atlantic Fleet—more destroyers and cruisers plus submarines and submarine tenders.

Another popular navy attraction is the Hampton Road Naval Museum. It is on the second floor of Nauticus, the National Maritime Center, in Norfolk (see selection).

Directions: Take the I-295 loop around Richmond and pick up I-64 east to Norfolk. After you cross the Hampton Roads Bridge Tunnel take Exit 564 for the naval base. Follow this to the very end, to where it intersects with Gate 2. This is the main entrance to the naval base.

Willoughby-Baylor House

All in the Family

William Willoughby's family roots extended back to the earliest days of the Virginia colony. His great-great-grandfather, Thomas Willoughby, had arrived here in 1610 at age nine. By 1636 Thomas had obtained a patent for 200 acres of Tidewater land on which Norfolk was later built. Thomas already owned the 500-acre Willoughby Plantation that is now Ocean View.

When William, prominent retail merchant and contractor, re-purchased the old family acreage, Norfolk was struggling to recover from the massive fire damage caused by Lord Dunmore's bombardment in 1776. In 1794 Willoughby built one of the first 20 brick townhouses in Norfolk. The townhouse reflected Federal and Georgian design. The furnishings you will see are in keeping with the 1803 inventory filed with the will at William's death. Hard use over the years resulted in the loss of all the original pieces.

In the front parlor you'll notice that the handkerchief table, card table and the tilt-top table all fold up. Furniture in the 18th century had to be versatile and movable to allow maximum use of space. The pair of Queen Anne mirrors that hang opposite each other, one in the parlor and the other in the adjoining dining room, were designed to reflect candlelight and not images; called mirrors when used downstairs, they were listed on inventories as looking glasses when used upstairs. The dining room table was once owned by James Madison's mother and was used in the White House during the Madison administration.

In the upstairs hall you'll find a sword chair, designed with an arm rest on only one side so that a man could sit and work while wearing his sword. There's also a dressing room with a gentleman's basin stand. The shaving cup is an ingenious contrivance with a saucer that held alcohol. The alcohol was lit and by the time it burned off, the water in the cup would be hot enough for shaving.

In the master bedchamber there is a curious device used for making inkles, the braided linen tapes used to secure clothes during the 18th century. Clothes were adjusted by inkles at neck, wrist and waist so that one size fit all. These small inkles prompted the expression, "don't have an inkling," meaning smallest idea. The last room on the tour is the children's room, in which you'll see a narrow chimney closet. The pattern on the children's dishes matches artifacts of china discovered during excavation.

The Willoughby-Baylor house is open April through December by appointment only, call (804) 664-6283. It is closed on Mondays and major holidays. Admission is charged.

Directions: From I-95 in the Richmond area, take I-64 east to Norfolk, then I-264 east. Exit on Waterside Drive and take an immediate right at St. Paul's Boulevard. Take a left onto Market Street, then the next right onto Cumberland Street. The house is at the corner of Cumberland and Freemason streets.

NORTHERN NECK

George Washington Birthplace National Monument

Planter's Paradise

On the western shore of the Chesapeake Bay lies Virginia's Northern Neck, first charted in 1608 by that intrepid explorer, John Smith. During the colonial period it was the port of call for many trading ships on their way to the West Indies and England.

The patriarch of one of America's first families arrived on one of those early trading ships. John Washington, great-grandfather of George, was a mate on an English ship that was trading for tobacco in 1657. It ran aground near Mattox Creek while sailing down the Potomac River on its voyage home. John Washington was so impressed with the land, the southern hospitality and the daughter of his host, Colonel Nathanial Pope, that he decided to remain. When he and Anne Pope were married, they were given 700 acres of choice land on Mattox Creek. He purchased additional land on Popes Creek and an American dynasty was begun.

It was here at Popes Creek Plantation that George Washington was born on February 22, 1732. The site is now the **George Washington Birthplace National Monument**. Because both progress and wars have bypassed this region, the grounds of the Washington plantation and the surrounding countryside look much as they did in the 18th century.

The natural beauty of the meandering Popes Creek, the broad views of the Potomac River and the gently rolling fields all can be enjoyed as you stroll along the park's trails. The land's historical significance is captured in the evocative film, *A Childhood Place,* shown at the visitor center. Fall leaves and migratory birds, snowy farmland, spring planting and summer wildflowers speak quietly and eloquently of the same seasonal shifts that influenced young George Washington. These natural rhythms form a bond between those who visit and those who once lived here.

George Washington lived on this family plantation until he was $3^1/_2$ years old when the family moved to Little Hunting Creek Plantation, now known as Mount Vernon. After his father's death when he was 11, George often returned to his early childhood home, inherited by his half-brother, Augustine.

The family home was destroyed by fire on Christmas Day 1779, while George was commander of the Revolutionary army. Oyster shells now delineate the foundations of the original home. A memorial house, erected in 1930–31, represents a house typical of the kind the moderately wealthy Washingtons could afford. Although most of the furniture is over 200 years old, only a small tea table and an excavated wine bottle are from the original house.

Both birth and death are remembered here. As you enter the grounds you'll see the miniature Washington monument, a single granite shaft erected in memory of George Washington in 1896. Nearby is the family burial grounds where George's father, grandfather and great-grandfather are all buried.

But it is the rebirth of nature that brings the long ago days to life. George Washington in his later years remembered fishing along Popes Creek. You can easily imagine the young boy making his way to the river and perhaps glimpsing an ocean-going trading ship from the shore. Today the National Park Service owns 538 acres of preserved shoreline, woods and pasture at

Popes Creek Plantation. Fields are still planted and tilled by 18th-century methods. During the summer months special demonstrations are given on sheep shearing, tobacco planting, harvesting and curing, soapmaking, candlemaking, dyeing and weaving. There are also colonial music programs featuring the spinet and other instruments.

The George Washington Birthplace National Monument is open daily from 9:00 A.M. to 5:00 P.M. except Christmas and New Year's Day. A nominal admission is charged. There is a picturesque picnic area overlooking Popes Creek. You can also picnic at nearby Westmoreland State Park. While at the park, you may want to take advantage of the Olympic-size pool or even spend a relaxing hour on the beach.

Also nearby (north off Route 3/301 on Route 218, just across the Potomac River bridge from Maryland) is **Caledon Natural Area**, a designated National Natural Landmark because of its bald eagle habitat. The hiking trails in this 2,579-acre natural area provide a chance to see one of the largest concentrations of bald eagles on the East Coast. Staff-led interpretive tours of their habitat are given from mid-June to Labor Day (reservations are recommended). There are five hiking trails at Celadon ranging from $7/_{10}$ miles to two trails of $1^1/_{10}$ miles. There are exhibits on the bald eagle at the visitor center in the Smoot House. For information on programs at Caledon Natural Area call (540) 663- 3861.

Directions: From I-95 take Route 3 east to Route 204. The George Washington Birthplace National Monument is $1^7/_{10}$ miles off Route 3 on Route 204.

Northern Neck

A Place to Really Stick Your Neck Out For

Locals have been heard to boast that even colorful characters who don't have a prayer of getting into heaven have had their turn in paradise by living in the **Northern Neck**. The Neck, which is Old English for peninsula, cape or isthmus is surrounded by the Potomac River on the north, Chesapeake Bay at the foot and Rappahannock River on the south. On the upper Neck are the birthplaces of two illustrious Americans: George Washington (see Birthplace selection) and Robert E. Lee (see Stratford Hall selection). Although their homes do not survive, James Monroe and James Madison were also born in the Northern Neck region.

The lower portion of the Neck also offers an array of historical and natural attractions. On a low bluff at the head of a branch of the Yeocomico River is the 1706 village of Kinsale. Named for an Irish seaport town in County Cork, the name is derived from the Gaelic, Cean Saile, meaning, "Head of the salt water." The community was a center of ship building in the late 1690s. Of 2,547 tons of shipping listed for the colony of Virginia in 1699, more than 900 tons were produced in and around this village. This active port officially became a town in 1784. During the War of 1812, Kinsale was burned by the British. Southern blockade runners used Kinsale as a base of operations during the Civil War, calling down the wrath of the Union army, who bombarded the town on numerous occasions.

When you visit you should stop at the still-active Kinsale Wharf at the foot of Steamboat Hill. On the Green in the heart of the village is **Kinsale Museum**, where you'll learn of the town's prominence as a steamboat port, connecting the Northern Neck with Washington and Baltimore. The museum is located in a late-19th-century barroom which, during the 1920s, was used as a meat market. Next to the museum is a soda fountain built in the late 1800s (now privately owned). The museum is open from May through October on Thursday, Friday and Saturday from 10:00 A.M. to 5:00 P.M. No admission is charged. You can pick up a walking tour brochure of this historic village. Kinsale is reached from Route 3 by taking Route 202 east then Route 203 north.

Heading down Route 202 you'll come to Heathsville, the county seat since 1681. You can take a walking tour of the historic district. The Northumberland County Historical Society's **Ball Memorial Library**, located behind the county courthouse, has extensive genealogical and historical records. Before leaving, stroll past the 1851 Courthouse and the 1844 Old Jail. The Historical Society is open Monday, Wednesday and Thursday from 9:00 A.M. to 4:00 P.M. and on the second and fourth Saturday of the month from 9:00 A.M. to 1:00 P.M. Also behind the courthouse is Hughlett's Tavern built in 1795 and later expanded into Rice's Inn. Now on the National Register of Historic Places, this old inn is currently being preserved and restored.

Take Route 360 east out of town for about three miles then make a left on Route 636, a Virginia Scenic Byway. Locally this route is called the **Northumberland Heritage Trail** and focuses on the region's three Fs: farming, forestry and fishing. The route takes you to a lookout with an excellent view of the Smith Point Lighthouse. The current one was built in 1897 but the first dated back to 1802. Your tour route provides an opportunity to utilize one of Virginia's two remaining free ferries, the Sunnybank Ferry that will take you across the Little Wicomico River. (The other is Merry Point Ferry that crosses the Corrotoman River in Lancaster County.) The Heritage Route ends just south of Reedville in Fleeton.

Located on a narrow peninsula between two arms of Cockrell's Creek, Reedville was established after the Civil War by Captain Elijah Reed who came to fish for menhaden, a small oily fish found in abundance in local waters. In 1874, he established a factory to press oil from the fish and process its by-products. The industry brought wealth to the region as you will see from the Victorian mansions along "Millionaires' Row," a section of Reedville's Main Street. The houses were built when Reedville boasted the highest per capita income of any town in the United States. This area is designated a historic district on the State and National Registers of Historic Places. Be sure to stop at the **Reedville Fishermen's Museum**, where you'll learn all about the menhaden industry. Models of fishing vessels and the tools of the trade are displayed along with equipment used by watermen from early Native Americans to modern fishermen. The porch of the Covington Building that houses the museum overlooks Cockrell's Creek where two fleets still set sail to fish for menhaden from May through December. Also part of the museum complex is the Walker House, representing a waterman's house at the turn of the century. The house was built by William Walker in 1875 on land purchased earlier that year from Captain Reed. Museum hours are from May through October daily 10:30 A.M. to 4:30 P.M. From November through April, the museum is open weekends only 11:00 A.M. to 4:00 P.M. Be sure to pick up a self-guided walking/driving tour brochure. Tour boats leave from Reedville for Tangier Island (see selection) and Smith Island.

In order to get to the southern section of the lower Neck, head west on Route 360 to Burgess and then south on Route 200. Just below Wicomico Church you can pick up another Virginia Scenic Byway, Route 679. Just off the Scenic Byway between Burgess and Kimarnock at the mouth of Dividing Creek on the Chesapeake Bay is the 203-acre **Hughlett Point Natural Area Preserve**, that opened in the fall of 1995. The preserve provides a glimpse of a tidal beach, saltmarsh and pine forest ecosystem. It is considered by locals as one of the best beaches for walking in the entire Northern Neck. There are trails and two observation decks. Commonly-sighted wildlife include wild turkey, bald eagles, osprey, swans and migratory waterfowl as well as deer and small mammals. The preserve is open daily from sunrise to sunset.

The Scenic Byway loops back into Route 200 just above Kilmarnock. At Kilmarnock head south on Route 200, then make a right onto Route 222 at the sign for **Historic Christ Church**. This Irvington church was built in 1735 by Robert "King" Carter (agent for Lord Fairfax, Proprietor of the Northern Neck) and presents the best example in the country of a virtually unchanged colonial church. This architectural gem with massive three-foot thick walls was built in the shape of a cross. It's equally imposing within, with a three-decker pulpit towering over the individually enclosed high-backed pews. Before exploring the church, watch the short slide presentation in the reception center. Hours are Monday through Friday 10:00 A.M. to 4:00 P.M., Saturday 1:00 to 4:00 P.M. and Sunday 2:00 to 5:00 P.M.

Robert Carter had this church built on the exact location of a 1670 church in which his parents were buried in the chancel on the understanding that his parents' grave would be moved to the new church's chancel. They remain buried under a large slate slab in Historic Christ Church. Outside are the tombs of Robert Carter and two of his wives. Descendants of Robert Carter include eight Virginia governors, three signers of the Declaration of Independence, two United States presidents and other distinguished Americans.

To complete your exploration of the Northern Neck return to Route 200 and head north back to Kilmarnock, then head west on Route 3. If you have time for a hike you'll pass the turn off for the **Corrotoman River Nature Trail**. This $1^6/_{10}$ mile trail (which takes about $1^1/_2$ hours to hike) meanders through a 1,000-acre forestry complex owned and managed by the Chesapeake Corporation. The trail map provides information on the plants and natural features you will observe. From several points along the trail you will see the western branch of the Corrotoman River, a tributary of the Chesapeake Bay.

Continue west to Lancaster where you'll find the **Mary Ball Washington Museum and Library**. The mother of the Father of our Country was born in Lancaster County. In the museum you'll see a 300-year overview of life in this area. The nearby 1797 Old Clerk's Office and the 1820 Jail are also open to the public and you can pick up a walking tour map of the Lancaster Courthouse Historic District. The museum and library is open Tuesday through Friday from 9:00 A.M. to 5:00 P.M. April through November it is also open on Saturday 10:00 A.M. to 3:00 P.M. The genealogical section of the library has county records dating from 1651.

Continuing west on Route 3 to Lively will afford another chance to get out and enjoy nature. From Lively take Route 683 south to **Belle Isle State Park**. There are two trails: the $1/_2$-mile Watch House trail and the $1^2/_{10}$-mile Neck Fields trail. The 733-acre park provides access to seven miles of the Rappahannock River as well as Deep and Mulberry Creeks, which provide a wide variety of wetlands. This diverse habitat is home to wild turkey, osprey and bald eagles. You may even spot white-tailed deer, fox, raccoon, opossum or groundhog. Naturalist guided canoe explorations of the salt marsh and shoreline habitats are available Thursday through Sunday from Memorial Day to Labor Day.

Back on Route 3 west, you will come to the town of Warsaw where you will discover the **Richmond County Museum and Visitor's Center**. This museum in the 1816 Old Clerk's Office on the Courthouse Green tells the story of rural life in this region

108

from colonial days to the present. Displays include domestic and agricultural memorabilia. Hours are Thursday and Friday 11:00 A.M. to 3:00 P.M. year-round and Saturday at the same times from April to December.

If being around all this water makes you want to get out and enjoy it, then pick up Route 360 south in Warsaw and head over the Rappahannock River to the town of Tappahannock where they offer cruises departing at 10:00 A.M. and returning at 5:00 P.M. Tuesday through Sunday from May through October. For more information or to book a cruise call (804) 453- 2628. Be sure to bring along binoculars as the boat passes eagles nesting in the trees and cliffs beside the river. The cruise takes you 20 miles up the river. After two hours on the water you'll land at **Ingleside Plantation Winery** (just outside Oak Grove and also accessible by car off Route 3). You'll get to taste and purchase some award-winning wines. One of the oldest and largest wineries in the state, Ingleside is also one of the few Virginia wineries to produce sparkling wine. This stop also serves as a lunch break—either a southern buffet at Ingleside or your own picnic. The last stop is at Wheatland's steamboat wharf. For an additional admission fee, you can tour the 1810 Federal-style farmhouse and the boxwood gardens. After this, you'll cruise back to Tappahannock.

Directions: From I-95 take Route 3 east to the Northern Neck.

Stratford Hall

These Siblings Weren't Rivals

The Washingtons were one of many families of prominence to have their roots in the Northern Neck. James Madison, James Monroe, John Marshall's father and the Lee brothers were all born in the region. The Washingtons (see George Washington Birthplace National Monument selection) and the Lees were virtually neighbors. Richard Henry Lee, who became a signer of the Declaration of Independence, was born the same year as George Washington, on January 20, 1732. His brother and fellow signer, Francis Lightfoot Lee, was born two years later on October 14, 1734. It is provocative to imagine the mutual influence Washington and the Lees might have had on one another had they grown up together.

The Lees were the only brothers to sign Declaration of Independence. It was Richard Henry Lee who actually proposed the resolution for independence from England at the Second Continental Congress. It is likely he would have been asked to draft the resolution had he not been called back to Virginia during the debate. It is perhaps best, as he was considered an orator, while Jefferson was noted as a superior writer.

Richard Henry Lee was an activitist. He established the first association in the colonies to boycott English goods, the Westmoreland Association. At the First Continental Congress his efforts in this direction led to the Continental Association, the first step toward a union of the colonies.

The father of these distinguished patriots, Thomas Lee, had held the highest office in the Virginia colony as President of the King's Council. In 1720 he built the family estate, **Stratford Hall**, on the cliffs overlooking the Potomac River.

Stratford Hall is far grander than the Washington home. It once encompassed 4,100 acres and even now includes 1,670 acres. Like Pope's Creek Plantation, it is still a working farm with a herd of 200 Black Angus. The house itself was an architectural anomaly in colonial America. It was not designed in traditional Georgian manner but in the Italian style with the major living quarters on the second floor. The design features an H-shaped great house with two clusters of four chimneys each. The great hall forms the center of the H, and it is considered one of the 100 most beautiful rooms in America. Like the rest of the house, it is furnished with 18th-century pieces.

Thomas Lee's great-nephew Light Horse Harry Lee was a military hero of the Revolutionary War. He went on to serve three terms as governor of Virginia. His son Robert E. Lee was born at Stratford Hall. Visitors can see the bedroom where Robert E. Lee was born. The adjoining nursery contains a fireplace with two bas-relief winged cherubs said to be favorites of the young Lee.

Stratford Hall is open 9:00 A.M. to 4:30 P.M. except Thanksgiving, Christmas and New Year's Day. Admission is charged. If you decide not to picnic on the grounds, try the Log Cabin Plantation dining room that is open from 11:30 A.M. to 3:00 P.M.

Directions: From I-95 take Route 3 east at Fredericksburg. Take Route 2 to Lerty and turn left on Route 214 for Stratford Hall.

PORTSMOUTH

Portside

Deserves a Bow

They no longer charge a bale of hay for the ferry ride across the Elizabeth River; now it's 75 cents. That's still an inexpensive way of getting out where the action is—the busy Norfolk-Portsmouth Harbor.

This waterway has been important since the earliest days of the Virginia colony. An exploration party led by Captain John Smith sailed up the Elizabeth River in 1608. Adam Thoroughgood, who arrived in 1621 as an indentured servant, operated the first ferry service in 1636 (see Adam Thoroughgood House in Virginia Beach selection). Adam owned a small skiff and had two oarsmen who would take passengers across the river. Stories were told that his helpers would hide in the marsh grass until enough passengers arrived to make it profitable, but then the stories also claimed that Adam was paid in bales of hay.

Ferry service between Portsmouth and Norfolk, the oldest continuous public ferry in the country, reached its zenith in the 1940s when there were diesel ferries for passenger cars. Once the tunnel connected the two cities in 1955, the ferry service was discontinued. In the early 1980s, ferry service resumed and has proven quite popular. The ferry runs daily throughout the year and has extended hours from April through October. The ferry leaves **Portside** on the hour and the half hour and Waterside in Norfolk at 15 and 45 minutes past the hour.

The *Carrie B* offers $1^1/_2$-hour afternoon cruises and $2^1/_2$-hour sunset sails. The *Carrie B* is a replica of a 19th-century Mississippi riverboat. It cruises past the world's largest working shipyard, the Norfolk Naval Shipyard, founded in 1767 when Virginia was still a British colony. During the Civil War when federal troops had to abandon the Norfolk navy yard, they sank the U.S. Frigate *Merricmack*. The Confederates raised the ship and in 1861–62 reconstructed the ironclad *C.S.S.Virginia* upon the hull of *Merrimack* in drydock here. This ship took part in the famous Battle of the Ironclads that changed the course of shipbuilding. This is the nation's oldest drydock, but technology has kept pace with the changes in ship design. The navy sends many of its modern supercarriers, submarines and missile ships here for repairs.

The *Carrie B* leaves from Norfolk, stopping at Portside 15 minutes later. From mid-April through October, cruises sail at 12:10 and 2:10 P.M. There are sunset cruises at 6:10 P.M. from June through Labor Day.

Whether you opt for the brief ferry trip or the longer cruise, your interest in nautical matters is likely to be piqued. Portside has two museums to satisfy your curiosity. The **Portsmouth Lightship Museum** at London Slip is located in a ship that never sailed but gave long service. Lightships combined the attributes of lighthouses and buoys; their lighted masts resembled the former and they floated like the latter. They had an additional benefit in that they could move from place to place. As they changed

Portside Marketplace along the banks of the Elizabeth River in Portsmouth bustles with activity from April through October. Visitors enjoy al fresco meals at open air restaurants and there is nightly musical entertainment.

---

locations they frequently changed names. The lightship now permanently docked at London Slip was first called *Charles,* then *Overfalls, Nantucket Relief, Stonehorse* and, just before retiring in 1964, it was called *Cross Rip.* In addition to seeing the inside of one of these old lightships you'll see Coast Guard equipment, uniforms and old photographs. You are welcome aboard at no charge Tuesday through Saturday from 10:00 A.M. to 5:00 P.M. and Sunday from 1:00 to 5:00 P.M.

Open during the same hours is the adjacent **Portsmouth Naval Shipyard Museum.** One of this museum's most interesting displays is the 1776 map of Portsmouth. An audiovisual program uses the map to acquaint you with life in colonial Portsmouth. You'll also see the plans of John L. Porter for the conversion of the *Merrimack* (these are the plans he hid in his home nearby, see Portsmouth Walking Tour selection). Old tools, weapons, ship models and uniforms fill the cases at this maritime museum.

During the summer months you can enjoy an al fresco meal at the Portside's Marketplace. Seafood is the specialty at many of the stalls—steamed shrimp, crabcakes, clams and oysters vie with other fare. If you prefer a restaurant, sample one of the many fine establishments in the Olde Towne historic district, located a few short blocks from the Portside Waterfront.

Directions: From I-95 south in the Richmond area, take I-64 east to the Norfolk-Portsmouth area. In Hampton, exit on I-664 south and cross the Monitor-Merrimac Bridge Tunnel. Take I-264 east into Portsmouth, then take the Crawford Street exit and follow Crawford Street for $1/_2$ mile to the Visitor Information Center at Portside.

Portsmouth Walking Tour

Harboring a Spirited Past

Portsmouth boasts the largest concentration of antique houses between Alexandria and Charleston, South Carolina. You'll see more sites on the National Register of Historic Places here than in any other Virginia city. It is not quantity, however, that captivates visitors on a walking tour of Olde Towne—it's the diversity of architectural styles.

The old English city checkerboard pattern was laid out in 1752 by Colonel William Crawford, prominent merchant and ship owner. You get the tour map by stopping at the Portside Visitor Center, then follow the red brick sidewalks into America's past on the **Olde Towne Lantern Tour**. Portsmouth plaques on the street lanterns indicate stops on the walking tour.

Begin your walk on London Boulevard at 108, the Cassell House that Captain John McRae built in 1829. You'll want to pay close attention to the details of these houses. The Cassell House features a handcarved arched frame door with a fanlight and stone lintel. The gabled roof reflects Dutch influence.

The house at the corner of London Boulevard and Crawford Street has two names. The first, Murder House, does not recall a heinous crime but the pronunciation of the owner's family name, the Murdaughs. Since the Civil War it's been called by its second name, the Pass House, because the Federal adjutant general headquartered here granted passes to enter and leave Portsmouth. This is the first example you'll see of the aboveground basement homes copied from Hull, England, that were ideally suited for this low-lying location.

The now-respectable office building at 216–218 London Boulevard was once a sailor's tavern called The Red Lion. Recent renovations uncovered a cockfighting pit in the cellar.

Move up London Boulevard to Middle Street and turn right. Several visitors have heard, but only one has seen, the ghost of the Ball-Nivison House at 417 Middle Street. According to that eyewitness, a professor in an academic gown carries not his books but his head under his arm. John Nivison, prominent

Portsmouth attorney, certainly kept his head when he bought this Dutch Colonial home in 1784. It is one of the many "tax dodger" homes in town, so named because the British taxed only full floors, leaving the dormer floor tax free.

When the Marquis de Lafayette returned to Portsmouth in 1824, 50 years after the Revolution, he stayed at the Ball-Nivison. Lafayette was 19 when he joined the fight for American independence. He returned, an elderly statesmen, to a hero's welcome. The **Lafayette Arch** at Crawford Street and London Boulevard commemorates his visit.

The Gothic Revival house at 370 Middle Street is full of gingerbread touches like the wooden lattice and patterned bargeboard gables. Victorian woodwork, called jigsaw, is featured on the porch at 371 Middle Street. Just a few steps down the street is another elaborate porch at 365.

Continue up the 300 block of London Boulevard to the corner of Court and Queen streets and you'll see the pink granite Court Street Baptist Church, considered by some architectural historians to be one of the four best examples of Romanesque design in the country. The words "In God We Trust" were added to our money at the suggestion of Mark R. Watkinson, a former pastor of this church.

The corner of Court and High streets was Towne Square on William Crawford's plans. On the four corners there was a church, market, courthouse and a jail. This took care of moral and practical needs. Only Trinity Church remains; it is Portsmouth's oldest church dating from 1761.

Norfolk burned during the American Revolution but not Portsmouth. The city was saved by Lt. John Dickey of the British Royal Navy. He had been captured and brought to Portsmouth, but instead of spartan imprisonment he enjoyed the hospitality of Tory sympathizers. Dickey repaid the city by intervening when Lord Dunmore was ready to turn the British guns on Portsmouth. General Cornwallis, too, spent time in Portsmouth. He was headquartered here before his ill-advised move to Yorktown. British supporters made him welcome, but he decided the town was difficult to defend. The Revolution might have lasted longer had Cornwallis remained in Portsmouth.

At 420 Court Street, a Victorian house built in 1870 has stylish floor length windows with semi-elliptical arched tops. Be sure to notice the ironwork, particularly where it crests over the porch. The 400 block of London Boulevard looks like a Currier and Ives print. The small frame house at 412 will remind you of Williamsburg. A row of colorful cottage-style houses built in the mid-to-late 1800s have a wealth of architectural details. Along Washington Street you'll find another group of 19th-century homes. Smuggled medicines destined for the Confederate army were hidden beneath the hearthstones at 412 Washington Street.

Turn right on North Street. At the corner of North and Dinwiddie streets is the Federal-style house built in 1799 by Colonel Dempsey Watts. During the Black Hawk War, the chief of the warring tribes was brought to Portsmouth to see the "big canoes" and hear the "big boom" of the *U.S.S. Delaware* cannons. Impressed, the Black Hawk Chief returned to the Watts House where he was entertained as a guest of the nation.

Turn left to explore the 300 block of Court Street. Like many of the English basement houses, 336 has been lowered so that the main floor is close to street level. The ghosts at the Maupin House 326, are, legend has it, pet bull terriers.

The Harth House at 320 Court Street is reputedly the oldest house in Portsmouth still faithful to its original design. This early 19th-century basement house has a Greek Revival portico. Notice the door's transom light with rectangular panes and the brass doorknob and knocker.

The William Peters House at 315 Court Street, with its Classical Revival look, suggests the Battery homes of Charleston, South Carolina. The Porter family lived here during the Civil War. John L. Porter hid the plans for the conversion of the salvaged Union ironclad *Merrimack* into the Confederate ship *Virginia* in the walls of his home. When Union General Benjamin Franklin Butler, who was in charge of this Confederate city, appeared to inspect their home, one of the ladies tripped him on the stairs. This was not as ill-advised as you might think. The general's nickname was "Spoon" Butler; he had a habit of purloining family silver. When Miss Porter tripped him, silver spoons bounced out of his uniform pockets as he tumbled down the stairs. Only Butler's dignity was harmed, but luckily for the Porter family he did not return to complete his inspection.

Years later when Butler ran for president on the Radical Reconstruction ticket, a campaign banner was hung in Portsmouth recalling the general's 1865 Civil War victory. To the slogan "Butler Hero of Five Forks" a local opponent added, "and the Lord only knows how many silver teaspoons."

On the corner of Court and North Street is the Bain House, built on one of William Crawford's original lots. The old Elks Club across Court Street is built in the Romanesque style. The 300 block of North Street has another group of mid-19th-century basement houses. The first city mayor, George M. Grice, who served from 1858 to 1861, lived at 314 North Street.

The **Hill House**, 221 North Street, was built in the early 1800s by Captain John Thompson. His nephew, John Thompson Hill, the second owner, gave his name to the house and it remained in the family until 1962. Many original 19th-century pieces still fill the house which is open for tours Wednesday, Saturday and Sunday from 1:00 to 5:00 P.M. Admission is charged.

The Grice-Neeley House, 202 North Street, suggests New Orleans with its wrought-iron balcony and graceful stairs. To complete your walking tour turn right on Crawford Street. You'll pass three mid-19th-century houses, the Benthall-Brooks Row. Brooks, a sea captain, built these houses in the 1840s one floor at a time. He built the basement story for all three and waited a year; then built the second floor and waited another year. He finished the three houses the third year. Perhaps he knew what he was doing; the row houses have survived more than 150 years.

Other interesting tours of the Olde Towne Historic District are the African American Heritage Trolley Tours, the Olde Towne Ghost Walk and Historic Civil War Day.

On weekends in the spring and fall and daily during the summer you can take a 75-minute trolley ride through Olde Towne Portsmouth and the **Norfolk Naval Shipyard's Trophy Park**. This latest addition to the tours features over 300 years of historical weaponry ranging from the Revolutionary War to World War I and II.

If you are searching for a cultural and aesthetic experience stop at the 1846 Courthouse, at Court and High streets, which features work from international as well as regional artists in temporary exhibitions. Three blocks up High Street, visit the state's largest children's museum. Formerly housed in the 1846 Courthouse, the expanded **Children's Museum of Virginia** offers over 60 interactive exhibits. It is open daily from 10:00 A.M. to 5:00 P.M. From Memorial Day through Labor Day hours are 9:00 A.M. to 9:00 P.M. Admission is charged.

Directions: From I-95 in the Richmond area, take I-64 east toward Norfolk/Virginia Beach. In Hampton, exit on I-664 south and cross the Monitor-Merrimac Bridge Tunnel. Take I-264 east into Portsmouth. Take the Crawford Street exit and follow Crawford Street for a half-mile to the Visitor Information Center at Portside. You can also take a ferry from Norfolk's Waterside to Portside.

TIDEWATER AREA

The Mariners' Museum

A Model Museum!

You know the feeling. You read a book, hear a joke, eat a fine meal—and can't wait to share your find. That's the reaction you'll have when you visit **The Mariners' Museum** in Newport News. Although the museum was founded in 1930, it's still a relatively undiscovered treasure.

The treasures here are the varied ships that ride the seas. The "jewels" of the collection, spotlighted in a darkened room, are the 16 miniature ships crafted by August F. Crabtree. These exquisite models represent the labor of a lifetime—each is a work of art. August Crabtree was born into an Oregon shipbuilding family in 1905. He worked for a time in a shipyard in Vancouver but enjoyed carving models more than building full-size ships. When Crabtree worked in Hollywood, he created the model of Lord Nelson's ship in the movie, *That Hamilton Woman.*

The Mariners' Museum purchased Crabtree's models in 1956. His work is exact in every detail. To outfit the tiny prehistoric men on the raft and dugout canoe, Crabtree trapped a mouse for its fur. The models reveal the artistry inherent in the construction of ships such as Queen Hatsheput's Egyptian fleet, circa 1480 B.C., or a Roman merchant ship, circa 50 A.D.

Some of the models have historical significance. One is the *Mora* on which William the Conqueror invaded England in 1066 and Christopher Columbus's *Santa Maria* and *Pinta*. Others are so intricately carved you'll need to use the magnifying glass attached to the display case to see the details. The hull on a 1687 English 50-gun ship is carved with 270 human, animal and mythological figures. An 1810 American brig is noted for its elaborate rigging.

The last of Crabtree's models was the first of Cunard's red-and-black funneled passenger steamers, the *Britannia.* One of the early passengers was Charles Dickens who complained his cabin was "an utterly impracticable, thoroughly impossible and profoundly preposterous box."

Entrancing as the models are, they fill only one of the museum's 14 galleries. The museum is also noted for the boardroom models done on a scale of one-quarter inch to a foot. These models were made by the shipbuilders for the ship owners' boardrooms. Many cruise ships are represented including the *S.S. Rotterdam* and the *Queen Elizabeth I.* The latter is done on a scale of three-eights inch to the foot and is over 28 feet long. The room where these models are shown has as its centerpiece the steeple-type engine from the *William Stewart*; only a foghorn could add to the ambience.

A ship modeler works several days each week in the Carvings Gallery surrounded by over 30 lifelike figureheads including a polar bear from the vessel used in Admiral Richard Byrd's Antarctic expedition. The museum has quite a collection of these carvings which once graced the bows of tall ships. As you enter the museum you'll see one of the most striking: the $1^1/_2$-ton gilded eagle with an $18^1/_2$-foot wingspan from the U.S. Navy frigate *Lancaster*. There are some unusual figures among the more traditional buxom female figureheads, such as an imperial-looking Queen Victoria, a threatening Hindu with a spear and even the Apostle Paul. When the Paul figurehead was purchased in Providence, Rhode Island, it was transported in an open rumble seat. The figure, wrapped in a blanket to prevent damage, looked so real that passersby took it for a dead body and called the police.

It takes a separate building to house the small craft, the most complete international collection in the Western Hemisphere. The oldest range from primitive skin boats to dugouts from Louisiana, Jamaica and the Congo. There are experimental racing yachts like the *Dilemma*, a Dutch yacht called a jotter, a Brazilian raft, a Chinese sampan, a Norwegian four-oared boat, a Venetian gondola, a Spanish sardine boat and a Portuguese kelp boat. The museum has expanded its Antique Boats Gallery to include additional boats, engines and photographs. The gallery setting suggests a 1930s dealer showroom. It showcases three original Chris-Craft boats including the 26-foot *Miss Belle Isle*, one of the oldest surviving Chris-Crafts.

Another gallery honors William Francis Gibbs, the architect who designed more than 6,000 naval and commercial vessels. He is best known for designing the superliners *SS United States* and *SS America*. The gallery features a recreation of Gibbs' glass-enclosed New York office, including many original personal effects, such as his drafting table, books and certificates. Photographs and memorabilia from his superliners are displayed.

The museum owns more than 35,000 items. There are many decorative pieces with nautical themes: Liverpool creamware, Staffordshire figures, Sevres and Derby ceramics and lovely scrimshaw work. Photographs, weapons, uniforms and ship models tell the story of important military confrontations at sea. The Chesapeake Bay Gallery covers fishing and boating on the bay from the time before European settlers first arrived.

For those with a scholarly interest in the sea, the museum has a 75,000-volume library as well as maps, journals and some 530,000 photographs. It is an amazing facility set in a 550-acre park and wildlife sanctuary. Within the park is 167-acre Lake Maury. There are fishing boats, athletic fields, picnic tables and the five-mile Noland Trail around the lake and through the woods.

The Mariners' Museum is open daily from 10:00 A.M. to 5:00 P.M. It is closed on Christmas. Admission is charged.

Directions: From I-95 in the Richmond area, take I-64 east to Exit 258A at Newport News and Route 17, J. Clyde Morris Boulevard, to the museum entrance. The route is well-marked.

Gracing the entrance to the Mariner's Museum in Newport News is this 1½-ton gilded eagle figurehead from the U.S. Navy frigate Lancaster. It has a wing span of 18½ feet.

Pamunkey and Mattaponi
Indian Reservations

Reminders of Once Powerful Nation

Side by side, reservations of the Pamunkey and Mattaponi can be visited, both tribes are survivors of the powerful Powhatan Confederation. Ten thousand years before the birth of Christ the Pamunkey Indians were working the soil of an area that would eventually become the Commonwealth of Virginia. When many of their neighboring Powhatans fled, leaving their homeland to the English settlers, the Pamunkey stayed. They remain on their Virginia reservation to this day.

Residents of the reservation near West Point worked for years developing their interpretive museum. Displays trace the tribe's origins in prehistoric Paleoindian days. The advances in both tools and agriculture during the Woodland Period become obvious as one sees specific examples of implements as they developed from archaic to modern. You can see the gradual improvement of tools in seven separate areas: cutting, hammering, chopping, grinding, piercing, scraping and tying.

The **Pamunkey Museum** also has an exhibit on changing styles of Native American pottery, from the primitive beauty of Woodland work through the decades to the designs of the 1990s. It is noteworthy that the 40s and 50s produced a garishly colored unauthentic-looking design, whereas the more recent pieces resemble very early works in form, clay, color and texture. Some fine examples of recent work are on sale at the gift shop, where you will also find Native American jewelry and souvenirs designed to appeal to young visitors. Museum hours are 10:00 A.M. to 4:00 P.M. Monday through Saturday and 1:00 to 4:00 P.M. on Sunday.

The nearby **Mattaponi Museum** eschews the organized, educational approach. Here, the collection of an entire people is jumbled together in a one-room display. Stuffed birds and local wildlife overlap ceremonial drums. Fossils dating from archaic man rest beside modern newspaper clippings about political figures. The artifacts span the entire history of the Mattaponi and the Powhatan Confederation. There is a headdress reputedly worn by Powhatan, a necklace that once belonged to Pocahontas and a tomahawk of Opechancanough's that reminds visitors of the more violent history between the Native Americans and the English settlers.

Opechancanough (pronounced Ope-can-canoe) is a tribal hero to the Mattaponi, who consider him a member of their tribe. Some historians dispute this, claiming instead, that he came from the West Indies. The Mattaponi revere him as one of the few Native Americans to perceive the eventual catastrophe of English domination. The museum includes several items that once belonged to Opechancanough.

One unusual item is a "mercy" tomahawk, used by the medicine men for those they could not heal. Several medicine bags, in which powerful amulets were carried, are on display. There is also a replica of the execution club, a snake-like club used for ritual killings. It was reputedly a club like this that Powhatan raised to kill Captain John Smith before Pocahantas's timely intervention. The museum is open by appointment only; call (804) 769-2194. A nominal admission is charged.

Directions: From I-95 just north of Richmond take Route 360 north for approximately 20 miles to Route 30, then head south for seven miles to Route 633. Turn right on Route 633 and travel eight miles to the Pamunkey Indian Reservations. Signs will direct you to the museum. The Mattaponi Reservation is almost directly across Route 30 from the Pamunkey Reservation. From Route 30, turn right on Route 640 and go one mile then make a left on Route 625 and travel $1^3/_{10}$ miles to the Reservation.

Smithfield and Fort Boykin Historic Park

You Can't Go Wrong in Isle of Wight County

In 1608 Captain John Smith journeyed to the Warrosquoyacke (War-a-squoy-ak) Native American area on the south bank of the James River to barter for food for the hungry Jamestown settlers. But **Smithfield** settlement was not named in his honor, but for Arthur Smith who, in 1637, patented 1,450 acres in Isle of Wight County. The county's name recognized the home of many of the area's settlers who came from England's channel island. In 1750, Arthur Smith IV had the land surveyed and laid out the town of Smithfield with four streets and 72 lots. In two years 59 lots were sold, each for four pounds, six shillings. By the time of the American Revolution all the lots in Smithfield were sold.

When you take an **Old Towne Walking Tour** of Smithfield you will see more than 15 structures from the 18th century. The tour, including over 60 points of interest, starts at **The Old Courthouse** and Clerk's Office at 130 Main Street. The courthouse, built in 1750, was the first building to stand in the new town of Smithfield. Architectural historians believe the rounded end of the main courtroom was copied from the Old Capitol in Williamsburg. When restoration was done at Williamsburg, workman came to Smithfield to study the copy in order to replace the original that had burned in 1749. The Smithfield courthouse was used until 1800, when the court was moved to the county seat, Isle Of Wight. (You can see the 1800 Courthouse after your walking tour, outside town on Route 258, Courthouse Road.) The 1750 Smithfield Courthouse was restored by the Isle of Wight branch of the Association for the Preservation of Virginia Antiquities and today it serves as a visitor center, open daily 9:00 A.M. to 5:00 P.M. It is closed on major holidays. Be sure to stop in and pick up a walking tour map.

Another Main Street tour stop should be **The Isle of Wight Museum**. Formerly a bank its architectural features include a Tiffany-style dome skylight, marble floor and decorative tile. Permanent exhibits include local fossils and Native American artifacts as well as a room-size country store with old post office boxes, a pot-bellied stove, an array of pharmaceuticals and even a Smithfield ham. Another exhibit explains Smithfield's meat packing industries. There are always changing exhibits as well. The main gallery also has a small theater showing a 15-minute slide program on the history of the region. Museum hours are Tuesday, Wednesday, Thursday and Saturday from 10:00 A.M. to 4:00 P.M., Friday 10:00 A.M. to 2:00 P.M. and Sunday 1:00 to 5:00 P.M. Admission is free.

The Todd House, stop seven on the tour at 22 Main Street, was built by cabinet maker Nicholas Parker in 1753. However, by 1767, it was the home of Captain Mallory Todd who started the business of curing and shipping hams that has made Smithfield world famous. Joyner's Smithfield Ham Shop at 315 Main Street and Smithfield Foods continues the tradition Todd started.

The Grove, at 220 Grace Street, has an interesting history. Thomas Pierce's estate, begun in 1780, once stood in a grove of oak trees, but they were cut and sold to the Russian navy during the Crimean War. In 1956, the house was restored by Lieutenant Governor and Mrs. A.E.S. Stephens.

Stop 21 of the walking tour puts you back on Main Street, #336 to #346, for Victorian Row. Five late-Victorian homes have typical embellishments such as bay fronts and gingerbread trim. Another delightful Victorian is the Pembroke Decatur Gwaltney House at 226 S. Church Street (stop 48). Built in 1876, until 1995 this house remained in the same family that founded the peanut business in Smithfield and later opened a meat curing and packing company. Stop 49, is Smithfield's most photographed Victorian house, built in 1901 for Pembroke Decatur Gwaltney, Jr. Farther down Church Street is the Goodrich House (stop 53), the only Victorian house in town with a Mansard roof and colored-glass cupola.

The last stop on the walking tour is Windsor Castle, built around 1750 by town founder Arthur Smith, IV. This stucco-covered brick house is probably not the first to be built on Smith's land. Actually, you might want to reclaim your car and drive to this Jericho Road house, although it is within Smithfield's Historic District.

Two miles south of Smithfield on Route 10 is **St. Luke's Church**. Known locally as "Old Brick", it is the country's only original Gothic church and the oldest existing church of English foundation in America. Vestry records indicate that the church was begun in 1632, several years before the Tower Church at Jamestown was started in 1638/39. The Mother Church of Warrosquyoake County had a congregation of 522 in 1634. It took more than four years to finish the exterior and more time was spent on interior touches. Gothic elements include buttresses, stepped gables, brick-traceried windows, a medieval timber-trussed roof structure and a three-story tower.

Records indicate that the interior was not finished immediately, in fact, there was a lapse of almost 25 years. The interior is Jacobean. From the founding fathers to modern worshipers, for more than 300 years prayers have been said in St. Luke's.

A number of the interior pieces have survived from the 17th century including a communion table and chairs, a silver baptismal font, silver wine ewers and candlesticks and a 1665 English organ. The church did not weather the vissitudes of time without being threatened. During the American Revolution, British troops under Colonel Tarleton (see Carter's Grove selection) camped in the church yard. St. Luke's Church at 14477 Benns Church Road is open 9:30 A.M. to 4:00 P.M. Tuesday through Saturday and 1:00 to 4:00 P.M. on Sunday. It is closed on Mondays and major holidays, and during the month of January.

From St. Luke's it is just a short drive down Route 17 to **Ragged Island Wildlife Management Area** at the foot of the James River Bridge. If you didn't do enough walking in Smithfield, you'll enjoy the nature trails and the panoramic view of the James River. You might want to bring binoculars as this is an excellent vantage point from which to spot a wide diversity of birds.

There's another park north of Smithfield that is also worth exploring and that is **Fort Boykin Historic Park**. A nature trail reveals traces of Fort Boykin, an installation that was part of American history from 1623 through every military campaign fought on American soil. Captain Roger Smyth received a commission to build the fort on May 11, 1623 to protect the colonists against, "Spaniards by sea and Indians by land." Smyth called his fort "The Castle" because of its imposing position on a steep cliff overlooking the James River. Refortified during the American Revolution, it stood guard over the James River, receiving its name from Major Francis Boykin, who served on General George Washington's staff.

Prior to the War of 1812, the fort was restructured in a seven-point star shape. This is the outline you see today. Local legend claims that the guns of Fort Boykin sank two British men-of-war during the second war with England. An attempted English landing was repulsed.

Refortified during the Civil War to protect the access to Richmond, it was discovered that guns from ships on the river could reach the fort but the fort's guns couldn't retaliate. The Confederates abandoned the fort and the Union forces landed and destroyed both of the forts magazines and burned all of the outbuildings. During the brief southern occupation, the Alabama poet Sidney Lanier was stationed at Fort Boykin. In the several months he spent at the fort, Lanier wrote several poems and started work on a novel.

Between 1862 and 1908 the fort reverted to wilderness, but efforts by a number of dedicated enthusiasts restored the ground. Today the trail takes visitors past a Civil War gun salient, the location of the old parade ground, two magazines, a well and flag mound. Flowers now grow where soldiers once marched. The fort is open daily from 9:00 A.M. to dusk. There are picnic tables and grills. From the high bluff overlooking the James River there is an excellent view of the navy's "Mothball Fleet," of ships no longer in active service.

Directions: From I-95 just north of Petersburg take Route 460 east to the Isle of Wight, or just north of Hopewell, take Route 10 east. From both of these you will turn on Route 258 which will take you into Smithfield. From I-64 take the James River Bridge Exit, Route 17 south to Route 258.

Smith's Fort Plantation, Bacon's Castle and Chippokes Plantation

Surry's Fringe Benefits

Originally part of the Jamestown colony, the land across the James River was included in Surry County when it was established in 1652. The name provided a link with Surrey, England, which most settlers would never see again. Today **Smith's Fort Plantation** offers a chance to see where Virginia's leading crop was developed, where rebels ruled a century before the Revolution, where farm land has been tilled since 1612 and evidence of what may be the oldest formal garden in the United States.

Captain John Smith built a fort in 1609 on the banks of Gray's Creek across from Jamestown. Five years after Smith's fort was built, John Rolfe, who settled in Virginia in 1610 and lost his wife shortly after arriving, remarried. He took as his wife Pocahontas, daughter of the Powhatan chief (see Henricus Historical Park selection). The Powhatan chief gave the couple tribal land that the English settlers had already commandeered. Rolfe used the land for experimenting with tobacco strains. Among the varieties he planted was the West Indian blend that became Virginia's number one cash crop.

The house you see today at Smith's Fort Plantation was not built until the 18th century. It is noted for its fine woodwork and period furniture. There is a small English garden and a trail leads to the ruins of the old fort. Smith's Fort Plantation is open for tours Tuesday through Saturday 10:00 A.M. to 4:00 P.M. and Sundays, NOON to 4:00 P.M. from April through October and weekends in March and November. Admission is charged.

124

Just as John Smith never lived at Smith's Fort Plantation, Nathaniel Bacon never lived at **Bacon's Castle**. This stately Jacobean house, once known as "Allen's Brick House," was built in 1665 by Arthur Allen, Speaker of the House of Burgesses and a good friend of Royal Governor Berkeley. The house is one of, if not the, oldest brick house in English North America. Although not the fortress its name suggests, it looks formidable with its Flemish gables and their matched triple chimney stacks. The house was extensively renovated both inside and out.

The house became a pivotal stronghold during the full-scale rebellion against Royal Governor William Berkeley, a century before the American Revolution. The rebels, led by Nathaniel Bacon, burned Jamestown to the ground in September 1676. Bacon then retreated to Gloucester and sent one of his lieutenants, William Rookings, to establish a base of operations in Surry County. On September 18, Rookings and his band of 70 men seized Arthur Allen's house. From there they ruled the county for the next three months until the rebellion was crushed.

Extensive archeological work was done on the grounds of Bacon's Castle. Archaeologists uncovered evidence of a 72,000-square-foot garden that may date from 1680, possible the oldest formal garden ever found in the United States. Although arranged in six sections with bisecting and surrounding paths, this was not an ornamental garden with mazes and decorative beds. It was a vegetable and herb garden (some of which flowered). Bacon's Castle is open concurrently with Smith's Fort Plantation from April through October 10:00 A.M. to 4:00 P.M. Tuesday through Saturday. Sunday hours are NOON to 4:00 P.M.

Another nearby plantation, in **Chippokes Plantation State Park** (named for a minor Native American chief friendly to the early settlers), has a model farm that demonstrates agricultural methods and crops from the 17th to the 20th century.

Chippokes has historical and horticultural significance. This land has been in continuous use for more than 300 years since it was first patented by Captain William Powell in 1612. Powell's heirs sold the land to Sir William Berkeley, the Royal Governor.

The antebellum plantation house was built in 1854 on the foundations of an earlier homestead. The mansion and out-kitchen can be toured, providing a look at life on a rural plantation in the days immediately before the Civil War. Behind the house is a six-acre garden, in bloom from spring through fall, with the peak season being late summer when the abundant crape myrtle blossom. There are 17th-, 18th- and 19th-century buildings on the grounds. Guided walks on weekends focus on historical reminders as well as the natural environment. An earlier home, River House, built in the 1700s, is not open for tours.

Chippokes may be visited daily from sunrise to sunset. The visitor center is open only from Memorial Day weekend to Labor Day weekend.

Directions: Take I-95 south of Richmond to the Route 10 Exit. Take Route 10 past Hopewell. All three attractions are just a short distance off Route 10. For Smith's Fort Plantation turn left on Route 31. For Chippokes turn left on Route 634 and for Bacon's Castle turn left on Route 617.

Virginia Living Museum

Window on the Natural World

The **Virginia Living Museum** in Newport News is part native wildlife park and part science museum and aquarium. A small planetarium and abundant botanical specimens provide a multidisciplinary introduction to Virginia's natural world. The museum is modeled on the renowned Arizona-Sonora Desert Museum in Tucson.

A living cross-section of Virginia's James River is the first exhibit. It covers 340 miles in 60 feet. It begins with the plants, fish and wildlife found in a mountain stream, then moves to a sluggish tidal river, next to the Chesapeake Bay and on into the Atlantic Ocean. The ocean tank has a loggerhead sea turtle. Young turtles are given to the museum, grow to maturity and then are released to the wild and the cycle begins again.

Young children enjoy reaching in and handling the specimens in the touch tank. They also enjoy the dinosaur exhibit that gives them a chance to place their hands on an authentic track made by a Kayentapus that roamed through Virginia over 210 million years ago. These bipedal dinosaurs were 126 inches high and $10^1/_2$ feet long. A sample of their footprints is nine inches long. These tracks were discovered by workers at the Culpeper Stone Company in a quarry near Stevensburg.

Another section of the museum concentrates on species survival, highlighting such basics as food, defense, reproduction and shelter. Creatures as diverse as a black widow spider, an octopus and a kestrel demonstrate various aspects of these vital functions. You will discover that if the kestrel could read it would be able to peruse a newspaper 100 yards away.

Certainly one of the most popular indoor areas is the two-story glass songbird aviary. These injured, abandoned and hand-raised birds have no fear of visitors and it's easy to get excellent close-up photographs of the colorful specimens. You'll see such elusive birds as cedar waxwings, summer tanagers and quail.

The bald eagle in its natural habitat exhibit at Virginia Living Museum is part of the native wildlife park, which includes a two-story glass songbird aviary. A small planetarium, abundant botanical specimens, aquarium and science exhibits are all part of this Newport News attraction.

From there the walkway leads outside along Deer Park Lake and past the habitats of native water animals like river otters, raccoons and beavers. A striking outdoor wetlands aviary gives you a chance to see glossy ibis, elegant herons and a variety of multi-hued ducks and other waterfowl. The aviary's overlook has three observation points so that you can see habitats representing marsh, swamp and bog. Only four percent of Virginia land is wetlands, but within that area live one-third of the endangered species in the state. The outdoor exhibits also include such woodland creatures as bobcats, deer, fox, opossum and skunk. You also can get a close look at a pair of bald eagles.

Depending on the time and length of your visit you may be able to include one of the museum's daily planetarium shows. During the summer there are three shows every afternoon and another on Thursday evening. The rest of the year there is only one afternoon show during the week. There is an extra charge for these shows. Another way to explore space is through the museum's telescope. The observatory offers solar viewing during regular museum hours and a chance to look at the stars on Thursday evenings.

The Virginia Living Museum is open from Memorial Day to Labor Day, 9:00 A.M. to 6:00 P.M. Monday through Saturday; on Sunday it opens at 10:00 A.M. The rest of the year hours are 10:00 A.M. to 5:00 P.M., except on Sunday when the museum opens at NOON. On Thursday evenings the museum opens from 7:00 to 9:00 P.M. It is closed on major holidays. For information on planetarium shows call (804) 595-1900.

Directions: From I-95 in the Richmond area, take I-64 east to Newport News. Take Exit 258A, the J. Clyde Morris Boulevard and a sign will indicate the museum on your left at 524 J. Clyde Morris Boulevard.

VIRGINIA BEACH

Virginia Beach

Surf-Fire Fun

There is more than sun, sand and surf at **Virginia Beach**, Old Dominion's ocean playground. If you like the ocean but don't like to lounge on the beach then you may enjoy the 27 miles of hiking and biking trails within the 2,770-acre **Seashore State Park** or a drive into the park to see some of the more than 336 species of trees and plants. During the summer the yucca plants, which provide oases of greenery on the park's mountainous dunes, blossom with bell-like white flowers.

The park, a Registered National Landmark, is open year round. The entrance is on U.S. Route 60, Shore Drive. There is a visitor center and museum where you obtain maps of the trails that fan out from the center. Many trails are sturdy wooden walkways that permit access to the swampy areas. If you set out in late afternoon, do apply insect repellent.

Across Shore Drive at Fort Story on Cape Henry are several historic reminders. The **First Landing Cross** commemorates the spot where the Jamestown settlers touched the shore of the New World on April 26,1607. Easter sunrise service is held here each year and on the April Sunday closest to the landing date, the Order of Cape Henry makes a pilgrimage to this National Historic Landmark.

One of America's first lighthouses, built here in 1791, provides mute testimony to the dangers of these waters. Funds for the **Old Cape Henry Lighthouse** were authorized by the First Congress. It was built with stones mined at Aquia Quarries, which also provided stones for the White House, the U.S. Capitol and Mount Vernon. During the summer months, for a small admission, you can tour the inside of the lighthouse. The Old Cape Henry Lighthouse is off Shore Drive via the west gate of Fort Story, or you can enter the east gate at the end of Atlantic Avenue.

One ship that went down despite Cape Henry Lighthouse was the Norwegian bark, *The Diktator*, which was wrecked off the shores of Virginia Beach in 1891. The citizens of Moss, Norway gave Virginia Beach a statue, *The Norwegian Lady*, to perpetuate the memory of the ship lost here. A second statue stands in the Norwegian city. The Virginia Beach statue is at 25th Street and Oceanfront.

An exhibit detailing this maritime tragedy can be seen at the **Lifesaving Museum of Virginia**. Since Virginia Beach grew up around the U.S. Life-Saving Coast Guard Station much of the town's early history is captured at this museum, which also includes maritime memorabilia from around the world. The museum, at 24th Street and Oceanfront, is open Monday through Saturday 10:00 A.M. to 5:00 P.M. and Sunday NOON to 5:00 P.M., from Memorial Day through September. From October to Memorial Day its hours are Tuesday through Saturday 10:00 A.M. to 5:00 P.M. and Sunday NOON to 5:00 P.M. It is closed on Thanksgiving, Christmas, New Year's Eve and Day. Admission is charged.

The **Virginia Marine Science Museum** (see selection) on General Booth Boulevard opened in 1986 and underwent a major expansion in 1995. It features the natural marine environment, encompassing four marine habitats and live vegetation, fish and birds. Admission is charged. It is open 9:00 A.M. to 5:00 P.M. daily with extended summer hours, call (804) 425-FISH.

The wide variety of things to do in Virginia Beach extends from museums and military installations to historic homes. There are two brick homes that have survived from the colonial period. The **Adam Thoroughgood House**, circa 1680, is one of the oldest standing brick houses in America built by early English settlers. The house was named for a young indentured servant who arrived in Virginia in 1621. After completing his servitude, he married a lady from a well-to-do family and used her dowry to pay the passage for 105 indentured servants to come to Virginia. In return for providing passage for these settlers, Thoroughgood was granted 5350 acres of land. It is on this land that his grandson built the house. The house is furnished with 17th-century antiques. Guides in period attire give tours from 10:00 A.M. to 5:00 P.M. April through December and from NOON to 5:00 P.M. January through March. It is closed on major holidays and on Mondays. Admission is charged. Because the Adam Thoroughgood House is owned by Norfolk, it is included on the Norfolk Automobile Tour, but is located in Virginia Beach. The house can be reached via Route 225, Independence Boulevard, off the Virginia Beach-Norfolk Expressway, Route 44.

Lynnhaven House, built between 1725 and 1730, is very much like the Adam Thoroughgood House, but the crafts and furniture represent the 18th century. Lynnhaven House is just off Route 225, at Independence Boulevard and Wishart Road. It is open for a nominal admission Tuesday through Sunday from NOON to 4:00 P.M. from June through September, and weekends from NOON to 4:00 P.M. in May and October.

If the present piques your curiosity more than the past, the Navy offers you much to see. There are tours of the Oceana Naval Air Station and you can watch the Navy's most advanced aircraft while enjoying a midday picnic at either of two parks: Observation Park on Oceana Boulevard or London Bridge Observation Park.

At Little Creek Amphibious Base you can actually board one of the home-ported ships. This is the largest base of its kind in the world and each weekend one of the ships has an open house. Passes onto the base are available at Main Gate 4 off Shore Drive between Independence Boulevard and Diamond Springs Road.

For information on these and other Virginia Beach activities, stop at the Virginia Beach Visitor Information Center at 2100 Parks Avenue at the end of Route 44. It is open daily from 9:00 A.M. to 5:00 P.M. with extended hours during the summer months. Before visiting call (800) 466-8038.

Directions: From I-95 in the Richmond area take I-295 and head east on I-64 to the Virginia Beach-Norfolk Expressway,

The Adam Thoroughgood House, circa 1680, is one of the oldest brick houses in America built by English settlers. It was built by the grandson of indentured servant Adam Thoroughgood.

Route 44. Take the expressway east to Virginia Beach. Turn left onto Route 60 for Shore Drive. For the Amphibious Base, exit from I-64 onto Route 13 north, Northampton Boulevard. Take that to Route 225 north, Independence Boulevard and then go left on Shore Drive, Route 60, to the base gate.

Virginia Marine Science Museum

They Put a Tiger in Their Tank

In recent years, the Tidewater region has opened or expanded a number of innovative museums that reveal diverse aspects of life on, in and around the water. Norfolk's Nauticus is a high-tech maritime wonderland and Newport News' Virginia Living Museum combines a native wildlife park, wetlands aviary and aquarium. Virginia Beach's **Virginia Marine Science Museum** has the world's largest collection of Chesapeake Bay fish and the Atlantic Ocean Pavilion that focuses on aquatic life off Virginia's coast.

As part of an expansion project begun in 1994, the museum expanded from 9 to 45 acres, adding a huge pool for harbor seals at the museum's entrance. The Atlantic Ocean Pavilion's 300,000- gallon aquarium recreates the Norfolk Canyon, a unique offshore geological formation. You can imagine you are diving deep into this submarine crevasse as you watch the schooling fish, sharks and other large ocean dwellers. The pavilion also has a 70,000-gallon sea turtle aquarium and a nearby hatching laboratory. The interactive oceanographic exhibits get young visitors involved in the experience.

Another significant focus of attention is Owls Creek, the waterway behind the museum. Boardwalks allow access to various points in the wetlands surrounding the buildings and along the creek bank. There is a river otter habitat with underwater viewing, a shorebird aviary, an interactive micro-marsh that directs your attention to insects of the marsh and a macro-marsh with animals that frequent this wetlands area. Another pavilion offers scientific exhibits on the creek and wetlands area. Trails through the salt marsh have explanatory signs and a series of observation platforms.

The museum maintains visitor favorites like the touch tank where children can hold a starfish, feed a horseshoe crab and grasp the contours of a hermit crab's home. There's also the larger touch tank where you can really get the feel of a stingray or tiger shark. Decoy makers and museum staff keep visitors entertained with explanations of their craft and stories of the fish that swim in Virginia's waters.

A towering six-story IMAX 3D Theatre takes this impressive viewing experience to new heights, in three dimension! It's one of the biggest screens on the East Coast. Located in the new east wing with this giant screen is a museum cafe and gift shop. The museum is open from mid-June through Labor Day on Monday through Saturday from 9:00 A.M. to 9:00 P.M. and on Sunday until 5:00 P.M. The rest of the year it closes daily at 5:00 P.M. Admission is charged.

Directions: From I-95 in the Richmond area take I-64 east to Virginia Beach. Turn east on Route 44 and exit right on Birdneck Road. Turn left on General Booth Boulevard and the museum will be immediately on your left.

WILLIAMSBURG

Anheuser-Busch Brewery Tour

Six Million Bottles of Beer on the Wall

For the hearty (or the thirsty) the **Anheuser-Busch Brewery Tour** provides a zesty look at the mechanization large companies have introduced to perform age-old processes. The self- guided walking tours are offered from 10:00 A.M. to 4:00 P.M. daily. Although the front door closes every day at 4:00 P.M., later visits are possible from adjacent Busch Gardens Williamsburg.

Your self-guided tour takes you above the action. Through large picture windows you look down to the floor below to watch the process that turns out no fewer than 70,000 gallons of beer a day on which the annual tax is $1,099,400,000. You'll immediately be struck by the fact that there are so few workers on the floor. The process is highly automated.

Taped messages provide information on each step of the beer-making process. First the grain mixture is prepared and cooked for a period of time, then sent to fermentation tanks and finally to the huge lager tanks. The liquid remains in the lager tanks for approximately 21 days before being bottled. Empty bottles on endless conveyor belts feed into a filter machine and come out full—as many as six million bottles of beer a day. Another area of operations turns out five million cans per day.

Your experience of the brewery process is somewhat sanitized. You get no aromas from the vats and tanks, but you do get a taste. Anheuser-Busch offers tour participants of drinking age two samples from their many products. Hot dogs, salads and

Visitors to Busch Gardens learn impromptu Bavarian folk dances in Rhinefeld, the park's German Village.

pizza are sold, along with soft drinks, at the Hospitality Center—making this an excellent spot for a mid-day break.

Although interesting, the brewery tour is not the major Anheuser-Busch attraction; most of the action is at the adjacent **Busch Gardens Williamsburg**. This 360-acre theme park features quaint European hamlets: Banbury Cross and Hastings, England; Heatherdowns, Scotland; New France and Aquitaine, France; Rhineland and Oktoberfest, Germany; plus San Marco and Festa Italia. There are rides, a wide variety of shops, restaurants and shows.

Busch Gardens is open daily from mid-May through Labor Day. It is open weekends-only from late March or early April until mid-May and again after Labor Day until the end of October. Admission varies according to age and length of stay. The park opens at 10:00 A.M., but closing time varies by season. Call (804) 253-3350 to check. They also operate the largest waterpark in Virginia, Water County USA just outside Williamsburg.

Directions: From I-95 in the Richmond area, take I-64 east to Route 199 and follow signs to Busch Gardens.

Bassett Hall

Putting on the Dog

On November 27, 1926, under an ancient oak tree behind the 18th-century home of Burwell Bassett (nephew of Martha Washington), John D. Rockefeller, Jr. and Reverend W.A.R. Goodwin first met to plan the restoration of Williamsburg, the 18th-century capital of the colonies. As they strolled back to town, Rockefeller said if he came back to Williamsburg he'd like to picnic beneath the oak.

It became easy for Rockefeller to picnic at Bassett Hall after he purchased the 585-acre estate in 1936. From this comfortable vantage point the Rockefellers watched the rebirth of Williamsburg. John D. Rockefeller, Jr. ultimately spent $60 million on the restoration of the venerable city and contributions by other family members brought the figure to $100 million.

A tour of Bassett Hall reveals a great deal about the Rockefeller life style. From the moment you enter the informal sitting room, the first room on the self-guided, audiotaped tour, one decorative influence is immediately apparent—Mrs. Rockefeller's folk art collection. There are 200 pieces from her extensive collection in this home and more than 400 pieces at the nearby Abby Aldrich Rockefeller Folk Art Center (see selection).

Bassett Hall represents a mix of decorating styles. In the hall passageway, which in colonial times served as the summer living room, you'll see a collection of Chinese export paintings. The paint was applied on the back side of the glass. Such paintings had to be carefully shipped, for if the glass broke the picture was lost.

In the formal parlor there is another unusual style of painting called mourning pictures. Painted by school girls and much in vogue after the death of George Washington, these depicted graveyard scenes full of tombstones. There are additional examples of these morbid works upstairs, though the master bedroom has stenciled pictures with cheerful subjects such as flowers, fruits and birds. Throughout Bassett Hall you see objects acquired by Mrs. Rockefeller's sister, Lucy, on her travels. She purchased the crocheted bedspread in the master bedroom from the Royal School of Needlework in England. Mrs. Rockefeller herself was a talented needleworker, as a trunk full of rugs made by her attests.

In the sitting room of the new wing there is an unusual painting of General Washington crossing the Delaware. The faces of all the men in the boat resemble George Washington.

Back downstairs you'll see the formal dining room, which Mrs. Rockefeller described in a letter to her son David as "the most pleasant room in the house." Although the dining room is quite elegant, when the heads of state from around the world attended the Summit of Industrialized Nation in May 1983, they enjoyed lunch in the garden overlooking the oak allée.

Explore the grounds before you end your tour of Bassett Hall. There are three original outbuildings: a smokehouse, kitchen and dairy. A modern teahouse, or orangery, was added by the Rockefellers.

Bassett Hall is open daily 9:00 A.M. to 4:45 P.M., except Wednesday, by appointment. Appointments can be arranged at any Colonial Williamsburg ticket office. Admission is by Colonial Williamsburg's Good Neighbor Card, Patriot's Pass or Museums Ticket.

Directions: From I-95 in the Richmond area, take I-64 east to Colonial Williamsburg. An alternate route is via Route 5 east from Richmond. You may want to stop at the Colonial Williamsburg Visitor Center upon arrival to obtain maps, brochures and tickets.

Carter's Grove and Wolstenholme Towne

Everything Old Is New Again

Your journey to **Carter's Grove** takes you from the bustling town of Williamsburg to the splendid country estate of Carter Burwell.

A return trip to Williamsburg along a one-lane carriage road through quiet woods and across wooden bridges, offers an opportunity to reflect on the well-dressed burgesses who passed the same scenery on their way to an evening's entertainment at Carter's Grove.

Current visitors to Burwell's mansion stop at a reception center where exhibits trace four centuries of history on this remarkable land. In the 1970s, when archeologists were digging for the plantation outbuildings, they uncovered a historical bonanza: the remains of **Wolstenholme Towne**, the 17th-century Martin's Hundred settlement that all but disappeared in 1622.

A group of British adventurers settled at Martin's Hundred and obtained a patent for 21,500 acres from the Virginia Company. Then in 1618 the company sent 220 settlers to Virginia who established a palisaded fort which they named in honor of Sir John Wolstenholme.

The remains of the fort have been uncovered as well as the remains of farmsteads, storehouses, dwellings and graves of settlers, some of whom were buried in haste after the Native American attack of March 22, 1622. The attack cost 58 settlers their lives; 20 more were captured and the homes and fields of almost all were destroyed. It was the end of Wolstenholme Towne.

The short two-year life of the town, plus its abrupt end, makes this an archeological time capsule. Many of the artifacts uncovered, some from sites that survived the massacre, have been of inestimable value. Two closed helmets are unique discoveries; no others have been recovered in America. The helmets have details not found on those exhibited in England. A dish made in 1631 is the oldest dated example of British colonial pottery-making.

After viewing the orientation film, *A Thing Called Time*, you follow a path to the overlook pavilion where you hear the site archeologist, Ivor Noel Hume, narrate a recorded drama about one settlement. Recorded messages are delivered at nine locations along the walk. There is also a detailed painting to help you imagine what the town looked like more than $3^{1}/_{2}$ centuries ago. Because there was not sufficient data to permit a complete reconstruction, only the outlines and partial building facades of the 1620 site have been reconstructed.

In total six sites dating from 1619 to 1645 have been explored. There are still others awaiting excavation including small farmsteads that survived the massacre and date from the period 1650 to 1750, the year when Carter Burwell began building his plantation house.

Burwell inherited the land from his mother, Elizabeth, the daughter of Robert "King" Carter whose vast estate encompassed 300,000 acres. In his will King Carter stipulated that this portion of his land must always bear the name Carter's Grove.

Over a million bricks were used to build Carter Burwell's imposing Georgian mansion. Great care was expended on the carved interior woodwork. Burwell brought English carpenter Richard Baylis and his family to Virginia so that he could devote all his energies and skills to creating the elaborate designs you see today. It took 500 days just to complete the hallway design. Carter Burwell did not have much time to enjoy his completed home (he died six months after it was finished), but it was held by the Burwell family until 1838.

It is furnished with period pieces collected by Mr. and Mrs. Archibald McCrea who purchased Carter's Grove in 1928 and restored it to its colonial elegance. No description of this historic estate is complete without the two legends told and retold about events that are reputed to have occurred here before and during the American Revolution. According to one story George Washington and Thomas Jefferson had their marriage proposals rejected while courting at Carter's Grove. The Refusal Room is where Washington is supposed to have asked Mary Cary, a Carter cousin, to marry him and where Jefferson is said to have proposed to Rebecca Burwell, his "fair Belinda."

The second legend dates from 1781 just before the Battle of Yorktown when British Colonel Banastre Tarleton was headquartered at Carter's Grove. Tarleton, believing that the Virginians were looting his supplies, wanted to rouse his sleeping men so he rode his horse up the grand staircase slashing the stair rails with his saber. Though the story may be apocryphal the scars on the stair rails are real.

Carter's Grove is open daily from 9:00 A.M. to 4:00 P.M. During the summer months it stays open until 5:00 P.M. It can be toured independently but it is also included on the Williamsburg Patriot's Pass. Tickets are available at the Colonial Williamsburg Visitor Center or the Carter's Grove Reception Center.

Directions: From I-95 in the Richmond area, take I-64 east to Colonial Williamsburg. Follow the Carter's Grove signs to Route 60. You will return to Williamsburg by the Country Road.

Gardens of Williamsburg

Floral Tribute

Williamsburg's enduring appeal is in its complete evocation of Virginia's colonial capital. Its public and private buildings are seen within the context of the 18th century rather than the hubbub of the 20th century. Brick walks flank the broad streets on which carriages and wagons still travel. As you glance over the picket fences you'll see the gardens of yesterday blooming again.

The town of Williamsburg was laid out by Governor Francis Nicholson in the area called Middle Plantation, established in 1699 on a broad ridge between the York and James rivers. This stockaded outpost provided a line of defense for Jamestown against Native American attacks. After the third Jamestown fire the capital of the colony was moved to Middle Plantation. It was renamed Williamsburg in honor of King William III. The town grew to a population of 1,800, but this was greatly increased when the General Court and the House of Burgesses were in session.

Nicholson's plan divided the city into one-half acre residential lots; sufficient land for a house, dependencies and a garden. English garden styles popular in the reign of William and Mary, 1687–1709, were copied in the elegant formal gardens of the Governor's Palace and the backyards of private homes.

Alexander Spotswood, the first of the seven governors to live in the Palace, was determined to make the garden the finest in the colonies, even if he personally had to pay to do it. He succeeded admirably and the garden he envisioned has been reconstructed and replanted. Of enormous help in this restoration was the discovery in Oxford University's Bodleian Library of an 18th-century engraving showing plantings near the Palace. Extensive archeological investigation revealed the location of paths, walls, steps, gates and the parterres (beds). To speak of the Palace garden as a single entity is confusing because there are several separate gardens—the maze, the upper and lower ballroom gardens and the falling garden.

The maze is perhaps the most popular. Young and old delight in tackling the mysteries of this conceit. The prickly leaves of the native American holly used to create this natural puzzle discourage short cuts. The design was copied from Hampton Court's maze, a favorite of the English nobility.

The upper ballroom garden reveals another component of many English gardens, the "Twelve Apostles." These sentinels, cylindrically shaped topiaries, keep constant watch over the garden. The extensive use of holly and boxwood means that the gardens remain green all year. Spring and summer bring masses of color to the 16 diamond-shaped beds of the upper garden and the long beds and borders of the lower level. Pleached (interlaced) allees flank the lower garden, making natural tunnels that provide both shade and privacy. The garden was an ideal spot for courting in the 18th century; it was one of the few places that a private conversation was possible.

You too might enjoy an escape to the gardens of Williamsburg. Many visitors are so busy trying to see the buildings, they miss

Ten landscaped garden acres surround the Governor's Palace in Colonial Williamsburg. There is a formal box garden, bowling green, ballroom garden, holly maze, fruit garden and terraced gardens sloping to a canal and fish pond.

the spirit of this remarkable place. The sense of continuity is keenly felt amid the living reminders of the past.

A few of the private homes open their garden oases to the public. A map denoting them is available at the visitor center. George Wythe (pronounced like Smith) spent tranquil hours away from disputatious lawyers in the pleasure garden of his home on Palace Green (see Private Homes selection). His neighbor and town mayor, Thomas Everard, added an unusual feature to his garden, a small duck pond. Many of the shops and taverns have gardens. You can enjoy an alfresco meal at King's Arms, Chowning's or Shields Tavern (see Tavern selection).

A garden symposium is held each April. Williamsburg's Historic Area is generally open daily from 9:00 A.M. to 5:00 P.M., and until 6:00 P.M. during the summer months.

Directions: From I-95 in the Richmond area, take I-64 east to Williamsburg. Use Exit 238 onto Route 143 (you'll bear right off I-64). This is quickly followed by a right onto Route 132. You'll turn left onto feeder road Route 132Y into the Colonial Williamsburg Visitor Center. Just follow the green shield signs to Colonial Williamsburg.

Public Hospital, DeWitt Wallace Decorative Arts Gallery and Abby Aldrich Rockefeller Folk Art Center

Mind Over Matter

The last of the reconstructed 18th-century Williamsburg public buildings, the **Public Hospital**, opened in 1985, a full century after it was destroyed by fire. When the hospital originally opened in 1773 it was the first institution in America devoted solely, as the law stated, "for the Support and Maintainance of Ideots, Lunatics, and other Persons of unsound mind."

During the first year there were only 12 patients who endured the harsh conditions you will become aware of as you tour the Public Hospital. A reconstruction of one of the original 24 primitive cells illustrates conditions prevalent during the Age of Restraint, which lasted from 1773 until 1835. The cell contains only a straw mattress and chamber pot. Patients were manacled. The windows were barred and the doors padlocked. A taped vignette helps re-create the lot of these early victims of mental illness who were treated by cold water plunge baths and harsh drugs.

The opposite side of the viewing room at the Public Hospital has a 19th-century apartment representing the period of Moral

141

Management from 1836 to 1862. This approach was based on the realization that the patient suffered emotional problems, needed kindly and respectful treatment, plus work and recreational activities to fill their time in confinement. The room contains a quilt-covered bed, table, chairs, rug and even a violin and newspaper.

Many of the "tools" of the mental health trade were recovered from the on-site excavations. The museum section of the hospital contains a strait jacket, Utica crib (a wire cage-like bed for violent patients), a tranquilizer chair and more benign objects like the sports equipment and games used in later years.

This new addition to Colonial Williamsburg certainly runs the gamut of "pain and pleasure," because after the horrors of the mental ward come the delights in the adjoining **DeWitt Wallace Decorative Arts Gallery**, built with funds contributed by DeWitt and Lila Wallace, co-founders of the Reader's Digest Association. The gallery is reached by elevator or stairs from the hospital lobby. On entering this bi-level museum you go through an introductory gallery that suggests the scope of this incredible collection. More than half of the 8,000 items on display have never, or only rarely, been shown, so it is indeed a new look at some very old items from the 17th, 18th and early 19th centuries.

Around an attractive central court you'll see the master works exhibit with selected pieces from the diverse small study galleries which branch off this core area. The prize pieces are the matched portraits of George III and George Washington that flank a throne-like ceremonial chair. Painted in the same pose, the two pivotal figures present a study in contrasts; the King with his full figure outfitted in elegant finery and the uniformed Washington with his military bearing and piercing gaze.

Study galleries at the museum include textiles, ceramics, glass, metals, prints, paintings and maps plus special rotating exhibits. A major collection of early 18th-century furniture and accessories was donated to the gallery by Miodrag and Elizabeth Ridgely Blagojevich. This important collection contains items too splendid for the modest means of the 18th-century Williamsburg residents.

The museum is open daily 10:00 A.M. to 6:00 P.M. Admission is by Colonial Williasmburg Good Neighbor Card, Patriot's Pass, Museums Ticket or Annual Museums Ticket available at the visitor center.

The Public Hospital and DeWitt Wallace Decorative Arts Gallery are at 325 Francis Street between South Henry and Nassau streets. Parking is available at a lot on Nassau Street. A cafe at the gallery is ideal for lunch, tea or snacks.

If you enjoy decorative arts you should also include a visit to the **Abby Aldrich Rockefeller Folk Art Center** on your itinerary. Mrs. Rockefeller, mother of the late Governor Nelson Rockefeller, was one of the first to collect American folk art. Her substantial collection serves as the nucleus for this small museum on South England Street adjacent to the Williamsburg Craft House. The exhibited work includes folk painting, decorated household furnishings, quilts, weather vanes, toys, ceramics and signs. The museum is open daily from 10:00 A.M. until 6:00 P.M. Admission is with the same ticket as the DeWitt Wallace Decorative Arts Gallery.

Directions: From I-95 in the Richmond area, take I-64 east to Colonial Williamsburg following the signs to the historic area.

Williamsburg's Private Homes and Businesses

Making Sense of the Past

The smells, sounds and sights of Colonial Williamsburg can best be sensed in the private homes and shops. The pungent hot gingerbread cookies at the Raleigh Tavern Bakery, the fragrance of leather permeating the harnessmaker's shop on Duke of Gloucester Street, the delicate floral scents emanating from the many small gardens half hidden behind the fences and walls of the private yards are all part of the total experience. So are the sounds that fill the air: the giggle of visitors trying on hairpieces at the wigmakers, the strident clatter of the blacksmith at work and the rattle and tinkle of the percussive instruments shown on "The Other Half" tour.

The sights of Williamsburg include more than 88 original buildings and an additional 400 reconstructions . You can get a real feel of what it was like to live in this town by visiting just three private homes: the Peyton Randolph House, George Wythe's House and the Brush-Everard House.

The original owner of the **Peyton Randolph House** was Sir John Randolph, the only colonial Virginian to be knighted. He was First Clerk of the House of Burgesses, then the member representing the College of William and Mary and finally Speaker of the House of Burgesses. When Sir John died in 1737 his wife inherited his Williamsburg home. On her death it passed to his son, Peyton, for whom it is named.

Peyton Randolph's career paralleled his father's. He, too, studied law in London after attending William and Mary. He, too, was sent to England on behalf of the colony. He was elected to the House of Burgesses in 1748, and in 1766 he, too, was chosen speaker. It was up to him to guide the Assembly through the tumultuous debates that led to the Revolution.

The Randolph's home is sectional. The western-most section of the house, built in 1715, was Sir John's home. He also purchased the house on the adjoining lot. Later the two homes were connected to make one large residence. The furnishings are stylish yet comfortable; it is definitely a home, not a museum. The paneled rooms exude a warmth that was enjoyed by two French guests. Count de Rochambeau used this house as his headquarters during the siege of Yorktown. When Lafayette returned to America 50 years after the Revolution he, too, stayed here.

After Peyton Randolph's death, Thomas Jefferson purchased his library. When the federal collection in Washington, D.C. was burned by the British during the War of 1812, Jefferson donated his extensive collection of books to the Library of Congress. Thus the combined libraries of Jefferson and Randolph became the nucleus of the national collection.

If Sir John was the most distinguished lawyer in Virginia in the first third of the 18th century, then another Williamsburg resident, George Wythe, may well lay claim to this distinction in the last third. While his neighbor, Peyton Randolph, was serving the colony in England, Wythe acted as attorney general. Wythe, a member of the House of Burgesses, was a good friend of Governors Fauquier and Botetourt. However, when the time came to choose sides, without hesitating, he joined the patriots and signed the Declaration of Independence for Virginia.

The document's author, Thomas Jefferson, was at one time a law student in Wythe's Williamsburg home. And in 1776 the Jefferson family stayed at the Wythe house for several weeks. A popular teacher, Wythe became America's first professor of law at William and Mary in 1779.

The **George Wythe House** was used by George Washington as his headquarters during the Yorktown siege. After the hostilities ended Rochambeau moved here from the Randolph House. Centuries later this Georgian mansion became the home of the Reverend W.A.R. Goodwin. Perhaps living here made him more attuned to the urgency of restoring Williamsburg to its former glory. In any event it was he who had the idea for Rockefeller's restoration. George Wythe established a mini-plantation in the heart of Williamsburg. You can see his outbuildings and gardens.

Like the books at the Randolph house, those at the **Brush-Everard House** also have a Jeffersonian connection, though not direct. This library was compiled from a list of 300 basic books Jefferson had recommended to a Virginia planter. The Brush-Everard House represents the 18th-century middle class life style. A modest frame house, it was built in 1717 by John Brush, gunsmith, armorer and the first keeper of the colony's Magazine (see Public Buildings selection). After passing through the hands of several owners, the house was purchased by Thomas Everard who was mayor of Williamsburg in 1766 and again in 1771. Everard enlarged the house, embellished the interior and added a small pond.

To see how John Brush would have practiced his craft visit the gunsmith shop near the Capitol. It is just one of many colonial crafts you can see demonstrated. There is a milliner, printer, bookbinder, blacksmith, cooper, bootmaker, wheelwright, harnessmaker, cabinetmaker, wigmaker and musical instrument maker.

For a look at Williamsburg from a different perspective sign up for "The Other Half" tour. Half of the city's population were African Americans and this two-hour walking tour tells you about them. The tour, which begins at the Greenhow Ticket Office, focuses on slave culture, racial interaction, African American music and the differences between plantation and town life.

Admission to all the homes and shops mentioned here is included in the basic ticket sold at the visitor center. All are generally open from 9:00 A.M. to 5:00 P.M. The days and times do change depending on the season.

Directions: From I-95 in the Richmond area, take I-64 east to Colonial Williamsburg and follow the signs to the visitor center.

Williamsburg's Public Buildings

Officially Speaking

There will always be an England, and on this side of the Atlantic you can find reminders of it in Colonial Williamsburg's public buildings. The governor, in his Georgian Palace, symbolized the power of the English king in the colony. The Virginia House of Burgesses meeting in the Capitol argued that they should receive the rights of Englishmen they considered their due. Lord Dunmore, fearing the vehemence of their argument, ordered his British Marines to secretly remove the powder from the Williamsburg Magazine. He hoped to keep ammunition out of the hands of angry colonists. And Bruton Parish Church was named for an English parish in Somerset that was the home of some of this colonial city's leading citizens.

The **Capitol** was built in Williamsburg in 1699 after the seat of government was moved from Jamestown. It had been less than a year since the last of several statehouses in Jamestown had burned to the ground. To prevent a similar fate in Williamsburg the wary burgesses ordered the building constructed without chimneys. There would be no warming blaze, no flickering candles and no smoking of the "noxious weed."

All that was fired up was the temper of the legislators. A constant barrage of complaints forced a reversal. In 1723, chimneys were added and the ban on smoking and candles was lifted. The fate that had been feared occurred on January 30, 1747, when the building was gutted by fire. Rebuilt, it burned again in 1832 after it had been abandoned by the legislators who moved with the government to Richmond.

Although it was the second Capitol building that had echoed to the impassioned words of Patrick Henry and the stirring debate about independence in 1776, it was the first Capitol that was reconstructed by Colonial Williamsburg. Two factors influenced this decision: there were more detailed records available about the first building and it was more architecturally distinct. One wing of the H-shaped building contains the Hall of the House of Burgesses, and the other wing was used by the General Court for their twice-yearly sessions. Upstairs there were committee rooms, a council chamber and a conference room where both burgesses and councilors met for morning prayers and held joint conferences.

The line between public and private is blurred in so far as the lavish **Governor's Palace** is concerned. It was the private home of a public figure. Seven royal governors and the first two elected chief executives of the state of Virginia—Patrick Henry and Thomas Jefferson—lived here.

The Palace was built from 1708–1720 during the term of Lieutenant Governor Alexander Spotswood. The last of the king's men was Lord Dunmore who fled the Palace in early June 1775. It was Governor Norborne Berkeley, Baron de Botetourt, whose tenancy is evoked when you tour the Palace. Botetourt was governor from 1768 until his death in October 1770. A detailed room-by-room inventory taken at that time of the 16,000 objects in the Palace's 61 rooms enabled Colonial Williamsburg to refurnish the palace as it was then. Additional help came from the daily records that were kept by Botetourt's butler, William Marshman.

When you tour the elegant public rooms and the governor's private quarters a colonially attired guide will help you imagine what it was like to visit the Palace more than two centuries earlier. The outbuildings are more suggestive of a Virginia plantation than a European palace, but the gardens delightfully blend influences of both continents (see Williamsburg Garden selection).

To complete your exploration of the town's public buildings stop at the **Courthouse of 1770**. Mock trials reveal judicial practices in the 18th century. The Courthouse stands on Market

Square, one of the community's social, political and economic centers. Townsfolk would flock to the square to hear important announcements; this is where they heard the Declaration of Independence proclaimed from the Courthouse steps. Troops were mustered on the square green, and twice each week farmers brought in their produce. Within the Courthouse two courts, the James City County Court and the Williamsburg Hustings Court met regularly. County courts acted as the main agents of local government in the Virginia colony, exercising both executive and judicial powers. The municipal court, also known as the Hustings Court, exercised civil jurisdiction over Williamsburg.

In front of the Courthouse of 1770 on Market Square Green are the instruments of local justice: the pillory with holes in a wooden frame for the miscreant's head and hands and the stocks that had ankle holes in its wooden frame. Those awaiting trial or in debt were incarcerated at the **Public Gaol**, described by a colonial chronicler as a "strong sweet prison." Only the General Court could try offenses punishable by death or mutilation. The county and municipal courts levied sentences that subjected felons to discomfort and public humiliation.

You'll discover that conditions in the Public Gaol were little worse than those in the Public Hospital (see selection). In fact, the gaol served for a time as a madhouse as well as a military prison, though the military had their own public buildings the **Magazine and Guardhouse**.

The Magazine was the arsenal of the colony, a sturdy brick repository of arms and ammunition. It was built in 1715 at the request of Governor Spotswood and has survived to this day. At the time of the French and Indian War (1754–1763) the Magazine held more than 60,000 pounds of gunpowder. It was at this time that the high protective wall and Guardhouse were added.

On April 20–21, 1775, the Magazine claimed its paragraph in American history. Lord Dunmore, keenly alert to the mood of the Virginians, sent forces secretly to remove the powder from the Magazine, but the irate reaction forced the British to make restitution for the pilfered powder.

Prayers were raised at **Bruton Parish Church** in 1774 in hopes of averting the division from England. Most parishioners had come to feel that war was the only answer, however, by the time the bells of Bruton Parish Church rang out on May 15, 1776, heralding Virginia's first call for independence. They should have rung yet again centuries later when the rector of the parish, the Reverend W.A.R. Goodwin, conceived the idea for restoring Williamsburg. It was Goodwin who persuaded John D. Rockefeller, Jr. to develop his idea into a reality.

All of these attractions are generally open 9:00 A.M. to 5:00 P.M. Days and times vary depending on the season.

Directions: From I-95 in the Richmond area, take I-64 east to Colonial Williamsburg. The Capitol is located at the east end of Duke of Gloucester Street. The Governor's Palace is at the north end of the Palace Green. The Courthouse of 1770 is on Duke of Gloucester Street at Market Square. The Magazine and Guardhouse are directly across the street. Bruton Parish Church is one block west on Duke of Gloucester Street. The Public Gaol is at the east end of Nicholson Street; there is also a path that leads from the Capitol to the Gaol.

Williamsburg's Taverns

Capital Conviviality

During the 18th century there were 40 taverns in the Virginia capital of Williamsburg. Today there are seven, offering a variety of tavern experiences. Lodging is available in the historic area at Brick House and Market Square Taverns. Guided tours are given of Raleigh and Wetherburn's Taverns. You can dine at King's Arm, Christiana Campbell's, Shields or Chowning's Tavern and take in evening "gambols" at the latter.

Raleigh Tavern, which opened in 1932, was the first Williamsburg reconstruction. The colonial capital was the focal spot of rebellion in Virginia, and a great deal of the action took place at the Raleigh Tavern. When the Royal Governor dissolved the House of Burgesses, the members resumed their meetings at the Raleigh Tavern. Often merchants and medical practitioners arranged their schedules so that they stayed at the Raleigh while the Burgesses met.

The most expensive piece of tavern equipment was the billiard table in the gaming room, where ladies never ventured. You will see one of these old playing tables with ivory balls and hand-carved cues.

Ladies could attend the balls and formal functions given in the Apollo Room. Thomas Jefferson, in his diary, notes that he danced here with Rebecca Burwell, his "fair Belinda." The residents of Williamsburg gathered in the Apollo Room to celebrate the Treaty of Paris, officially ending the American Revolution. Some years later in 1824, Lafayette attended a party at the Raleigh celebrating the American victory at Yorktown. The tavern is open daily from 9:00 A.M. to 5:00 P.M. and is included on the Patriot's Pass and the Basic Williamsburg ticket. Behind Raleigh Tavern is the bake shop which still employs 200-year-old techniques to prepare gingerbread men and other delicacies for their customers.

Across Duke of Gloucester Street and down about half a block is **Wetherburn's Tavern**, which is also open for tours daily from 10:00 A.M. to 6:00 P.M. The archeological on-site dig helped insure the authenticity of this restoration. Pottery shards and tavern equipment unearthed in dry wells, the garbage dumps of the 18th century, enabled Colonial Williamsburg Foundation to furnish the tavern according to the inventory left by Mr. Wetherburn. Like many of his colonial contemporaries, Mr. Wetherburn had two wives. He mourned 11 days before marrying the widow of a fellow tavern keeper, thus securing her inherited goods including a good bit of silver.

As you will readily observe at both Raleigh and Wetherburn's, taverns in the 18th century were a combination hotel, restaurant, bar and community center. Unless he paid dearly for a private room, a guest was apt to sleep with three or four strangers—not just in the same room, but in the same bed! From this practice comes the expression "sleep tight." The ropes supporting the mattress were tightened each night, otherwise all the occupants would roll into the center of the bed. Slaves traveling with their masters slept either on the floor or in one of the dependencies.

Dining in the taverns of Williamsburg today is far different from what it was during the colonial period. The smaller taverns in the 18th century prepared only one meal; few had the luxury of a menu. Now at four taverns you can have a choice of colonial and traditional fare for lunch and dinner. The fare at **King's Arm Tavern**, the most elegant of the three, features a dinner menu of game pie, oyster pie, Cornish game hen and beef with Sally Lunn bread, Indian corn muffins, assorted relishes, vegetables and old-fashioned desserts to complement the meal. At **Christiana Campbell's**, dinner selections include clam chowder, Virginia ham, backfin crab imperial and southern fried chicken. **Josiah Chowning's** features Brunswick stew, barbecued ribs or pork barbecue; Welsh rabbit is a lunchtime favorite. The newest kid on these very old blocks is **Shields Tavern**, which opened in 1989. Featuring the food enjoyed by the lesser gentry and upper middling ranks of locals and travelers, the menu includes spit-roasted chicken, Chesapeake Bay poached seafood and a delightful greengage plum ice cream. The most accurate replication of 18th-century food offered at any of the Williamsburg taverns is the appetizer assortment, "Shields Sampler: A Tasting of 1750s Foods." Reservations are a must for these colonial dining experiences, and should be made well before your visit (as much as two months during the peak season) by calling (800) HISTORY. Be sure to confirm your reservation when you arrive. If you stay over in Williamsburg, you might want to drop in on the nightly "gambol" at Chowning's. These evenings of tavern games are very popular. You can play backgammon,

Seven of 40 Williamsburg taverns remain from the 18th century, offering a variety of lodging, dining and touring. The Brick House Tavern on Gloucester Street has advertised rooms since 1770.

---

checkers, chess, cards or learn such new "old" board games as "The Royal and Most Pleasant Game of Goose" and "Bowles' Royal Pastime of Cupid," or "Entertaining Game of Snake."

The **Brick House Tavern** has been advertising "12 or 14 very good lodging rooms" since 1770. Unlike many taverns of the day, it welcomed women guests. Today 18 rooms are available for any Williamsburg visitor who can get reservations.

Just two blocks away up Duke of Gloucester Street is **Market Square Tavern and Kitchen** where visitors have found accommodations for three centuries. The 18-year-old apprentice law student, Thomas Jefferson, rented rooms here while he studied with George Wythe.

Tavern rooms are available though the Colonial House program at Williamsburg Inn. In all there are 23 guest houses, each enhanced by period furnishings, and three taverns that offer lodging. For information or reservations, call (800) HISTORY.

Directions: From I-95 in the Richmond area, take I-64 east to Williamsburg. Use Exit 56 onto Route 143 (you'll bear right off I-64). This is quickly followed by a right onto Route 132. You'll turn left onto feeder Route 132Y into the Colonial Williamsburg Visitor Center.

JAMES RIVER PLANTATIONS

Berkeley and Westover

Side by Side

The story of Thanksgiving is inextricably linked to the Pilgrims at Plymouth Rock despite the fact that America's first Thanksgiving did not occur in Massachusetts. It took place in Virginia a full two years before the Pilgrims arrived in the New World.

John Wooflief, captain of the 40-ton *Margaret*, landed his small party of 38 settlers at Berkeley Hundred on December 4, 1619. They came ashore and gave thanks for their safe passage, reading the message prepared for their landfall by King James I, their English proprietor: "Wee ordained that the day of our ships arrivall at the place assigned for plantacon in the land of Virginia shall be yearly and perpetually kept holy as a day of thanksgiving to Almighty God." Each year on the first Sunday of November the landing of the *Margaret* and the First Thanksgiving are reenacted at **Berkeley**. (The house is called Berkeley; the settlement, Berkeley Hundred.)

This would be quite enough to secure Berkeley's place in history, but it holds yet another distinction. It is one of only two houses in America to be the ancestral home of a signer of the Declaration of Independence (Benjamin Harrison) and two presidents of the United States (William Henry Harrison and William Henry's grandson, Benjamin Harrison). The other house with this

Berkeley Plantation was the ancestral home of the Harrisons, two of whom became President. The first settlers celebrated Thanksgiving after landing in 1619, before the Pilgrims.

historic significance is the Adams ancestral home in Braintree, Massachusetts.

Berkeley is also credited with the first distillation of bourbon. In the early days at Berkeley Hundred the colonists worked hard to establish their settlement. George Thorpe, an Episcopal missionary, concocted a home-brew to encourage their efforts. His corn liquor proved more popular than their English ale.

The Harrison family acquired Berkeley in 1691, but it was not until 1726 that Benjamin Harrison IV built the Georgian-style main house, the oldest three-story brick house in Virginia. Benjamin Harrison's wife was Anne Carter, the daughter of Robert "King" Carter. It was their son, Benjamin Harrison V, who became a signer of the Declaration of Independence and three-term Governor of Virginia. He held elective office for 42 of his 65 years. His picture hangs over the mantle in Berkeley's northern drawing room.

Benjamin Harrison V's youngest son, William Henry, the future president, was born at Berkeley in 1773. He gained fame as an Indian fighter at the Battle of Tippecanoe and became Governor of the Northwest Territory. When William Henry Harrison ran for the presidency in 1840 he initiated campaign publicity. You see examples of his buttons and banners when you tour Berkeley. Although he was born to wealth and social position, Harrison was depicted on his commemorative handkerchiefs as a rude frontiersman standing in front of a log cabin home.

Harrison won the election and became the ninth president. He returned to Berkeley to write his inaugural address in the room where he was born. During the campaign, Harrison had been advised by party leader Nicholas Biddle to "say not one single word about his principles, or his creed—let him say nothing—promise nothing. . ." The opportunity to speak proved too tempting for Harrison; at better than two hours, his was the longest inaugural speech ever delivered. He paid a high price for his vanity; he contracted pneumonia from his prolonged exposure to Washington's cold, wet weather and died within 30 days. His vice president was his Sherwood Forest neighbor, John Tyler, whose smooth succession to the presidency set a precedent for future mid-term transitions. In 1888 Harrison's grandson, Benjamin Harrison, became the 23rd president.

Though Berkeley looks as if nothing had happened to it since colonial days, history tells us otherwise. In 1781, during the American Revolution, Benedict Arnold's troops plundered the plantation. Late in the Civil War, during July and August of 1862, General McClellan made Berkeley his headquarters. The Union army of 140,000 men camped on the grounds, during which time President Lincoln conferred twice with McClellan here. Linking the past with the present, the current owner of Berkeley, Malcolm Jamieson, is the son of a drummer who served with Mc-Clellan's army at Berkeley.

Berkeley's preeminent role in history is highlighted in a slide program that precedes the guided tour of the house. After the tour be sure to explore Berkeley's grounds and gardens. The plantation is open daily from 8:00 A.M. to 5:00 P.M. Admission is charged.

Next door to Berkeley is **Westover Plantation**. Although the mansion is not open, the views you can get of the house from various parts of the sweeping grounds are worth your time. Westover is considered an outstanding example of Georgian architecture. If Westover looks familiar it is because it is featured in the Williamsburg movie, *The Story of a Patriot*.

There are several dependencies on the grounds, including the kitchen, smokehouse, icehouse and necessary. The formal gardens were reestablished about 1900; within the garden you'll see the tomb of William Byrd II, founder of Richmond and Petersburg, buried here in 1744. Westover's grounds and gardens are open daily from 9:00 A.M. to 6:00 P.M. A nominal admission is charged.

Directions: From I-295 to the east of Richmond, take Route 5 along the James River toward Williamsburg. Berkeley and Westover, which are about 22 miles east of Richmond, are well-marked.

Sherwood Forest and Evelynton

Caretakers of the Past

It doesn't seem possible, but **Sherwood Forest** is today owned by President John Tyler's grandson, Harrison Tyler. John Tyler was 63 when he fathered his youngest son, Lyon, who in turn, at the age of 75 fathered his youngest son, the current owner, Harrison. It enables visitors to see a home remarkably unchanged by time. Few, if any, historic homes have retained as complete a collection of family furnishings, and nowhere else are you as likely to hear as many colorful anecdotes about them as you do here.

You learn that when John Tyler and his wife, Julia Gardiner, moved into the White House, Congress would not allocate any funds for redecoration. The Tylers brought their own furniture to the White House and took it back to Sherwood Forest at the end of John Tyler's term in 1845. Tyler, the 10th president (1841–1845), was the first to gain office by the death of his predecessor, William Henry Harrison. This was also the first and only time neighbors followed each other into this high office, as Tyler's home was next to Harrison's birthplace, Berkeley Plantation (see selection).

The house was under construction from 1660 to 1845. By the time it was finished its 301-foot length made it the longest frame house in America, the same length as a football field. One of the last extensions to be built was a narrow ballroom, added specifically for dancing the Virginia Reel. Sherwood Forest is the only James River plantation to have a ballroom. The long hall on the other side connecting the kitchen with the main house was called the colonnade and used as a "whistling walk," and storage area. Legend has it that slaves carrying dishes to the dining room had to whistle as they walked, to prove they weren't sampling the fare.

According to family legend one room at Sherwood Forest is haunted by the Gray Lady. The family sitting room, known since 1840 as the Gray Room, is connected by a narrow staircase with the nursery above. The children's nurse customarily brought the youngest child downstairs to rock in front of the fireplace. When the youngster died, the devoted nurse was inconsolable. Since that time a phantom rocker has been heard at night in this room.

Behind the house is a ginkgo, one of 37 tree varieties at Sherwood Forest that are not indigenous to the area. The ginkgo was brought to America by Admiral Perry when President Tyler reopened the trade routes to the Far East.

The house and grounds at Sherwood Forest opened to the public on March 29, 1993, President Tyler's 203rd birthday. Tours are given daily 9:00 A.M. to 5:00 P.M., except Thanksgiving, Christmas and New Year's Day. Admission is charged.

As you travel Route 5 toward Richmond you'll pass other James River plantations. One that opened to the public in 1985 after being closed for 20 years is **Evelynton**. The land on which Evelynton stands was occupied by the Powhatan Indians prior to the arrival of English settlers. It became part of William Byrd's colonial holding and he gave it to his wife, Lucy Parke. It was intended to have been a dowry for their daughter, Evelyn, who died tragically after a broken romance.

Evelynton was purchased in 1847 by Edmund Ruffin, Jr., son of the Confederate who fired the first shot of the Civil War at Fort Sumter in April 1861. The plantation house was burned during the Civil War. During the Peninsula Campaign in 1862, Confederate troops led by Generals J.E.B. Stuart and James Longstreet skirmished with Federal forces on Evelynton Heights. The armies returned to the James River area in 1864 in the last days of the war as the Southern army retreated from Petersburg to Richmond and Appomattox. You can still see breastworks from the 1862 confrontation below the house.

Evelynton Plantation remained in the Ruffin family throughout the difficult years of Reconstruction, although Edmund Ruffin, Sr. did not choose to survive what he viewed as the indignities of Yankee domination. Ruffin fired a fatal shot and joined his dead comrades. In 1935 the current Georgian Revival house was commissioned by Mrs. John Augustine Ruffin, mother of the present owner, Edmund Saunders Ruffin. Constructed of 250-year-old bricks on the foundation of the earlier house, it certainly looks as if it had survived from colonial days. The house stands at the summit of a long cedar and dogwood allee, overlooking the meandering Herring Creek and James River.

Evelynton underwent a major interior facelift in 1985. The furnishings have been collected by the Ruffin family and include period American and English pieces plus European additions from the early 20th century.

You can tour the house, gardens and grounds. There is a formal English boxwood garden and a fully stocked boxwood nursery and garden center. The gift shop, in a century-old corn crib, is filled with mementos of the past, a comprehensive book section and one-of-a-kind treasures.

Evelynton is open daily from 9:00 A.M. to 5:00 P.M. except Thanksgiving and Christmas. Admission is charged.

Directions: From the Richmond area take I-295 east, to Exit 22A, Route 5. Take Route 5 east toward Williamsburg. Evelynton and Sherwood Forest are on the right; both are well-marked. From the Williamsburg and Virginia Beach area, take I-64 to Route 199, Exit 242, toward Jamestown. At Route 5, turn left and travel west approximately 20 miles. Both Evelynton and Sherwood Forest are on the left.

Shirley and Edgewood Plantations

Family Trees

It did not take many years for the English who settled at Jamestown in 1607 to discover that one path to the wealth they craved was tobacco. To that end they began spreading out, establishing plantations to grow the golden weed. One of the earliest of these plantations was **Shirley**; the name first appeared on records in 1611, although it would be two more years before the estate was inhabited.

For three centuries and ten generations Shirley has been held by the Hill-Carter family. Though the intricate family tree dates back to 1660, the house was not built until 1724 when Edward Hill III began constructing it for his daughter Elizabeth and her

Shirley Plantation has been held by the Hill-Carter families since 1660. Tobacco was being shipped from here seven years before the Pilgrims landed at Plymouth Rock.

husband John Carter, son of Robert "King" Carter. Architectural historians trace the inspiration for this square-shaped home to the Governor's Palace in nearby Williamsburg (see Public Buildings selection), completed in 1720. Rather than the Georgian hyphen and wings design, Shirley has a basement and three stories. Like the numerous dependencies, the brick house is built in the Flemish bond pattern. On the roof is a carved pineapple, symbol of hospitality.

Shirley is noted for its hospitality—to horses as well as presidents. The family silver has been used to serve George Washington, Thomas Jefferson, John Tyler and Theodore Roosevelt. Not one of the presidents, however, had his own silver cup like Nestor, the family's champion racehorse. After a victorious race Nestor was offered wine from his cup, reversing the practice of offering the loving cup to the owner.

Family lore abounds at Shirley. One story that is told and retold concerns the frieze over the fireplace in the dining room. It may have been told one too many times. One of the current younger generation at Shirley, after hearing repeatedly about an earlier Carter youngster who whittled all but four acorns out of the carved frieze, decided to make his own mark and eliminated all but one before his mother stopped him in mid-crime.

Fortunately the frieze is not the carved work for which Shirley is noted. That honor belongs to the hanging staircase. This square, not curved, staircase rises without visible means of support, and each tread is gracefully scrolled.

The parlor at Shirley is historically, rather than architecturally, significant. It was here that Anne Hill Carter married Governor Henry "Lighthorse Harry" Lee. Their son, Robert, would spend several boyhood years at Shirley. History also marked this plantation during America's early struggles. Like so many of the James River plantations, Shirley had troops on her soil during both the Revolutionary War and the War Between the States.

Shirley is still a working plantation producing corn, barley, wheat and soy beans. The grounds have a full complement of dependencies—a large two-story kitchen, smokehouse, dovecote, stable and barns. You can visit Shirley daily except Christmas Day from 9:00 A.M. to 5:00 P.M. Admission is charged.

At nearby **Edgewood**, just three miles from Shirley, the family tree is likely to be one of the 18 decorated Christmas trees that fill this Carpenter's Gothic house from October well into January. Here the ambience is not Revolutionary or antebellum but Victorian, a delightful change of pace.

The house was built in 1849 by Spencer Rowland, a New Jerseyite who fell in love with the South. His daughter, Lizzie, likewise fell in love with the South, or at least a young southerner from a nearby plantation, perhaps even Shirley. Lizzie was in her mid-twenties when she moved to Edgewood and lost her heart. Then she lost him to the Civil War. Her ghost is said to haunt the bedroom where she died and her name is etched on the window through which the apparition peers, forever searching for her handsome beau on his spirited horse.

Dot and John Boulware purchased this house in 1978. They have repaired and refurbished the 14 large rooms that evolved into a bed and breakfast. Dot offers Victorian teas and luncheons and if you call ahead she wears a Victorian dress for the house tour. The bedrooms are a treasure trove of Victoriana, with old-fashioned clothes laid out casually to enhance the decor. One overnight guest mistook the decor for a gesture and wore the antique nightshirt to bed.

You can visit Edgewood daily from 11:30 A.M. to 4:00 P.M. To pre-arrange visits, teas, luncheons or accommodations call (804) 829-2962.

Directions: From I-295 east of Richmond, take Route 5 for about 25 miles to Shirley Plantation on the right and Edgewood on the left.

JAMESTOWN

Jamestown, The Original Site (Colonial National Historical Park)

Best of Both Worlds

Two side-by-side attractions in Jamestown tell the same story by very different approaches. One, a national park, lets you use your imagination to rebuild and repopulate the Jamestown settlement. The second, Jamestown Settlement, a living history museum operated by the Jamestown-Yorktown Foundation, provides a re-creation of the ships on which the settlers arrived in the New World and the fort they built (see selection).

If you arrive at **Jamestown, The Original Site (Colonial National Historical Park)** with a proficient 17th-century vocabulary you'll be able to banter with your colonially-attired interpreter on one of the frequent walking tours. Try dropping a "Heaven forfend," "Shodikans," or "Fie on it," in your conversation. Substitute "nay" or "aye" for "no" or "yes." Use "a" in place of "to," as in "go a town." Or try "me" to replace "I" as in "me feels" and "me thinks." You'll have a wonderful time.

Visitors to this 1607 settlement are often greeted as if they had just stepped off a ship from England. Park personnel in the guise of settlers at James Cittie wax enthusiastic about the opportunities for advancement in Virginia. They will tell you that the road to riches is tobacco, not gold, as the first arrivals so mistakingly believed. Park rangers conduct site tours on a regular basis.

Although only foundations and a crumbling tower from the 1639 church remain from that early era, the visitor center helps your imagination rebuild and repopulate the once thriving town. A 15-minute film provides the background on those first intrepid adventurers who set sail from England at Christmas time in 1606 on the *Discovery, Susan Constant* and *Godspeed.*

After a four-month Atlantic crossing made under difficult and cramped conditions (you can board a reconstruction of one of their ships at Jamestown Settlement adjacent to the National Park), the settlers arrived at a land where they had to hunt, grow and build everything necessary for their survival. The exact site of their James Fort is not certain, but there is a path along several streets of their town. Artifacts that have been recovered are on display in the visitor center museum. There is also a museum shop that offers some fine reproductions of the pottery and glassware once made at Jamestown.

The seven-mile loop trail gives a clear picture of the natural environment the first settlers tamed in order to establish their community. The marsh and woodland is little changed since the early 1600s.

Before leaving the park be sure to stop at the **Glasshouse**, located just inside the entrance. Here, in an open-sided timber and thatch shelter, craftsmen reproduce the first "factory-made" exports of the colonies. The green-colored glass, its tint due to the iron oxide in the sand, was sent back to England. You can watch craftsmen deftly blow down a long tube to form a jug or pitcher. A second glassmaker quickly adds a molten piece to form a graceful handle. The glass is at a temperature of between 2,000 and 3,000 degrees when first removed from the dome-shaped furnace. Soon after shaping, it's returned to another 800 degree oven for slow cooling to prevent cracking.

Jamestown, The Original Site (Colonial National Historical Park), is open daily, except Christmas, from 9:00 A.M. to 4:30 P.M. with extended hours spring through fall. A nominal admission is charged per car.

Directions: From I-95 in the Richmond area, take I-64 to the Williamsburg area. Then take the Colonial Parkway nine miles to Jamestown Island. Turn right to reach the Colonial National Historical Park. An alternative route is to take I-64 to Exit 242A and turn onto Route 199 west. Drive five miles to the intersection with Route 31 and turn left. Jamestown Island, the Original Site, and Jamestown Settlement are four miles farther on the left.

*Full-size reproductions of the three ships that carried 104 set-
tlers from England to Virginia in 1607 are moored at Jamestown
Settlement. The largest,* Susan Constant, *can be boarded.*

Jamestown Settlement

Powhatans, Pocahontas and Pioneers

Just outside the boundaries of Jamestown, The Original Site (Colonial National Historic Park), is **Jamestown Settlement.** This state-operated history museum of 17th-century Virginia has recreations that help young and old gain a deeper understanding of the past. It's one thing to read about a confined cabin, rustic fort or spartan Native American village and quite another to climb aboard the *Susan Constant*, to hear the wind whistle through a wattle-and-daub house or to step inside a Powhatan dwelling. Jamestown Settlement offers these options as well as the chance to explore extensive gallery exhibits.

Start your visit with "Jamestown: The Beginning," a 20-minute docudrama that describes the origins and early years of America's first permanent English colony. Three themed exhibit galleries featuring artifacts from the 16th and 17th centuries explore circumstances that led to English colonization of the New World, the culture of Virginia's Powhatans and the colony's development in the 17th century.

The first English settlers in the Jamestown area were sponsored by the Virginia Company of London. Men and company alike were anxious to make fortunes by taking advantage of the foothold on the continent. They planted a few crops and built a rough stockade and crude huts within two months of their arrival on May 14, 1607. Food was obtained by Captain John Smith in trade from the local tribes. Explorations led by Smith in the spring and summer of 1608 enabled him to map much of the surrounding area.

A fire in January 1608 burned the first fort. It is likely that the harsh winter weather helped to convince the settlers that sturdy houses were essential, and the second time they were more careful in their construction. They rebuilt the fort, church, storehouse and guardhouse. These and other buildings from the fort have been recreated at Jamestown Settlement. You'll also see replicas of the three ships that brought the settlers to America. Interpreters dressed in period clothes are at the fort and dock to answer questions.

Perhaps the best known Native American to become involved with the Jamestown settlers was Pocahontas. The museum has a small permanent exhibit that features several artists' renditions of Pocahontas, favored daughter of Powhatan, the leader of about 32 Algonquian-speaking tribes in coastal Virginia. There is a European engraving that depicts the legendary December 1607 incident when 11-year-old Pocahontas rescued Captain John Smith from execution by her father. The only reference to this occurence was in Smith's subsequent account of his experiences with the Native Americans and many historians doubt the incident took place. Two items on display—a cameo brooch and small stoneware jug—were reputedly given to Pocahontas when she and her English husband John Rolfe visited London. A 17th- or 18th- century painting of Pocahontas shows her in English attire.

A vivid evocation of the Powhatans who inhabited Tidewater Virginia awaits you at the tribal village and its ceremonial dance circle. Youngsters are amazed to learn that Native Americans in the East did not live in tepees. The dwellings in the village are based on archeological findings and drawings made by an Englishman during an earlier attempt to colonize Virginia.

Authentically dressed interpreters explain how the Native Americans prepared their food and constructed their utensils and tools. The houses are furnished as they would have been in the early 17th century, with fur-covered ledges along the walls for sleeping, woven mats on the earth and a central fire for warmth. Extended families shared the houses. The dance circle may have been used by the Powhatans to celebrate harvests, seasonal changes and other significant events.

Jamestown Settlement is open daily 9:00 A.M. to 5:00 P.M. except Christmas and New Year's. Admission is charged. A combination ticket with the Yorktown Victory Center is available.

Directions: From I-95 in the Richmond area, take I-64 to the Williamsburg area. Then take the Colonial Parkway nine miles to Jamestown Island. Turn right to reach Jamestown Settlement. An alternate route is to take I-64 to Exit 242A and turn onto Route 199 west. Drive five miles to the intersection with Route 31 and turn left. Jamestown, The Original Site (see selection) and Jamestown Settlement are four miles farther on the left.

YORKTOWN

Nelson House

There's Nothing Half-Way About This Nelson

The **Nelson House** in Yorktown is filled not with furniture, but with voices from the past. Exemplifying the best traditions of the National Park Service, the free, living history programs performed here bring to life this important American family.

If you've ever wandered through a historic house and thought

163

about the stories it could tell, you'll appreciate the Nelson House Drama. Three actors perform this mini-drama as they re-create prominent Nelson family members and servants. The presentation brings alive the tumultuous days when America sought her independence. The program is given every half hour from 12:30 P.M. to 4:00 P.M. except 3:00 P.M. throughout the summer.

The Nelson's family home was built around 1711 by "Scotch Tom" Nelson, an Englishman born near the Scottish border and rumored to be tight-fisted, or "scotch," with his money. Young Thomas Nelson, Jr., just seven when his grandfather died, went on to play a pivotal role in Virginia history.

Following colonial tradition he was educated in England at Cambridge University. When he returned to the colonies he served as a member of the Royal Governor's Council. But as the dispute grew between crown and colony, he sided with his fellow Virginians and became one of the signers of the Declaration of Independence.

The Nelson House still bears reminders of Thomas Nelson, Jr.'s military career during the Revolution. As brigadier general of the Virginia militia he directed his men to fire at his own home because it was serving as headquarters for British Commander Lord Cornwallis. You'll see two cannonballs embedded in the east wall. They were placed in the wall in the 20th century to fill scars left from the siege of 1781.

The Revolution not only threatened the very walls of Nelson's house, it also cost him a substantial fortune. He personally outfitted and provisioned his men during the Virginia campaign. Despite his financial reverses, the Nelson family house was the scene of a lavish gala honoring Lafayette on his return in 1824 to celebrate the victory at Yorktown.

Visitors are as welcome now as they were in the 18th century at the "house of two chimneys," open daily from mid-June to mid-August from 10:00 A.M. to 4:30 P.M. and in the spring and fall from 1:00 to 4:30 P.M. Hours may vary, depending on funding. Before leaving, be sure to explore the restored formal English garden. For information on the living history dramas call (804) 898-3400, extension 58.

While in Yorktown take the time to stroll along Main Street. Just to the right of the Nelson House are two interesting homes. The Dudley Diggs House was built in the early 18th century and during the Revolutionary years was the home of a council member for Virginia. You'll also see the Sessions House built in 1692 and believed to be the oldest house in Yorktown.

To the left of the Nelson House on Main Street there are five buildings of historical interest. Just across Read Street is the customs house, reputedly built in 1721. Across Main Street is another 18th-century residence, the Pate House. Next door is

164

Somerwell House, which survived the siege of 1781 to become a hotel during the Civil War. Across Church Street is the medical shop, reconstructed to look as it did during the 18th century.

Facing the medical shop on Main Street is the Swan Tavern and dependencies, now operated as an antique shop. Swan Tavern was built in 1722 by "Scotch Tom" Nelson in partnership with Joseph Walker. You can pick up a walking tour map at the National Park Service Visitor Center.

Directions: From I-95 in the Richmond area, take I-64 east to the Colonial Parkway. Follow Colonial Parkway to Yorktown.

Yorktown Colonial National Historical Park

The World Turned Upside Down

The rights proclaimed in the Declaration of Independence—life, liberty and the pursuit of happiness—were grounded in the rights the colonists felt were due them as Englishmen. These rights and privileges were asserted from the beginning; the first permanent settlement at Jamestown had a representative legislative assembly in 1619. At Williamsburg, colonists again heralded the cause of man's natural rights in their 1776 "Declaration of Rights." The final battle to insure these rights took place at Yorktown.

This Yorktown victory is given depth and substance at the National Park Service Visitor Center at the **Yorktown Battlefield**. A free museum with exhibits and a movie provides an ideal introduction to your battlefield tour.

It was the end of September 1781, the seventh year of the American Revolution, and Cornwallis had moved his British troops into Yorktown following his campaign through Virginia and the southern colonies. Washington responded by moving his men from their New York camp down to Virginia, hoping to arrive before Cornwallis escaped by sea with his army.

For three weeks Washington's men dug siege lines around the British who were forced by a French blockade to hold their positions. With his army surrounded and his escape cut off, Cornwallis had run out of options. On October 14 two important British redoubts fell. (A painting in the Old Senate Chamber at the Virginia State Capitol captures this dramatic action. See Capitol selection.) On October 17, a red-coated drummer appeared on the British inner defense line and beat a parley. The guns were silent at last. On October 18 surrender terms were drawn up at the home of Augustine Moore, and the next day the

British army surrendered. It would be another two years before the peace treaty was signed, but the war was, in fact, over.

A popular exhibit at the museum is the gun deck and captain's cabin from the *Charon*. The *Charon* was a 44-gun frigate the British lost during the Battle of Yorktown. Also on display are the British regimental colors surrendered to Washington on October 19, 1781.

Before starting your drive, take the time to view the battlefield from the visitor center observation deck. The seven-mile tour marked by red arrows, includes six main points of interest: British inner defense lines, grand French battery, second Allied siege line, redoubt 9 and 10, the Moore house and surrender field.

A second Allied encampment tour extends nine additional miles and is marked with yellow arrows. Its significant stops include: the American artillery park, Washington's headquarters, the French cemetery, the French artillery park, the French encampment loop and an untouched British redoubt.

Yorktown Battlefield at Colonial National Historical Park is open daily 8:30 A.M. to 5:00 P.M. with seasonally extended hours. Admission is free.

Directions: From I-95 in the Richmond area, take I-64 east to the Colonial Parkway. Follow the Colonial Parkway to Yorktown.

Yorktown Victory Center

The American Revolution: See It, Hear It, Feel It!

The Virginia peninsula, a 15-mile wide strip, encompasses the historic triangle of Jamestown, Williamsburg and Yorktown. On this land the first permanent English settlement was established, the colonial capital of Virginia thrived and the War for American Independence ended. At the **Yorktown Victory Center** the story of the revolutionary struggle is told, from the beginning of colonial unrest to the formation of a new nation.

The victory at Yorktown was the culmination of a war that had begun more than six years earlier. Events that led to hostility between the colonies and Britain are chronicled along the "Road to Revolution," an open-air exhibit walkway. Sections of a time line, interspersed with quotes and illustrations, connect three themed pavilions that explore the impact of three issues: treaties, taxes and tea.

At the end of the walkway, the museum exhibition building offers an introductory look at the Declaration of Independence before leading into a series of themed galleries. Attention is paid to three groups—African Americans, Native Americans and women—to whom the early documents regarding freedom and equality did not apply.

History is not composed of just big events; it includes personal stories of ordinary individuals. Ten individuals provide a unique perspective in the "Witnesses to Revolution" gallery. Making up this group are two African American slaves who support opposing sides in the colonial conflict, a Mohawk chief who wants to keep his people neutral, a loyal British Virginia plantation owner, two Continental army soldiers, a woman captured and adopted by the Seneca Indians just before the outbreak of war and three civilians who reflect on the homefront. The words you hear are their own, taken from diaries, letters and other sources. The exhibit also includes graphics, artifacts and life-size cast figures.

Pivotal events from the issuing of the Declaration of Independence to the significant victory at Yorktown are captured in photomurals along the ramp that connects the first theme gallery with the "Converging on Yorktown" gallery. Yorktown and Gloucestertown were on opposite banks of the York River. Multinational armies, clashing for one of the last times in this epoch struggle, converged on these small communities. One of the center's prized exhibits is a pair of pistols that belonged to Marquis de Lafayette, who was on hand in 1781 to witness the British defeat he had helped to bring about. Again there are "witnesses" from the various countries represented here—American, British, French and German. This personal look at the events that occurred in Yorktown is also presented in an 18-minute film, "A Time of Revolution." Individuals in encampments around Yorktown reflect on the struggle.

Yet another gallery tells the story of ships sunk or scuttled in the York River, "Yorktown's Sunken Fleet." A re-creation of the bow portion of the British supply ship *Betsy* is the focal piece of the exhibit. Artifacts from the *Betsy,* the most extensively studied wreck in the area, add another dimension to the exhibit. There is a video on the excavation of the *Betsy* and a detailed scale model.

Outdoors, in re-creations of a Continental army camp and an 18th-century farmsite, costumed interpreters re-enact and discuss daily life during and just after the Revolution. The camp has two furnished officers' tents—one for the company commander and one for the regimental surgeon. There are several soldiers' tents and a massive earthen "kitchen," designed to serve a company of soldiers. Activities in the camp include demonstrations of musket loading and firing, 18th-century medical practices, military drills and music and meal preparation. Visitors are "recruited" into military service or given the opportunity to prepare an herbal remedy.

Originals of many of the reproductions used in the encampment are exhibited in the Mathews Gallery. These include uniforms, weapons, musical instruments, medical equipment, personal documents and belongings.

The farmstead represents a typical small farm in post-revolutionary Tidewater Virginia. Interpreters at the site engage in domestic activities, such as preparing flax and wool and making candles. During your visit you may be invited to help out in the field or kitchen.

The Yorktown Victory Center is open daily except Christmas and New Year's Day from 9:00 A.M. to 5:00 P.M. During spring and fall weekends and daily during the summer there is a children's discovery room with participatory activities. Admission is charged. A combination ticket is available that includes Jamestown Settlement (see selection); both are operated by the Jamestown-Yorktown Foundation.

Directions: From I-95 take I-64 to Exit 247. Take Route 143 to the traffic light and turn left onto Route 238. The Victory Center is four miles farther on the right, on Old Route 238.

Since October 1, 1867, the lighthouse on Assateague Island has guided visitors around the southern end of the island. You can reach the lighthouse via a woodland trail and see the original light mechanism there.

═══════Eastern Shore═══════

Virginia's coastal region is a slender 70-mile finger of land
bordered on one side by the Atlantic Ocean and on the
other by the Chesapeake Bay. The 17.6 mile Chesapeake
Bay Bridge- Tunnel, the world's longest bridge-tunnel complex,
connects the peninsula with Virginia's mainland. Here the
beaches are unspoiled, giving you a sense of what this region
was like when the first European settlers arrived. The Native
American names of the fishing villages are reminders of those
on hand to greet the new arrivals. You can hear the voices of the
past in the accents of Tangier Island natives, see colonial government buildings in Accomac and Eastville and taste the bounty
of the sea enjoyed by all the region's inhabitants.

Life is enjoyed at a leisurely pace as you walk the unpopu-
lated shore of the Chincoteague National Wildlife Refuge or
travel by boat along the shore or to the barrier islands that lie
off shore. Nature stimulates the senses: listen to the gulls
screech, feel the spray from the crashing waves, smell the salty
air and watch the crabs scurrying along the beach.

CHINCOTEAGUE ISLAND

Little Horses, Loads of Fun

Chincoteague is linked to the Delmarva Peninsula by a five-mile
causeway. The island and neighboring Assateague Island, are
key stop-over areas on the Atlantic Flyway, the seasonal migration path for hundreds of species of birds. More than 316 species
have been sighted at the **Chincoteague National Wildlife Refuge**
and **Assateague Island National Seashore**. Binoculars and a
birding book are a must; even the most avid birders may find
themselves stumped by the more seldom-sighted varieties. Accessible hiking and biking trails provide alternative methods of
exploring various sections of the refuge. The automotive Wildlife

171

Loop, open from 3:00 P.M. to dusk, is yet another way to see a great deal of the refuge. Visitors may also enjoy walking along the unspoiled seashore where there is no sign of man's intrusion.

You'll need no book to identify Chincoteague's wild ponies, although Marguerite Henry's children's novel *Misty* makes excellent family reading before your trip. Legend says the wild ponies are descendants of ponies that survived the wreck of a Spanish galleon. The ponies may approach stopped automobiles, but they should not be fed. One look at their uncombed manes, shaggy coats and the forelocks over their eyes tells you that these are not domesticated animals and should not be petted.

The best place to spot the wild ponies is from the Woodland Trail overlook or from the concessionaire's land tour to the northern portion of the refuge. There are roughly 150 ponies on the Virginia portion of the island traveling together in groups of 2 to 20 animals. One of the most popular events in this part of the state is the annual pony swim and penning held during the last week in July. The Virginia ponies are herded across Assateague Channel to Chincoteague.

Refuge hours vary according to the season: May through September hours are 5:00 A.M. to 10:00 P.M., April and October hours are 6:00 A.M. to 8:00 P.M. and November through March from 6:00 A.M. to 6:00 P.M. There is a nominal per automobile entrance fee that is good for seven days.

One of the most enjoyable ways to see Chincoteague and the National Wildlife Refuge is on a guided cruise aboard the *Osprey*. The 90-minute voyage takes you down the southern end of Chincoteague and along the southern tip of Assateague. Your knowledgeable guides will point out the landmarks and identify the wildlife you will spot along the way. You'll even learn to give directions like a native: south is "down the marsh," north is "up the neck," west is "over the bay" and east is "to the beach." Tickets can be purchased at the Refuge Motor Inn on Beach Road just before the bridge to Assateague Island. Another option is the 90-minute Wildlife Safari Land Tour (tickets are sold at the Wildlife Refuge Center) that travels through areas of the refuge not accessible to automobiles. Here too, knowledgeable naturalists will identify the flora and fauna as you make your way around the sanctuary. For ticket information and schedules for the cruise and safari call (804) 336-6155.

Chincoteague has two small museums: the **Refuge Waterfowl Museum** and the **Oyster & Maritime Museum**. The former has a fascinating collection of decoys plus exhibits that reveal the history of hunting water fowl along the coastal waterways. Weapons, boats, traps, art and carvings augment the extensive decoy collection. The museum on Maddox Boulevard is open

Each year in late July the Chincoteague wild ponies are rounded up. The ponies swim the quarter mile channel between Assateague and Chincoteague islands and are auctioned off to benefit the Chincoteague Fire Department.

daily during the summer months from 10:00 A.M. to 5:00 P.M. Admission is charged. Just up the street is the Oyster & Maritime Museum with display cases of shells and fossils. This museum has ambitious expansion plans. Hours are the same with the exception of Sunday when it is open from NOON to 4:00 P.M. Admission is charged. Both museums are seasonal, opening only from May to September.

Just five miles before reaching Chincoteague you'll pass **NASA Visitor Center at Wallops Flight Facility.** If you're traveling with children, they are sure to spot the rockets and re-entry vehicles exhibited in front of the center. Since 1945 Wallops has launched roughly 12,000 rocket research vehicles and about 20 earth satellites. The history of this significant space research is presented at the center. There are scale models of space probes, satellites and aircraft as well as full-scale planes and rockets. Space suits, a moon rock brought back by the Apollo 17 mission and exhibits on the Hubble space shuttle make this a worthwhile stop. The center is open daily from 10:00 A.M. to 4:00 P.M. from July 4th to Labor Day; at other times it is closed on Tuesday and Wednesday. There is no admission charge.

Directions: For Chincoteague take I-64 east past Norfolk and then take Route 13 north through the Chesapeake Bay Bridge Tunnel for 80 miles to Route 175. Take Route 175 east to the Chincoteague National Wildlife Refuge.

Kerr Place and Onancock

On the Waterfront

Scottish merchant John S. Ker (the original spelling) built his two-story brick house in 1799 on 364 acres of land that his wife, Agnes D. Corbin Ker, inherited. He died shortly after the manor house was completed, and his son Edward inherited the estate on the death of his mother. With Edward's death in 1826 the house passed out of the family and was owned by several families before **Kerr Place** was sold to the Eastern Shore Historical Society in 1960.

The Society offers tours of the restored rooms on the first floor and the exhibit and period rooms on the second floor. The furnishings are period pieces from 1799 to 1840. Great effort has been made to restore the original room colors and decorative architectural touches like the plaster moldings and the faux marble doorposts. There was no indication of draperies in the downstairs rooms; instead they had interior folding shutters like the ones visitors see at each window. The distinctively patterned

174

wooden pianoforte was crafted by Conrad Graf of Vienna, Austria in 1804. It is thought that the Hepplewhite sideboard was owned by a Kerr cousin.

In one of the second floor bedrooms there are mannequins with period clothes including an 1800 gold moire dress with a snail lace shawl and an 1880 wedding dress. Another room has a small copy of a portrait of General John Cropper, the highest ranking Revolutionary officer from this area, along with his traveling wine case. A family cradle and bed from the late 18th century are also exhibited. The museum room has a doll collection, fans, Native American artifacts and a trunk with five broad arrow markings that might have belonged to Captain John Smith. The latter is the oldest piece in the house.

In 1981 the Garden Club of Virginia began a grounds restoration project. No evidence of gardens or specific grounds ornamentation were discovered. While retaining the high-branched shade trees, shrubs were added as they might have been planted in the early 19th century. These shrub islands, or shrubberies as they were originally styled, incorporate flowering shrubs around a small tree. Behind the house, a walkway bordered by flowers leads to an arbor. Specimen trees are planted on the lawn. Kerr Place, 69 Market Street, is open Tuesday through Saturday from 10:00 A.M. to 4:00 P.M. Admission is charged. It is closed on Sundays, Mondays and holidays. The house is in the picturesque town of **Onancock** (the Indian word for foggy place). The town originally called Port Scarburgh, was founded in 1680 and served as the county seat until 1693.

Kerr Place is just a few blocks from the marina on Onancock Creek, a great spot for lunch or to board excursion boats to Tangier Island (see selection). This secluded deep-water harbor is only $2^1/_2$ miles from the Chesapeake Bay. From June through mid-September, daily cruises leave Onancock each morning, returning in the afternoon: for information call (804) 891-2240 or 787-8220.

While at the harbor you can enjoy lunch at the **Hopkins & Bros. Store**, built by Captain Stephen Hopkins in 1842. Now a Virginia and U.S. Historic Landmark, it's one of the oldest general stores on the East Coast. General merchandise and regional arts and crafts are sold in the store and local seafood is served in the restaurant that overlooks the harbor. Most of the fixtures and equipment in the store are original. Tangier Island cruise tickets are sold from the same window that steamboat tickets were sold over a hundred years ago. This was a major stop for steamboats plying the Chesapeake Bay.

Not far from Onancock in Nassawadox, The Nature Conservancy schedules boat trips to **The Virginia Coast Reserve**, a barrier island wilderness area. The Atlantic's last totally unspoiled frontier contains approximately 40,000 acres of sandy beaches, salt marsh and upland terrain. Its significance as a privately protected natural area is recognized by its designation by the United Nations as a World Biosphere Reserve.

The reserve sponsors natural history field trips to many of the islands for the hardy explorer. Neither the boats nor the islands have public facilities and there is no protection from the elements. The open boats make it easy to spot the plentiful waterfowl and migratory birds. The islands are breeding grounds for geese, loons, ibises, egrets, hawks and even the rare peregrine falcon. Before joining one of these expeditions be sure to liberally apply both sunscreen and insect repellent.

To obtain a schedule of trips and workshops call the Virginia Coast Reserve at (804) 442-3049.

Directions: From I-64 in Norfolk take Route 13 across the Chesapeake Bridge Tunnel and continue up Route 13 to the turnoff for Onancock. You'll make a left turn on Route 179. Kerr Place is located $1^1/_2$ miles on the right.

Tangier Island

Virginia's Island in the Sun

In 1608 Captain John Smith, who charted so many of Virginia's waters, stopped at an island in the Chesapeake Bay and named it **Tangier** after the Moroccan coast he thought it resembled. Located 15 miles from the Maryland shore and 20 miles from the Virginia mainland, Tangier was a hunting and fishing grounds for the Pocomoke Indians. An Englishman named West purchased the island from the Pocomokes in 1666 for two overcoats. In another two decades John Crockett, who was attracted by the rich oyster and crab grounds, bought part of the island from West and settled in Tangier with his family. Even today the fewer than 1,000 residents of this isolated island retain an old English accent more reminiscent of 17th-century Elizabethan England than 20th-century Virginia.

It is hard to image 12,000 British soldiers on this tiny $3^1/_2$-by-1-mile island, but this was their staging area for the attack on Baltimore in the War of 1812. The beach from which they embarked has now been reclaimed by the sea. Erosion, an ever-present threat, has made the islanders put their small white frame houses far back from the shore. There are only a few cars; visitors tour on golf carts along the narrow roads, or ride bikes they rent or bring aboard the excursion boats. Inquire about arrangements when you make reservations for the island trip; call (804) 453-2628.

Getting to Tangier is half the fun. During the summer months the ferry, *Chesapeake Breeze*, leaves Reedville at 10:00 A.M. (a two-hour drive from Richmond) and returns at 3:45 P.M. Reedville is the center of the Chesapeake Bay menhaden fishing industry and on your way across the bay you're likely to see fishermen setting their big nets around huge schools of fish. It's an $1^1/_2$ hour trip to Tangier, but the breeze off the water makes it pleasant even on the hottest summer day. You can also catch the boat at Onancock (see selection) or from Crisfield, Maryland. From mid-May through October the cruise ship *Stephen Thomas* sails from Crisfield daily at 12:30 P.M. and begins the return trip from Tangier at 4:00 P.M., call (410) 968-2338 for details. Sailing year-round is the U.S. mailboat *Courtney Thomas* that also leaves Crisfield's dock at 12:30 P.M. daily and arrives in Tangier about 1:15 P.M. Since the captain is an islander, he does not return to the mainland until the following day so overnight accommodations are necessary for mailboat passengers. For additional information call (804) 891-2240.

Although the ferry schedule allows only a brief three hours on the island, you'll want to spend part of that time enjoying lunch at Mrs. Crockett's Chesapeake House. Many passengers return just to repeat the experience. Meals are served family style with enormous platters of crab cakes, clam fritters, Virginia ham, hot corn pudding, fresh vegetables, homemade rolls and pound cake, all washed down with pitchers of iced tea. Those who want to stay can find overnight accommodations at the Chesapeake House, but reservations are required far in advance; call (540) 891-2331. Other popular restaurants are The Fisherman's Corner and The Islander. If you want to stay overnight on Tangier there are two bed & breakfasts: Bay View Inn (804) 891-2396 and The Sunset Inn (804) 891-2525.

Directions: From I-95 in the Richmond area, take I-295 east of the city and pick up Route 360. Follow Route 360 to Reedville for the Tangier Island cruise. From Virginia's Eastern Shore, take the excursion boat from Onancock.

Virginia's Delmarva Peninsula

Courthouses and Coastline

From the south, Virginia's Eastern Shore is accessible by crossing the Chesapeake Bay in and on the world's longest bridge-tunnel ($17^6/_{10}$ miles in all). A Heritage Trail guides you to the many points of interest in Northampton County.

The southern tip of the Delmarva Peninsula, 651 acres, is protected as the **Eastern Shore of Virginia National Wildlife Refuge** with public access along a half-mile interpretative trail. The trail winds through a mixed hardwood forest, past an old graveyard to the top of a World War II bunker, once part of Fort John Custis. Bring binoculars because this vantage point offers a panoramic view of the refuge's marshes, barrier islands, bays, inlets and the Atlantic Ocean. From late August until early November you are apt to see large groups of migrating birds waiting for favorable winds and weather conditions before crossing the bay. Two endangered species have been sighted at this refuge: the bald eagle and peregrine falcon. More frequently sighted birds include the American woodcock, northern harrier, American kestrel, snow goose, great blue heron, glossy ibis, great horned owl, osprey and bobwhite.

Quite close to the refuge is the state's newest 375-acre park, located just three miles from the northern terminus of the Chesapeake Bay Bridge-Tunnel. The park's name **Kiptopeke**, honors the younger brother of the Accawmacke King, whose tribe once fished these waters and hunted on this peninsula. Kiptopeke, which meant big water in the Accawmacke language, greeted Captain John Smith in 1608 and befriended the first Europeans who settled this area. The park has a fishing pier, boat ramp, swimming beach and picnicking and camping facilities. Fishing is particularly good because of the row of nine surplus World War II concrete ships that form a breakwater just 1,500 feet off shore. This site was once the ferry terminus for visitors crossing the bay; long-range plans call for turning the old ferry terminal into a visitor center.

Long before this became the first park on the Eastern Shore, bird population studies were done here; the hiking and interpretative trails lead to a hawk observation area. At the Raptor Research Area naturalists observe and band hawks, kestrels, osprey and other birds of prey from September to early November. There are designated areas where visitors can quietly observe this banding. Also banded are migrating songbirds like warblers, wrens and thrushes and a wide variety of waterfowl.

There are trails through the upland hardwood forest area and along the southern beach. Boardwalks allow access to Kiptopeke's dunes. Park personnel offer interpretative programs during the summer months; for a schedule of the evening campfire programs, afternoon hikes, canoe trips and fishing clinics, call (804) 331-2267. One increasingly popular event is the Eastern Shore Birding Festival held on the first full weekend in October.

Continuing north of the bridge-tunnel for six miles, off Route 13 on Route 644, is the Custis family tomb where John Custis IV is buried. His home, Arlington, built in 1657, was the largest house in colonial Virginia. Arlington Plantation was Martha Custis's home before her marriage to George Washington.

Moving up the peninsula you can vear off Route 13, to see the region's prosperous railroad town, **Cape Charles**, in 1884 the southern terminus of the New York, Philadelphia and Norfolk Railroad. The town is noted for its large white bay-front homes and its churches—there seems to be one on every corner. See if you can pick out the "Sears" homes, ordered from the catalog, shipped by the railroad and put together by local contractors. A handy guide to this community and others along this peninsula is Kirk Mariner's *Off 13 The Eastern Shore of Virginia Guidebook.*

In **Eastville**, the Old Courthouse houses the oldest, continuous court records in the country. The Declaration of Independence was read here on August 13, 1776. Local government began in 1632 with the colonial commissioners, or justices as they were later called, meeting as a court. Before the courthouse was built in 1677, they met in private homes. The court records from these early gatherings have survived and are filed in this courthouse. Built in 1731, it was the third to serve this region. You can pick up the keys for the Old Courthouse, the Old Clerk's Office and the adjacent Debtor's Prison in the new courthouse that also stands in the complex. While the courthouse has been completely restored the other buildings have had little improvements. Cases with Native American artifacts and colonial memorabilia can be seen in the Old Clerk's Office, while the Debtor's Prison, built sometime in the early 1740s, (although some architectural historians date it around 1814) still retains its spartan look. This complex is a designated Virginia Historic Landmark and is listed on the National Register of Historic Places.

Heading north the next major point of interest is Onancock (see Kerr Place selection). Meandering farther north to **Accomac**, you will see another courthouse and debtor's prison complex. This quaint community has an abundance of restored colonial architecture. The courthouse was built in 1899, but the records in the clerk's office date back to 1663 (only Eastville predates these documents). It is insightful to look at the *Accomack County Orders 1714-1717* for the conflicting messages inscribed on the flyleaf: one reads "God Save the King" while beneath it in another handwriting is "God Damn the King." The Debtor's Prison, built in 1783, contains a small museum focusing on regional history. It is worth strolling the quiet streets of Accomac and enjoying the rich detail on the private homes and public buildings.

Before heading east to Chincoteague (see selection) railroad buffs will want to make a brief stop in Parksley to see the **Eastern Shore Railway Museum**, in the old Parksley Station. The small museum has a modest collection of railroad memborablia, an 1890s maintenance shed and several railcars on sidings. The group operates train excursions; call (804) 665-6271 for ticket and schedule information.

Directions: Take I-64 past Norfolk and then take Route 13 north through the Chesapeake Bay Bridge-Tunnel. The Heritage Trail begins when you cross over onto the peninsula.

Central Virginia

O ne of the few cities in the country that boasts it served as two capitals, Richmond has a distinguished history. Virginia's state capital was for a time the capital of the Confederate States of America. A stellar array of distinguished men left their mark on Richmond: Thomas Jefferson was its architect, Patrick Henry its spokesman, Edgar Allan Poe its poet, and Robert E. Lee its general.

Homes of the Founding Fathers enrich this region, Thomas Jefferson's Monticello is a mecca for historians from around the world. Less well known is Poplar Forest, Jefferson's nearby getaway. Also nearby is Ash Lawn-Highland, the home of Jefferson's friend and fellow president James Monroe. James Madison's Montpelier is still a work-in-progress and it's fascinating to watch the interpretation evolve. From an earlier page in history, the still-evolving Henricus Historical Park is well on its way to providing a glimpse of the community where Pocahontas spent four years.

The Civil War years come to life at Jefferson Davis's White House of the Confederacy and at battlefields where the ground was wrested from the control of the southern army. Richmond, City Point, Petersburg and the final days at Appomattox all tell the story of the ultimately unsuccessful attempts of the Confederacy to secure their capital.

This region encompasses the foothills of the Blue Ridge where you can see Crabtree Falls, the highest east of the Mississippi River, tidal rivers you can explore by excursions from Hopewell, the multi-faceted Orange County above Richmond and recreational opportunities at Smith Mountain Lake.

Appomattox Court House National Historical Park

Surrender to Its Appeal!

In 1861 Wilmer McLean, merchant and sugar importer, lived with his family along a stream near a sleepy Virginia community. The town was Manassas Junction, the stream was Bull Run, and the first battle of the War Between the States was fought there. General Beauregard used McLean's home as his headquarters. Town folks say that a Yankee cannonball went through the McLean's outside kitchen during the general's stay spoiling his dinner. A year later the armies of the North and South clashed once more on the hills and fields around McLean's home. He decided Manassas wasn't safe and moved his family to **Appomattox Court House**, an obscure county seat in the central Piedmont region. It is one of the ironies of history that the war which began in Wilmer McLean's front yard ended in his parlor!

There are 27 restored or reconstructed buildings at Appomattox Court House National Historical Park. Your first stop should be the visitor center where a 15-minute chronological slide program will acquaint you with the dramatic events from April 1 through 12, 1865, leading up to the final surrender. A second program, *Honor Answers Honor*, uses first person accounts to recapture the emotions felt by those on both sides of the surrender field.

After this slide program you'll walk the quiet country lanes to the area where the stacking of arms ceremony took place. Imagine the emotions of the battle-weary Confederates as they marched between the Union soldiers and discovered that their former enemies were presenting arms. When you tour the **Clover Hill Tavern** you'll see some of the paroles printed for the surrendering army. The presses had to turn out 28,231 passes for the Confederates who laid down their arms.

At the reconstructed **McLean House** you'll learn that only a few of the furnishings are original. Not only did the surrender take place in Wilmer McLean's parlor, but Federal officers took some of his furniture when they left. Some purchased pieces and others, it is said, stole them; all wanted souvenirs of Lee's surrender to Grant.

The stacking of arms ceremony was ironically on the fourth anniversary of its opening salvo. The surrender of the infantry of Lee's Army of Northern Virginia took place on April 12, 1865, exactly four years to the day after Fort Sumter was fired on by Confederate batteries.

Appomattox Court House National Historical Park is open daily from 9:00 A.M. to 5:00 P.M. except Thanksgiving, Christmas, New Year's, and the birthdays of George Washington and Martin Luther King. There is a visitor admission fee for those 17 and older. Informative programs are given during the summer months.

Directions: From I-95 in the Richmond area, take Route 360 west to Jetersville, then Route 307 to Route 460. Go west on Route 460 to Appomattox. Take Route 24 east for three miles to Appomattox Court House National Historical Park on the right.

The war that began in Wilmer McLean's front yard, along Bull Run, ended in his parlor at Appomattox Court House. General Robert E. Lee surrendered his Army of Northern Virginia to General Ulysses S. Grant on Palm Sunday, April 9, 1865 bringing an end to the Civil War.

Quartermaster Museum

Head for the QM, PDQ!

One of the world's most complete military uniform collections can be seen at the **Quartermaster Museum** at Fort Lee. The uniforms date from the 1700s to the present and include boots, helmets and all kinds of special gear such as fearsome looking gas masks and padded dog-training suits.

Many well-known military leaders are remembered. The museum has General George S. Patton's 1944 jeep with its "steamboat trombones" or air horns and General Dwight D. Eisenhower's 1940 mess jacket and his "pinks and greens" dress uniform. Amid the many presidential banners used by Taft, Wilson, Harding, Truman and both Roosevelts is the original 50-star flag presented to President Eisenhower.

The museum reveals the diverse functions of the Army Quartermaster Corps which range from providing housing, food, clothing and transportation to arranging funerals. You'll learn how much the rations of the U.S. soldier, now considered the best in the world, have changed from the fire cakes and water that were standard fare at Valley Forge.

The Corps also quarters and equips animals used by the military. There's a delightful old recruitment poster that tells potential soldiers, "Join the Cavalry and Have a Courageous Friend. . . . The Horse is Man's Noblest Companion." The era of the horse soldier is illustrated by a display on the Ninth and Tenth Cavalry, whose Black ranks were known as the "Buffalo Soldiers." You'll also see a reconstructed saddler's workshop and a blacksmith shop.

In the military funeral exhibit, look for the elaborate black caisson used in the funeral of General George Pickett in 1875 and Jefferson Davis on May 31, 1893. There is also the architect's original model for the Tomb of the Unknown Soldier at Arlington Cemetery. A somber black drum used in the funeral cortege of John F. Kennedy causes many a visitor to stop and stand solemnly before it.

There is so much to see that visitors with special interests can spend hours. The Hall of Heraldry alone has thousands of examples of crests, patches, plaques and flags. Special exhibits and selections from the stored collection make this an interesting spot to revisit. The QM, as it is called, is open Tuesday through Friday from 10:00 A.M. to 5:00 P.M. and on weekends from 11:00 A.M. to 5:00 P.M. It is closed on Thanksgiving, Christmas and New Year's Day. There is no admission charge.

Directions: From I-95 in the Petersburg area, take the Fort Lee Exit (signs also indicate directions to the QM Museum). The QM is located on Route 36, east between Petersburg and Hopewell. The museum is just inside the main gate of Fort Lee. You do not need a special pass; Fort Lee is an "open post."

Red Hill, The Patrick Henry National Memorial

Country Sage

No one visits **Red Hill** by accident; greater numbers should visit by design. This is the last home and burial place of Patrick Henry, the "voice of the Revolution." Henry argued against the ratification of a United States Constitution containing no Bill of Rights. Some attribute his lack of prominence to his Revolutionary role of speaker, not scribe. He left few papers or letters behind. This neglect lends irony to his gravestone inscription, "His Fame His Best Epitaph," since Henry's fame has diminished. Although school children recognize his famous quote, "Give me liberty, or give me death," they know nothing about the man.

This is quite an eclipse for a man once heralded as the "first national hero," the "idol of the country," and "the noble patriot." A visit to Patrick Henry's last home, Red Hill, near Brookneal, introduces you to this fascinating Founding Father. Patrick Henry was the first elected governor of Virginia, which declared independence from England on June 29, 1776. He served five one-year terms in all and was so popular among Virginians that he could have served more. In 1794 he retired from a lucrative law practice at age 57 and moved to Red Hill. This was the favorite of the four Virginia plantations he owned at the time of his death. He called it "one of the garden spots of Virginia," no doubt because of its sweeping view of the Staunton River Valley, which remains little changed today.

Today's visitor is greeted at the visitor center where a 15-minute video on Patrick Henry and Red Hill is shown. The center's museum room houses the largest existing collection of Henry artifacts and memorabilia. Perhaps the most famous of these is Peter Rothermel's painting "Patrick Henry before the Virginia House of Burgesses." This impressive canvas, measuring 8 ft. by 7 ft., depicts Henry's Stamp Act speech during which he defied fellow members of the colonial legislature who critized his opposition to taxation without representation by declaring, "If this be treason make the most of it."

You'll explore the Red Hill buildings and grounds with the help of a self-guided walking tour brochure. The house, a reconstruction of the original which burned in 1919, has three downstairs rooms—the master bedroom, children's bedroom and family room. The last two of the Henry's 17 children were born in the master bedroom. Several pieces of furniture throughout the house are Henry originals.

The Henry family relaxed and entertained in the parlor. Two of their daughters were married there. It was in this room that Patrick Henry died on June 6, 1799. A Chippendale corner chair is identical to the one he was resting in when he died.

After leaving the house, the visitor can explore its dependencies, which include a kitchen, privy, smokehouse, servants' quarters, carriage house and stables. Although Henry had finished riding the circuit of county courthouses by the time he retired to Red Hill, he did continue to practice law in the office building you'll see on the estate. Henry also taught law here to several of his sons and grandsons.

In the Henry house's front yard stands the national champion Osage orange tree, certified as such by the National Forestry Association. This multi-trunked giant with its gnarled roots and striated bark rises to a height of 60 feet and has a crown spread of 85 feet. It is an impressive sight.

You can take the garden walk to the family graveyard. It contains the graves of Patrick Henry, his wife Dorothea, and several members of his family, including his youngest son John in whose family Red Hill remained until it was purchased by the Patrick Henry Memorial Foundation in 1944. In 1986 it became a national memorial, although it is still operated and maintained by the foundation.

Red Hill is open daily 9:00 A.M. to 5:00 P.M. except from November through February when it closes at 4:00 P.M. It is closed on Thanksgiving, Christmas and New Year's Day. Admission is charged.

Directions: From I-95 in the Richmond area pick-up Route 360 southwest to the Keysville . Then take Route 15 until it intersects with Route 40. Take Route 40 to within two miles of Brookneal and follow well-marked signs to Red Hill.

Sayler's Creek Battlefield Historical State Park

Botched and Bloody Battle

Seventy-two hours before General Lee surrendered at Appomattox, April 1865, he lost over half his army in the war's last major Virginia battle at **Sayler's Creek**. Total Confederate losses were estimated at 8,000 with 6,000 taken prisoner—the largest number of men ever to surrender in a single action on this continent. Five generals and numerous high-ranking officers were captured. As the stragglers were rejoining the main force, Lee looked around and exclaimed, "My God! Has the army dissolved?"

What caused such a debacle? A combination of factors bedeviled Lee's ragged and starving army as they fled Petersburg and Richmond. Heavy spring rains caused frequent rerouting and mudsoaked roads were often impassable for the wagons, resulting in loss of communication. The army was heading for Amelia Court House where they hoped to be reprovisioned. When supplies did not arrive, a day was wasted on a fruitless search for food. This gave Union forces time to catch up.

On April 6, a third of Lee's army under General Anderson and General Ewell bogged down—literally—in the swampy bottom land of Sayler's Creek and were overtaken by Federal troops under General Wright. Though the Richmond clerks, sailors and artillerymen who made up the Confederate force repulsed the first attack, they came under the artillery batteries and were stopped. The entire force surrendered.

186

The wagon column under General Gordon that the Confederates were trying to salvage had already crossed the creek but here, too, they were stopped by a numerically superior Union force commanded by General George Armstrong Custer. While General Gordon and a few men escaped, the wagons and almost all of Lee's dwindling supplies were lost along with three-fourths of the men. The defeat of the Confederate army at Sayler's Creek was just three days before Lee's surrender of the Army of Northern Virginia at Appomattox Court House (see selection).

Today there is an auto route at Sayler's Creek Battlefield Historical State Park. Overlooking the battlefield is Hillsman House (not open to the public) which was used as a field hospital by both armies. Interpretive signs and audio programs reveal details of this climactic encounter. This state park is open Memorial Day through Labor Day at no charge.

Directions: From I-95 just to the south of Richmond, take Route 360 west. Just past Jetersville, turn right on Route 307. Make another right on Route 617 and head north. The battlefield auto route markers are at intervals along Route 617.

CHARLOTTESVILLE

Ash Lawn-Highland

Accomplished Protege

Improbable but true, three of America's first five presidents died on July 4: Thomas Jefferson and John Adams on the very same day in 1826 and James Monroe in 1831. After 50 years of public service Monroe had hoped to retire to Highland (now called **Ash Lawn-Highland**), his rural Virginia home. His long years of government work, however, had so impoverished him that he was forced to sell Highland. The loss was undoubtedly easier to bear because earlier that year his good friend and neighbor, Jefferson had died.

Monroe built Highland at Jefferson's urging. The Sage of Monticello wanted to create "a society to our taste." He envisioned surrounding himself with a coterie of interesting and stimulating friends. The young James Monroe, who had studied law with Jefferson after the American Revolution, was happy to oblige his mentor.

In 1793 Monroe spent $1,000 for 1,000 acres adjoining Monticello. Before he could begin building, President Washington, another Virginian with whom Monroe had close ties, having served under him at Valley Forge, appointed Monroe Minister to France. In the entrance hall of Ash Lawn-Highland is a copy of the Leutze painting, *Washington Crossing the Delaware*, which portrays Monroe holding the flag behind his commander. Not wanting the house project to languish while Monroe was out of the country, Jefferson enlisted the help of James Madison and the two of them, with Monroe's uncle, Joseph Jones, began the planning of Monroe's house. Jefferson also sent his gardener over to begin landscaping the grounds. Monroe dubbed his home a "cabin-castle" because, though the exterior was simple, the interior was furnished with Neoclassical French Empire pieces that the Monroes acquired aborad. On your tour of the house you'll see a portrait of their daughter Eliza's life-long friend, Hortense de Beauharnais, daughter of the Empress Josephine, who became Queen of Holland and the mother of Napoleon III. There is also a portrait of the headmistress of the French school attended by Eliza and Hortense. In the drawing room you'll see a marble bust of Napoleon Bonaparte, a gift to Monroe. The study has a copy of the Louis XVI desk used by Monroe when he was president.

Monroe, like his friend George Washington, was taller than average. The highpost bed was big enough to accommodate his six-foot frame. Although it is the only Monroe piece in the master bedchamber, the rest of the furnishings are from Monroe's time. You'll learn that the wooden working parts of the case clock were greased with fat. This attracted mice and may have provided the inspiration for the popular nursery rhyme.

Ash Lawn is operated today by James Monroe's alma mater, the College of William and Mary. Thomas Jefferson and John Tyler were also alumni. The college maintains the 535-acre estate as a 19th-century working plantation. A dozen peacocks strut in the boxwood garden and an abundance of nature can be enjoyed year-round. Spring and summer bring flowers and herbs, as well as the Ash Lawn-Highland Summer Festival, two months of opera, musical theater and family entertainment. Vegetables are harvested in the fall and in winter Christmas trees can be cut at Ash Lawn-Highland. Traditional farm crafts are demonstrated throughout the year.

Ash Lawn-Highland is open March through October from 9:00 A.M. to 6:00 P.M. From November through February, hours are 10:00 A.M. to 5:00 P.M. It is closed on Thanksgiving, Christmas and New Year's Day. Admission is charged.

Directions: From I-95 in the Richmond area take I-64 west to Charlottesville, then use Exit 121. Follow signs to the Charlottesville/Albemarle County visitor center and continue past that, then turn left on Route 53 past Monticello. Make a right turn on Route 795, the James Monroe Parkway, for Ash Lawn-Highland.

Historic Michie Tavern

Where Southern Hospitality Prevails

Historic Michie Tavern is one of the oldest homesteads remaining in Virginia. It was originally located on a well-traveled stagecoach route some 17 miles northwest of the present site. To accommodate the many travelers seeking food and shelter at his home, William Michie opened his dwelling as an "Ordinary" in 1784.

Michie (pronounced Micky) Tavern's museum hostess will tell you about young William. His father, "Scotch John" Michie, was deported to Virginia in 1716 after taking part in the Scottish Jacobite Rising. When John arrived in Virginia he began acquiring land; ultimately he handled more than 11,500 acres. The land on which his son would eventually build Michie Tavern was acquired from Major John Henry, father of Patrick, another rebel against England.

William Michie also played a role in the struggle against England. He was part of the Continental army that wintered with Washington at Valley Forge. He signed the Albemarle Declaration of Independence in 1779. It was after the Revolutionary War that William Michie obtained a license to operate his "Ordinary."

After the guide's introduction you will make your way through the tavern. Each room has a recorded narration that portrays 18th-century tavern life through living history interpretation. Visitors feel like they are listening in on colonial conversations. The tavern has about 50 items that once belonged to the Michie family. The first room on the tour is the gentlemen's parlor with its adjoining tap room. The tap bar is a very small enclosure, so built as to bar the public from its access. The tavern-keeper became known as the bar tender—a phrase still widely used.

From the gentlemen's parlor you'll move across the hall to the ladies' parlor. After the Revolutionary War road conditions and travel by coach improved. Female travelers were no longer an oddity and it was in the proprietor's best interest to set aside a special room for women. The woodwork and furnishings are more elaborate here.

The upstairs ballroom served many functions including additional sleeping space, a place for church worship, dancing lessons and school. Entertainers, traveling doctors and dentists would set up "shop" in this room. It is the thought of so many long-ago balls, however, that strikes the most romantic chord. It was here, legend proclaims, that the first waltz was danced in the colonies. Although no surviving account can document this story, old-timers claim the event was recorded in the margins of the tavern log book that mysteriously disappeared in the 1950s.

The story proclaims one of Jefferson's daughters had just returned from France where she had learned a "radical" new dance step. She danced it gaily in the arms of a dashing officer. Onlookers were shocked and her chaperone quickly escorted her from the floor. According to reports, she was harshly scolded.

Back downstairs you will see the keeping hall where food was kept warm before serving. This room holds a fine selection of spinning equipment. One special piece is a yarn winder which was invented to count thread. A small wooden peg (known as the weasel) pops loudly after each revolution of the wheel (known as the monkey). The "monkey" chases the "weasel" as in the nursery rhyme, *Pop Goes the Weasel*. Other handy kitchen items include the hand-carved cheese press, apple peeler, cole slaw shredder and French-fried potato cutter.

The narration continues as you tour the dependencies— kitchen, necessary, springhouse, well house and smokehouse. If you have problems with steps you may want to skip these buildings. Your tour ends beneath the tavern in the wine cellar that now houses the **Virginia Wine Museum**. After your tour you may continue to the "Ordinary" and enjoy a colonial buffet. Michie's hospitality didn't end with the 18th century. The "Ordinary" still serves fried chicken, blackeyed peas, stewed tomatoes, cole slaw, southern beets, green bean salad, potato salad, corn bread, biscuits and apple cobbler. Lunch is available from 11:30 A.M. to 3:00 P.M. daily in four dining rooms and an outdoor courtyard.

The thread of preservation continues with the **Sowell** (pronounced Soul) **House**, an early 19th-century structure that was reconstructed on the Michie Tavern site. Tours of this house focus on the architectural development of the house and the way that it reflects events in the life of the Sowell family—both personal and national. Before leaving you should also tour the **Meadow Run Grist Mill** which houses the General Store. The mill was moved 50 miles to this new location. It is an appropriate addition because the Michie family owned and operated a mill and general store. Their family history is further preserved through the interpretation. The tavern was relocated at this site in the 1920s and the move itself became an historic event. The Michie Tavern is significant as an example of the early preservation movement.

Michie Tavern is open 9:00 A.M. to 5:00 P.M. with the last tour beginning at 4:20 P.M. Admission is charged and includes both the tavern and grist mill.

Directions: From I-95 in the Richmond area take I-64 west to the Charlottesville area. From I-64 take Exit 121A, Route 20. Just past the Thomas Jefferson Visitors Bureau, turn left on Route 53. Michie Tavern is on the right just before the entrance to Monticello; both are well marked.

Monticello

The Sage of Monticello Grew Other Spices

Monticello is one of the most interesting homes in America because Thomas Jefferson was one of the most original thinkers of his, or any, age. His home reveals the breath and scope of his interests.

President Taft said that in Charlottesville, "they still talked of Mr. Jefferson as though he were in the next room." When you visit Monticello and sense the individuality of its designer, it is easy to feel that Mr. Jefferson is in the next room.

Thomas Jefferson inherited the land on which he built Monticello at his father's death in 1757. He had played on the mountaintop as a child while growing up at neighboring Shadwell. Jefferson occasionally took time out from his law studies with George Wythe in Williamsburg and explored his Virginia hilltop, perhaps planning the home that he eventually built. The year after he finished reading law, 1768, he began to level the top of his 867-foot mountain so that he could begin building. He named his estate "Monticello," or little mountain. The design, like the name, is Italian. Jefferson used architectural books to design his house. He borrowed heavily from the Palladian style popularized by Andrea Palladio.

Like so many of the skills Jefferson acquired, his architectural artistry was self-taught. He was an enthusiastic innovator in all that he attempted. One of the features that would become a Jeffersonian trademark was the dome he added to his house. His was the first private house in America to have a dome. His dome-room is only reached by a pair of narrow staircases, so visitors cannot enjoy an up-close look at this architectural feature. Jefferson loved domes but disliked obtrusive staircases.

Another innovation was the seven-day clock Jefferson designed for the entrance hall. Cannonball weights indicated the day of the week. Saturday's marker is below the hall on the basement level and can be seen in the archeological exhibit area. Jefferson even designed a special ladder for the weekly winding of the clock. The hall also boasts antlers brought back by Lewis and Clark from their trip to the far west, as well as mastodon bones that Clark found in Kentucky.

When you tour Monticello you quickly become aware of Jefferson's practical turn of mind. In the study there is a marvelous device that allowed him to write with one pen while a second connected pen made a copy of the letter. Jefferson designed his bedroom so that he could have access to his bed from either the bedroom or the sitting room; the bed itself is a room divider. He also designed beds to fit in alcoves to conserve space. His prac-

ticality extended to other areas of the house. There is a lazy susan door in the dining room that allowed the kitchen staff to set
the prepared dishes on the door shelves and then simply turn
the door, fully stocked, for service in the dining room.

Much as Jefferson enjoyed designing, building and embell-
ishing his mountaintop home, his real passion was for horticulture. Indeed, this great leader, who served as President of the
United States, Vice-President, Secretary of State, Minister to
France and Governor of Virginia, once said, "I have often thought
that if heaven had given me a choice of my position and calling, it should have been on a rich spot of earth...and near a good
market...No occupation is so delightful to me as the culture of
the earth..."

The gardens of Monticello are not to be missed. Visitors should
plan their day so that they can include an hour-long escorted
tour of the garden, offered daily April through October. Jefferson's creativity certainly extended to his garden. As he proudly
proclaimed, "I am become the most ardent farmer in the state."
In his later years he would say, "Though an old man, I am but
a young gardener."

He was 23 years old when he began the garden diary he would
keep until two years before his death. His precise records have
enabled the Thomas Jefferson Memorial Foundation to accu-
rately restore the landscape to its appearance following Jefferson's second term as president in 1809. A grid, drawn by Jefferson in 1778, gives the exact location of 300 trees. In all, his
notes and planting plans indicate the position of 900 trees. His
enthusiasm for fruit trees unquestionably exceeded their use-
fulness. Even on his busy estate there weren't enough people to
consume the fruit from 300 trees. Jefferson's orchard was one of
the most extensive in America; he planted 122 varieties of ten
different types of fruit.

He also enjoyed experimenting with vegetables in his massive
1,000-foot vegetable garden located on a terraced area above the
orchard. Peas were one of Jefferson's favorite vegetables and he
grew 20 kinds of English pea. In total he cultivated 250 varieties
of vegetables. Jefferson once said that the "greatest service which
can be rendered any country is to add an useful plant to its culture."

Monticello is open daily except Christmas from 8:00 A.M. to
5:00 P.M. March through October and from 9:00 A.M. to 4:30 P.M.
November through February. Admission is charged. You can purchase a Presidents' Pass at the Charlottesville-Albemarle Visitors Bureau, a discounted combination ticket for Monticello, Historic Michie Tavern and Ash Lawn.

Directions: From I-95 in the Richmond area, take I-64 west to
Charlottesville. Take Exit 121, Route 20 south, off I-64. From

Route 20, turn left onto Route 53, the Thomas Jefferson Parkway, to Monticello. Traveling from the Washington D.C. area take I-66 west to Route 29 south, the Warrenton exit. Follow Route 29 south to Charlottesville. Take Route 250 West bypass to I-64 east toward Richmond. From I-64 take Exit 121 A, the Monticello exit. This will put you on Route 20 south and you will proceed as outlined above.

CHESTERFIELD

Chesterfield Museum Complex

Go Directly to Jail

Four historically significant buildings await visitors to the Chesterfield Courthouse complex: a county museum, the 1892 jail, a 1917 Colonial Revival Courthouse and a Federal-period plantation house called Magnolia Grange. They are all operated by the Chesterfield Historical Society.

The **Chesterfield County Museum** is housed inside a replica of the county's 1750 courthouse. This modest museum may have greater appeal for county residents than casual visitors, but it does encompass an important bit of Virginia history. The state's earliest inhabitants, Appomattox and Monocan Indians, are represented by a collection of stone implements and a 17th-century dugout canoe.

An historic document from 1749 has a fascinating past. Called the Commission of Peace, it had established the county of Chesterfield. In 1865 Edward Jeffries of the New York Infantry stole it. Then, 90 years later on April 6, 1955, a county resident saw an advertisement for the document's sale. He purchased it and had it returned to its rightful place in Chesterfield.

Three county firsts are commemorated. It was in Chesterfield in 1700 that the French Huguenots established the first commercial coal mines in America. This was also the location of the first iron mines, established in 1619 and eliminated along with the Henricus settlement (see selection) in the 1622 massacre. The first railroad in Virginia was also in this county.

Visitors to the Chesterfield County Museum can see a well-stocked country store, reflecting the years from 1900 to 1940. Old medicine jars hold long-forgotten nostrums. There are such arcane items as a hog scraper, shotgun shell crimper, Cresoline lamps (the forerunners of vaporizers), cherry seeders and a device for watering baby chicks. On the counter there is a 1922 account book from the general merchandise store; some youngsters are amazed to learn that a store would "carry" a customer.

Downstairs at the jail, visitors can see police and fire department artifacts. The old cells upstairs are definitely a crime deterrent—small, dark, cold and totally inhospitable. One prisoner who was determined to escape jumped the jailer. The jailer, who was getting on in years, fortunately had been forewarned by a prison trustee. He pulled his revolver and shot the prisoner dead. He was buried on the sheriff's farm until relatives could claim the body.

The 1917 Colonial Revival Courthouse is open for tours. It houses changing exhibits, a gift shop and a local history/genealogy library that is open daily for researchers. Museum offices are also located in the courthouse.

The last part of the complex, **Magnolia Grange**, is across Route 10 from the Court Green. Built in 1822, it is one of the finest Federal period houses in Virginia. The building has been restored to represent the early 19th-century life-style of an affluent Virginia planter. The architecture and furnishings reflect the Greek Revival influence, except for an upstairs bedroom that is decorated in the Victorian style, popular in the 1890s.

The Chesterfield County Museum Complex is open Monday through Friday from 10:00 A.M. to 4:00 P.M. and on Sunday 1:00 to 4:00 P.M. Admission is charged to tour Magnolia Grange and the museum. Call the Chesterfield Historical Society at (804) 748-1026 for further information.

Directions: From Richmond take I-95 south to Route 288, Exit 62. Take Route 10 west to the Chesterfield Courthouse. The museum is on the right.

Henricus Historical Park

Pocahontas Slept Here

Born in 1595, Pocahontas was the favorite daughter of Chief Powhatan, a significant distinction as he fathered approximately 100 children. When the English settlers arrived in Virginia they encountered the Mattaponi tribe ruled by Powhatan's Confederation (see Mattaponi Indian Museum selection and Jamestown Settlement).

The inquisitive Princess Pocahontas was fascinated by the English and she frequently visited their fort. Most historians believe that her 1607 "rescue" of Captain John Smith, when she was 12, was part of an adoption ritual intended to welcome a foreign captive into the tribe. It wasn't long before Pocahontas discovered what it was like to be a captive. In 1613, two years after Captain John Smith returned to England, Pocahontas was kidnaped by Captain Samuel Argall. After ransom negotiations between Argall and Chief Powhatan broke down, Pocahontas was taken to the new Citie (sic) of Henricus.

This was the second permanent English settlement. Although John Smith claimed Jamestown was the "fittest place for an Earthly Paradise," its low-lying terrain proved to be too swampy. Henricus was established by Sir Thomas Dale, a sea captain and temporary deputy governor of the Virginia colony, along with 350 settlers in 1611 on a bluff above the James River. The Native Americans attacked the settlement constantly and it was in hopes of securing peace that Argall took Pocahontas hostage. She was taught Christianity by Reverend Alexander Whitaker and at age 18 or 19 was baptized in Henricus's church, taking the name Rebecca. In 1614, Rebecca (after obtaining a divorce from her Native American husband) married John Rolfe, a young English planter and had a son they named Thomas. It was John Rolfe who developed a sweeter tasting tobacco hybrid while living near Henricus. In 1616–1617 the Rolfes traveled to London where Pocahontas dazzled the English court. Pocahontas died in London in 1617 after a brief illlness. The peace achieved by Pocahontas presence at the settlement broke down and a massacre in 1622 virtually destroyed Henricus. On Good Friday, May 22, 1622, Powhatan's warriors came to Henricus and, after entering the settlement, they used the colonists' own weapons to slay them.

This historic site was overlooked for centuries, but in 1985 the **Henricus Historical Park** opened (although it wasn't until 1995 that the access road to the park opened). This is still a work in progress. The Henricus Foundation plans to add a four-acre village with a recreation of Mt. Malady, the first hospital in North America, as well as the church where Pocahontas was baptized. Three more watchtowers and other settlement buildings will be constructed. There will also be a visitor center to provide orientation. Already in place is a fort with a watchtower and firing platforms, a wattle and daub settler's home (intended for six men since women didn't arrive in the colony until 1619) and a small fence-enclosed garden planted with corn and tobacco. There is also a $1^1/_4$-mile walking path along the James River. A free boat dock is available for those who travel to the park by water.

The Henricus Historical Park reconstructed area is open at no charge Thursday, Friday and Sunday NOON to 5:00 P.M. and Saturday 9:00 A.M. to 5:00 P.M. The park area is open March through October from 8:00 A.M. to 8:00 P.M. and until 6:00 P.M. the rest of the year.

A special Publick Day is held annually on the third Sunday in September. A lively celebration includes historical reenactors, colonial crafts, children's games and musket companies, a

Native American exhibit and period food like Indian corn soup, Brunswick stew, gingerbread cookies and sassafras tea.

Directions: From I-95 take Exit 61A, and travel east on Route 10 for about one block to Old Stage Road. Take Old Stage Road north for two miles to Coxendale Road and make a right; continue on that for a $1/_2$ mile to Henricus Road.

HOPEWELL

City Point Unit and Appomattox Manor

Who's Living on the Eppes's Lawn?

During the American Revolution, George Washington received the rank of lieutenant general. This rank was not bestowed again until late in the Civil War when on March 9, 1864, President Abraham Lincoln made Ulysses S. Grant general-in-chief of all Union armies, which included more than a half million soldiers across the United States.

Grant lost approximately 18,000 men at the Wilderness battlefield, roughly another 19,000 at Spotsylvania, where the fiercest 24-hour period of the war occurred at the "Bloody Angle," followed by about 12,000 more at Cold Harbor near Richmond. Nevertheless, Grant decided to cross the James River and attack Petersburg, the railroad center of the Confederacy. Much of General Robert E. Lee's supplies were brought from the deep South to his army through the Petersburg rail lines. Grant realized that if the rail lines were severed, Lee's supply line would be restricted which might hasten Lee's defeat.

For four days in June of 1864 Grant's army hit hard at the southern line just outside Petersburg. When the aggressive attack did not break the city's defenses Grant decided to dig in and start siege operations. Thus began a nine and a half-month siege, the longest siege in American history. Grant's headquarters was located at **City Point**, it soon became the largest logistical and supply operations of the entire war. During the Siege of Petersburg, City Point was one of the world's busiest ports. Enormous quantities of war materials were off-loaded at the half-mile stretch of wharves along the James River. These supplies provisioned over 100,000 Union troops and 65,000 animals. Tons of supplies were also shipped to the army by the railroad, which had supply lines leading directly to the front.

Telegraph lines linked Grant to the battlefront, Washington D.C. and other theaters of war. Seven hospitals were built at City Point, over 6,000 patients a day could be treated at the largest facility. Support facilities also included a bakery which produced more than 100,000 rations of bread each day.

President Lincoln met with Grant at his City Point headquarters on two occasions. In March and April, 1865, Lincoln spent two of the last three weeks of his life at City Point and nearby Petersburg and Richmond.

When you tour City Point it is fascinating to discover that Grant refused the spacious accommodations available in the Eppes's **Appomattox Manor** and lived in a tent from June until a crudely constructed officers' cabin was completed in November 1864. The cabin, which for a time stood in Fairmount Park, Philadelphia, has been moved back. It is located on the manor's east lawn and you can view the interior through the front door and windows.

Appomattox Manor, the ancestral home of the Eppes family since 1763, serves as a visitor contact station. The east wing and portions of the west wing were added around the central portion before the Civil War. Although there are 23 rooms, only three are open to the public and only two decorated with original Eppes's family furnishings. At the center you can view a 15-minute video, shown every half hour, on Grant and the supply system established at City Point. The attractive porch offers a view of both the river and grounds including several of the original outbuildings. There are six interpretive markers on the grounds.

The City Point Unit, which is part of the Petersburg National Battlefield, is open daily at no charge from 8:30 A.M. to 4:30 P.M. It is closed on Christmas and New Year's Day. If you have time you may want to take the Hopewell (see selection) and City Point Historic District Walking Tour. A map will point out houses occupied by Union generals and several other homes in the community that belonged to the Eppes family.

Directions: Take I-95 to the Hopewell Exit. Take Route 10 into Hopewell. Once you cross the Appomattox River, turn left at the second traffic signal onto Main Street, which will change into Appomattox Street. Follow Appomattox Street to Cedar Lane, turn left. At the end of Cedar Lane turn left into the National Park Service parking lot.

Hopewell New and Old

Historic Time Tunnel

You can explore Hopewell's history, enjoy the city's diverse neighborhoods and view wildlife at an island refuge. Tour options include walking tours of the City Point National Historic

District, self-guided driving tours of Crescent Hills, a ferry ride to see waterfowl and a boat excursion along the James River.

One of the newest additions on Hopewell's City Point National Historic District Walking Tour harkens back to the region's earliest days. The **City Point Early History Museum at St. Dennis Chapel** has artifacts that trace the history of regional Native Americans and colonial settlers. The story of the town, its inhabitants and illustrious visitors is examined from the past into the 20th century. Museum hours are Monday through Saturday 10:00 A.M. to 4:30 P.M. from April through October. A nominal admission is charged.

The town of City Point was established in 1613 by Englishman Sir Thomas Dale. City Point withstood Native American raids and Revolutionary War skirmishes. The town played a significant role during the Civil War (see City Point Unit selection). In 1923, City Point was annexed by the city of Hopewell.

St. Dennis Chapel was built in 1883 by sailors and marines who were anchored off City Point. Although the chapel was converted to a private residence in the early 1900s, restoration has brought back its ecclesiastical features including a stained-glass rose window and tall steeple.

The chapel is just one of the points of interest on the walking tour of the four-block historic district located at the confluence of the Appomattox and James rivers. Along the tour route are audiovisual exhibit centers that provide architectural and historical details of the houses you pass as well as information about the activities that occurred when City Point served as the headquarters of the Armies of the United States.

After your walking tour, take a self-guided driving tour through the 1920s **Crescent Hills** subdivision of Hopewell. M. T. Broyhill, founder of the real estate company that bore his name, needed up-scale residences for plant executives at ANCO (now Allied Signal Corporation) and others moving to the area because the industrial upsurge creating a housing demand that could not be met by existing communities. He felt the need was too acute to wait for the normal building schedule, so Broyhill ordered an entire subdivision of homes by mail from Sears, Roebuck and Company.

Broyhill ordered the Sears homes in a variety of models and his company customized each home for the buyer—adding a porch, changing a door or window treatment, reversing a floor plan and other modifications. The 40 custom-kit homes were built of high-quality materials and the subdivision is still one of Hopewell's most affluent and attractive neighborhoods. You can pick up a driving tour map at the Hopewell Visitor Center at Randolph Square on Route 10 (open daily, except major holidays, 9:00 A.M. to 5:00 P.M.), or by calling (800) 863-8680.

There are two options that will get you out on the water. One is a pedestrian ferry to **Presquile National Wildlife Refuge**. (The second is a boat excursion along the James and Appomattox rivers.) The island refuge is five miles north of Hopewell in the James River. In order to visit, call the refuge manager at (804) 733-8042, the only access is by a government owned and operated pedestrian ferry that leaves from the very end of Old Bermuda Hundred Road, State Route 827.

The two-mile-long island has a rich history. Native Americans hunted and fished on the island. English settlers established Bermuda Hundred here in the early 1600s, the first settlement established after Jamestown. In 1660, William Randolph moved to the island and lived here for many years. Many notable Virginians are related to Randolph including Thomas Jefferson, John Marshall and Robert E. Lee. During the Battle of Petersburg, Union troops used the island, then called Turkey Bend, as an observation post. In 1952, the island was bequeathed to the government by Dr. A.D. Williams, who had used the property as a country estate and dairy farm.

The island is now a resting spot for between 9,000 and 11,000 migrating Canada geese. The wetlands is also the winter home of wood ducks, black ducks and mallards. A farming program on the island provides forage for the migrating and resident wildlife. Winter flocks average 3,000 Canada geese and 1,000 ducks. A small number of bald eagles have been sighted nesting along the river and in trees beside the farm fields. White-tailed deer are frequently spotted, the more elusive red fox, muskrat, beaver, opossum, eastern grey squirrel and woodchuck are only occasionally glimpsed. There is a $3/4$-mile nature trail that will provide an opportunity to spot the waterfowl and wildlife. Be sure to bring binoculars. The best time to see a high population of waterfowl is from October through November (but it can be quite brisk, so bundle up). During the legal deer hunting season a portion of the refuge is open to hunters. The refuge office is open Monday through Friday from 7:30 A.M. to 4:00 P.M.

To take advantage of the second option, take an excursion aboard the *Pocahontas II*. Hopewell can claim its share of the Pocahontas legend, because the town was the home of her only granddaughter, Jane Rolfe Bolling. The original *Pocahontas* sailed on April 25, 1893 offering excursions on the James River between Richmond and Norfolk for $2.50. The boat nicknamed "Old Pokey" gave passengers ample time to savor the plantations along the lower James River. It was replaced in 1993 by a 65-foot cruise boat and the tradition of offering a narrated cruise through the heart of Plantation Country continues. Trips leave from Hopewell's city marina from April through October. You can enjoy a buffet meal or a moonlight party cruise. Call (800) 405-9990 for information and reservations.

200

Directions: From I-95, or I-295, take Route 10 east to Hopewell. Hopewell is 20 minutes from downtown Richmond and less than an hour from Williamsburg.

Weston Manor and Flowerdew Hundred Plantation

What a Wedding Gift!

Christian Eppes Gilliam, whose mother was descended from Pocahontas and whose cousin was married to Thomas Jefferson's daughter, was delighted with her wedding present. Who wouldn't be happy with a vast plantation overlooking the Appomattox River? By 1789 Christian and her husband William had completed **Weston Manor**, an elegant, formal 13-room dwelling—the very essence of the Tidewater plantation house.

The house was rich in architectural details and the land rich in history. In 1607, around the time Jamestown was settled, Captain Christopher Newport led an exploratory party 30 miles up the James River. They were entertained on the banks of the Appomattox River by Queen Opusoquoinuske and a group of Appomattox Indians. Later in 1635, the land on which they met was included in the 1,700 acres granted to Captain Francis Eppes by crown patent.

Weston Manor, the three-story colonial frame farmhouse that you see today is a classic example of Virginia Georgian architecture. The manor's distinctive moldings, wainscoting and chair rails are 85 percent original. The central arch accented with a paneled keystone in the 28-foot entrance hall is particularly attractive. The spiral stairway features concave paneling, a walnut handrail and hand-carved supports. The old heart-of-pine floor still shines despite its long and hard use. If you look closely you can see some of the original wooden floor pegs.

Although now beautifully restored and furnished with period reproductions, the house did suffer damage during the War Between the States. The house was shelled by a Northern gunboat. In fact, a cannonball was fired through the dining room window into the ceiling. It may well have served as a reminder of the hazards of war to the officers under General Grant's command who were billeted at Weston Manor during the siege of Petersburg. General Philip Sheridan was one of the officers quartered here. A windowpane scratched with his authenticated signature is displayed in the parlor.

Before its occupation by Union troops, Weston was the temporary residence of 12-year old Emma Wood, who kept a jour-

In 1618 Flowerdew Hundred was granted to Governor George Yeardley making it one of the New World's earliest English settlements. Around 1621 a windmill was built at Flowerdew. No traces of this windmill were found but a replica of an 18th-century windmill was added in 1978.

nal. Visitors hear about little Emma's wartime adventures and of post-war ghosts that "run rampant" in the manor.

Today this stately manor house serenely overlooks the Appomattox River. A community outdoor stage has been built on the riverbank. Sunday afternoon concerts are given during the summer months. Weston Manor is open for tours Monday through Saturday from 10:00 A.M. to 4:30 P.M. April through October. The tour lasts an hour and a nominal admission is charged.

Just downriver from Weston Manor on the south bank of the James is **Flowerdew Hundred**, one of the earliest English settlements in North America. The land originally inhabited by prehistoric people was granted to Governor George Yeardley in 1618. Secrets from the past have been uncovered by archeologists. Artifacts dating from 9000 B.C. to the Civil War era are on display in the Flowerdew Museum.

The visitor center/museum is located in the only pre-Civil War building, originally a schoolhouse, still standing. An 1820s detached plantation kitchen has been reconstructed on the foundations of the original kitchen. The guided tour encompasses this building and the windmill. In 1978, an 18th-century style windmill was built to commemorate the 1621 windmill. It illustrates windmill technology through the Revolutionary War. Flowerdew Hundred is a 1,400-acre working farm.

Flowerdew Hundred Plantation is open April through November, Tuesday through Sunday from 10:00 A.M. to 5:00 P.M. At other times it is open by appointment; call (804) 541-8897. Admission is charged. There are picnic facilities on the grounds.

Directions: From I-95 head south of Richmond to the Hopewell Exit, Route 10. Follow Route 10 into the city. Weston Manor is located near the Hopewell Yacht Club off 21st Avenue on the Appomattox River. There are Hopewell Historic Marker signs to direct you. For Flowerdew Hundred take Route 10 East (8 miles east of Hopewell). Turn left on Flowerdew Hundred Road, Route 639. The entrance is five miles off of Route 10.

LYNCHBURG

Anne Spencer House

At Home with the Arts

Anne Spencer, noted African American Virginia poet, was an individualist with a questing mind and an indomitable spirit. Her Lynchburg home reflects both. Tours of the **Anne Spencer House** are conducted by her only son, Chauncey Edward Spencer, whose reminiscences of his mother add a personal dimension few other homes on the National Register of Historic Places can match.

Chauncey is quick to point out, "Mother was the intellectual." It is readily apparent that her family and friends recognized and encouraged her creative muse. Her daily routine, after 26 years as a librarian at Dunbar High School, was clearly that of a thinker and poet. She worked in her flower garden and wrote in the garden cottage during the later afternoons. She would frequently stay in her garden cottage during dinner, eating from a tray while she worked long into the night.

The garden cottage was added by her husband, Edward Spencer, to give Anne a retreat where she could work undisturbed. The name she gave her cottage-studio, Edankraal (Ed and Ann's place), reveals their close relationship. Many of her poems touch on her love of flowers and her garden oasis. A tender sentiment is expressed in the following Anne Spencer poem:

He said:

"Your garden of dusk
is the soul of love
Blurred in its beauty
And softly caressing;
I, gently daring
This sweetest confessing
Say your garden at dusk
Is your soul, My Love."

Both the garden and house provide an intimate look at Anne Spencer. The house has remained as it was during the 72 years she lived here. It rings with her vibrant spirit. "Lines to a Nasturtium" is printed on a nasturtium decorated wallpaper that covers a kitchen cupboard.

The house was built for Edward Spencer and his family in 1901 and he continued to work for years expanding and decorating it. He added several guest rooms. The Spencers kept an open house for all those interested in meeting and talking with Anne Spencer. Travel for African Americans in the 1920s and '30s was difficult because so few accommodations were available. Their children often referred to their home as an overground, not underground, railroad. The Spencer home became a stopover for many political and literary figures. James Weldon Johnson, Field Secretary of the NAACP, was instrumental in thrusting Anne Spencer on the national horizon. He and H.L. Mencken sought a publisher for her poems. Johnson's friendship led to a wider circle of contacts.

Visitors to the Spencer home included Booker T. Washington,

Paul Robeson, Charles Gilpin, Marian Anderson, Dr. George Washington Carver, Langston Hughes, Carl Van Vechten, H.L. Mencken, Thurgood Marshall, W.E.B. DuBois, Martin Luther King, Jr., Jackie Robinson, Mary McCloed Bethune and many others. The Rev. Adam Clayton Powell and his bride honeymooned at the Spencer home.

The Anne Spencer House is open by appointment only. To arrange a visit call (804) 846-0517.

Directions: From I-95 in the Richmond area take Route 360 southwest to Burkeville. From there pick up Route 460 west to Lynchburg. At Lynchburg turn right on Route 501, then take the Buena Vista off ramp to Kemper Street. Take Kemper Street to 12th Street and turn right. Drive two blocks on 12th to Pierce Street and turn right. The Anne Spencer House is at 1313 Pierce Street. There is an Historical State Marker at the front of the house.

Point of Honor and Lynchburg Museum

Hill Street Greys

Lynchburg, which Thomas Jefferson described as "the most interesting spot in the state and the most entitled to general patronage for its industry, enterprise and correct course," has two important hills that bring in focus a great deal of its fascinating past. The first, a residential area known as Daniel's Hill, gets its name from Judge William Daniel, Jr., who inherited the property in 1839. Its handsome Federal-style mansion, situated on 737 acres overlooking the James River basin, was built by Dr. George Cabell, Sr., in 1815.

Dr. Cabell (you'll find a street named for him) called his place **Point of Honor** because he is said to have built his house on a dueling ground. He treated his most illustrious patient, Patrick Henry, with mercury—a remedy that neither cured nor comforted the patient. Dr. Cabell lost his life in 1823 from an injury sustained in a riding fall. His legacy, Point of Honor, remains.

Point of Honor was home to a number of prominent Lynchburg families after Judge Daniel lived there. Just before the War Between the States the mansion grounds were developed as a residential community. A five-block walk down Cabell Street includes ten points of interest, but Point of Honor is the neighborhood's most significant spot.

Picture a two-story house with long porches across the front on both the first and second floors. Point of Honor is not boxy but many-angled, so the porches meet octagonal bays not right angles. The polygonal rooms in these bays are light and airy because each has three large windows. You might think to look at Point of Honor that there is an architectural link with Thomas Jefferson's Poplar Forest that was being built at the same time just outside of Lynchburg. But although Jefferson and Cabell were friends there is no indication that Jefferson had any input in the design of Point of Honor.

Interior design touches to note include the wallpaper in the parlor, a copy of the 1814 original called "Monuments of Paris." The downstairs, or best, bedroom has an exact duplicate of the original bed hangings on the four-poster bed. The house and gardens can be toured 1:00 to 4:00 P.M. daily. A small admission is charged.

Lynchburg's second major hill was once owned by the city's founder, John Lynch. He sold the property to the city in 1805 for one dollar and the city built a courthouse on the site in 1814. Although the structure you see today is called the Old Court House, it is actually the second courthouse on the site, dating from 1855 Its design is based on the Parthenon and the stucco over the brick facade was scored to give it the look of sandstone.

Inside the Old Court House is the **Lynchburg Museum**. Its exhibits trace the development of Lynchburg from its early days as a hub of eastern markets and western mountain goods. The recreated 1855 Hustings courtroom represents the time when aldermen were elected to preside over and judge legal cases. The museum is open from 1:00 to 4:00 P.M. daily. There is a small admission charge.

If you take the Courthouse Hill walking tour, you will see 14 points of interest in all. One of them, Monument Terrace, is just across Court Street. You needn't climb the 135 steps of Monument Terrace in order to appreciate this city landmark. At the top of the terrace is a Confederate memorial and at the foot, a statue of a World War I soldier. The walking tour also takes you past four churches, a mere sampling of the city's total of 126 churches. It is no wonder that Lynchburg is often referred to as the city of churches.

Directions: From I-95 in the Richmond area take I-64 west to Charlottesville and then Route 29 south to Lynchburg. In Lynchburg continue on Route 29 Alternate. Proceed to Main Street and turn right onto Rivermont Avenue. Turn right again onto D Street and follow the signs to Point of Honor, located at Cabell and A streets. For the Lynchburg Museum take Cabell Street to the intersection with Rivermont Avenue and turn left on Rivermont. Take Rivermont to 5th Street and make a right, go one block to Court Street and turn left. The museum is at 9th and Court streets.

Poplar Forest and Miller-Claytor House

On Jefferson's Trail

The visionary design can be discerned despite the ruinous inroads time has inflicted on **Poplar Forest**, Jefferson's country retreat, 70 miles south of Monticello just outside Lynchburg. Restoration work still continues on the masterpiece Jefferson created at the peak of his architectural maturity.

Jefferson acquired the land through his wife, Martha Wayles Skelton Jefferson, whose father owned the Lynchburg acreage. Jefferson designed the house as an escape from the crush of visitors that engulfed him at Monticello. Based on a Palladian plan, the house has four equal octagonal rooms grouped around a square dining room with an overhead skylight. It was the first octagonal residence in the New World.

Work on Poplar Forest began in 1806, and in 1812 Jefferson said, "When finished, it will be the best dwelling house in the state, except that of Monticello; perhaps preferable to that, as more proportioned to the faculties of a private citizen."

You can imagine Jefferson reading in the bright, airy rooms. Today, Jefferson's private sanctuary where he said he enjoyed the "solitude of a hermit," is open to the public. Hours are 10:00 A.M. to 4:00 P.M. from April through November, Wednesday through Sunday. Closed on Thanksgiving. Group tours by appointment year-round; call (804) 525-1806.

When Jefferson traveled to Poplar Forest he often stopped for a visit at the **Miller-Claytor House**. You can add this stop to your outing. This modest house was the fourth house built in 1791 in the new town of Lynchburg. Legend has it that on one of Jefferson's visits he took a bite of a "love apple" growing in the yard. It is believed to be the first time that a tomato, generally considered poisonous, was eaten in this part of the country.

The Miller-Claytor House at Miller-Claytor Lane and Treasure Island Road in Riverside Park is open May through September, Thursday through Monday, from 1:00 to 4:00 P.M. To arrange a tour, call (804) 847-1459. There are 12 sites of interest along Rivermont Avenue. They include richly embellished private residences, Randolph-Macon Women's College and the Centenary United Methodist Church. Architecture runs the gamut from Beaux Arts to a Swiss Chalet style with Queen Anne influence.

Directions: From I-95 in the Richmond area take Route 360 southwest to Burkeville, then take Route 460 to Lynchburg. Or take I-64 west to Charlottesville, then Route 29 south to Lynchburg. The visitor center is at 12th and Church streets.

Jefferson's country retreat 70 miles from Monticello Poplar Forest was the New World's first octagonal residence. It was here Jefferson escaped the crush of visitors and enjoyed the "solitude of a hermit."

South River Meeting House

A Quiet Place

The history of the Lynch family and the **South River Meeting House** are entwined. John Lynch established a ferry service across the James River in 1757 near what is now Lynchburg. After the ferry prospered he divided 45 acres on the hills above the ferry house into town streets and lots. In 1786 Lynch obtained a charter that authorized the establishment of the town of Lynchburg and he sold the lots. He earmarked some of the land for community purposes. Two acres were set aside for a burial ground and a large hillside tract for the courthouse which cost the city only one dollar. At the time that John Lynch first settled in the area his mother, Sarah, had given two acres for the first Quaker meeting-house. In 1791 John provided ten acres for the third meeting-house, school and cemetery.

The stone meeting-house, begun in 1791 and completed in 1798, is what you see today. The earlier log structures were destroyed by fire. This is an economical and ecumenical house of worship. It passed from the Quakers to the Methodists, and then to the Presbyterians. Appearances changed with denominations, but the meeting-house has been restored to the way it looked in the 1790s.

Despite their generosity to their fellow Quakers, the founding family was not exempted from the strict discipline of their group. John Lynch's mother was "read out of meeting" because she married a non-Quaker. She was eventually reinstated in the fellowship, but two of her children were also "read out:" her oldest son, Charles, because he took an oath as a member of the House of Burgesses and John Lynch because he "too unguardedly gave way to a spirit of resentment."

It is interesting to learn that the term "Lynch Law" is derived from Charles Lynch's band of determined patriots who took the law into their own hands. Lynch organized and led a group of Virginians who protected their community from the lawless Tories. Malcontents who were captured were tried by the patriots and flogged; the sentence was never death. Although it was called Lynch Law, at the time it did not carry the connotation it does today. Colonel Charles Lynch was even commended for his service by the Virginia legislature, which at the same time exonerated him from all charges of acting outside the legal system.

Tours of this old meeting-house are conducted by volunteers wearing traditional Quaker garb. You'll see that this old church is divided into two distinct meeting-rooms to separate the sexes during the service. Each side conducted its own meeting and men and women could be "read out" by their own meeting. You'll learn how a Quaker meeting was conducted and what is was like to be a Quaker in Lynchburg in the 18th and early 19th century.

Just outside the meeting-house is the church burial ground. The Quakers did not hold burial services. You'll observe that there are no tombstones; the graves are marked with simple field stones. John Lynch, who died on Halloween in 1820, does, however, have a marker on his grave. It was placed there by the city of Lynchburg.

You can arrange to visit the South River Meeting House from 9:00 A.M. to 4:00 P.M. daily. At least three days prior notice is needed for a costumed guide; call (804) 239-2548.

While you're in Lynchburg you may want to visit the Thomas Road Baptist Church where Pastor Jerry Falwell has seen his congregation grow from 31 members to 21,000. He built Liberty College on 4,000 acres overlooking Lynchburg. In 1971 Lynchburg Baptist College had 100 students; it expects to have 50,000 by the year 2000.

Directions: From I-95 in the Richmond area take Route 360 southwest to Burkeville, then take Route 460 west to Lynchburg. From Route 460 take Candlers Mountain Road, Route 128, west.

At Wards Road and Candlers Mountain Road intersection continue straight ahead; the road becomes Sheffield Drive. Turn right onto Fenwick Drive from Sheffield Drive and right again on Fort Avenue. The South River Meeting House is at 5810 Fort Avenue.

NELSON COUNTY

Crabtree Falls and Woodson's Mill

Highest Falls East of the Mississippi River

There are those who argue that **Crabtree Falls** is technically not a waterfall but a series of five striking major cascades and a series of smaller ones that, in total, tumble a staggering 1,200 feet. Just to give you a contrast, the height of Niagara Falls' Horseshoe Falls (the wider of the two) is 162 feet, while the American Falls is 167 feet.

The hiking trail that leads to the falls offers numerous scenic delights. The trail crosses an arched wooden bridge spanning the Tye River and meanders through the forest to the first overlook just 700 feet from the lower parking lot (off Route 56). It continues up the mountainside to additional overlooks. If you make it to the top, you'll have a splendid panoramic view of the mountains surrounding you and the cascading falls at your feet. The trail ends at Crabtree Meadows, but a half mile past the open meadow there is a link-up with the Appalachian Trail.

The water is highest at the falls from winter through spring, but fall is a colorful season to hike this trail. Good hiking boots or comfortable walking shoes are recommended. The trail does get icy during the winter months so exercise caution.

If you head south of Crabtree Falls, you can visit **Woodson's Mill**, which is on the National Register of Historic Places. Historians consider this a significant example of a still-operational 19th-century mill. For the past two centuries—though not continuously—wheat, corn and other grains have been ground by water power from Piney River. Currently five tons a week are ground at Woodson's Mill.

The mill, originally called "Big Piney Mill" was constructed in 1794 by Guiliford Campbell. Only the foundation remains of that first mill. The present structure was completed in 1845 and expanded soon after the Civil War. It is a four-story post-and-beam double overshot gristmill, one of the few of its kind in the country. In 1900 the mill was purchased by Dr. Julian Woodson, who was a medical doctor, a dentist and a miller. His mill became such a center of community life that it may have contributed to his later election as state senator.

There were a number of decades when the mill stood idle, but in 1983 it was purchased by J. Gill Bokenbrough, Jr. who is president of the First Colony Coffee and Tea Company of Norfolk. The head miller is Steve Roberts of Massies Mill. Today two water wheels run the mill: a small Fitz-type wheel that provides the mill's electricity and the large $12^1/_2$-foot steel Fitz wheel that drives the two runs of millstones. Woodson's Mill is open on Saturday from 8:00 A.M. to 3:00 P.M. There is an operational cider press at the mill and picnic tables on the grounds.

If you head northeast from Crabtree Falls you will reach **Wintergreen Resort**, an excellent spot from which to explore Nelson County. This year-round vacation mecca has 36 holes of championship golf, 17 ski slopes and trails, 25 tennis courts, an indoor-outdoor spa, 30 miles of marked hiking trails plus riding trails, six swimming pools and a 20-acre lake. Day guests may use many of the recreational facilities; for information call (804) 325-2200. The resort hosts a wide range of special events.

Directions: From I-64 take Exit 99 (Afton Mountain) and follow the signs to the Blue Ridge Parkway south. Stay on the parkway to Route 56 east. Turn left on Route 56 and follow the signs to Crabtree Falls. From I-81 take the Raphine exit. Turn east onto Route 56 toward Steeles Tavern. Cross the Blue Ridge Parkway and continue on Route 56 to Crabtree Falls. For Woodson's Mill continue west on Route 56 to the intersection with Route 151, then head south on Route 151/56. Turn right on Route 778 and head west for two miles to Lowesville. The mill is on the left just across the river. For Wintergreen, at the intersection of Routes 56 and 151, head north on Route 51, then bear left on Route 664. Wintergreen is between Blue Ridge Parkway mileposts 13 and 14 (see Blue Ridge Parkway selection). For more information call the Nelson County Division of Tourism at (800) 282-8223.

Swannanoa

Opulent Love Nest

Swans mate for life and this romantic constancy appealed to Sallie May Dooley. You can see her fondness for swans at Maymont, the Dooleys' Richmond home (see selection) and in their palace atop Afton Mountain. Major James Dooley named the $2 million summer home **Swannanoa** as a testament to their love.

Dooley, an executive with the Chesapeake and Ohio Railroad Company, hired more than 300 artisans to build the 52-room marble palace. Work began on this Virginia replica of the Villa de Medici in Rome in 1903 and was completed in 1912. The affection that James Dooley bore his wife is evident in the numerous likenesses of her that grace the mansion. There is a 4,000-piece stained-glass window created by Tiffany for $100,000 that portrays her image in the midst of Swannanoa's Italian Garden. Her likeness can also be seen in the fresco on the domed ceiling above the staircase. The mansion's Italian Renaissance style is apparent in the Carrara and red Sienna marble entrance hall.

On the first floor there is a Florentine-style dining room with tooled leather-covered walls and a carved and coffered ceiling. The adjoining breakfast room has frescos of morning glories on the walls. It is thought the major choose the Latin quotations that are carved in the library's woodwork. The most formal room is the Louis XV ballroom with its original gold damask wallcovering and ceiling painting. The marble mantel is signed by the artist who worked at Maymont, Rafael Romanelli. He carved exquisite cherubs; one is seen throwing a piece of wood into the fire while another blows it with the bellows. The Persian Room was Major Dooley's private study. Decorative appointments are from the Far East including the teak wood mantel, window and doorfacings.

After the Dooleys both died in the early 1920s, the estate was purchased by a golf and country club. The club's decorating sense left something to be desired; it painted the walls and the white marble a drab brown color and covered the hand-carved oak mantles with the same nondescript hue. After the club lost its backing in the stock market crash, Swannanoa was abandoned for 15 years. There are stories from the 1930s of cows roaming the halls and children roller skating in the house. In 1948, it was leased by Walter and Lao Russell, founders of the University of Science and Philosophy.

The Russells were on their honeymoon looking for an ideal place for their work and teaching. When she saw Swannanoa, Mrs. Russell ignored its deterioration, insisting that she recognized it from a vision that had come to her two years earlier. Within six months they had restored the estate sufficiently (including removing the layers of brown paint) to open it to the public as a World Cultural Center. It was the Russells' belief that science and religion were in harmony, not at odds. Students came from around the globe to study their "Science of Man."

The Russells were an exceptional couple. Although Walter left school when he was nine, he became an architect, scientist, sculptor, painter, musician and author. There was a considerable age difference between Walter and Lao; he was 77 when they married and she was 43, yet she always said he was the

Major James Dooley built a 52-room marble palace as a testament to his love for his wife, Sallie May Dooley. Years later it became the home of Walter and Lao Russell, founders of the University of Science and Philosophy.

youngest man she knew. When Walter was in his sixties he became a champion figure skater. At age 69 his competition was all under the age of 30 and he won three first prizes. Russell designed several hotels in New York including the first Hotel

Pierre. He received a doctorate of science and was noted as the official sculptor and painter for Theodore Roosevelt and Franklin D. Roosevelt. Mrs. Lao Russell was also a sculptor, author, teacher, lecturer and, for 40 years, the president and managing director of The University of Science and Philosophy at Swannanoa. Walter died in 1963 and Lao in 1988, but the Russells' presence is still strongly felt at Swannanoa.

In the gold ballroom, one of Lao Russell's favorite rooms, is the original clay model of the head of the Christ figure sculpture. Walter sculpted the figure including the head, but Lao did not feel he was capturing the facial contours satisfactorily so after he went to bed she would slip downstairs and change his work on the head, doing all the final shaping. Many of the large paintings on the walls cover holes that were made when the estate was derelict and people took clippings out of the silk damask walls. In the center of the ballroom is the *Four Freedoms*, a large sculpture Walter Russell did for President Franklin D. Roosevelt. Also on view is his painting the *Might of Ages* with figures from history such as Columbus, Napoleon, Washington and Sitting Bull. Another of Walter Russell's sculptural masterpieces is the Mark Twain Memorial. The furnishings, artwork and books you see were all added by the Russells.

The terraced gardens spread out behind the palace. Here too you'll discover the Russells' sculpture. From the vision that brought them to this mountaintop home, they created *The Christ of the Blue Ridge*. Mrs. Russell believed she saw Christ looking over a valley, and that the valley proved to be Rockfish Valley which Swannanoa overlooks. The garden also has a marble-columned pergola, a meditation pond with fish and a "peace pole" inscribed with four languages.

Swannanoa is open daily year-round from 9:00 A.M. to 5:00 P.M. Visitors can tour the first floor and gardens, or take an extended tour of all three floors and the mansion's tower. Admission is charged and there is an added fee for the extended tour.

Directions: From I-64 take Exit 99; bear to the right on Route 250 and follow the signs to Route 610 and the entrance to Swannanoa.

Walton's Mountain Museum and Oak Ridge Estate

Hamner Nailed His Subject

Earl Hamner, Jr., author of the fictional account of the Waltons popularized on television, grew up in Depression-era Schuyler (pronounced Sky-ler), in the shadow of the Blue Ridge Mountains. This rural town now has about 300 people, but once it was a bustling community with a soapstone plant that employed 1,500 people. The plant is no longer operational but you can see the post office, convenience store and several churches. It's the old Schuyler Elementary School that travelers come to see—it has been converted to the **Walton's Mountain Museum**.

The school that Earl and his brothers and sisters attended is now a museum dedicated to the popular television show based on Hamner's fictional account of his childhood experiences. Earl Hamner, Jr. is the original John-Boy and the museum includes replicas of sets from the show. You'll recognize the bedroom where John-Boy retreated to write. An Underwood like the one that Earl Hamner, Jr. used when he began writing lends a note of authenticity as does the 1930s period furniture. The bedroom has a display case filled with memorabilia sent by Earl Hamner and cast members. In the case is the Emmy awarded to Hamner, photographs of the cast and the Hamner family, dolls representing characters on the show and stories about the show.

Fans of the show will also recognize the kitchen where meals were prepared over an old wood cookstove like the one you'll see. The family sat on long benches at an identical wooden table. A wooden icebox and antique hutch complete the picture. It's easy to picture John and Olivia surrounded by their children in the living room with its sofa and stuffed chairs. There is also the Atwater Kent radio and organ that Ben often played. Visitors linger longest in Ike Godsey's Store with its drink box, scales and barrels of penny candy. This now doubles as a gift shop and locally crafted items are sold. The museum shows a 30-minute "Waltons" documentary that has interviews with Hamner and cast members plus clips from the show.

The Walton's Mountain Museum is open daily March through November from 10:00 A.M. to 4:00 P.M. Admission is charged. The museum has a special resource center with a 380-volume collection of Hamner's scripts, diaries and other writings. The collection is not open to the general public but may be used by researchers; call (804) 831-2000.

To the west of Walton's Mountain Museum is the home of another Nelson County native who made good, Thomas Fortune Ryan. Orphaned at age 10, he was raised by his mother's family, the Fortunes. When he left Nelson County at age 17, he soon proved the prophetic significance of this family name, embarking on a career as a financier and stock investor. He became one of the ten wealthiest men in the country with a net estate of more than $130 million. Ryan was director, share holder or officer of the Morgan Guaranty Trust, the Southern Railroad, American Tobacco Company and Equitable Insurance. He owned vast rubber plantations in Mexico and diamond mines in Africa. He was one of the most substantial Catholic philanthropist in America. He amassed a renowned art collection.

In 1901, Ryan purchased the **Oak Ridge Estate**, once owned by merchant and tobacco planter Robert Rives. Rives sold goods to Jefferson's estate and his son studied with the great man at Monticello. The influence of Jefferson's architectural ideas can be seen at Oak Ridge, particularly in the outbuilding used as an office by Rives and Ryan.

When Ryan purchased Oak Ridge he added two wings and a third floor to the 1802 Rives manor house. He also constructed more than 80 outbuildings including a rare rotunda Crystal Palace-style greenhouse, carriage house, railroad station, three-story farm manager's house, children's cottage, chauffeur's garage, dairy complex and springhouse/teahouse. Ryan added the latest technology to his estate; he had his own power plant to generate electricity as well as a 700,000-gallon water reservoir. Ryan's goal was to make his estate a showplace for farming, livestock, agricultural technology and gardening. To further the latter goal he added a formal Italian garden and rose garden. To provide recreational diversion there was an indoor horse training track and a mile-long race track which plans to open again when restoration is complete.

The first floor rooms have been restored to the splendor of the Ryan years. Some three-quarters of the furnishings are from Ryan's residency, with a few reminders of earlier owners. The floors are original (from 1908) and are appropriately made from oak. All but one of the 12 fireplaces, each a distinctive design, are operational. In the parlor, highlighting the property's antebellum history, are the handwritten will of Robert Rives and an inventory of the mansion made at his death in 1845. The stained-glass windows on the stair landings feature oak leaves and acorns, a motif that can be seen throughout the house.

Items in the library, or antebellum sitting room, represent the era of Thomas Fortune Ryan's ownership. His estate was the first in the county to have phone service and an Oak Ridge Telephone directory recalls that distinction. There are also photographs from the period and an original obituary of Ryan. In 1907 Ryan underwrote a series of reproductions for the Jamestown Exposition (see Norfolk Naval Base selection). The collection included 23 portraits of English kings and queens, statesmen and explorers plus Pocahontas in English dress. After the Exposition the pictures hung at Oak Ridge for 30 years before they were donated to the University of Virginia. Several have been loaned back to Oak Ridge and hang in the library and other rooms. On the mantel is a bust of Thomas Ryan made in 1909 by Auguste Rodin.

It is thought that the John Barry Room, named for a relative of

Ryan's first wife, was the bedroom of Robert Rives. Later it served as Ryan's private office. The room now has memorabilia of Commodore Barry, a distinguished naval captain in the American Revolution. He received commendations from George Washington and is credited with establishing the peacetime navy after independence from England. The mahogany-paneled dining room, with Ryan's original table, was the scene of lavish entertainment. Tradition holds that although he served his guests elegant multicourse dinners, his favorite meal was pig's feet and salad greens. Rooms added by Ryan to the original Federal-style dwelling include the spacious formal drawing room and the more casual breakfast room, with its own paintings of the estate from 1908.

In 1989, the 4,800 acre Oak Ridge estate was acquired by the Holland family. Work continues on the mansion's upstairs rooms, the outbuildings and gardens. The estate is the largest property now under historic restoration in Virginia. Guided tours of the mansion's first floor and the immediate plantation grounds are available by reservation; call (804) 263-8676. The estate is also open to walk-in visitors when festivals and living history events are scheduled.

Directions: From I-64 at Charlottesville, take Route 29 south. Then take Route 6 east; midway between Faber and Esmont take Route 800 south to Schuyler. The museum is on Route 800 at the intersection with Route 17. For Oak Ridge Estate, return to Route 29 and head south to Lovingston. Just past Lovingston take Route 653 east (Oak Ridge Road) for 2.4 miles to the Oak Ridge Estate entrance.

ORANGE COUNTY

Montpelier

Our Father's Keeper

President James Madison's **Montpelier**, acquired by the National Trust for Historic Preservation in 1984, was the last home of one of America's Founding Fathers to pass into public hands. This 2,700-acre estate in Virginia's Piedmont affords a tantalizing glimpse of the Madison family plantation. But you need to realize that this plantation is presented in a distinctly different manner than more familiar sites like Washington's Mount Vernon and Jefferson's Monticello. Montpelier is a work in progress—ongoing archeological work is revealing new facets of the plantation grounds while architectural historians are still uncover-

217

ing new dimensions to the mansion. Many of the rooms are unfinished and unfurnished. Several of the lavishly appointed rooms represent the duPont years, the final private owners of the estate.

James Madison's family arrived in Virginia in 1653 and his grandfather acquired and settled the Montpelier estate in 1723. James (who was actually Jr.) was born on March 15, 1751, the eldest of 12 children. He was educated and pursued a career in law and politics. There are historians who claim that America's greatest contribution to western civilization is the thinking of James Madison. His work in formulating and winning approval for the Constitution and Bill of Rights shaped the framework for modern democracy not only in the United States but around the world.

Madison's public service career spanned 53 years. He served as a delegate to the Continental Congress. He was a member of the Virginia House of Delegates, a United States congressman, Thomas Jefferson's secretary of state and United States president from 1809 to 1817. After his second presidential term, Madison retired to Montpelier with his wife Dolley, whom he had married in 1794. He died breakfasting in the dining room on June 28, 1836.

The Montpelier mansion has changed a great deal over the years, but docents help you see the stages of the main house beginning with the central and earliest portion of the house that was built in 1760 for James Madison, Sr. After James and Dolley were wed they moved into one wing of the house, with her son John Payne Todd by her first marriage. For the first five years that Montpelier was open to the public, it was thought that the newlyweds occupied what was essentially a duplex in the northern section of the mansion. But archeological research uncovered an interior doorway indicating the two suites were connected.

During the last years of his father's life, James began work on a 30-foot addition to the northeast end of the house. The dining room was added and the front portico work was completed by 1800. Nine years later, additional projects were launched including interior renovation and the addition of one-story wings at each end of the house. The mansion's first inside kitchens were in the basements of these wings. After consulting with his good friend, Thomas Jefferson, Madison had the entire mansion stuccoed.

After the death of her husband, Dolley Madison moved to Washington. She sold Montpelier in 1844; most of the furniture had already been sold at auction. For over five decades the estate changed hands frequently, until in 1901 it was purchased by William duPont, Sr. The duPont family made significant alterations and additions to the house and grounds. The last owner, Marion duPont Scott, added a steeplechase course. The Montpelier Hunt Races that she inaugurated are still held the first weekend each November.

When you visit, you will view a brief audiovisual program on Madison's career before touring the first floor of the 55-room mansion. Some of the rooms reflect the senior Madisons and the 1760s, during the president's youth. The post White House years are captured in other rooms with furnishings from the 1820s. The lifestyle of the senior duPonts during the Gilded Age is depicted in the Morning Room and Adam Room. These rooms are noted for ornate plasterwork, elaborate chandeliers, embossed silk wallpaper and other elegant decorative touches. The distinctive Art Deco period is captured in Marion duPont Scott's Red Room with photomurals of her beloved horses. After touring the house, wander through the two-acre garden, with its photogenic temple, added by Madison in 1811. Madison took the extravagant step of hiring a French gardener, who was paid a generous $700 a year. Madison's terraced garden covered four acres, including the two-acre formal area that has been restored by the Garden Club of Virginia. You can also take a tree walk, using a self-guided brochure that pinpoints over 40 species of trees. Madison introduced trees and exotic plants from around the world, like the large cedar of Lebanon at the entrance to the formal garden. With all the changes the main house experienced over the years, one constant was the unobstructed view from the portico of the Blue Ridge Mountains. The grounds fluctuated from the early days as a colonial-era working plantation to the later country equestrian years. You will see elements from each as you drive around the 2,700-acre estate past more than 100 buildings. They include smaller houses, barns, a bowling alley, stables and a family cemetery where both James and Dolley Madison are buried. Much of the acreage is open pasture and the stables are still filled with horses.

Montpelier is open daily March through December from 10:00 A.M. to 4:00 P.M. and weekends only in January and February. It is closed on Thanksgiving, Christmas and New Year's Day. There is a well-stocked Country Store Museum Shop with a nearby picnic area. Admission is charged.

Directions: From I-95 take the Fredericksburg exit and proceed west on Route 3 to the intersection with Route 20. Make a left on Route 20 to Orange. Montpelier is four miles southwest of Orange on Route 20.

Orange County

Paint the Town Orange

Virginia's largest county, created in 1734, extended to the Mississippi River in the west and north to the Great Lakes. Orange

County not only encompassed great distances, it also witnessed great events and was home to great men. Lieutenant Governor Alexander Spotswood took charge of the Virginia colony in 1710. Four years later he settled with a group of German immigrants on the banks of the Rapidan River, in what two decades later would be Orange County. His palatial home and the settlement were both called Germanna. When William Byrd of Westover (see selection) visited the mines and furnaces, he called Spotswood's home "The Enchanted Castle." The remains of Fort Germanna and Spotswood's home are being excavated and studied.

In 1716, Spotswood led a group of settlers over the Blue Ridge Mountains. He wanted to show his colonists that the mountains could be crossed and that rich land lay waiting for them. Spotswood called the prominent men who traveled with him the Knights of the Golden Horseshoe. One of the Knights was James Taylor II, who patented 13,500 acres, which included most of what is today the town of Orange. His 1722 house, Bloomsbury, still stands (it is not, however, open to the public). Two of Taylor's great-grandsons became president of the United States: Zachary Taylor (born in Orange County) and James Madison (see Montpelier selection).

While the area had only a peripheral brush with the American Revolution—a British raiding party scoured the area for several days and Lafayette marched through the county—it was the scene for numerous engagements during the Civil War. In 1862 a skirmish was fought in the town streets of Orange. Two railroad lines that supplied the Confederates ran through the county and the area had several soldiers' hospitals. The Army of Northern Virginia retired to Orange County for nine months after Gettysburg. General Robert E. Lee repulsed Grant when his Army of the Potomac crossed the Rapidan River into Orange County in the fall of 1863. Both armies then spent the winter camped across from each other along the river's banks. Lee and his staff officers attended St. Thomas' Episcopal Church in Orange.

With spring, the Union army under Grant recrossed the Rapidan into the eastern region known as the Wilderness. The armies met in one of the bloodiest battles of the war (see Wilderness Battlefield selection). Although that battle was a costly draw at best for Grant, he continued his attacks in Virginia driving first to Richmond and then on to Appomattox.

There are many reminders of Orange County's rich past. The **James Madison Museum** honors the country's fourth president and the man who was primarily responsible for the drafting and ratification of the U.S. Constitution and its Bill of Rights. Exhibits reveal the many facets of Madison's life, including many personal possessions from James and Dolley Madison's nearby home, Montpelier.

One of the focal pieces is Madison's favorite chair made from campeachy wood, a type of mahogany grown in Mexico. Other exhibited pieces include a four-poster bed, chest, game table and library table. There are books from Madison's own collection and correspondence from his years as president. Fashions worn by Dolley Madison are also exhibited. A short video is shown on Montpelier, Madison's life-long home.

In addition to the historical exhibits about Madison, the museum also has a Hall of Agriculture with early farm equipment and machinery and a restored 1730s "Patent" house. This is singularly appropriate as Madison was described by Jefferson as the "best farmer in the world" because of his innovative farming methods. Farm equipment on exhibit includes a reaper, seed cleaner, corn sheller, wooden cider press, fodder cutter, husker, wagon and several varieties of plows.

The James Madison Museum, 129 Caroline Street, is open year-round on weekdays 9:00 A.M. to 4:00 P.M. and on weekends from March through November from 1:00 to 4:00 P.M. It is closed on weekends from December through February and on major holidays. Admission is charged.

Right beside the museum is **St. Thomas Episcopal Church**. This church was built in 1833–34 according to plans designed by Thomas Jefferson for Christ Church, Charlottesville. Jefferson's church was built in 1824 and torn down in 1895. St. Thomas Episcopal Church, the only surviving example of Jefferson's ecclesiastical design, is based on Chalgrin's St. Philippe de Roule, a church Jefferson admired in Paris. It is likely that the church in Orange was built by one or more of the master builders who worked with Jefferson at Monticello and the University of Virginia. These artisans worked in the Orange area during the 1820s and 1830s and were responsible for the duplication of Jefferson's architectural designs throughout the region. The church window on the left side near the front was done by Tiffany; it is just one of the church's many vibrant stained-glass windows.

In addition to serving as a house of worship during the Civil War, it also was used as a hospital and shelter following the Battles of Cedar Mountain, Fredericksburg, Chancellorsville, the Wilderness and Spotsylvania Courthouse. St. Thomas' Church is included on the Virginia Landmarks Register and the National Register of Historic Places.

A walking tour route (copies can be picked up at the adjacent museum) begins in front of the church and encompasses the historic sights in Orange, now designated a Historic Main Street Community. The route is $1^1/_2$ miles long and passes 21 points of interest. While you explore Main Street, stop at the **Ed Jaffe Gallery** to see the work of this internationally known sculptor.

Gallery hours are Thursday, Friday and Saturday from 11:00 A.M. to 5:00 P.M.

After exploring the town of Orange, head south to nearby Gordonsville (here too you will find a self-guided walking tour handout). Just off Main Street is the **Exchange Hotel Civil War Museum**. The spacious columned veranda of the 1860 Greek Revival hotel beckons visitors as it once welcomed passengers alighting from the Virginia Central and Orange & Alexandria Railway in the pre-war years. Civil War skirmishes and battles in the Orange County area resulted in this hotel being transformed into the Gordonsville Receiving Hospital. Trainloads of Confederate wounded were unloaded at the hotel's railroad platform. In 1864 alone, 23,000 men were treated at the hospital, including 6,000 in one month. The grounds became a sea of mud, tents and crude sheds while the surrounding fields were mass burial grounds for more than 700 soldiers. The hotel's once gleaming floors were blood stained, the stairways gouged and the paint faded.

With war's end, the railroad resumed passenger service, the hotel was renovated and business again flourished. With the railroad's demise in the 1940s, the hotel went into a steady decline and within several decades was as derelict as it had been in 1865. It wasn't until the 1970s that local residents recognized the hotel's historic significance and restored it to its former glory. Some of the rooms are decorated to recall the hotel years while others serve as exhibit rooms for Civil War memorabilia including weapons, uniforms, battle flags, medical equipment, surgeons' tools and period photographs. The third floor rooms reflect the years that the hotel served as a hospital with a four-bed ward room and an actual operating table.

The museum is open Tuesday through Saturday 10:00 A.M. to 4:00 P.M. from mid-March through December. During the summer months it is open Sunday 12:30 to 4:30 P.M. Closed on major holidays. Admission is charged.

There was one area ruin that couldn't be rebuilt or restored and that was the mansion Thomas Jefferson designed for James Barbour, who served as governor of Virginia from 1812 to 1814. The house burned on Christmas Day in 1884 but the massive brick walls and columns remain standing. The **Barboursville Ruins** are just west of Gordonsville on Route 33 on the grounds of the **Barboursville Winery**. These dramatic ruins provide an exciting backdrop for the Four County Players' August weekend productions of "Shakespeare at the Ruins."

The Zonin family, who now owns the winery, live in the brick dependence that the Barbour family renovated after the fire. Four Zonin brothers continue the wine tradition begun by their family in Italy more than a century ago. In 1976 they expanded their operation to Virginia, where Thomas Jefferson once dreamed of developing a flourishing wine industry. Roughly 100 acres of their 830-acre property are currently planted and plans are to expand. Luca Paschina, the General Manager and Winemaker, was trained in Alba, Italy. Be sure to stop at the winery and sample its award-winning wines. Barboursville Vineyards is open for tastings and sales Monday through Saturday from 10:00 A.M. to 5:00 P.M. and Sunday 11:00 A.M. to 5:00 P.M.

If you are in the Gordonsville area around lunch or dinner, be sure to stop at the Toliver House Restaurant, renowned for their fried chicken and traditional southern cuisine. The restaurant is at 209 N. Main Street; for reservations or additional information call (540) 832-3485. For information on Orange County sites and events call the Visitors Bureau, (540) 672-1653.

Directions: From I-95 at Fredericksburg, take Route 3 exit west. Turn left on Route 20 for Orange; this will become Main Street when you enter town. To reach Gordonsville head south on Route 15. For Barboursville head west on Route 33. Turn left on Route 777 and you will soon see the entrance for Barboursville Vineyards.

PETERSBURG

Blandford Church

Memorial Day Birthplace

Memorial Day observances began at **Blandford Church** on Well's Hill in Petersburg, Virginia, on June 9, 1865 and not on the last weekend in May as it is observed today. It was the following year that Mary Cunningham Logan, wife of General John A. Logan, saw young school girls placing flowers on the graves of slain Confederate soldiers on May 26th, the day set aside by Mississippi to commemorate the fallen. When Mrs. Logan learned from the girls' headmistress, Nora Davidson, that they intended to hold a "Decoration Day" every year, she urged her husband to propose extending the gesture nationwide. As commander-in-chief of the Grand Army of the Republic, General Logan spearheaded the work for the establishment of an official Memorial Day. His objective was achieved when, by Act of Congress, the occasion was first celebrated across the country on May 30, 1868.

The history of Old Blandford Church does not start with the War Between the States. The church, the oldest building in Petersburg, was built in 1735. The earliest date on a gravestone is

1702. It marks the grave of Richard Yarbrough, who died at the age of 87. When the British lost the Revolutionary War, the Church of England (or Protestant Episcopal Church as it was then called) lost members. In the year 1799 only six services were held at Blandford Church, one a memorial service for George Washington. The church was abandoned entirely by 1819.

The city of Petersburg added a new roof to the deteriorating building in 1882. But is was not until 1901 that the Ladies Memorial Association of Petersburg undertook its reconstruction. During the Civil War, Blandford Church had served as a hospital for wounded Confederate soldiers. More than 30,000 Confederate dead were laid to rest in the church cemetery. To honor these sons of the South the Ladies Association of Petersburg commissioned Louis Comfort Tiffany to design windows for the rebuilt church, one for each of the southern states plus the three border states of Maryland, Missouri and Kentucky. Each state had to raise the money for its window (about $400).

Louisiana's window, commissioned and paid for by the Washington Artillery of New Orleans, was the only regiment represented. All the states paid except divided Kentucky which had already arranged its own memorial. Tiffany donated the 15th window, the "Cross of Jewels." This window, even more than his other works, has the iridescence of jewels. Tiffany, an experienced chemist, developed a unique technique for adding crushed copper, gold and cobalt for special depth and lustre. No one has ever been able to duplicate Tiffany's artistic creations. On the morning after his death, at his direction, his formula and notes were destroyed.

The church contains several memorial plaques. One honors the men who lost their lives in the Battle of the Crater. Their gallant commander, General William Mahone, who led the crater charge is, at his request, buried in the churchyard with the unknown Confederate soldier. A plaque on the church wall has a poem attributed to the Irish actor Tyrone Power, grandfather of the Hollywood star, written before the restoration when the church was still in ruins.

> Thou art crumbling to the dust, old pile,
> Thou art hastening to thy fall,
> And 'round thee in thy loneliness
> Clings the ivy to thy wall
> The worshippers are scattered now
> Who knelt before thy shrine,
> And silence reigns where anthems rose,
> In days of "Auld Lang Syne."

The historic graveyard has been the scene of more than one duel. On one notable occasion two suitors, R.C. Adams and

James B. Boisseau, fought for the affections of Ellen Stimson and were both mortally wounded. Dr. Ira Ellis Smith, who was called to their sides, failed to save his patients, but he saved Miss Stimson by marrying her.

You can visit daily from 10:00 A.M. to 5:00 P.M. Admission is charged.

Directions: Take I-95 to Petersburg. Take the Wythe Street Exit and go east on Wythe Street for one block, then turn right on Crater Road, Route 301-460. Blandford Church is located on Crater Road at Rochelle Lane.

Centre Hill Mansion and Trapezium House

Front and Centre but No Right Angles

Two totally different homes in Old Towne Petersburg evoke the 19th century. **Centre Hill**, overlooking the town, is the third hilltop home of the wealthy Bolling family. In 1823 when Robert Bolling was 64, he built Centre Hill for his fourth wife. The architectural eclecticism of Petersburg is nowhere more evident than at Centre Hill, built in the Federal style but remodeled twice. Robert Buckner Bolling who inherited the house from his father in the late 1840s added a Greek Revival look to Centre Hill. At the turn of the century, Mr. and Mrs. Charles Hall Davis purchased the house and remodeled it along the then-popular Georgian Revival style.

It is the affluent era before the siege of Petersburg that is recreated today at Centre Hill. Your entrance to the house is less dramatic than it would have been in the 1850s. Entrance is through the basement where one can view a service tunnel. This tunnel was used as an entryway to the house by the slaves who used the basement as a work area.

Centre Hill has some unique furnishings. On the marble mantlepiece is a clock commemorating Lord Nelson's victory at the Battle of the Nile. In the dining room is the forerunner of the wet bar, a zinc sink, ideal for wine and beverages. But it is the 24-karat, gold-trimmed dinner service that has an interesting story. If you think you have troubles with delivery service today, consider that it took five years for these dishes to get here from the Minton factory in England. The ship on which they were sent had to bypass the Union naval blockade around Petersburg. Then the shipment had to be smuggled past Grant's forces surrounding the city. The dishes finally were delivered during the Christmas season of 1864 and by that time there was no food to serve on them. During that Christmas season there were only "starvation balls."

The President's Room is an upstairs bedroom named in honor of the day in May 1909 when incumbent William Howard Taft rested here after dedicating the Pennsylvania Monument in Petersburg. He was the third president to visit Centre Hill. John Tyler visited as a personal friend of the Bollings. Abraham Lincoln stopped once to confer with General George Z. Hartsuff when this was his Petersburg headquarters.

You too can visit Centre Hill from 10:00 A.M. to 5:00 P.M. daily except on major holidays. There is a charge. Parking for Centre Hill is located at Tabb and Adams streets.

The **Trapezium House,** just a few blocks away, is named for its odd shape. Its owner, Charles O'Hara, an Irish bachelor, was a bit odd himself. There are absolutely no right angles in his house—walls, stairs, floors, windows and even the mantles were all set at an angle. Legend has it that O'Hara built the house in 1816 in response to a warning from a West Indian slave that right angles harbored evil spirits.

O'Hara kept a pet monkey, parrot and white rats. He may well have found the animals more compatible than his boarders. His mistrust of people is obvious from the way he numbered logs beside the fire so that no one would steal from his stockpile. This house at Market and High streets can be toured for a charge 10:00 A.M. to 5:00 P.M. daily except major holidays. It is also closed from October through March.

Directions: Take I-95 to Petersburg, then use Exit 52 onto West Washington Street into Old Towne. Turn right on S. Sycamore and proceed to the end of the street. Then turn right for the visitor center parking lot.

Petersburg National Battlefield

Monumental Blow-Up

Do you know where the greatest manmade explosion before World War I occurred? It happened at Petersburg, Virginia, during the longest siege in American warfare. Had the Battle of the Crater turned out differently, the siege might have ended after little more than a month instead of ten long months later. It might even have helped bring an earlier end to the War Between the States, although the war was certainly fought on more than just this front.

General Ulysses S. Grant marshalled his army against Petersburg on June 15, 1864 after a failed frontal assault on Richmond, the Confederate capital. In the early days of the siege, a plan evolved to tunnel under the Confederate lines. Coal miners and other men from the 48th Pennsylvania Infantry began digging a 511-foot tunnel (when you add the two galleries used for powder magazines the total length was 586 feet). At 4:45 A.M. on July 30, 1864 they exploded four tons of powder beneath the Confederates. The southern troops had heard rumors that the Yankees were trying to dig beneath their lines, but they didn't know where or when. The Confederates even sunk countermines to try to find the tunnel. Petersburg had buzzed with tales of the tunnel for weeks.

The gigantic explosion on July 30th created a 170 × 60-foot crater that was 30 feet deep. The African American division, selected to lead the charge after the explosion, was replaced at the last minute with an untrained force out of fear that the Union command would be accused of needlessly sacrificing African American troops. The use of a poorly prepared division brought an unnecessary loss of life. The eruption sent men and equipment hurtling into the sky panicking the Union troops, who had entered the crater out of curiosity and without proper leadership from their regimental commanders. The Union casualties came to 4,400 while the Confederates, against whom the attack was launched, suffered only 1,500 casualties.

You can see the crater and the tunnel entrance on a **Petersburg National Battlefield** auto tour. Park at Stop 8 and take the short trail to the crater. Exhibits and audio stations provide more details. To obtain a more complete picture of the longest siege any American city has been forced to withstand, be sure to see the map presentation at the visitor center. The War Room has a nine-foot, three-dimensional map that traces the action on what was the largest battlefield of the Civil War. After this introduction, walk the short loop trail from the visitor center to the Dictator, a formidable cannon. Although this is not the mortar positioned at Petersburg, it is an original 17,000-pound seacoast mortar. The Dictator lobbed 200-pound shells into Petersburg just $2^1/_2$ miles away.

From mid-June to mid-August, the park presents a living history program. There are artillery demonstrations daily at 11:00 A.M., 2:30 and 4:30 P.M. (except Monday and Tuesday). It's exciting to watch soldiers representing Louisiana's Washington Artillery, with their battleflag flying, gallop up the hill past the earthenwork remains of Fort Stedman. Their six-horse team pulls the cannon and timber. Horses were so vital to the war effort they were always carefully unhitched before the cannon was placed in position. The men fire the 12-pound Napoleon field gun according to standard Civil War drill.

The gun crew carefully explains each step of the firing, does a practice drill and then suggests visitors cover their ears—the Napoleon makes a mighty noise. You'll learn that the 12-pound balls could travel for one mile. Then you can examine the "table of fire" on the ammunition chest that gun crews used to determine projectory and the amount of powder needed to hit the target. At NOON and 3:30 P.M. the smaller 24-Pounder Coehorn Mortar, which had a $^3/_4$-mile range, is fired. Between firings the crew and their horses can be found resting beneath the trees near Fort Stedman.

During the summer other soldiers representing the 200th Pennsylvania Volunteer Infantry are on hand daily from 9:00 A.M. to 6:00 P.M. at auto Stop 3. They'll show you around their camp and talk about camp life. You'll learn that during the summer the infantry men shared dog tents, forerunner of the army pup tents. The name came from the men's claim that they weren't fit for a dog to sleep in. There is also a winter hut of the type that was shared by two officers or from four to six enlisted men. Near the living quarters is a surgical field tent, far more primitive than anything seen in the TV show *M.A.S.H.* A member of the medical branch of the Union army tells you about the hazards of Civil War field medicine.

It is the maze of connecting earthenwork trenches that fascinate visitors most. It's one thing to read about siege lines and another to walk behind the earthen embankments and imagine being under fire with no greater protection than a mound of dirt. There were 70 miles of trenches around Petersburg and Richmond.

Also in the camp area is the Sutler Store where soldiers could buy supplies and the latest newspaper (which meant it was only two weeks out-of-date). Members of the U.S. Sanitary Commission are on hand as they would have been during the long siege to hand out provisions and medical supplies. They were the forerunners of the Red Cross volunteers.

It is certainly more interesting to visit Petersburg National Battlefield when you can take advantage of these programs that recreate military life in 1864. If you have time you can also join a 20-minute conducted walking tour that begins at Confederate Battery 5, auto Stop 1. The walking tours are given daily. Check at the visitor center desk for times. All of these excellent interpretative programs are provided at no charge.

Directions: Take I-95 to the Petersburg area and exit on Route 36 east. Turn left on Wythe Street and continue on to Petersburg National Battlefield, two miles away.

Siege Museum

The Echoes Remain

"You can still find the old city if you look, you can hear it if you listen," says Petersburg native Joseph Cotten as he narrates the inspiring movie shown at the **Siege Museum** about the ten months Petersburg was under siege. It was a time of courage and a time of fortitude; no other American city has endured such a long trial.

Petersburg became the Union target because General Ulysses S. Grant believed it was "the key to taking Richmond." He felt that in order to take Petersburg, he needed to sever the five railroad lines that fed the city. At the Siege Museum, the civilians' side of the last great struggle of the War Between the States is told. They suffered almost daily shelling.

The museum's exhibit of shells reveals that the never-ending bombardment left few buildings unmarked. Shells flew so thick and fast they even met in midair, as you will discover. The relatively small size of most of the shells meant that almost all of the damage was repairable.

Personal accounts from diaries and letters lend poignancy to the fear and hunger the townspeople endured. Although they had little to share, ladies smuggled what they could to the men protecting the city. They carried food, supplies and messages beneath their crinolines. Miss Anne Pigman ran the blockade disguised as a poor market woman. Fortunately gallantry was observed by both sides. Had she been required to lift her skirts even an inch, she would have revealed not only smuggled goods but her $60 shoes, a sure giveaway. The expensive shoes are now on display in the museum.

The display on "The City and Its People" recreates a portion of a typical Petersburg parlor and an office from the Bank of the City of Petersburg. There's also a children's desk and school box indicative of the normal routines the citizens tried to follow.

A more comprehensive look at banking in Petersburg is given at the visitor center located in the **Farmers Bank Museum** in Old Towne, easily located by following the bright red Petersburg Tour markers. Banks in the 1800s were primarily for the wealthy, so the Farmers Bank was established to serve the common man. The bank museum has a cashier's office with a printing press used to print Confederate money, a teller's office with a small safe made at the Petersburg ironworks, plus a bank vault where you can see the hidden chamber beneath the regular vault. You'll learn that when customers applied for a loan, directors would vote with marbles. The black marble indicated a no confidence vote, hence the derivation of the word "blackball." The Farmers Bank Museum is closed October through March.

The visitor center and Siege Museum are located within a block of each other. Except for holidays both are open daily, 10:00 A.M. to 5:00 P.M. There is a small charge for the Siege Museum. On your stroll from one to the other you can browse through the boutiques and antique shops in Old Towne. Along the main street, there are several excellent places for lunch.

Directions: Take I-95 to Petersburg, Exit 52, Washington Street. Follow Washington Street to the fifth traffic signal and turn right onto Market Street. At the second traffic signal turn right onto Bank Street. The Siege Museum is at 15 W. Bank Street and free public parking is available behind the museum. For additional information on Petersburg call the Petersburg Visitor Center, (800) 368-3595.

RICHMOND

Agecroft Hall

15th-Century England in 20th-Century Richmond

You needn't cross the Atlantic to enjoy an old English country house. A 15th-century Tudor manor house built in Renaissance England a decade before Columbus sailed to America now stands above the James River just outside downtown Richmond.

Agecroft was purchased by Thomas C. Williams, Jr., in 1925 when industrialization around Lancashire threatened to destroy the house. Brick by brick and beam by beam, it was taken down, numbered and shipped to Virginia where it was painstakingly reassembled over the next three years.

A ten-minute slide introduction to Agecroft provides details of this amazing move. Special architectural features and unusual furnishings are pinpointed so that you will be sure to notice them on your tour. Your first glimpse of Agecroft's interior is the great hall. The enormous mullioned window in this room survived the Atlantic crossing intact—not a single pane was broken!

As you tour the house you'll learn about the life style of the Tudor and early Stuart period, 1485 to 1650. Rushes cover part of the floor in the great hall. In centuries past, such long reeds were often left for a month or more before they were swept up. Each day more rushes would be added to cover the food and refuse on the floor until they reached a depth of 12 inches or more. The rushes provided insulation and moderated the irregularity of the rough stone floor. When you see the rush lamp you'll learn the derivation of the expression "burning the candle at both ends." Although not literally a candle, the rush was formed into a wick and lit at both ends.

In the withdrawing room there are several unusual chairs. The draught chair was a precursor of the wing-backed chair. A three-legged chair attests to the difficulty of balancing on the stone floors. Its massive legs provide a strong point of contact and the stretcher base provides a place off the cold floor to put your feet while seated.

The next room is the eating parlor. Although there are forks on the table these were used only for the dessert course. The apostle spoons on display reveal the derivation of yet another expression "born with a silver spoon in your mouth." These spoons were the traditional Christening gift for affluent families and bespoke a comfortable background. The covered cups reveal a less comforting practice. Cups were covered to protect diners from poison, not infrequently employed in Tudor times to remove those who stood in the way of someone else's advancement.

The staircase to the upstairs rooms is a work of art; it is not original to the house but comes from the priory at Warwick. Upstairs you'll get another view of the great hall from the minstrels' gallery. Then you'll see the north bedroom. Here again you'll discover a concern for safety. The Elizabethan bed has an elaborately carved tester. Not merely decorative, it also protected the slumberer from bits of falling plaster. Another rare reminder of earlier times is the laundry counter on which the servants kept track of the bedlinens and nightwear they collected from each room.

Each bedroom contains an elaborate and quite different bed. In the second there is a 1629 bed from Bridgewater Castle in Somerset. It is the third bed that is really a stunner, a polychrome bed from the 1600s with its original red, green and yellow paint.

After your house tour you'll step outside to see the exterior architectural features. One windowpane at the far end of the terrace contains a royal reminder. On June 12, 1645, King Charles I, used his diamond ring to carve the name William Dauntesey on it.

Before leaving be sure to allow time to explore the gardens. The sunken garden is copied from Hampton Court. There are three additional gardens you'll want to explore: the knot garden, formal garden and herb garden. The latter contains only herbs grown during the reign of Elizabeth I.

Agecroft Hall is open year-round Tuesday through Saturday from 10:00 A.M. to 4:00 P.M. and Sundays from 12:30 to 5:00 P.M. Admission is charged.

Directions: Take I-95 to Richmond. From downtown take Cary Street west to Malvern Avenue on your right and Canterbury Road on your left. Turn left on Canterbury Road. Canterbury Road merges with Sulgrave Road. Agecroft is at 4305 Sulgrave Road. There is free parking on the grounds.

*In Richmond you can visit a furnished Tudor manor house built
in England in the 15th century. Agecroft Hall was brought to the
shores of the James River beam by beam, brick by brick, in 1925.*

The Edgar Allan Poe Museum

Mastering the Macabre

Some individuals—like Edgar Allan Poe—stride across life with great elan. He came by his dramatic flair quite naturally, having inherited it from his father, his mother and his maternal grandmother, all of whom were actors. Poe's biographers believe that David Poe deserted his family before his early death. Poe's mother, Elizabeth Arnold Poe, died in Richmond in 1811 when Edgar was just under three. A plaque in St. John's Cemetery commemorates her passing, but the exact gravesite is unknown.

The Edgar Allan Poe Museum in Richmond is a complex of buildings that surround the Old Stone House of 1737–39. When the Marquis de Lafayette toured Richmond on his triumphant return to America in 1824, he stopped at this old landmark. Among those who escorted him was Edgar Allan Poe, a member of the Morgan Junior Riflemen. Poe's grandfather had served with Lafayette during the Revolution. The Old Stone House is only blocks away from the former site of Poe's first Richmond home.

To acquaint visitors with Richmond and the Poe connection, the museum's first display is a scale model of Richmond circa 1809–1849. Museum docents retrace Poe's footsteps around the old city. He spent more time here than in any other city. He grew up, married and first gained national recognition for his writing in Richmond's *Southern Literary Messenger*.

Guided tours of the museum's large collection of Poe memorabilia add details to the portrait of this genius. In 1826 when Poe entered the University of Virginia, founder Thomas Jefferson was still on hand to greet incoming students. Perhaps no remarks were exchanged between these two great American intellectuals, but it is interesting to imagine their paths crossing.

Poe was adopted unofficially after his mother's death. His foster father refused to give him enough money to cover his tuition, living expenses and mounting debts. Consequently Poe traveled to Boston and enlisted in the army. Although he was appointed to West Point, he deliberately broke minor rules and was dismissed. He was to gain international recognition as a writer of indisputable genius, but Poe spent much of life in poverty.

When Poe left Richmond he was distraught over the forcible rupture of his engagement to Elmira Royster, his childhood sweetheart. But his romance with Elmira was rekindled when he returned to Richmond in 1849, about two months before his death. As both of them had lost their first spouses, they became engaged again. He gave his final public reading at the Exchange

Hotel. Of course his popular poem "The Raven," published in 1845, was on the program.

The Poe Museum's exhibition galleries (including "The Raven Room") contain materials that bring his well-known poems and tales to life. In the Memorial Building you will see some of the worldly goods Poe possessed at the time of his death: a trunk, his wife's mirror and trinket box, a walking stick, a pair of boot hooks and other items associated with his life. In the Enchanted Garden, created to complement Poe's poetry, the bust of Poe overlooks a green oasis amid the bustle of downtown Richmond.

The museum is open year-round from Tuesday through Saturday, 10:00 A.M. to 4:00 P.M. Sunday and Monday hours are 1:00 to 4:00 P.M. with guided tours given on the hour. It is closed on Christmas Day. Admission is charged.

Directions: From I-95S take Richmond Exit 74B, the Franklin Street exit, and travel east on Main Street. From I-95N take Exit 74C, 17th Street, and travel east on Main Street. The Edgar Allan Poe Museum is on the left at 1914–16 E. Main Street.

The James River and Kanawha Canal Locks

Locks Link to Past

There are two things you should know about the **James River and Kanawha Canal**. It was the first canal system built in America, and it is one of the coolest spots in Richmond on a hot summer afternoon. Beneath the 13th Street arched overpass, built in 1860, there is a picnic pavilion shaded from the sun and cooled by the canal. Display cases in the pavilion provide the history on this significant canal.

It was George Washington's dream to have a "Great Central American Waterway" linking the Atlantic Ocean to the Ohio River. In order to realize that dream the James River had to be made navigable for carrying tobacco and other goods. From the earliest days, settlers had encountered the obstacle of seven miles of rapids at the falls. On May 24, 1607, ten days after landing at Jamestown, a party of 21 explorers including Captain John Smith, sailed up the James River only to be halted by these falls. The falls broke the connection between the Atlantic Ocean some 125 miles down the river and the 200 miles of navigable river extending into the Alleghenies.

Land along the falls was sold in a lottery by Colonel William Byrd II in 1737, and again by his son, William Byrd III, in 1768.

This settlement formed the nucleus of the city of Richmond. Although early lot purchasers hoped the James River would be cleared for navigation, it was not until George Washington became president that the work was actually started. In January 1785, the Virginia Assembly established the James River Company, with Washington serving as its first president, with the object of "clearing and improving the navigation of the James River."

By the end of 1789 large boulders were removed from the James River and two short canals were built around the falls. In 1800 an eastern terminus called the "Great Basin" was built in Richmond between the area that is now 8th, 12th, Canal and Cary streets. The next step needed to complete the canal system was to connect the Great Basin in the town of Richmond with the docks located in the Tidewater below Shockoe Creek—the Tidewater Connection. Between 1810 and 1812, 13 wooden locks were built by Ariel Cooley.

In 1826, Charles Crozet, Chief Engineer for the canal, proposed that Cooley's decaying wooden locks be replaced with stone locks. He estimated the cost at $350,000. By 1854 when the five stone locks and two basins Crozet recommended were finally open to commerce, the price tag was $850,000.

The canal has not been used since the end of 1870, but you can still visit restored locks number 4 and 5 of the Tidewater Connection at the Canal Locks park. Each of these large granite-blocked locks is 100 feet long and 15 feet wide. This National Historic Landmark is open at no charge from 9:00 A.M. to 5:00 P.M. daily. The Tidewater Connection and the surrounding park was preserved by the Reynolds Metals Company incorporating the canal path and lock system into the design of the Reynolds Wrap Distribution Center.

Directions: The James River and Kanawha Canal Locks can be seen in downtown Richmond at 12th and Byrd Streets. Parking is available alongside the canal.

John Marshall House

Virginia Is—and Was—for Lovers

In an era when their contemporaries were marrying for wealth and position, John Marshall and Mary "Polly" Willis Amber married for love. It was a love that was to last a lifetime and influence the career decisions of a major figure in American history.

John Marshall, who was to become Chief Justice of the U.S. Supreme Court, met Polly Ambler when she was a girl of 14. When Marshall first proposed Polly burst into tears; he was taken aback and left in despair. A cousin of Polly's caught up with

Marshall as he was leaving and gave him a lock of Polly's hair. Marshall kept the talisman and proposed again several years later. She accepted and they were married in 1783 when he was 28 and she was 17.

Along with his good fortune in obtaining the hand of the girl he loved, Marshall also inherited the law practice of Edmund Randolph who relinquished it to run for governor of Virginia. With this practice and his own clients, Marshall had a thriving practice. He also had a growing family and in 1788 John Marshall purchased a one-block lot in the center of Richmond. While their house was being built the Marshalls lived in a small two-story cottage on the grounds. They moved into the two-story brick house in 1790. The main house still stands, though the large kitchen dependency, laundry, smokehouse, carriage house and Marshall's law office are gone.

The **John Marshall House** itself has been open to the public since 1913, and it contains the largest collection of Marshall memorabilia in existence. The Marshall silver, returned to the house for his 225th birthday celebration, is here as is the French porcelain purchased by Marshall when he was Ambassador to France in 1797. His wife's invalidism and nervous disorders meant that Marshall did far more of the housework and child care than men typically did in the 18th century. Although Polly did not enjoy entertaining, he frequently invited 30 fellow attorneys for his "lawyer dinners."

His tenure as ambassador was one of the rare times Marshall accepted an appointment away from Richmond. As chief justice, he was able to do much of the case work at home. When you look at the portrait of Polly Marshall at age 33, you can see why he was reluctant to leave her. She was a gorgeous woman despite her ill health that came in part, from bearing 10 children and suffering several miscarriages. Marshall also had health problems; he had over 1,000 gallstones removed with only alcohol for an anesthetic. Despite their problems both lived long lives, Polly Marshall to age 66 and John to just prior to his 80th birthday.

John Marshall may well have attributed some of his long life to his wine cellar. He spent a tenth of his income on wine. His Richmond home boasted a superb wine cellar that has been restored. A reproduction of a sundial John Marshall set in place in the 18th century can be seen on the lawn.

The John Marshall House is open Tuesday through Saturday from 10:00 A.M. to 5:00 P.M. Admission is charged, either for this house alone or as a Court End block ticket that provides reduced admission to three houses and St. John's Church on a self-guided walking tour which includes ten additional points of interest. The block ticket provides admission to the Marshall House, the Wickham-Valentine House and the John Brockenbrough House

which served as the White House of the Confederacy (see selections).
Directions: From I-95 south, take Exit 74C to Broad Street west. Travel to 9th Street and make a right. The John Marshall House in at 818 East Marshall Street on the corner of 9th and Marshall streets.

Lewis Ginter Botanical Garden and Three Lakes Nature Center

Natural Oasis

An already delightful garden retreat has ambitious plans: the **Lewis Ginter Botanical Garden** intends to become one of the world's outstanding gardens with exceptional seasonal floral plantings. Only the initial stage of the first of three phases was achieved when the garden opened in 1984. This provides a great opportunity to literally watch a garden grow.

One completed area is the three-acre Henry M. Flagler Perennial Garden, showcasing the plants available to southeastern gardeners. There are approximately 12,000 plants representing 655 species and cultivars. This includes the trees and shrubs as well as green and flowering plants. Something is in bloom year-round, although January is the slowest month. The winding brick path leads past a stream and small pond to the garden's focal point—a large stone pavilion at the end of the central bed.

The Grace E. Arents Garden was created on the grounds adjacent to the house in the late teens and early 1920s by the niece and heir of Richmond businessman Lewis Ginter. The house, which served as a sort of country club, was called Bloemendaal House, Dutch for "flower valley." Grace Arents created a botanical garden in memory of her uncle. The property was once part of a 217-acre track of land owned by Patrick Henry, governor of Virginia. Over the years the design of the garden changed, but key elements remained. In 1990 the Garden Club of Virginia began restoring the garden, relying on recovered remnants to pinpoint where the walkways, central beds, sundial, arbors and summer house once stood. As in Miss Arents time, the annuals create an ever-changing look.

A timeless look is achieved in the English cottage garden, with its knot garden and old roses. The herb collection includes culinary and medicinal varieties. The children's garden has an international collection with varieties native to Africa, Asia, North and South America. The botanical garden also has the American Ivy Society's Standard Reference Collection. With 190 different cultivars, it is the world's largest and most accurate collection. A wildflower meadow, shrub border and rhododendron collection are also in place.

Another specialty area is the Martha and Reed West Island Garden with an exotic display of bog and wetland plants. This is located in the lake area between the perennial garden and Lora and Claiborne Robins Tea House and Gardens. Lunch is served in this Japanese-inspired teahouse daily from 11:30 A.M. to 2:30 P.M. After walking along the lake and crossing a picturesque footbridge you'll see the colorful lotus pool, which is at its peak in mid-summer.

Currently the visitor center and "Shop in the Garden" are located in the Bloemendaal House. The house can be toured, except when special events are in progress. Long-range plans call for an attractive new visitors' pavilion and what can only be described as a crystal palace for conservatory plants.

The grounds open daily at 9:30 A.M. and close at 4:30 P.M. Visitor center hours are the same Monday through Saturday; on Sundays it opens at 1:00 P.M. A nominal admission is charged.

Not far away in Henrico County the Division of Recreation and Parks has equipped **Three Lakes Park** with a nature center and observation deck. It offers families a place to get outside, let children play and also see an indoor-outdoor fresh-water aquarium. Among the specimens in this 50,000 gallon tank are bluegill, largemouth bass, redbreast sunfish and channel catfish. The nature center has a wide variety of hands-on nature-related exhibits. There are also hiking trails around the lakes. The park is at 400 Sausiluta Drive; call 804-672-5100 for details on the county parks.

Directions: From I-95 south take Exit 83B, Parham Road west. Get into the lefthand lane immediately. At the traffic light, turn left on U.S. 1. Continue on U.S. 1 to the second traffic light, and turn right onto Lakeside Avenue. The Lewis Ginter Botanical Garden is at 1800 Lakeside Avenue on the right. If you are traveling north on I-95 take Exit 80, Lakeside-Hermitage. Go to the traffic light and turn right onto Lakeside Avenue. Travel north on Lakeside Avenue until you see the garden entrance on the left.

Maymont

May Be the Place for You

A one-day visit to **Maymont** is a multi-dimensional excursion. You can tour the Victorian-Romanesque Maymont House, stroll through the Italian and Japanese gardens, explore the carriage collection, drop by the children's farm, see the indoor nature center and the outdoor wildlife habitats, ride the tram around the estate or treat yourself to the luxury of a carriage ride.

Maymont stands, as does much of Richmond, on land granted to William Byrd in 1675 by the English crown and sold by his grandson to pay his debts in 1769. The land was acquired by James Henry Dooley in 1886. At that time the Dooleys were living on Franklin Street, a fitting in-town address for one of Richmond's most affluent families. Because of the growing noise, pollution, crime and overcrowding in the inner city, however, Dooley acquired 94 acres on the outskirts of the city and later added 11 more.

The Dooleys' 33-room mansion on this acreage was designed in an early medieval style enjoying a vogue during the last quarter of the 19th century. It is still decorated in the height of fashion—for the 1890s. Furnishings were purchased by the Dooleys on their travels around Europe and were chosen in a mixture of historical and exotic styles.

The ornately decorated rooms in this, one of the only Victorian estates open to the public in Virginia, make it easy to understand why the late 19th century was called the Gilded Age. In the library, the first room you see, there are several unusual items. The Italian Renaissance winged-lion chair the Dooleys may have found in Italy always elicits questions from visitors because of its unusual design. The ceilings feature such Victorian touches as stenciling and strapwork. Stenciling, which originally adorned modest homes in the form of folk art, was later adopted and embellished by the more sophisticated. Strapwork, which had its origins in fine Elizabethan and Jacobean houses, is a ceiling design done with wooden moldings.

Both the pink and blue drawing rooms utilize French decorative styles. The former is decorated with Louis XV furniture to complement the rococo, 18th-century French architectural details, such as the ceiling frescoes and the 14-karat gold-plated chandelier and sconces. The drawing room has a parquet floor, highly touted in an 1884 edition of *Godey's Lady's Book*. It is said that Mrs. Dooley made visitors put on flannel shoe covers to protect her floor. The stained-glass windows demonstrate another favorite decoration of the Victorian period. The blue drawing room is done in the neoclassical style and has Louis XVI furnishings.

The dining room walls are covered with painted canvas "tapestries," very popular during the Gilded Age. The porcelain is copied from Rutherford B. Hayes's White House china. The enormous, ornately carved mahogany and rosewood cabinet was made in France in the 1850s and displayed at the Paris Universal Exposition.

You'll also see the upstairs bedrooms. The most interesting is the Swan Room filled with furniture featuring swan motifs. A large swan bed competes for attention with a table made of silver and narwhal (a single tusk whale) by Tiffany and Co.

In addition to turning the main house into a display of Victoriana, the many dependencies at Maymont have been turned to good use. The first dependency to be built may predate the mansion. Now called the "mews," it serves as a gift shop. The carriage house contains a sizeable collection of 19th-century horse-drawn vehicles. Carriage rides are given from 1:00 to 4:00 P.M. on weekends April through October, weather permitting. The old hay barn houses a nature center.

There are also wildlife habitats on the grounds. The most noticeable member of the grasslands community is the American bison, a species at one time native to Virginia. Another habitat is the black bear exhibit, located in an old quarry and pond area. The forest edge has its own denizens—raccoons, foxes, chipmunks, elk and deer. A variety of owls and hawks populate the bird of prey exhibit. Maymont's aviary includes wild turkey and many types of waterfowl. Domestic animals are at the children's farm.

The gardens of Maymont should not be missed; indeed, they are the primary reason many visitors return. The first of the diverse gardening styles to be observed is the English pastoral landscape that surrounds the house. The objective of this style was to make the grounds look natural even when planted with trees and shrubs that were not indigenous to the area. The Dooleys imported 185 varieties of exotic trees from six continents.

Between 1907 and 1910 the Dooleys built a three-tiered Italian garden. The garden's multi-level terraces are enhanced by statuary, a formal cascade fountain with terraced pools, a wisteria-covered pergola (or arbor) plus a promenade overlooking the secret garden.

The formal cascade fountain contrasts with the naturalistic waterfall flowing into the Japanese garden, a renovation done in 1976. The current garden includes trained and pruned trees and shrubs, raked sand pools, meandering paths, stone lanterns and delicate bridges.

The Maymont grounds are open 10:00 A.M. to 5:00 P.M. daily November through March and 10:00 A.M. to 7:00 P.M. April through October. Exhibits are open NOON to 5:00 P.M. Tuesday through Sunday from September through May and 10:00 A.M. to 5:00 P.M. Tuesday through Sunday, June through August. The last tour of Maymont House begins at 4:30 P.M. Donations are requested. For additional information or group reservations call (804) 358-7166.

Directions: From I-95 and I-64, take Exit 78, The Boulevard and travel south for two miles to The Boulevard's end at the

The Dooleys' magnificent 33-room neo-Romanesque mansion overlooks the 105-acre Maymont Park with its Italian and Japanese gardens, carriage collection, children's farm, indoor nature center and outdoor wildlife habitats.

Columbus statue. Follow Maymont signs through Byrd Park and into the parking area at the Hampton Street Gate. If you want to enter Maymont near the children's farm, turn right at the Columbus statue, then make a left onto Pump House Drive at the Carillon, left onto Shirley and right into the parking area.

Meadow Farm Museum at Crump Park

Confederate Line

With attention focused on agrarian life in these days of crisis for the American family farm, why not plan a timely visit to **Meadow Farm Museum**? In 1975 this 19th-century farmhouse, along with 150 acres of pasture and woodland, was given to Henrico County by Elizabeth Adam Crump in memory of her husband, the late Adjutant General of Virginia, Sheppard Crump.

Reminders of man's interaction with this land date from prehistoric time when Native Americans camped along North Run

241

Creek. It was acquired by the Sheppard family in 1713. The farmhouse you'll visit was built almost a century later in 1810 by Mosby Sheppard. Earlier in 1800 Mosby had uncovered the details of a planned slave uprising, Gabriel's Insurrection. The idea of a slave revolt terrorized southern slave owners, and encouraged men like John Brown whose 1859 Harpers Ferry raid was an attempt to get munitions to help slaves seize their freedom.

According to Sheppard family stories, Meadow Farm had its own brush with history one memorable day in 1864. Major General George Custer, with some of his Union cavalry, raided Meadow Farm before continuing on to Yellow Tavern five miles away, where a confrontation occurred that cost J.E.B. Stuart his life.

Your visit to Meadow Farm begins with a video in the orientation center introducing you to the Sheppard family during the year 1860. The center also features a series of exhibits which expand on the topics of rural southern life. About 80 percent of the furnishings now in the farmhouse belonged to the Sheppards. The dining room, hallway and one upstairs bedroom were built in 1810. In 1820, as the family grew, a downstairs master bedroom and an additional upstairs bedroom were added. By 1858, a third two-story section was constructed that gave the family the luxury of a formal parlor and added two bedrooms.

The Sheppards' ten children slept upstairs as did the governess and tutor, a "teacher of English." During the prewar years the family had 17 slaves. It's hard to imagine that many people being supported by such a modest farm. John Mosby Sheppard was able to afford his sizeable household because he also had a thriving medical practice. His office at Meadow Farm is typical of a mid-19th-century doctor's office.

An 1840 outbuilding similar to the one used by Dr. Sheppard stands on the site of his old office. Dr. Sheppard's diploma from the University of Pennsylvania Medical College hangs on the wall. The shelves and tables are cluttered with old medicine jars and bandages. Dr. Sheppard mixed many of his own medicines, but did purchase, from an apothecary, quinine for fevers and laudanum to kill pain. He normally charged his neighbors two dollars for an office visit and four dollars if he had to go out at night. Delivering a baby cost ten dollars. Except during the Civil War, his fees remained substantially the same during his 37-year practice.

After touring Meadow Farm Museum, there is a nature trail to explore. North Run Trail traces the evolution of an old farm field into a forest where you may spy a red-winged hawk. At the farm pond, you may see nesting water birds or turtles basking in the sun.

There are also picnic and playground areas at Crump Park and special events scheduled throughout the year. They include the

Memorial Day Civil War Battle and Encampment in May, an Old-Fashioned Fourth, September Civil War Day, the Harvest Festival in October and a Yuletide Fest. There is an admission to the museum, but admission to the park is free.

Meadow Farm Museum is open Tuesday through Sunday NOON to 4:00 P.M. from the first Saturday in March until the second Sunday in December and on weekends from mid-January through February. Crump Park is open daily from dawn to dusk year-round.

Directions: From I-95 just before Richmond take I-295 west toward Charlottesville to Woodman Road South Exit. Follow Woodman Road to Mountain Road and turn right; continue two miles to park entrance on the right.

Richmond Children's Museum and Maggie L. Walker Historic Site

Hands Full of Fun

"Let a child be your guide" suggests the **Richmond Children's Museum**. Since opening in 1981, this hands-on, lively and innovative museum has been a favorite with youngsters and their families.

No hands-off policy here! Interaction with the exhibits and participation in the programs is encouraged at this museum. Everyday exhibits include Playworks, The Cave, StagePlay, In My Own Backyard, Mickey's Mouth and the Art Studio. Together children and adults can learn through independent exploration or by attending one of the many weekly programs, workshops or performances. Tomorrow's artists, environmentalists, doctors, bankers, retailers, farmers and TV personalities may well visit the museum today.

The Richmond Children's Museum is open Tuesday through Saturday from 9:00 A.M. to 5:00 P.M. and Sunday from 1:00 to 5:00 P.M. From June through August, the museum is open on Monday from 10:00 A.M. to 5:00 P.M. A nominal admission is charged.

Just a few blocks from the Children's Museum in the Jackson Ward Historic District is the **Maggie L. Walker National Historic Site**. Maggie Walker was the first woman in America to found and become president of a bank. She achieved her success in spite of the fact she was an African American woman in poor health. In her later years she was paralyzed from the waist down and confined to a wheel chair.

The house at $100^1/_2$ East Leigh Street was Maggie Walker's home from 1904 until her death in 1934. The 22-room house is fitted with Walker family pieces and looks as it did in the 1920s. There is no charge for the tours which are offered Wednesday through Sunday from 9:00 A.M. to 5:00 P.M. It is closed Christmas, New Year's Day and Thanksgiving.

The Maggie L. Walker House is just a block away from the park dedicated to Bill "Bojangles" Robinson, who grew up in this Richmond neighborhood. The famed tap dancer is shown in a life-size statue that looks as if he were going to dance down the bronze steps and off the pedestal.

Directions: From I-95, take the Coliseum exit. At the first traffic light, turn left on Jackson Street. Go three blocks to Navy Hill Drive. Turn left, the Richmond Children's Museum is at the end of the block on the left. For the Maggie L. Walker House take Sixth Street to Broad Street. Take Broad Street to Second Street and turn right. Continue on Second Street to Leigh Street.

Richmond National Battlefield Park

Double Jeopardy

"On to Richmond" was a battle cry heard with chilling frequency during the War Between the States. Seven Union drives were launched against the capital of the Confederacy. The North sought the psychological victory of capturing the symbol of southern independence as well as the military advantage of disabling the principal supply depot for the Confederate army.

Two Federal drives nearly succeeded: McClellan's in 1862 and Grant's in 1864. You can trace them at **Richmond National Battlefield Park's** Chimborazo Visitor Center with the help of an audiovisual program, exhibits and park rangers. An annotated park map routes you along the 60-mile battlefield trail; you can rent or buy auto tape tours.

There are five tour stops along the McClellan route (marked in red). The first is Chickahominy Bluff from which General Lee watched the opening engagement of the Seven Days' campaign. You can see earthwork fortifications that protected his position.

The next stop is Beaver Dam Creek, a Federal defensive position that was part of the three-mile Union line that Lee tried to break on June 26, 1862. Along the short trail at Gaines' Mill, you can walk the steep hillside used by the same Union forces who had defended Beaver Dam Creek. They tried in vain to hold the line against determined Confederate assaults. A battlefield landmark, the restored Watt House (seen from the exterior only), exemplifies the middle-class farms around which the Seven Days' campaign was fought.

Another stop is Malvern Hill where the last of the battles raged. So fierce was the fighting that afterward a Confederate officer mourned, "It was not war—it was murder."

The last stop along the red route is Drewry's Bluff where Fort Darling protected the James River (and thus Richmond). This Confederate fort even repulsed the Monitor, the formidable Union ironclad.

Only an ardent Civil War buff would want to explore both 1862 and 1864 routes on the same day; most people return later to cover Grant's drive (the blue route). If you've stopped before at the Chimborazo Visitor Center, you can begin the blue route at the Cold Harbor Visitor Center where there are picnic facilities. The facility is staffed daily during the summer months and signs direct you along a one-mile interpretive walking trail or a $1^1/_4$ mile auto route. Both take you past well-preserved Civil War trenches that proved impregnable against frontal attack and influenced battlefield tactics. The nearby Garthright House was used as a field hospital. It is not open, but the exterior has been restored to look as it did in the 1860s. Some portions of the house date from the 1700s.

South of Richmond, the action shifts to Fort Harrison where there is another small visitor center open daily in the summer and on weekends in spring and fall. On occasional summer weekends, Fort Harrison offers living history programs. Miles of breastworks connected the smaller forts that surrounded Fort Harrison. A self-guided trail leads you though the fort. The self-guided driving tour continues to Fort Brady on the James River.

Richmond National Battlefield Park's Chimborazo Visitor Center is open 9:00 A.M. to 5:00 P.M. daily except Thanksgiving, Christmas and New Year's Day. There is no admission charge.

Directions: From I-95 northbound use Exit 74C; if you are traveling south, take Exit 74B. Take East Broad Street to the Chimborazo Visitor Center at 3215 East Broad Street.

St. John's Church and St. Paul's Church

Chapels of Liberty

Necessity often forced the Founding Fathers to mix church and state. On one historic occasion in 1775 the Second Virginia Convention chose **St. John's Church** as their meeting place because it was the largest public gathering place in Richmond. On the fourth day of their week long convention Patrick Henry deliv-

St. John's Church, made famous by Patrick Henry's immortal "liberty or death" oration in 1775, was built by the great-great-great-grandson of Pocahontas in 1741.

ered his famous "Liberty or Death" speech (see Scotchtown and Red Hill selections).

This historic occasion is reenacted on summer Sundays at 2:00 P.M. from the last weekend in May through the first Sunday in September and on the Sunday closest to March 23, the day on which Henry delivered his impassioned plea. Join with costumed actors portraying Henry, Washington, Jefferson and other Virginia delegates as they debate the future of the American colonies. You are indeed where history happened. Later during the Revolutionary War, Benedict Arnold quartered his troops in St. John's while occupying Richmond.

St. John's, 35 years old when the Revolution began, is the oldest church in Richmond and one of the oldest surviving wooden buildings in the city. It was built in 1741 on land given to Henrico Parish by William Byrd II. Although the church has been largely restored since colonial days, the high pulpit, flooring, transept and many of the pews are original.

Guided tours of the church are given for a nominal admission, Monday through Saturday from 10:00 A.M. to 4:00 P.M. and Sunday from 1:00 to 4:00 P.M. The last tour starts at 3:30 P.M. St. John's is closed on major holidays. Sunday Episcopal worship services are held at 8:30 and 11:00 A.M. with a NOON coffee hour and reception. During hours when tours are conducted the Chapel Gift Shop is open in the old Victorian Gothic Keeper's house.

Also historically significant is **St. Paul's Church** at 815 East Grace Street. You can attend services at NOON Monday through Friday and 11:00 A.M. on Sunday at this church where both Robert E. Lee and Jefferson Davis worshipped. The President of the Confederacy was attending service on Sunday, April 2, 1865, when he received word that Petersburg had fallen and the Union army was marching on Richmond. The fear that spread through the congregation was quickly confirmed by Davis's order to evacuated the city. St. Paul's Church is open Monday through Saturday from 10:00 A.M. to 4:00 P.M. and Sunday 1:00 to 4:00 P.M.

Directions: Take Exit 10 from I-95. St. John's is located at 2401 East Broad Street down from the Richmond National Battlefield Park (you can follow the battlefield signs). For St. Paul's Church take Broad Street to 8th Street and turn left. Make a right on Grace Street.

Science Museum of Virginia

There's Magic to Do

At the **Science Museum of Virginia**, touch, observe and explore the impact of science on your life from astronomy to computers, from flight to crystals and from illusions to electricity—all within the grandeur of a renovated historic railroad station.

There are no "do not touch" signs here! More than 250 interactive exhibits make the worlds of science and technology entertaining as well as educational for all ages. The fun starts as you walk through the parking lot past a solar-electric car and its charging station. When you enter the museum, you will want to stop at the Foucault pendulum in the grand rotunda and watch as it shows the earth's rotation.

As you walk through the museum, you learn to identify stars and constellations in "Night Visions." Tell your innermost thoughts to Dr. Know, a computerized counselor in "Computer Works." Examine gem specimens from around the world in "Crystal World." Climb aboard a Piper Cub and dream of flying through the clouds while in "Aerospace." Play a quick game of laser pool or investigate the world of sound in "Science Sense". In "Electriworks" you can create sparks at the Van De Graaff generator and compare wattage usage of major appliances. Pause to telegraph a message to a friend while passing through "Telecommunications." Cause a head-on collision in "Force and Motion."

Take time to watch one of the daily demonstrations. Friendly volunteers and staff will draw you into the phenomena of air pressure, electricity and illusions. You can also be part of the action through large-screen films and multimedia planetarium shows in the museum's **Ethyl Universe Planetarium and Space Theater**—Virginia's only OMNIMAX theater. The five-story theater, with its tilted-dome, 76-foot screen and 108 speakers, provides sight and sound from every direction. You'll travel as you never have done before—through space to explore distant planets and stars.

The Science Museum of Virginia is housed in the former Broad Street Station, which was designed by John Russell Pope. Pope also designed the National Gallery, the National Archives Building and the Jefferson Memorial in Washington, D.C. The building is included in the National Register of Historic Places.

Plan to spend $1^{1}/_{2}$–2 hours exploring the exhibits, and another hour each for the film and planetarium show. There are varied admission prices for exhibits and theater depending on your choice and age. Don't miss the museum store with its collection of science and aeronautically related toys, books, posters, jewelry and T-shirts.

The Science Museum's exhibit areas are open daily. Winter hours are Monday through Saturday 9:30 A.M. to 5:00 P.M., Sunday NOON to 5:00 P.M. During the summer the museum stays open on Friday and Saturday until 7:00 P.M. The Ethyl Universe is open Monday through Thursday 11:00 A.M. to 5:00 P.M., Friday and Saturday until 9:00 P.M. and Sunday 1:00 to 5:00 P.M.

The museum opened a satellite science center in Danville and the **Virginia Aviation Museum,** a division of the Science Museum, is located near the Richmond International Airport. This shrine to the "golden age of aviation" enhances the Science Museum's aerospace exhibits with its extensive collection of historic flying machines, dioramas on World War II, a special exhibit on Admiral Richard E. Byrd, early flight memorabilia, navigational devices and the Virginia Aviation Hall of Fame.

As you take an hour's walk through aviation history, you'll get a close look at a World War I Spad VII, see Captain Dick Merrill's 1930s open cockpit mail plane and have the opportunity to view the *Stars and Stripes*, one of three aircraft Commodore Byrd took with him on his first expedition to Antarctica. Aeronautical buffs will enjoy an aviation film in the comfortable Benn Theater as well as talking with the volunteers, who are all aviation enthusiasts.

Throughout the year the Virginia Aviation Museum hosts special events, such as Toss Across America in May, Flight Day in June and a celebration of the Wright Brothers' first flight in December. On the third Thursday of every month, experts in the aeronautical field present free, topical lectures. Call (804) 236-3620 for scheduling details.

Museum hours are daily 9:30 A.M. to 5:00 P.M. Admission is charged. There is a museum store with toys, books, posters and T-shirts.

Directions: From I-95 take Exit 78; the Science Museum of Virginia is located at 2500 West Broad Street in Richmond. For further information call (804) 367-1013 or (800) 659-1727 during museum hours or (804) 367-0000 for a 24-hour recorded message. For the Virginia Aviation Museum, take I-95/I-64 east to Exit 47A; the museum is at the Richmond International Airport.

Scotchtown and Barksdale Theatre

Not-So-Canny Country

A man's home may be his castle, but if he plans to build an actual castle something less than grand may be a disappointment. It was a grandiose dream that inspired Charles Chiswell in 1717 to obtain a land grant from the King of England of 9,976 acres in New Kent County, now Hanover County, Virginia. He envisioned an entire transplanted Scottish community with himself as laird of the castle and hired Scottish architects and laborers to build his town.

The main house (Chiswell named **Scotchtown**), mill and a small group of outbuildings were all that were finished when disease decimated the workers and the project was abandoned. A disillusioned Chiswell lived in the main house until his death in 1737.

Scotchtown's next owner, Charles's son John Chiswell, also had his dreams shattered—his by a too hastily delivered sword thrust. Chiswell's intemperate remarks in a tavern in Cumberland County provoked Robert Routledge into throwing his drink into Chiswell's face. Without thinking Chiswell unsheathed his sword and killed Routledge on the spot. He was immediately arrested and, again acting hastily, committed suicide rather than face certain conviction. Perhaps he was correct in assuming the trial would go against him. Feelings were strong because of Chiswell's unprovoked attack on Routledge and the young man's family were suspicious that Chiswell's death may have been faked. To make sure that it was Chiswell in the coffin, the Routledges demanded it be opened before burial to prove he had indeed perished by his own hand.

Things did not run smoothly for Patrick Henry's family either after they acquired Scotchtown in 1771. Sarah Shelton Henry was left at this rural Virginia home with six children and 30 slaves while Patrick Henry fulfilled his many political commitments. In the seven years the Henry family lived at Scotchtown, he served in the House of Burgesses in Williamsburg, the First and Second Continental Congresses in Philadelphia and the Second Virginia Convention at St. John's Church in Richmond (see selection).

Some historians have conjectured that when he delivered his famous "Liberty or Death" speech at St. John's Church his thoughts may have included, in addition to the plight of the American colonists under British tyranny, the unfortunate curtailment of his own wife's liberty. Due to her deteriorating mental condition, she was kept locked in one of the cellar rooms at Scotchtown until her death in 1775 at the age of 36. She was cared for there by Dr. Thomas Hinde and a nurse, as well as by Patrick Henry's mother and sister.

Patrick Henry's second wife, Dorothea Dandridge, whom he married in 1777 while living in the Palace at Williamsburg, did not want to live at Scotchtown and the plantation was advertised for sale in the *Virginia Gazette* in 1778. The years of Patrick Henry's residency are recaptured in this restored plantation house.

The personality of Patrick Henry is imprinted on the house. Henry enjoyed holding dances in the Great Hall and playing a spinet similar to that exhibited in the Ladies' Parlor. An enthusiastic, versatile musician, he taught himself to play the flute while recovering from a broken collarbone. One of the most evocative family pieces is the writing desk in his bedroom that is believed to have been made by his father. It was said you could always tell when Henry was approaching the main thrust of his political speeches by his habit of raising his glasses to the top of his head allowing his eyes to pierce his audience. That well-known pose of his is captured on canvas in a portrait hanging at Scotchtown.

Portraits of the Sheltons, his first wife's family, hang throughout the house. Many are primitive paintings, so called because only the head was done from life. There are two portraits of Dolley Payne Madison, wife of President James Madison, who lived at Scotchtown from the age of 11 months until the age of three, while her father rented the property (some historians believe he was the overseer of the plantation).

Eighteenth-century furnishings reveal a great deal about life in colonial America. The carver type rocker in the children's bedroom has two distinct sections on the back enabling either young or older ladies to use it for drying their hair. They would drape their hair through one of the two openings so it would not get the back of their garments wet. It was the custom of the day to take baths only seasonally. Patrick Henry was frequently accused of being untidy; Thomas Jefferson particularly chafed at his countrified ways.

As you wander around the grounds looking at Patrick Henry's old law office and the other outbuildings, it is not hard to imagine the great man himself strolling beneath the trees. Scotchtown is open April through October on Monday through Saturday from 10:00 A.M. to 4:30 P.M. and on Sunday from 1:30 to 4:30 P.M. Admission is charged.

Patrick Henry worked both before and behind the bar. If you are staying overnight in the Richmond area don't miss the chance to visit **Barksdale Theatre** in historic Hanover Tavern, where Patrick Henry often helped out in the taproom. As the wine list at this dinner theater proudly claims, they've been "Serving Fine Wines Since 1723." In 1754 18-year-old Patrick Henry married Sarah Shelton, daughter of Hanover Tavern owner, John Shelton. The young couple lived with her parents for three years while Patrick tried to earn a living at store keeping, farming and finally the law.

When the Barksdale Theatre opened in 1953 it was the nation's first dinner theater. You'll dine by candlelight at this tavern that once hosted both George Washington and Lord Cornwallis, though not on the same evening. We know from Washington's diaries that when business or politics brought him to Richmond he often sought dining or lodging at Hanover Tavern. The tavern's Washington Room has a large portrait of Washington over the fireplace, and back in a corner alcove there is a small portrait of Cornwallis, who left without paying the bill for his 18-day stay.

When you make reservations for dinner and the profession-
ally-performed play that follows, request a guided tour of the
Hanover Courthouse and **Old Jail** directly across from the tavern. Tours are given at no charge 30 minutes before the buffet
dinner. It was at this courthouse that Patrick Henry delivered
what is considered by many historians the first attack on the
tyranny of George III. Barksdale Theatre is open Wednesday
through Saturday; call (804) 798-6547.

Directions: From I-95 take Ashland Exit, Route 54. Continue
through Ashland for $8^1/_2$ miles to Route 671 and turn right. Make
another right turn on Route 685 for Scotchtown. Parking is available on the grounds and there are picnic tables in a tree-shaded
grove. Barksdale Theatre is only 15 minutes from Scotchtown.
Take Route 54 past the I-95 intersection to Hanover Courthouse.
The courthouse is on the left and the Hanover Tavern is on the
right. From I-95 take Ashland Exit, Route 54 east.

Valentine Museum and Wickham House

The Museum of the Life and History of Richmond

Mann S. Valentine Sr. (1786–1865), his son Mann S. Valentine
II (1824–1892) and grandson Granville Valentine (1860–1943)
exemplify the **Valentine Museum**'s theme that people create
their own histories by what they chose to save and collect. As
exhibit curator Jane Webb Smith explains, "The individual histories people developed were often transformed into museums."
Certainly the Valentines were collectors.

The senior Mann amassed a fine arts collection and the next
two generations gathered archeological material. Their collections were exhibited privately and publicly. Granville took the
histories and the items his family collected and established the
Valentine Museum in 1898, then reorganized it in 1930.

Five interpretative periods in the history of the Valentine family are covered in the exhibit "Creating History." Over the years
the Valentine Museum changed its definition of culture and its
interpretation of history to reflect the changes in social as-
sumptions and interpretations of the past. Items from the collection of each generation are included. Another exhibit showcases the Valentines' nationally-acclaimed costume and textile
collection.

Valentine Museum docents also conduct tours of the adjacent
Wickham House. John Wickham, prominent Richmond attorney,
had this elegant neoclassical, 17-room mansion built on the highest hill in the city in 1812 at a cost of $70,000. Now a National

Historic Landmark, the house has been restored to its 1820s splendor.

On entering the house you'll see 18-inch brick walls overlaid with stucco to look like marble. The cantilevered staircase winds upward to an opening shaped like an artist's palette. The banister is carved with magnolia seed pods, dogwood blossoms and periwinkle. The oval ladies' parlor is unusually beautiful. On its walls are paintings of scenes from Homer's *Iliad*, done during Wickham's residency and subsequently overpainted. Only recently discovered, they have been carefully uncovered and restored. The restoration also re-created mantels of carved Italian marble and period window treatments.

Mr. Wickham conducted his law practice from his very masculine library. His most famous case was the successful defense of Aaron Burr in his trial for treason before Chief Justice Marshall at the Virginia State Capitol. The dining room has the original Wickham porcelain dining service, that arrived intact from China in 1814.

The grandeur on the first floor is not matched on the second floor. The upstairs rooms were bedrooms and work space for the 31 people who lived in the house (the extended family and servants). It was here that Mrs. Wickham bore many of her 17 children. There are also work areas in the basement.

The garden is the oldest in continuous use in Richmond. It is maintained in accordance with the original landscape specifications. Within the garden you'll find the sculpture studio of Edward V. Valentine, a noted 19th-century artist and brother of Mann Valentine. You'll see the tools of his trade and both completed and unfinished work. Valentine's best known piece is the "Recumbent Lee" in the Lee Chapel on the Washington and Lee University campus (see selection).

The Valentine, the Museum of the Life and History of Richmond, and Wickham House are open Monday through Saturday from 10:00 A.M. to 5:00 P.M. and Sunday from NOON to 5:00 P.M. Admission is charged but block tickets can be purchased as part of a Court End Tour that includes the Marshall House, Brockenbrough House (White House of the Confederacy) and Wickham House (see selections).

Now that you have a perspective on Richmond's past, walk down 9th Street to City Hall and take the elevator to the Skydeck. From here you get a great view of the city and can enjoy lunch at umbrella-shaded tables.

Directions: From I-95 take Exit 74C, Broad Street west. Continue on Broad Street to 11th Street, then turn right. Follow 11th Street to Clay Street and turn left. Make another left on 10th Street and the Valentine Museum parking lot will be on your left. From I-64 take Exit 43, 5th Street south. Continue on 5th to Marshall Street and take a left. From Marshall take another left on 11th and left again on Clay Street. Make a last left on 10th Street and the parking lot will be on your left.

Virginia Museum of Fine Arts and the Fan

State of the Art

Richmond's **Virginia Museum of Fine Arts**, America's first state-wide arts system, opened in 1936. In December 1985, it effectively doubled its gallery space with the addition of the West Wing, containing the collections of the two gallery sponsors: the Mellons and the Lewises.

Lofty, oversized rooms hold the Sydney and Frances Lewis art nouveau, art deco and contemporary art collections. Paul and Rachel Mellon's fine selection of impressionist and post-impressionistic art is hung in smaller, more intimate rooms.

These were added to the museum's already exciting collection, which spans the past 5,000 years of art. Surrounding the classical court are the galleries of the ancient world, Asia, the classical era and ancient America.

A life-size statue of the Roman Emperor Caligula, dating from the first century A.D., is one of the museum's prize pieces. But this is not the work best remembered by Virginia schoolchildren; their favorite is the Egyptian mummy sarcophagus (a stone coffin). Another piece in the Egyptian collection, the *Seated Scribe*, has an interesting story. The two halves of the *Seated Scribe* were acquired separately, the top part added 13 years after the bottom was purchased by the museum. The figure now looks as it originally did in the years between 663 and 525 B.C. during the Saite period in the XXVI dynasty.

Another visitor favorite is the lovely gallery of Fabergé Easter Eggs and Russian Imperial Jewels. The museum also has a prized set of Gobelin tapestries illustrating the story of Don Quixote. In order to match the splendor of the new wing, the older galleries underwent extensive refurbishing at a cost of roughly $100,000 per gallery. Skylights were uncovered to let in new light on the old masters—Degas, Goya, Matisse, Picasso, Monet, Brueghel and Gainsborough.

The Virginia Museum also houses **Theatre Virginia**, one of America's leading professional residential theaters. This 32-year-old, 500-seat theater puts on six Broadway and Off-Broadway plays a year from October through May. During the summer the museum hosts Thursday evening jazz and pop music programs in the garden.

The Czarevitch Egg of lapis, diamonds and gold, which con-
cealed a miniature portrait of the Czarevitch Alexis, is in the
outstanding Fabergé egg collection at the Virginia Museum of
Fine Arts. Virginia Museum of Fine Arts

The Virginia Museum's sculpture garden is itself one of the most beautiful spots in Richmond. It is equally pleasant for a morning stroll, an al fresco lunch, afternoon tea or an evening concert. The garden's focus is the massive fountain. The sound of its cascading water seems to lower the temperature on warm summer days. The public cafeteria is adjacent to the garden, with trees and umbrellas to provide shade for those who enjoy eating outside. Colorful blossoms enhance the sculpture, some of which is on loan from the Whitney Museum of American Art, the Hirshhorn Museum and the Museum of Modern Art.

The Virginia Museum is open Tuesday through Sunday from 11:00 A.M. to 5:00 P.M. and Thursday evenings until 8:00 P.M. It is closed on Monday and major holidays. Visitors are asked to make a donation. Seniors and children under 16 are free.

The Virginia Museum is located in the **Fan**, a district of restored homes, charming cafes, arty boutiques and antique shops. The Fan encompasses 85 blocks and extends north to Monument Avenue, south to Main Street, east to Laurel Street and west to the Boulevard. The once decaying turn-of-the-century townhouses have been reconstructed and are now popular with the faculty and students of Virginia Commonwealth University. A brochure covering the Fan district highlights 41 points of interest including museums, parks, monuments and homes. One of the favorite neighborhood eateries is Strawberry Street Cafe at 421 North Strawberry Street. You will understand why once you get a look at its cheery red and white tablecloths, the stained-glass decorative arch, an old-fashioned bathtub with salad fixings and blackboard drawings of cafe specialties.

Directions: From I-95/I-64 take Exit 78 and travel south $1^1/_2$ miles on the Boulevard to the museum, located in Richmond's West End at the corner of the Boulevard and Grove Avenue.

Virginia State Capitol

Capital Idea!

Age isn't everything, but it means a lot in Richmond. The **Virginia State Capitol** is the second oldest working capitol in the United States (after Annapolis, Maryland). The Virginia Capitol has been in continuous use since it was built to Thomas Jefferson's specifications in 1788. Jefferson modeled this Classical Revival building after Maison Carree, an ancient Roman temple he admired in Nimes, France.

The Virginia State Capitol does have a dome, as did all of the buildings that Thomas Jefferson helped design, but it is not visible from the exterior. The rotunda dome, 10 feet below the roof, can only be seen from within.

Beneath the skylighted dome stands the life-size statue of George Washington done by French artist Jean Antoine Houdon. Houdon visited Mount Vernon, and George Washington posed for this work, the only Washington statue done from life. Houdon carved it from Carrara marble and exhibited the statue in the Louvre before shipping it to America in 1796. As you look at the statue you can almost feel the trouser legs gathered into the tight boots. The veins are clearly visible beneath the taut gloves, even the strands of braid on the epaulets can be discerned.

When Lafayette saw the statue he said, "This is the man, himself, I can almost realize he is going to move." How fortunate that he appreciated the work of Houdon because the sculptor also did a bust of Lafayette, which is displayed in the Rotunda. Lafayette and John D. Rockefeller are the only two non-Virginians honored in the Capitol. Encircling the statue of the first president are niches containing busts of the seven other Virginia presidents—Thomas Jefferson, James Madison, James Monroe, William Henry Harrison, John Tyler, Zachary Taylor and Woodrow Wilson.

A portrait of the second honorary Virginian, John D. Rockefeller, who merited this distinction for his work in restoring Colonial Williamsburg, hangs in the Old Senate Chamber. The chandelier-lit chamber has two additional paintings. One depicts the three ships that first brought settlers to Virginia in May 1607: the *Susan Constant, Godspeed* and *Discovery*. The other large painting shows the Revolutionary forces storming the British Redoubt Number 10 during the Battle of Yorktown on October 14, 1781.

The final room on your Capitol tour is the Old House of Delegates chamber, scene of many historic events. The Virginia House of Delegates met here from 1788 to 1906 as did the Confederate Congress while Richmond served as the capital of the Confederacy. In 1807 Aaron Burr was acquitted of treason in a trial before U.S. Chief Justice John Marshall. More than 50 years later on April 23, 1861, Robert E. Lee stood in this room and accepted command of the Virginia armies. A bronze statue of Lee now stands on the very place he stood.

Lee is one of many Virginians honored here. There are busts of such Revolutionary statesmen as George Mason, Richard Henry Lee, Patrick Henry and George Wythe. Some of the Confederate heroes also commemorated are Stonewall Jackson, J.E.B. Stuart, Joseph E. Johnson and Fitzhugh Lee. Two non-Virginians who figured prominently in the destiny of the South are also represented—Jefferson Davis, President of the Confederacy and his Vice-President, Alexander H. Stephens. Finally there are busts of Henry Clay, Matthew Fontaine Maury, John Marshall, Sam Houston and Cyrus McCormick.

One item not to be missed in this chamber is the Edwardian-style mace that rests on a table in front of the Speaker's chair. This symbol of government was presented to the Virginia House of Delegates in 1974 by the Jamestown Foundation. The mace was made in England of silver with a 24-karat gold wash.

You can tour the State Capitol any day of the week at no charge. From April through November the hours are 9:00 A.M. to 5:00 P.M. From December through March Sunday hours change to 1:00 to 5:00 P.M.

Directions: The Virginia State Capitol is on Capitol Square between 9th and 11th streets in downtown Richmond.

The White House and Museum of the Confederacy

FFV

The two-story townhouse of Dr. John Brockenbrough at 12th and Clay streets in Richmond has survived the vicissitudes of time. The design is traditionally attributed to Robert Mills, architect of the Washington Monument.

The house has not, however, remained unchanged. In the 1850s the Brockenbrough House was architecturally altered to include a third floor and a cupola; Victorian features were also added to the interior. One of the finest in Richmond, the house was purchased by the city in June 1861 for Jefferson Davis, president of the Confederacy. When he would not accept it as a gift the city rented it to the southern states to be used as "**The White House of the Confederacy**." The Davis family was in residence until March 1865 when Varina Davis and her four children fled.

During Reconstruction, 1865–1870, the former White House was used as U.S. Army headquarters for Military District Number 1. Alterations were made when it was converted to use as a public school, but by 1890 it was in such sad repair the city considered tearing it down. It was saved by the Confederate Memorial Literary Society, a group that evolved from a ladies' organization devoted to tending the Confederate graves at Richmond's Hollywood Cemetery. The addition of the word "literary" gave justification for the transfer of this former city school to private hands. It also reflected the national interest in the South evoked by the late 19th-century literary movement of southern authors.

The house was repaired and opened as a museum by the Confederate Memorial Literary Society in 1896. The very existence of this museum prompted donations from throughout the South, and the collection grew.

By 1976 a new Museum of the Confederacy had been built adjacent to the old Brockenbrough house. The personal effects of Robert E. Lee, including the sword he wore at Appomattox, are the museum's most prized pieces. There are military weapons and uniforms belonging to Stonewall Jackson, J.E.B. Stuart, Joseph E. Johnston and A.P. Hill. Many uniforms, letters and mementos from the soldiers who fought the battles the generals planned are on display. Dresses, jewelry and letters from the women who fought the battles at home are also prominently featured.

With the opening of the new museum, work began on restoring the White House to its appearance during the Davis residency. The ground floor houses an exhibit introducing visitors to the Jefferson Davis family. Above it, on the first floor are the public rooms of the Executive Mansion that served as the social center for the political and military leaders of the Confederacy. The second floor is restored to reflect the family quarters with nursery, private office and master bedroom. The third floor has curatorial and educational facilities.

The neoclassical Brockenbrough House is included in the Court End block ticket (see John Marshall and Wickham House selections). It, along with the Museum of the Confederacy, is open Monday through Saturday from 10:00 A.M. to 5:00 P.M. On Sunday it opens at NOON. Admission is charged.

Directions: From I-95 or I-64 eastbound take Exit 74C, Broad Street. Go west on Broad Street. From Broad Street turn right onto 11th Street and go straight to Leigh Street. Turn left on Leigh Street and go one block to 10th. Turn right onto 10th and you will see a parking deck on your right. A shuttle bus will take you to 12th and Marshall, one block from the museum. Bring your parking ticket to be validated.

Wilton and Tuckahoe

Randolph Riches

Wilton, like neighboring Agecroft Hall, was dismantled and moved brick by brick to a new location. But Wilton's journey was far shorter, a mere 14 miles up the James River rather than the 3,000 miles across the Atlantic that Agecroft traveled (see Agecroft selection).

Wilton, a Georgian brick plantation house, was built for William Randolph III between 1747 and 1753. William, like others in his family, served in the Virginia militia (as a colonel) and was a delegate to the House of Burgesses. William married Ann Carter Harrison of Berkeley (see selection) in 1743 and reared eight children at Wilton. Many noted historical figures enjoyed the hospitality of his 2,000-acre plantation.

An entry in George Washington's diary reads, "March 25, 1775. Returned to the Convention in Richmond. Dined at Galt's and went to Mrs. Randolph's of Wilton. 26 Stayed at Wilton all day." One of the bedrooms is decorated to look as it did during Washington's visit. Thomas Jefferson frequently visited his cousins at Wilton. His mother was a Randolph from nearby Tuckahoe.

At the end of the American Revolution from May 15 to 20, 1781, General Lafayette made Wilton his headquarters. He moved on to Richmond when Cornwallis crossed the James River and headed in Wilton's direction.

Today you can enjoy the hospitality of Wilton, thanks to the efforts of The National Society of the Colonial Dames of America in the Commonwealth of Virginia. In 1933, Wilton faced demolition and a museum was negotiating for the parlor paneling. The Colonial Dames, under the direction of Mrs. Granville Gray Valentine, saved the house. Although Wilton stood empty for years, it has now been beautifully restored and furnished with 18th-and 19th-century period pieces.

Your tour begins in the central hallway. The so-called back door was the main, or river, entrance when the James was the main highway between plantations. One of the finest antiques at Wilton is the mahogany tall case clock in the hallway, made in 1795 by Simon Willard. Before you leave the hall, be sure to take a close look at the stair railing crafted from a single piece of walnut.

The parlor is included in Helen Comstock's book, *100 Most Beautiful Rooms in America* (now out of print). The 12 carved pillars are among the most attractive features of the room. The alcoves that flank the marble fireplace add to the parlor's symmetry. The earliest record of furnishings is an 1815 family inventory, the basis for the current furnishing and interpretation of the period rooms.

In all, you'll see copies of ten family portraits painted to hang at Wilton around 1755. The originals are owned by the Virginia Historical Society. The Garden Club of Virginia has also made a contribution by landscaping the grounds. Be sure to stroll around the grounds after your tour.

Wilton is open Tuesday through Saturday from 10:00 A.M. to 4:30 P.M. and Sunday 1:30 to 4:30 P.M. The last tour begins at 3:45 P.M. It is closed on Monday (except by advance appointments), national holidays and during the month of February. Admission is charged.

After touring Wilton why not head just a little farther out of town to **Tuckahoe Plantation**. You will need to call (804) 784-5736 for an appointment. If you feel you recognize the house on your first visit, it is probably because you remember the country scenes filmed here for Williamsburg's orientation film, *The Story of a Patriot*.

Thomas Jefferson lived at Tuckahoe, his mother's home, between the ages of two and nine. The schoolhouse where Jefferson began his studies is matched on the other side of the main house by the plantation office. The rare outbuildings and H-shaped house are, according to architectural historian Frederick Nichols, "the most complete plantation layout in North America dating from the early 18th century."

Tuckahoe's interior features some of the most important architectural ideas of the early Georgian period. The house is still a home, and the family who live at Tuckahoe often conduct the guided tours. They have a wealth of old stories to share with visitors.

Directions: From Richmond center take Main Street to Cary Street, Route 147 west. At the 6900 block of Cary Street, turn south on Wilton Road. Follow Wilton Road to the James River. Ample parking is available on the grounds. To reach Tuckahoe from Wilton turn left on Cary Street and continue to River Road. Turn right on River Road. When you pass Parham Road South it is 4.6 miles farther down River Road to Tuckahoe's entrance on the left. The entrance road is flanked by white pillars and there is an historical marker.

SMITH MOUNTAIN LAKE

Booker T. Washington National Monument

Up From Virginia

The slide presentation at the **Booker T. Washington National Monument** is inspirational, but that is not surprising. The subject is the phenomenal journey of a young boy, born here in slavery, who grew up to found Tuskegee Institute and become an unofficial advisor to three United States presidents. The images of this 15-minute program are poignant and the evocation of the life of young Booker T. Washington striking. It sets the stage for your walking tour of this pre-Civil War plantation.

The Plantation Trail takes you through a partial reconstruction of James and Elizabeth Burroughs's 200-acre tobacco farm. It was typical of the area's working-class farms on which slaves were used to grow a cash crop of tobacco. A reconstructed kitchen cabin stands near the location of the original cabin where a slave child, simply called Booker, was born in the spring of 1856. Like many slave cabins of the period, it has no windows, just crude openings and a bare earth floor. Booker, his mother Jane, his brother John and his sister Amanda slept on rags piled in the corner of a similar cabin. The slide show quotes young Booker on the discomfort of a new flax shirt. It felt like chestnut burrs pressed against his skin. He also complained about the slaves' crude wooden shoes.

As a child, Booker carried water, fed the livestock, took corn to the mill and fanned flies away while the Burroughs family ate. Though his ambition as a boy was to "secure and eat ginger-cakes" like his owner's daughters, he developed more ambitious goals. After Emancipation in 1865, he moved with his family to West Virginia. Life was still hard, but he was finally permitted to learn reading and writing. His workday at a salt furnace began at 4:00 A.M. and he studied the alphabet at night. When he heard about the Hampton Normal and Agricultural Institute for African Americans, he became determined to attend although he had no idea where it was located or how he could get there.

Booker walked and begged rides across Virginia to reach Hampton. His experiences at this school changed his life. Because of his outstanding scholastic performance, the principal at Hampton recommended Washington for a position as principal at a school in Tuskegee, Alabama. When Washington arrived in Tuskegee, there were no teachers, classrooms, supplies or campus. Washington, however, established the school and made it successful.

Booker T. Washington's roots were in the rural Piedmont farm where he lived as a slave and he referred to his early days on the plantation throughout his life. In fact, his most autobiographical book was called *Up From Slavery*. It is amazing to reflect, as you walk the paths of this out-of-the-way farm, that a slave boy born here ended up having tea with Queen Victoria and informally advising Presidents McKinley, Roosevelt and Taft.

The National Park Service maintains the farm today. On this living historical farm are reconstructed 19th-century buildings, farm animals, a kitchen garden and fields of tobacco and other crops. During the summer months, interpreters dressed in 19th-century garb are on hand. The visitor center at Booker T. Washington National Monument is open year-round. Park hours are

A reconstruction of the slave cabin in which Booker T. Washington was born near Rocky Mount is a part of the National Monument commemorating his life as an educator.

from 9:00 A.M. to 4:30 P.M. daily, except Thanksgiving, Christmas and New Year's Day.

While in the area you may want to visit nearby **Smith Mountain Lake**, a state park rivaling Lake Tahoe in beauty and sports opportunity, according to Virginia enthusiasts. With 525 miles of shoreline, this is the largest lake within Virginia's boundaries. The Blue Ridge Mountains form a backdrop for fishing, boating, swimming and camping at this 22,000-acre manmade lake. There are numerous marinas and campgrounds around the lake.

The well-stocked lake offers record-size striped bass and muskies. Altogether 5,000 acres have been set aside for hunting, fishing and wildlife development. Local game includes squirrel, rabbit, raccoon, woodchuck, whitetail deer and an occasional bear. Game birds include dove, quail and wild turkey.

There is a Smith Mountain Dam visitor center with energy exhibits and an overlook. Guided tours are given but call ahead for scheduling details at (540) 985-2587. For information on all the activities in the Smith Mountain Lake area call (800) 676-8203.

Directions: From I-81 in the Roanoke Valley, take I-581 south to Route 220 to Rocky Mount. At Rocky Mount follow directional signs north on Route 122 to the park. For the lake continue north on Route 122.

——Shenandoah Valley——

The 200-mile long Shenandoah Valley bisects a region with world renowned natural wonders such as the striking Natural Bridge and the dazzling underground world of Luray Caverns. Many visitors seek the tranquility of the vast stretches of unspoiled wilderness that make up the George Washington and Jefferson National Forests and the scenic terrain along the Blue Ridge Parkway.

At the Museum of American Frontier Culture America's roots are traced back to the farm traditions of the European countries from which the early pioneers emigrated. While an in-depth look at the frontier they settled is presented at Virginia's Explore Park.

Significant historical figures have cut a swath through this region. George Washington surveyed the Natural Bridge and Thomas Jefferson owned it. Jefferson surveyed the scenically splendid Falling Spring Falls in the Allegheny Highlands. Stonewall Jackson lived in Lexington and taught at VMI. During the Civil War Jackson established his headquarters in Winchester, near where George Washington had an office when he was still a British officer. Six months after Appomattox, Robert E. Lee accepted the presidency of Washington College and moved to Lexington. Technology was advanced when in 1831 on a rural farm in this region, Cyrus McCormick invented the mechanical reaper, beginning the American Agricultural Revolution. Woodrow Wilson's birthplace still stands in Staunton and World War I and II military leader George C. Marshall's exploits are recognized at a museum on the VMI parade grounds.

In the heart of this valley is Roanoke with its still active century-old open-air farmer's market, cultural center, stimulating art scene, restaurants and the Grand Old Lady of hospitality, the newly restored and refurbished Hotel Roanoke. For a luxurious mountain getaway there is The Homestead.

ALLEGHANY HIGHLANDS

Shenandoah Valley's Southernmost Point

Natural beauty, recreational options, historical sites and craft shops all abound in southwest Virginia's **Alleghany Highlands**. When Douthat State Park, just seven miles north of Clifton Forge, was established in the 1930's as Virginia's first state park, the tranquil natural setting along the lake was carefully preserved. It is now a National Historic Landmark. Within the park, trout fishermen can try their luck in the lake or along Wilson Creek; both are stocked regularly. There are boat rentals and a boat ramp. The lake has a designated swimming area. The park's cabins, lodges and campground provide overnight accommodations. There is also an extensive trail system; several trails lead to scenic waterfalls.

If you head west of Clifton Forge, just past Covington on Route 220 north, you will be able to see one of the area's most splendid falls from your car window. Officially named **Falling Spring Falls**, they are known locally as Jefferson Falls because Thomas Jefferson surveyed them and included them in his "notes on the state of Virginia," published in 1778. He wrote: "The only remarkable cascade in this country is that of the Falling Spring in Augusta. It is a water of the James River where it is called Jackson's River. It falls over a rock about 200 feet into the valley below and while not as wide as Niagara it is again half as high." There is an easily missed overlook, so keep alert for the falls on your left.

Nineteen miles north of Covington, scenic **Lake Moomaw** is part of George Washington National Forest (see selection). Popular with sports enthusiasts—fishermen, hunters, campers and hikers—the lake has a 43-mile shoreline with mountains rising from its banks giving it a natural beauty that may remind travelers of the fjords of Alaska and Norway. The water isn't as cold as those waters and there are two swimming beaches. Since this is a manmade lake, caution must be exercised because there are submerged stumps, logs and rocks. The lake's 2,530 acres accommodates both fishermen and water skiers. There are shoreline fishing access trails and boat launching facilities, including fishing platforms and facilities for the physically challenged. Trophy-size bass, bream and brown and rainbow trout can be caught. The national forest on the lake shore is surrounded by the 13,428-acre T.M. Gathright Wildlife Management Area, which is especially known for its wild turkey population. Bald eagles nest around Lake Moomaw; eagle perches have been built in secluded areas to encourage these endangered birds. Five waterfowl islands below the McClintic Bridge encourage ducks and geese to nest on Lake Moomaw.

The lake was created in 1965 when the 257-foot-tall Gathright Dam was built on the Jackson River. There is a visitor center near the dam maintained by the Army Corps of Engineers who constructed the dam. One of the prime fishing spots is directly below the dam.

Another regional scenic attraction, just three miles west of Covington, is the graceful **Humpback Bridge**, the state's oldest standing covered bridge. The first bridge over the James River was built here in 1820. It was washed away and the second was also lost. The third bridge remains standing. It was built in 1857 as part of the Kanawha Turnpike, which eventually extended into Kentucky. The 120-foot-long bridge has no middle supports and the center is eight feet higher than the ends giving it a hump-back appearance. This was originally one of three hand-hewn oak bridges within a mile of each other, but it is the only one still standing. The framework and abutments are original, though the roof, floorboards and exterior walls have been replaced over the years. Traffic stopped rolling over this bridge in 1929. After being neglected for many years it became part of a community wayside park in 1954. The bridge, now on the National Register of Historic Places, is the country's only surviving curved-span covered bridge.

Craftsmanship on a smaller scale can be appreciated and acquired at specialty shops in Covington and Clifton Forge. The **Craft Shops of Covington**, 120 West Main Street, is a regional market featuring handcrafted pottery, textiles, jewelry and collectibles. You can watch artists at work, take classes and purchase supplies. The shops are open NOON to 6:00 P.M. daily except Sunday when it opens at 1:00 P.M. In nearby Clifton Forge you will find the **Alleghany Highlands Arts & Crafts Center** where juried work is exhibited and sold. Oil paintings, watercolors and graphic arts, framed and unframed, are available. The center also features pottery, wooden ware, jewelry, stained glass, needlework, quilts and fiber art. Hours for the center from May through December are Monday through Saturday 10:30 A.M. to 4:30 P.M. The rest of the year it is closed on Monday. Be sure to notice the center's exterior architectural details: there is an elaborate decorative brickwork and cast concrete cartouche on the top of the two buildings that house the center.

Railroad buffs will want to stroll around Clifton Forge where there is a 1906 two-story frame C&O Railroad Office Building and Station Yard that recalls the hectic 1920s when a hundred trains passed through town each day. On the south side of Main Street is the brick C&O Freight Depot, which the C&O Historical Society Inc. plans to restore as a railroad interpretative center. The C&O Historical Society has its exhibits in the 1891 W.W. Pendleton building. It is one of the largest collections devoted to one rail line. They sell memorabilia and are known as the: "Keeper of the Chessie Kitten." Calendars and railroad related books are also available. The society has an extensive collection of railroad cars, documents, photographs and artifacts. The cars can only be toured by making an advance appointment; call (800) 453-COHS. The society office is open Monday through Saturday from 8:00 A.M. to 5:00 P.M.

Directions: From I-81 take I-64 west to Clifton Forge and Covington. For Douthat State Park take Exit 27 off I-64 and follow Route 629 north. For Falling Spring Falls take Route 220 north of Covington; the falls will be on your left. For Lake Moomaw from Covington take Route 220, Hot Springs Road, to Route 687, Jackson River Road. From Route 687 pick up Route 638 which will take you to Lake Moomaw and Gathright Dam. For the Humpback Bridge take Exit 10, the ramp to US 60 at the Callaghan interchange. Go east on Route 60 about a half-mile; the wayside park is on the right. For the Craft Shops of Covington take Exit 16 and turn left at the light onto Route 60 and take that into downtown Covington. The Crafts Shops are on the corner of Route 60 and Main Street. For the Alleghany Highlands Arts & Crafts Center take Exit 24 or 27 off I-64 and follow Route 60 Business west to the midtown parking lot in Clifton Forge. The center is at 439 East Ridgeway Street.

Blue Ridge Parkway

So Near and Yet So Far Removed

It is astonishing to learn that the **Blue Ridge Parkway** lies within a one-day drive of a sizeable portion of the United States population living between New York and northern Florida. More than 20 million people a year travel the parkway's 469 miles. Yet the parkway remains unspoiled, although it is crowded on most pretty weekends from May through October.

The Blue Ridge Parkway begins where the Shenandoah National Park ends at Waynesboro, Virginia and continues to the beginning of the Great Smoky Mountain National Park in Cherokee, North Carolina. The idea of a scenic parkway is generally credited to Virginia Senator Harry F. Byrd who in 1933, suggested to President Franklin D. Roosevelt that the two national parks be connected. Construction began September 11, 1935 and the last seven-mile segment around Grandfather Mountain in

North Carolina opened five decades later on September 11, 1987. This scenic parkway was designed to be savored, not rapidly consumed. The ten visitor centers and 275 turnouts provide ample opportunities to enjoy the scenic overlooks, explore the many trails and visit areas of special interest.

Milepost zero of America's longest national park is at Rockfish Gap and from there both the numbers and the road climb. Elevations range from a low of 649 feet around the James River (milepost 63.8), where there is a visitor center and a restored lock of the James River Canal (see James River and Kanawah Canal selection) to a high of 6,047 around Devil's Courthouse in North Carolina.

The planners of the Blue Ridge Parkway sought to conserve not only the natural beauty of the southern Appalachian highlands but also the cultural and historical resources. **Humpback Rocks** at milepost 5.8, for example, features exhibits on the home life of mountain settlers. A self-guided trail leads to a restored pioneer farm where visitors get a first-hand look at what life was like for those who literally carved homesteads out of wilderness. They hewed the logs for their cabins and picked the rocks for the foundations and fireplaces. In addition to their houses, they built barns and pens for their animals and bins for their crops. The rustic cabin is furnished and has "live-in" occupants who recreate life on this mountain farm every day from May through October.

Of course, on the parkway the fun is in traveling along the mountain tops while gazing over the mesmerizing valleys of Virginia. This is a drive you'll want to take slowly; the 45-mile-an-hour speed limit and the winding macadam road make that a requirement even if it's not a preference.

One of the most scenic spots along the parkway is the **Peaks of Otter** at milepost 86. It is one of only two spots on the Virginia portion of the parkway offering overnight accommodations. For reservations at Peaks of Otter Lodge call (540) 586-1081. In Virginia the toll-free number is (800) 542-5927. Rocky Knob, at milepost 174, offers overnight cabins. For reservations call (540) 593-3503. The Virginia portion of the parkway also has four campgrounds: Otter Creek (near the James River), Peaks of Otter, Roanoke Mountain and Rocky Knob. For information on these campgrounds call (540) 857-2458.

The Peaks of Otter drew visitors even before European settlement. The Iroquois and Cherokee once used the area as a "Warrior's Path." Supplies for the Revolutionary War were carried along a valley road. From 1845 to 1859 Polly Wood operated an ordinary, or inn, for travelers through the Alleghenies. You can visit Polly Wood's Ordinary on weekends or take part in occasional living history programs on this site.

At Sharptop, near the Peaks of Otter on the Blue Ridge Parkway, visitors marvel at the view. The Parkway and Skyline Drive through Virginia's highlands form one of America's most scenic highways.

Another location for living history is the Johnson Farm built about 1850 and farmed through the 1930s. Today it is used to recreate farm life of the 1920s. Back in 1867 Robert E. Lee climbed the summit of the Peaks of Otter; today you can ride a bus to the top of Sharp Top Summit. You can also hike one of the six trails. For an easy and short walk take the $^8/_{10}$-mile Elk Run Loop; if you want a real workout, try the $3^3/_{10}$-mile moderately difficult Harkening Hill Loop.

Do save enough time to continue your drive as far as **Mabry Mill** at milepost 176, perhaps the best-loved spot on the entire parkway. Ed Mabry made his money in the coal mines of West Virginia and came back to the southern highlands of Virginia to purchase land. He quickly gained a reputation for fixing things at the blacksmith shop he set up in the Meadows of Dan area. Today the ring of hammer and anvil resounds from the shop Ed Mabry built. He went on to build a gristmill and sawmill. Customers claimed the Mabrys produced the "best cornmeal in the country." You can test that claim yourself by buying a sample of the cornmeal and buckwheat flour still sold at Mabry's Mill.

The weathered gray frame mill with its giant wheel sits beside a stream in a sylvan setting. Amateur shutter bugs and professional photographers line the stream bank vying for the perfect shot. Mabry's Mill, which served the community as a mill from 1905 until 1935, now serves as the central attraction of the National Park Service exhibit on mountain industry. The exhibit depicts the work of a tanner and shoemaker and, on summer weekends, other craftsmen including a blacksmith.

Traveling beyond the Virginia border into North Carolina, the parkway leads to the scenic charms of Linville Falls, Craggy Gardens and Mt. Pisgah. You should drive all the way to the end of this magnificent mountain drive.

Directions: From I-95 in the Richmond area, take I-64 west past Charlottesville to the beginning of the Blue Ridge Parkway. The parkway can also be reached from numerous exits off I-81, most notably in the vicinity of Roanoke and Buena Vista.

George Washington & Jefferson National Forests

Combining Forces

George Washington and Jefferson National Forests, once separate entities, have combined to provide over 1.8 million acres of natural beauty extending from Winchester to Big Stone Gap. The

George Washington portion of the national forest encompasses over a million acres of northern forests spreading across the Blue Ridge, Massanutten, Shenandoah and Allegheny mountain ranges. Its highest point is 4,463-foot Elliott Knob, just to the west of Staunton.

Within the George Washington section there are 1,700 miles of roads from interstate highways to rough woods roads and 910 miles of hiking trails, with an additional 45 miles of motorized trails. These trails range from short paved interpretative walks to longer hiking loops and even more challenging backcountry long distance trails.

Three interpretative trails can be entered near the **Massanutten Visitor Information Center**, off Route 211 just three miles east of New Market. Families particularly enjoy the short walks like Discovery Way, a $2/_{10}$-mile paved trail that begins just south of the visitor parking lot. Another option is the Massanutten Storybook Trail, a paved $1/_4$-trail that offers a scenic overlook of Page Valley and the Blue Ridge Mountains. Interpretative signs reveal the geological story of the development of this mountain range. (To reach this trailhead, take Route 211 east of New Market for five miles then turn left on Chrisman Hollow Road, FDR 274, and head north for $1 1/_2$ miles.)

For the visually impaired, there is the Lion's Tale National Recreation Trail, a $1/_2$-mile sensory trail that deals with forest ecology. (Follow above directions but continue 8 miles past the Massanutten Storybook Trail on Chrisman Hollow Road.)

There are numerous loop trails offering an array of scenic delights. One of the most popular is the three-mile Crabtree Falls Trail. Along the trail you'll see five cascading waterfalls that drop a total of 1,200 feet; it's the highest drop in the Blue Ridge Mountains. The best spot to enter this trail is from Route 56, east of the Blue Ridge Parkway and Montebello. The five-mile loop trail to the rocky peak of 4,032-foot Mount Pleasant affords outstanding views of the countryside. This is not an easy hike but it will reward your effort. Long distance trails include the Appalachian National Scenic Trail, the Wild Oak National Recreation Trail, the Shenandoah Mountain Trail and the Great North Mountain Trail. For those who prefer to see the sights from the comfort of their car, there is the Highlands Scenic Tour, a 20-mile scenic drive through the mountains. Details on any of these trails and additional recreation options within the national forest are available at the Massanutten Visitor Information Center (open May through October) and at various ranger district offices throughout the forest.

Now linked with this northern forested area is the Jefferson National Forest, roughly 710,000 acres in west-central Virginia. Here you'll find more than 1,100 miles of trails, 500 miles of trout streams, six fishing lakes and four swimming lakes. Four trails are especially noteworthy: the Appalachian National Scenic Trail, the Cascades National Recreation Trail, the Mount Rogers National Recreation Trail and the Virginia Highlands Horse Trail. Few hikers can manage the total 2,000-mile distance of the Appalachian Trail, but within Jefferson National Forest it is possible to sample 300 miles of this historic walkway up the eastern United States. For the weekend hiker, the four-mile round trip Cascades National Recreation Trail that leads to a striking 66-foot waterfall is ideal. Another scenic four-mile hike is offered along the Mount Rogers National Recreation Trail from the Fairwood Valley to the Appalachian Trail near Mount Rogers, the highest point in the state. Finally, there is the 68-mile horseback and wagon train trail. The open grassy meadows of Pine Mountain's high country near Mount Rogers is only open to hikers and horseback riders. There are, however, two scenic byways that let automobile passengers enjoy the mountain vistas.

You can link up with the 16-mile Big Walker Mountain Scenic Byway near Wytheville. It takes you past old farms, through forested areas, by the trail heads for numerous hiking options, to scenic overlooks, picnic spots, fishing ponds and campgrounds. At Big Walker Lookout, there is a swinging bridge and observation tower that can be enjoyed from April through October. The Mount Rogers Scenic Byway provides automobile passengers a look at the natural beauty of this area during its scenic peak in the autumn when the leaves turn. Another scenic area within the Jefferson National Forest is the Guest River Gorge (see selection).

To obtain information on the George Washington and Jefferson National Forests you can call the forest supervisor's office at (540) 265-6054.

Directions: From I-81 take Route 211 three miles east of New Market for the Massanutten Visitor Information Center. You will be able to pick up trail maps and complete information on recreational options within the national forest.

The Homestead

One of America's Oldest and Most Prestigious Resorts

The Homestead, one of the most venerable resorts in the country, first opened as an inn in 1766. The medicinal properties of the mountain springs had been noted as early as the 1600s. Local legends claim a Native American messenger went to sleep one winter night in the hot springs' water and discovered its rejuvenating effects. Dr. Thomas Walker, a medical missionary who charted this territory, wrote in his journal on July 9, 1750, "We went to Hot springs and found six invalids there. The spring is warmer than new milk and there is a spring of cold water within 20 feet of the warm one."

Thomas Jefferson is credited with designing Warm Springs' first men's bathhouse in 1761; it's the oldest spa structure in America. In 1766, Lieutenant Thomas Bullitt, who was stationed on the frontier at Fort Dinwiddie, built an inn he called The Homestead. Legend has it he opened the hostelry because so many uninvited guests were arriving at his home to stay while they sought the curative effects of the hot springs. Although only Thomas Jefferson's visit is documented, it is believed that George Washington and Alexander Hamilton also enjoyed the water of Warm Springs, as Hot Springs was called during the Revolutionary War.

Bullitt died in 1778 and a series of absentee landlords owned the property before it was acquired in 1832 by Dr. Thomas Goode who improved the bathhouses. By 1846 he announced the opening of a "modern hotel." Goode placed glowing testimonials and accounts in *Harper's Weekly* and other periodicals claiming the waters cured gout, rheumatism, liver diseases, paralysis, neuralgia, enlarged glands and spinal irritations.

After Goode's death in 1858, another series of absentee owners ran the property for decades. During the Civil War, The Homestead was used as a Confederate hospital. In 1891, a group of stockholders in the Chesapeake and Ohio Railroad purchased the hotel and land. M.E. Ingalls, a member of the syndicate, became president of The Homestead, and in 1914 his family purchased controlling interest in the resort. The railroad connection proved helpful, as a branch line of the C&O was built to Hot Springs in 1891–1892, providing passenger service until 1970. In 1892, the spa was built and the first tee of the golf course and first tennis court added. Buildings that remain from this early period include the spa, casino (added in 1893) and eleven cottages (which now house specialty shops).

After a fire destroyed the old wooden frame hotel, the main section of today's Homestead was built in 1902. The west wing was added in 1903, the east wing in 1914 and the tower section in 1929. This new resort attracted the rich and famous; such illustrious personalities as Henry Ford, Thomas Edison and John D. Rockefeller, Sr. visited The Homestead. Woodrow Wilson and Edith Bolling Galt spend part of their honeymoon at this resort. Thirteen former presidents, starting with William McKinley and ending with Lyndon Johnson, have visited here.

The recreational opportunities lured visitors. In October 1924, the William Flynn-designed Cascades course opened. It was ranked by *Golf Magazine* as one of the world's top 100 golf

In 1766, The Homestead opened as an inn for visitors enjoying the medicinal properties of the nearby mountain springs. Since that time the rich and famous have flocked to this venerable resort.

courses and ranked by *Golfweek* as Virginia's premier course. In 1933, the resort opened the Shooting Club, considered to be one of the nation's finest championship shooting facilities.

During World War II, The Homestead was used as an internment site for Japanese diplomats. On December 29, 1941, shortly after the attack on Pearl Harbor, 250 men, women and children arrived by train from Washington's Union Station (more arrived later).

The Homestead embarked on a period of recreational expansion in the 50s and 60s that included the opening of an outdoor pool and sun beach in 1954, an innovative southern skiing and ice skating program in 1959, bowling in 1962 and a third golf course in 1963. The resort is now managed and co-owned by Club Resorts Inc., who will become sole owners in 1999.

In 1994, the new ownership/management company began a $6.5 million renovation project that included both interior and exterior work on the hotel and cottages, grounds work and work on the recreational facilities. The Homestead has 521 guest rooms and 81 luxurious suites some featuring sun porches and fireplaces. Among the ten dining venues is the Dining Room which features live entertainment and dancing, plus The Grille, a sports bar, cafe, tavern and other options. A wine room holds thousands of bottles of outstanding wines. Guests can take a tour of The Homestead cellars or they can arrange to host a wine tasting. In addition to the boutiques located in Cottage Row the hotel has Palm Beach Corridor with exclusive shops.

The resort has three golf courses: the top-ranked 1924 Cascades course, the recently improved 1892/1913 Homestead course and the 1963 Lower Cascades course. Added in 1994 is a driving range and practice facility. There are eight Har-Tru and four all-weather tennis courts. While many sports enthusiasts don't think of Virginia as a ski destination, The Homestead has nine groomed downhill ski slopes. They offer night skiing, a half-pipe and snowboard park, ski shop, ski and snowboard rentals and a ski school. Winter sports fans also enjoy the Olympic-sized outdoor skating rink with day and nighttime sessions. The renowned Shooting Club features sporting clays, five-stand sporting, skeet, trap and a .22-caliber rifle/pistol range. There are also more than 100 miles of riding trails and 40 horses on the property. Carriage and pony rides can also be arranged. Three hiking trails begin in front of the hotel; for all except the short Promenade, sturdy walking shoes are recommended. One of the most popular hikes is along the Cascades Gorge Nature Trail which traverses a dozen waterfalls, climbing roughly 450 feet in about $1^1/_2$ miles. Another way to explore the trails is by mountain bike. A three-mile-long trout stream flows between the Cascades and Lower Cascades golf courses; gear and permits are available at The Outpost in Hot Springs.

Many guests return year after year, for the spa and hot springs. An indoor pool is fed by Hot Springs' 104 degree mineral water. Also offered are mineral baths, massages, loofah scrubs, combination baths, a tanning bed, saunas and a steam room. The bathhouses at Warm Springs, added in the late 1700s and early 1800s, still serve Homestead guests.

For information about staying at The Homestead call (800) 838-1766 or (540) 839-1766. There are a wide variety of vacation packages available.

Directions: Take I-64 west to Staunton, then pick up Route 250 west to Route 254. Take Route 254 west to Route 42, and follow that south to Route 39. Head west again on Route 39 to Route 220. Take Route 220 south to Hot Springs and The Homestead. From I-81, traveling south, take the Bridgewater exit, Route 257 and head west on that to Route 42, then pick up above directions. From Alexandria take the Beltway, I-495/95, to I-66 and travel west to I-81. Take I-81 south to I-64 west to Covington. Pick up Route 220 north to Hot Springs.

Luray Caverns

Hurray for Luray!

Once you have explored nature's handiwork beneath the hills of **Luray**, you can well imagine the awe Andrew Campbell and Benton Stebbins felt in 1878 when they discovered the labyrinth. With two helpers, young Billy Campbell, Andrew's nephew, and Trent Lilliard, they had been searching for a month for a cave in the hills outside this sleepy Virginia community in the Shenandoah Valley. They searched so long they became the butt of good-natured jokes around town. Being called a "cave rat" and "phantom chaser" discouraged young Trent and he gave up the quest. On August 13 the remaining searchers found a sinkhole on Cave Hill that looked promising. Digging all morning in the August heat they were cooled by air welling up from below. When they finally had an opening large enough Andrew Campbell was lowered into the cave. What he saw was beyond the trio's wildest dreams: a cavernous palace with columns of stalagmites meeting hanging stalactites, crystals that glistened like diamonds and pristine white formations that gave dramatic contrast to the onyx-colored walls.

At Luray you see the caverns just as they looked when discovered. Only the walks and lights have been added. There is no artifice, no colored lights nor special effects; none is needed to enhance the natural beauty of this subterranean fantasy world. The dripping stalactites continue forming just as they have for millions of years. The limestone base rock in the caverns was formed during the Paleozoic age over 400 million years ago.

The caverns opened several months after they were discovered and have been open every day since. One addition made in 1954 is worth noting: the Great Stalacpipe Organ in what is called the "Cathedral" room. *Ripley's Believe It Or Not* television crew filmed this one-of-a-kind organ. The stalactite formations have been tuned by reshaping and are played from a large organ console.

This is not the only musical attraction at Luray. On Tuesdays, Thursdays, Saturdays and Sundays at 8:00 P.M. you can hear a free 45-minute recital on the 47 bells of "The Luray Singing Tower," an outstanding carillon built on the grounds above the caverns.

While at Luray Caverns you can also explore the **Historic Car and Carriage Caravan**. The 75 vehicles in this collection are all polished and ready to go. There are some sporty models to see, including a 1908 Baker Electric, a 1927 Bugatti, a 1927 Rolls Royce that belonged to Rudolph Valentino, a 1930 Cord and a 1935 Hispano Suiza. You can also decide whether you would have preferred a Ford, Chevrolet or Dodge when you view all three manufacturers' models for 1915.

Admission covers both the caverns, a U.S. Registered Natural Landmark, and the historic vehicle museum. The first tour of the caverns is at 9:00 A.M. every day and the last tour is given at 7:00 P.M. from mid-June until Labor Day. From Labor Day to November the last tour is at 6:00 P.M. From November until mid-March the late tour on weekdays is at 4:00 P.M. and on weekends at 5:00 P.M. From mid-March until mid-June the last tour is at 6:00 P.M.

Directions: From I-95 take the Fredericksburg exit, Route 3 west to Culpeper. Then continue west on Route 522 to Sperryville and Route 211 to Luray. From the Washington Beltway I-495/95, it is a 90-minute drive; take I-66 west to Route 522 at Front Royal and pick up Skyline Drive, or Route 340 south. Then head west on Route 211 to Luray. From I-81 take Exit 264 at New Market and head east on Route 211. Luray Caverns is 15 minutes from the central entrance to the Shenandoah National Park.

McCormick Farm and Historic Museum and Wade's Mill

Reaping What You Sow

An historic mill on the farm where Cyrus McCormick was born and a working farm with an operational gristmill make a dandy country duo.

Walnut Grove Farm, while not widely known, is picturesque, educational and historical. The oak log gristmill, built in 1778, stands beside the blacksmith shop where, in 1831, Cyrus McCormick designed and built the first successful horse-drawn mechanical reaper. Twenty-two-year-old Cyrus worked with his father, Robert, who was also an inventor and tinkerer. They tested the reaper in John Steele's neighboring grain field. It was a two-man operation. Jim Hite drove the horse and Jon Anderson raked the grain. In half a day they had reaped six acres of oats, or as much as five men with scythes could harvest in a day. Despite such a demonstration, there were no buyers when Cyrus offered his marvel for sale at $50.

The following season the McCormicks harvested their own 50 acres with the new reaper. Gradually buyers were found. Between 1831 and 1846 when Cyrus left Walnut Grove at age 36, he built and sold 100 reapers and the price doubled to $100. The American Agricultural Revolution started slowly, but, unquestionably, this out-of-the-way Virginia **McCormick Farm** (now named for its famous native-son) was its birthplace.

In the blacksmith workshop, which was the only "factory" McCormick had during the 1830s, you'll see an anvil he used to build the first reaper. A working reproduction of the reaper has the place of honor among the numerous McCormick farm inventions displayed in the museum above the shop.

As part of the nation's bicentennial this old reaper was operated for a BBC program. Getting it out of the museum was like trying to take a ship from a bottle. It had to be disassembled to get it through the door and then rebuilt. This was not the end of the problems—a young horse harnessed to the noisy reaper bolted and ran it into a fence. Finally an old workhorse pulled it into the field for the film. The TV crew might better have used the models; the details are so exact on these scale-models they look full-size when photographed outdoors. You'll see models of the reaper and binder, as well as the combined reaper and mower.

The McCormick homestead, built in 1821, now serves as headquarters for the Virginia Polytechnic Institute's Shenandoah Valley Research Station. Visitors are welcome to explore the sheep barns and other livestock areas. There is also a picnic area and restrooms in the old slave quarters. The farm is open daily 8:00 A.M. to 5:00 P.M. at no charge. Located just a half-mile off I-81, it's a great place for an interstate break.

Down the road $4^1/_2$ miles is **Wade's Mill**, listed on the National Register of Historic Places. Captain Joseph Kennedy, who built two of the earliest mills in Rockbridge County, built this mill in 1750. In 1882, James F. Wade purchased the mill and it was operated by his family for four generations. A major historic renovation has returned the interior and mill workings to their appearance in the late 1880s. Power for the mill is supplied by a 21-foot water wheel fed by a nearby stream. The old-fashioned method of water-powered stone grinding uses stone burrs to slowly crush and grind the entire wheat kernel into flour, producing what many purists believe is a better tasting, more nutritious flour.

Wade's Mill produces a wide variety of flours with no bleaches, additives, preservatives or chemicals. The flours include wholewheat, buckwheat, cornmeal, cracked wheat, natural white and a buckwheat pancake mix. They also offer gift boxes with a variety of their products. These can be purchased in shops in Virginia, in D.C. Safeways or by mail. Write Wade's

Mill, Inc., Route 1, P.O. Box 475, Raphine, VA 24472. You can stop by the mill Thursday through Saturday from 9:00 A.M. to 5:00 P.M., April though mid-December.

Also in Raphine is **Buffalo Springs Herb Farm**, an 18th-century farmstead with a variety of theme gardens, a plant house stocked with herb plants and nature trails. The oldest section of the stone and brick house dates back to 1793. In a barn beside a rushing creek you can purchase dried flowers, herbal products, garden books and participate in a wide array of programs and workshops. For a current schedule call (540) 348-1083. The farm is open April through mid-December Wednesday through Saturday from 10:00 A.M. to 5:00 P.M. and Sundays in April and May and September through mid-December from 1:00 to 5:00 P.M.

Directions: From I-95 in the Richmond area, take I-64 west to Charlottesville. From Charlottesville take the scenic Blue Ridge Parkway south. Exit the parkway at milepost 27.2 on Virginia Route 56 to Steele's Tavern. At Steele's Tavern go south on Route 11 for about 100 yards and turn right on Route 606 to McCormick Farm. For Wade's Mill take Route 606 four miles past I-81. The mill will be on the right as indicated by the sign on Route 606. Just past the turn for Wade's Mill on the right on Route 606 is Buffalo Springs Herb Farm. Or from I-81 take exit 205 (Raphine/Steele's Tavern) and go west on Route 606 for Wade's Mill or east for McCormick Farm.

Natural Bridge

Don't Knock the Rock!

The key word is natural. If you ignore all man's intrusions, the rock bridge Thomas Jefferson called "the most sublime of nature's works" still enthralls.

Jefferson's enthusiasm was in part proprietal, since he owned the bridge. It and Niagara Falls were considered wonders of the New World. **Natural Bridge** was part of a 157-acre tract Jefferson acquired from King George III for 20 shillings, or less than $5, just two years before the Revolution. Once he had acquired it, Jefferson refused to sell the bridge, calling his ownership a "public trust" to make sure that it was available to the people.

The Natural Bridge is a massive geological structure rising 215 feet above meandering Cedar Creek. The bridge span is 90 feet long and 50-150 feet wide. Scientists theorize that the bridge was formed when Cedar Creek was diverted into a cave. Over time the roof of the cave collapsed, leaving the bridge as the most stable portion of the natural tunnel through the cave.

You'll rarely find a more impressive nature walk than the one along Cedar Creek. The steps down to the creek follow the smaller Cascade Creek. For those who have trouble walking there is a shuttle bus. Along your walk you will observe examples of fossilized moss being formed. One noticeable outcropping is just to the left of the first wooden bench along the trail.

The arbor vitae along the trail are some of the oldest and largest specimens in the world. The Monacan Indians found medicinal properties in the arbor vitae foliage. The Monocans considered the bridge a gift from God, they prayed at the bridge and used it as a thoroughfare. As you approach the bridge along Cedar Creek you'll see how the rocks are inclined. This effect was created 200 million years ago when the Appalachian Mountains were formed.

Across the creek on the steep wall beneath the bridge are the initials George Washington carved when he was surveying the area in 1750. He climbed up 23 feet to leave his mark.

On the other side of the bridge you'll discover picnic tables beside the creek. If you continue your walk you'll see the salt-peter cave. Nitrates mined from the cave during the War of 1812 and the Civil War were used to make gunpowder. The cave does not appear to extend any farther than the cavity you'll observe when peering into the opening. A short distance from the cave is the barely visible Lost River.

Far more interesting is the 50-foot drop of Lace Falls just down the trail. This is the last point of interest along the Natural Bridge walking trail. If you are staying through the evening you should plan to attend the Drama of Creation. Twice a night during the summer (once nightly during the winter) the 45-minute sound and light show is presented. The musical program is technically a bit passe and some purists might prefer listening to Strauss's *Also Sprach Zarathustra* or an equally dramatic work on their personal cassette while watching the impressive play of lights across the great chasm. The show goes on despite the weather, so dress appropriately.

Since 1978 the Natural Bridge caverns have been open to the public. First discovered in the 1880s, these are well worth investigating. The caverns have numerous flowstone cascades, deposits of calcite formed when water flows down the walls of a cave. One example, a dome-shaped mass, is one of the largest of this type of deposit to be found in the East. The caverns are also noted for their drapery-shaped deposits.

The beauty above and below make this excursion a double treat for nature lovers. Admission is charged to all three attractions—Natural Bridge, caverns and a wax museum. Children under six are admitted free. Natural Bridge is open 8:00 A.M. daily until dark when the Drama of Creation begins.

Directions: From I-95 in the Richmond area take I-64 west to Staunton and pick up I-81 south. Continue past Lexington to Exit 180, Route 11. Follow the well-marked Route 11 to Natural Bridge.

New Market Battlefield Historical Park

From Classroom to Conflict

The Battle of New Market is remembered as the first and only time in history that the entire student body of an American college marched into battle. The 257 brave cadets from the Virginia Military Institute joined General John Breckinridge's troops. Together they won the last Confederate victory in the Shenandoah Valley.

This 280-acre battlefield park is dedicated "to valor on the part of all young Americans in defense of their country." Most Virginia battlefields belong to state or federal governments, but New Market was purchased by a 1911 VMI graduate and given to the college. The Hall of Valor, which should be your first stop at the park, has a movie, *New Market—A Field of Honor*, that tells the story of the VMI soldiers. Their four-day march from the classroom to the battlefield was made in a torrential downpour. Their strategy classes had never dealt with the problem of advancing across a field so sodden that it sucked the shoes off soldiers' feet. Forever after, the land around the Bushong Farm has been called "The Field of Lost Shoes."

The young soldiers become more than statistics when you read the penciled note from Cadet Merritt to this father: "Dear Pa, I write you a few lines to let you know that I was wounded. I was in the battle here yesterday. . ." Cadet Merritt was one of 47 cadets wounded during the battle. Ten young boys lost their lives. You'll empathize with the grief another father must have felt as you read the telegram informing him of his son's death. There is a life-size portrait of Thomas Garland Jefferson, 17-year-old cousin of President Thomas Jefferson, who died from a fatal chest wound.

A dramatic stained-glass window includes, among the symbols of war, names of the ten cadets who died at New Market. Diaries, photo murals and models illustrating the variety of uniforms worn during the Civil War as well as battlefield mementos provide a glimpse of the war's full scope. All of the major campaigns in the state are covered in the museum's Virginia Room. The Hall of Valor salutes the brave of both North and South and tells more than the story of New Market. A second film covers Stonewall Jackson's Valley Campaign. Before the war Jackson was an instructor at VMI (see Stonewall Jackson House and Stonewall Jackson's Headquarters selections) and, along with the fallen cadets, he is enshrined in the pantheon of Civil War heroes at VMI.

From the Hall of Valor you move outside. The **Bushong Farm** around which the battle raged has been preserved to give you a look at 19th-century farm life. The original farmhouse was built about 1825 on land the family acquired on June 22, 1791. During the summer months you can tour two rooms of the house. Throughout the year you can see seven restored outbuildings including a wheelwright and blacksmith shop, a bake oven and summer kitchen. A trail leads from the house across the fatal field to the hilltops from which the Union forces made their last stand. A second trail takes you along the high bluffs above the North Fork of the Shenandoah River.

New Market Battlefield Historical Park is open daily 9:00 A.M. to 5:00 P.M. except Thanksgiving, Christmas and New Year's Day. Admission is charged. The Battle of New Market Reenactment is presented each year on the Sunday closest to May 15.

Directions: From I-95 in the Richmond area, take I-64 west to Staunton and I-81 north to New Market. The battlefield is directly off I-81 at Exit 264. Turn onto Route 211 west, make an immediate right onto Route 305, the George Collins Parkway. Travel to the end of the parkway, $1^1/_4$ miles to reach the Hall of Valor Civil War Museum, which is part of New Market Battlefield Historical Park. This is the third museum on the parkway.

LEXINGTON

George C. Marshall Museum and Library

War and Peace

George Catlett Marshall, one of only a few professional soldiers to be awarded the Nobel Peace Prize, was both a military genius and an inspired humanitarian. His European Recovery Plan rehabilitated the economies of that war-torn continent.

As the son of a Kentucky Democrat living in Republican Uniontown, Pennsylvania, young Marshall had no hope for an appointment to West Point. He chose instead to attend Virginia Military Institute, spending his spare time exploring Virginia's Civil War battlefields. He learned a great deal about the military strategies of legendary VMI instructor Stonewall Jackson.

Sightseers in Lexington may ride in style in a surrey through downtown and residential districts.

Today at the **George C. Marshall Museum**, you'll see an exhibit covering Marshall's years as staff officer in France, from 1917–1919. Damon Runyan wrote a newspaper column about him entitled, "American Sudan Drives According to Principles of Stonewall Jackson." Runyan was not the only one to discern the influence of Jackson. As early as 1913 while he was in the Philippines, Marshall was called upon to attack when his chief of staff fell ill. Marshall dictated the entire plan of battle without corrections. In commending the young lieutenant for his field orders, Major General J. Franklin Bell said, "He is the greatest military genius since Stonewall Jackson."

Photo murals and personal mementos at the museum trace Marshall's outstanding military leadership. The course of World War II is detailed in a 25-minute electric map presentation. For military buffs there is General George Patton's helmet, Field Marshall Rommel's map of El Alamein and General Gerow's operation of Omaha Beach.

Marshall's career as statesman and diplomat is also thoroughly covered. In the postwar years he served as President Truman's envoy to China with the rank of ambassador and as his secretary of state. It was in the latter capacity that he spoke at the Harvard Commencement program in June 1947 and outlined what has become known as the Marshall Plan. At the age of 70 by a special act of Congress Marshall became Truman's secretary of defense during the Korean conflict.

America is not the only nation to recognize Marshall's achievements. The museum displays medals from 16 countries including the George VI's Honorary Knight of the Grand Cross, Military Division of the Order of Bath. One award did not go directly to Marshall but to *Patton*, the movie about General Patton's drive across Europe. The producer of this Best Picture of the Year for 1970, Frank M. McCarthy, chose to have his Oscar displayed at the George C. Marshall Museum.

The museum has an innovative "Try on a Piece of History" program for young visitors. The Research Center houses an extensive archive containing the personal and private papers of General Marshall and other contemporaries as well as a library of more than 25,000 volumes specializing in 20th-century military and diplomatic history. The Research Center is available without charge to researchers of all ages.

The George C. Marshall Museum is open daily from 9:00 A.M. to 5:00 P.M. except during the months of November through March when the museum closes at 4:00 P.M. The Research Center is open weekdays from 8:30 A.M. to 4:30 P.M. Both are closed on Thanksgiving, Christmas and New Year's Day. Admission is charged for the museum.

Directions: From I-95 in the Richmond area, take I-64 west to Lexington, then exit onto Route 11. Just outside Lexington, Route 11 forks to the right onto Jefferson Street. The first right off Jefferson up Letcher Avenue takes you to the VMI parade grounds and to the George C. Marshall Museum. From I-81, take the Route 60 exit and head north into Lexington on Nelson Street. Follow Main Street to Letcher Avenue.

Goshen Pass and The Virginia Horse Center

Don't Pass This Up!

Matthew Fontaine Maury, the 19th-century scientist and VMI instructor known as the "Pathfinder of the Seas" for his pioneering work in oceanography, was inordinantly fond of **Goshen Pass**. He viewed it as the loveliest spot in the state. His funeral instructions stipulated that his body be carried through the pass when the rhododendron were in bloom. Although he died on February 1, 1873, the following May the cadets of Virginia Military Institute formed an honor guard and carried his coffin through Goshen Pass. Later the scenic, boulder-strewn river that meanders through the three-mile-long Allegheny Mountain pass was renamed the Maury River.

Native Americans used this narrow-wooded canyon pass to cut through the mountains. The elk and buffalo created a trail here as they crossed the mountain in search of food. Eventually wagons began widening this route and around 1880 the pass was the stagecoach thoroughfare. First called Dunlap's Gap, the name was changed to Strickler's Pass and then Goshen Pass.

A wayside park provides a base for those pursuing recreational opportunities. The park also has picnic and restroom facilities. Fishing, swimming, tubing, canoeing and hiking are all options. There is a walking trail on the north side of the river. In the spring the gorge is abloom with rhododendron and dogwood; later the laurel comes into flower. Low lying ferns and mosses are underfoot, while magnificent pines, hemlocks and evergreens provide a lush canopy throughout most of the year. Up from the wayside park there is a shady trail along Laurel Run, a sparkling mountain stream. Another spot with picnic tables and grills is Indian Pool, just 1.1 miles inside the pass from the Goshen Pass sign at the southern entrance. There is a parking area and steps with an iron railing lead down to the river. The walk takes you past a massive stone wall, and then along the river past a spot where the water falls over two rock ledges. At this picturesque spot you'll find picnic facilities. There is an overlook and monument to Matthew Fontaine Maury before you reach the main wayside park. Maury's plaque states that he was "The Genius Who First Snatched From Ocean and Atmosphere The Secret Of Their Laws." Past this park is one final parking area, just before the portion of the river called Devil's Kitchen. Just past this area is a turn-around if you want to return to Lexington.

On the way to or from Goshen Pass you might want to stop at **The Virginia Horse Center**, just outside Lexington on Route 39. Established by the Virginia legislature in 1985, it is one of the finest equine complexes in the country. The facility includes a 4,000 seat coliseum, outdoor arena and grandstands, and state-of-the-art barns that can stable over 700 horses. There are no horseback riding facilities for the general public. The center hosts shows, auctions, educational clinics, workshops and a horse festival in April. For scheduling information call 540-463-2194.

Directions: Just north of Lexington, I-81 south and I-64 west merge for a brief time. When they split at Lexington take I-64 west and then take Exit 55 onto Route 11 north for one tenth of a mile to Route 39 west. It is Route 39, designated a Virginia Scenic By-Way, that winds through Goshen Pass (which is only 12 miles outside Lexington).

Lee Chapel and Museum

Certain-lee, Master-lee!

On October 2, 1865, less than six months after the surrender at Appomattox, Robert E. Lee accepted the presidency of Washington College at an annual salary of $1,500. At 58, he was anxious for the chance to be of use to the "rising" generation.

Lee first lived in the president's house that Thomas "Stonewall" Jackson had shared with his in-laws during his 14-month marriage to Elinor Junkin, whose father was the college's president (see Stonewall Jackson House selection). Soon after Lee arrived he embarked on a building program.

His first project was the chapel that ultimately became known as the **Lee Chapel**. Lee lavished great enthusiasm on the chapel he requested the trustees build on campus. Work began in January 1867, under the close supervision of Lee and his son, Custis, a professor at neighboring Virginia Military Institute. It was completed in time for the 1868 June commencement. From then until his death in 1870, Lee attended daily worship service there with his students.

Lee's son also helped him formulate plans for a new president's home. Although unhappy that the house cost more than the $15,000 originally appropriated for it, he was pleased with several architectural details. The verandas were designed so that his wife, crippled with arthritis, could move her rolling chair across them. Lee was also happy to have his old friend, Traveller, nearby in a new brick stable adjoining the house. Reports from the 1860s indicate that Traveller certainly needed a refuge. Souvenir hunters had pulled out so much hair from its mane and tail that the warhorse shied away from people.

On the chapel's lower level, Lee established his office. He fashioned and furnished it, and it remains today as it was when illness forced him from his desk on September 28, 1870. The remains of Traveller are buried just outside the office. Today the rest of the lower level is a museum where reminders of both Lee and Washington can be seen.

A letter dated 1796 thanks George Washington for his gift of stock, saving the school from bankruptcy. Washington endowed the school with $50,000 of James River Canal Company stock that is still paying dividends. Students today each receive roughly $3 a year in residuals. Many of Lee's personal belongings are included in the museum collection. The portraits bring famous figures from history to life. Paintings include the Charles Willson Peale portraits of Washington and Lafayette and the popular Lee portrait done by Theodore Pine.

The lower level also contains the Lee family crypt where Lee is buried with his wife, parents and their seven children. Many visitors mistakenly believe Lee is buried in the chapel apse beneath the impressive Edward Valentine statue. Lee's widow chose the recumbent pose; she wanted to remember him as if he were sleeping on the battlefield.

Robert E. Lee died on October 12, 1870. Later in the month, when George Washington Custis Lee was elected to succeed his father as president, the college name was changed to Washington and Lee University. Both the Lee Chapel and the Front Campus Colonnade of Washington and Lee University are National Historic Landmarks. There is no charge to visit the Lee Chapel and Museum. Hours are 9:00 A.M. to 4:00 P.M. Monday through Saturday from mid-October to mid-April and until 5:00 P.M. the rest of the year. Sunday hours are 2:00 to 5:00 P.M.

Directions: From I-95 in the Richmond area, take I-64/I-81 west to Lexington. Take Route 11 exit off I-64 and travel south. Just outside Lexington Route 11 will fork right onto Main Street. Follow Main Street to the Washington and Lee campus. From the south if you are traveling on I-81 take Exit 188, Route 60 West.

Follow Route 60 West to Main Street. Turn left to Henry Street which will take you to the Washington and Lee campus. For information on this and all the Lexington attractions stop first at the Lexington Visitor Center at 107 East Washington Street.

Stonewall Jackson House

From Square Box to Stone Wall

Jackson was nicknamed Square Box and Tom Fool by his young charges at Virginia Military Institute who thought ". . . his classes too dull, his methods too rigid and his discipline too severe." It is said that when he was asked for clarification by a student he would simply repeat his statement using the same words and intonation. His lectures were not lightened by explanations or discussions. Yet those who survived the carnage of the War Between the States grew old bragging that they were taught natural philosophy or artillery tactics by Old Jack.

The teacher who memorized his lessons standing at his desk in his Lexington home went on to glory by standing firm at Bull Run. He became known as "Stonewall" after that opening Civil War battle when General Bee spotted Jackson's brigade and cried, "There stands Jackson like a stone wall. Rally behind the Virginians."

But it is the days Jackson spent in Lexington before the war that are remembered at the **Stonewall Jackson House**. A short slide program introduces you to the young, handsome Virginia instructor. He was a deeply religious and disciplined military man who began each day with a cold bath and a brisk walk around town before his morning devotions. During the week he taught his classes at VMI. On Sunday he founded and taught a Sunday School for African American youngsters. When he left for the war he earmarked part of his pay so that these religious classes could continue. Jackson regularly contributed a tenth of his income to the Presbyterian Church.

Two years after he arrived in Lexington he married Elinor Junkin, whose father was president of Washington College. The newlyweds lived on campus with Elinor's parents in what is now called the Lee-Jackson House. Their life together was brief; she died the following year in childbirth.

In 1857, after three years as a widower, Jackson married Mary Anna Morrison and in 1858 they purchased this house on Washington Street.

The furnishings you see today are personal possessions and period pieces that match the inventory made following Jackson's tragic death after the Battle of Chancellorsville in 1863. The first room on the tour is the kitchen, which is furnished with a six-burner wood cookstove. The Jacksons owned one like it which was valued at $50 on the estate inventory. On a 20-acre farm at the edge of town Jackson, with the help of three slaves, grew much of the food for his table. He would often supervise the preserving of his crops, keeping an eye on the kitchen slaves and lending a hand to seal jars of tomatoes.

In Jackson's study there is a desk like the one he stood before while memorizing his lessons. In the parlor are a loveseat and two chairs that belonged to the Jacksons. Representing Jackson's one extravagance is a piano like the one he purchased for Mary Anna for $500. Even though he was a devout church-goer he was known to occasionally waltz his wife around the parlor. (He learned to waltz and polka while serving in the Mexican War.) Jackson's rocking chair is in the bedroom. An early picture of Jackson reveals just how handsome he was without his beard. Legend has it that he vowed not to shave until the South was victorious, a story that is suspect as he did carry his shaving kit with him to war. At least one British journalist described him during the war as having ". . . thin colorless cheeks, with only a very small allowance of whiskers; a cleanly-shaven upper lip and chin. . . ."

The dining room was used every morning and evening for Bible reading and prayers. On Sunday evenings slaves in the neighborhood would join the Jacksons for devotions. Before ending your visit be sure to view the exhibits that focus on General Jackson, the Civil War era and life in Lexington during its "golden age."

The Stonewall Jackson House, at 8 East Washington Street, is open for guided tours 9:00 A.M. to 4:30 P.M. Monday through Saturday and 1:00 to 4:30 P.M. on Sunday. During the summer it stays open until 5:30 P.M. Admission is charged.

To discover other city sites associated with Jackson, stop at the Historic Lexington Visitor Center just down Washington Street at number 106. You'll realize that this is a town with character when you read the historic plaque on the house next to Jackson's. It says:

N.O.N. Historic Marker
On this Spot
February 29, 1776
Absolutely Nothing Happened.

While you are exploring the 19th-century houses, inns and quaint shops, join Lexington natives at the Sweet Things Ice Cream Shoppe at 106 W. Washington Street. Here you can get homemade ice cream in homemade waffle cones—a double delight. For an extra taste treat try a waffle cone sundae.

Directions: From I-95 in the Richmond area, take I-64 west. At Staunton head south on either I-81 or Route 11. From I-81 take Exit 188B, then follow the signs to Lexington's visitor center. If you are on Route 11 it will divide and you should take Main Street, not Route 11 By-Pass. From Main Street, turn left on Washington Street for the Stonewall Jackson House.

Theater at Lime Kiln and Lenfest Center

Artful Presentations

The *Roanoke Times & World News* may be guilty of regional boosterism in calling the **Theater at Lime Kiln** "one of the most agreeable spots in the western world." But there is no denying that this is, to quote another claim, "the most unusual theater setting in the United States." Performances take place in an outdoor amphitheater amid the ruins of a 19th-century lime quarry and kiln where stone masons once worked and the kilns burned red-hot 24 hours a day.

The professionally presented musicals, plays and concerts are often family oriented and there are annual performances scheduled specifically for children. Many of the works performed from Memorial Day through Labor Day are original plays that focus on the history and culture of Virginia and the southern mountains. Sunday concerts feature a wide range of music from the classics to zydeco and from folk to gospel. The increasingly popular Family Folk Tale Festival offers a rotating repertory of one-act plays based on Appalachian fairy tales and legends. The box office opens in mid-April; for schedule and ticket information call (540) 463-3074.

There are also two theaters for student and professional productions at Washington and Lee University's **Lenfest Center for the Performing Arts**. The attractive lobby has a gallery of art from the American West. Call (540) 463-8000 for the schedule of performances.

At the Lexington Visitor Center, 106 East Washington Street, you can pick up brochures on the galleries in Lexington, including the popular Artists in Cahoots at 1 West Washington Street. This cooperative gallery, run by local artists and craftspeople, always has innovative original pieces. The gallery is open Monday through Saturday 10:00 A.M. to 5:00 P.M. and Sundays 11:00 A.M. to 3:00 P.M.

Directions: From I-81 take Exit 188B toward Lexington; you will be on Route 60 west, Nelson Street. Continue on Nelson Street through Lexington, go under the bridge at Washington and

291

Lee University and continue .4 miles and make a left onto Borden Road (this is across from the athletic fields). Borden Road
will bear right through a residential community. The entrance
to Lime Kiln is .2 of a mile on your left. From I-64 east take Exit
50 toward Lexington; you will be on Route 60 east. Continue on
Route 60 for five miles and make a right at the Shell gasoline
station onto Belle Road, Route 666. The entrance to Lime Kiln
is at the end of Belle Road. Once in Lexington you will see small
white and blue directional signs to the Theater at Lime Kiln.

VMI Museum

From RAT to VIP

On November 11, 1839, 23 men reported to the Franklin Literary Society Hall in Lexington. They became the first Virginia
Military Institute cadets when their sole instructor, Major Francis Smith, assumed command of the old arsenal and established
the nation's first state supported military college. The history of
VMI and its well-known graduates unfolds at the museum located on the campus parade grounds.

For 146 years VMI has trained officers who have made outstanding contributions to the military. The young cadets study
in spartan surroundings as you will learn in the museum's cadet
exhibit room. This is just part of the cadet life exhibit that details their surroundings, uniforms, ROTC program, and VMI's
sport, academic, military and spiritual program. The collection
of VMI rings dating from 1848 to the present is enormously popular.

The first graduates barely completed their college years before
being called to serve in the Mexican War, 1846–48. A captured
Mexican general's war chest with its silver goblets provides a
look at what the Mexican high command considered roughing
it.

Three years after the Mexican War in 1848, Thomas Jonathan
Jackson resigned his army commission and joined the faculty at
VMI. He found the peacetime army too tedious and unreward-
ing for a man anxious to make his reputation. As a teacher of
natural philosophy and artillery tactics his students found him
dull, rigid and severe (see Stonewall Jackson House selection).
The blackboard from his classroom is displayed at the museum.

Jackson's genius became apparent when he led the Stonewall
Brigade in the War Between the States. The VMI Museum displays the uniform Jackson wore as a teacher as well as his battlefield raincoat, a poignant reminder of his senseless death af-

Cadets parade in front of the Barracks on the campus of the Virginia Military Institute. Stonewall Jackson of Civil War fame taught at VM I and George C. Marshall was a gifted graduate.

ter the Battle of Chancellorsville. Jackson was wearing the Indian rubber raincoat on May 3, 1863, when he was accidentally shot in the arm by one of his own men. The bullet hole is clearly visible; it seems too small to have caused such a big hole in the Confederate command. After his arm was amputated Jackson contracted pneumonia and died within a week. It also interesting to discover that while teaching at VMI, Jackson had escorted cadets to stand guard at the hanging of John Brown. A further historical footnote to that event, John Brown's lawyer was a VMI graduate. One of the museum's most popular items is Little Sorrel, Jackson's favorite horse. Little Sorrel died in 1886; he was not stuffed but rather his hide was mounted over a plaster of Paris form. The saddle was made by H. Peat, saddler to the queen of England.

It was not only teachers who marched off to battle during the Civil War. The small butternut jackets on display remind visitors how young the boys were who were sent off to join General Breckenridge's battle-worn regulars. The southern general was ordered to stop the northern push into the crucial Shenandoah Valley. The Union troops numbered 6,300 against Breckenridge's 4,900. To augment the ranks the 157 cadets at VMI were ordered out of the classroom into battle. Ten cadets lost their lives on May 15, 1864, at the Battle of New Market (see New Market Battlefield selection).

Jackson is only one of the illustrious professors profiled in this museum. Following him so closely that they used the same microscope, was physics professor Matthew Fontaine Maury (see Goshen Pass selection), noted for his marine charts. A small section of the Trans-Atlantic cable is exhibited. As Cyrus Fields, who laid the cable, explained, "Maury provided the brains, I provided the brawn." Another faculty member, John Mercer Brooke, designed the armor for the *Merrimack*, the ironclad the Confederates called the *Virginia*. Brooke also invented a device to bring up samples from the ocean floor. One of VMI's most gifted graduates was George Catlett Marshall (see George C. Marshall Museum selection), and his accomplishments are proudly noted.

Today when cadets enter the barracks through the Jackson Arch, they are reminded of Stonewall's determination. Carved overhead are his time-honored words: "You may be whatever you resolve to be." The museum shows that many VMI graduates have followed his advice.

The museum is open at no charge weekdays 9:00 A.M. to 4:30 P.M.; Saturdays 9:00 A.M. to NOON and 2:00 to 5:00 P.M. and on Sundays 2:00 to 5:00 P.M. Visitors who would like a free cadet escorted tour of the post can stop at the VMI Visitor Center in Lejeune Hall. They are given twice a day; call for specific times at (540) 464-7306. You can also pick up a walking tour map and wander the campus on your own.

Directions: From the Richmond area, take I-64 west toward Lexington. From I-64, exit on Route 11. Entering Lexington, Route 11 forks to the right; make an immediate right onto Letcher

Avenue. Follow Letcher Avenue to the VMI parade grounds and the VMI Museum in Jackson Memorial Hall.

ROANOKE

Center in the Square and Historic Farmer's Market

Action Around the Square

Years ago malls revolutionized suburban shopping; in a similar fashion Roanoke has creatively combined the city's cultural offerings into one exciting location called **Center in the Square**. When you add the adjacent Historic Farmer's Market with its shops, stalls and eateries you have an especially appealing one-stop attraction.

Since Center in the Square opened in 1983, it has been the focal point of Roanoke. The action even moves out of this world at Hopkins Planetarium, part of the **Science Museum of Western Virginia**, one of the three museums in the complex. Regular weekend presentations explore the universe on the 40-foot dome, and other shows such as *To Fly* and *Space Shuttle* have extended runs. On the second Friday of each month there is a live sky-show lecture.

The Science Museum of Western Virginia has plenty of family appeal with its hands-on exhibits featuring geology, weather and the flora and fauna of Virginia. Anyone who has ever despaired at the often misleading local television weather forecast will enjoy playing anchor at the museum's studio. A weather map and other props are in place; all you have to supply is the jargon and you're ready to roll tape. Television is also featured in an exhibit on energy designed to test endurance, not imagination. You bike your way to fleeting fame; the faster you pedal, the clearer your screen image becomes.

There is so much to see, touch and discover you may end up spending more time than you anticipated. Just don't forget there are two more museums to explore at Center in the Square plus the Mill Mountain Theatre, which offers year-round performances.

You'll learn how the city got its name at the **Roanoke Valley Historical Society Museum**. The town was first called Big Lick because animals frequented this part of the Shenandoah Valley for the rich salt deposits. Following the animals came the Native Americans whose shell beads were called "rawranoke." The Historical Society has collected more than legends. Their displays begin with Native American baskets, bowls and beads, then move to the belongings of settlers along the Valley Trail. Life on the frontier can be better understood after viewing such artifacts as mill equipment, a blacksmith's work table and farm implements. The turbulent times of the War Between the States and the Reconstruction period are also covered.

From the state of fashion to the state of art, Roanoke is enjoying an active artistic renaissance with galleries proliferating around Center in the Square. Within the center you'll find the **Art Museum of Western Virginia**. Rotating exhibits include nationally and internationally known artists as well as folk art from the southern mountains. Permanent collections demonstrate American works from the 19th and 20th centuries. Educational opportunities can be found at Art Venture, a children's center.

The science museum charges admission, both for the planetarium and for the exhibits. There is also an admission to the history museum but the art museum is free. Hours for the Science Museum of Western Virginia, the Art Museum of Western Virginia and the Roanoke Valley Historical Society Museum are Tuesday through Saturday from 10:00 A.M. to 5:00 P.M.(the history museum closes at 4:00 P.M. on weekdays) and Sunday 1:00 to 5:00 P.M. Only the science museum is open on Monday.

Across the street from Center in the Square is **Studios on the Square**, an artists' cooperative where painters, sculptors, carvers, weavers, potters and others artists produce and sell their work. Adjacent to the center is the **Historic Farmer's Market** with two main areas of interest: the market building with its specialty shops and ethnic food booths, plus colorful street stalls offering local produce. Shops run the gamut from chic, like Wertz's Country Store with its basement level wine shop, to neighborhood merchants and flower vendors. Some shops are closed on Sunday. The Historic Farmer's Market is open six days a week, year-round. Be sure to take advantage of the wonderfully diverse restaurants in this area. You can have a world taste tour at Carlos Brazilian International Cuisine (312 Market Street) or the Mediterranean Italian and Continental Cuisine Restaurant (127 Campbell Avenue). For American fare and hamburgers famous throughout the region try 309 First Street Fine Food & Drink (309 Market Street). For information on Roanoke attractions call (800) 635-5535.

An elevated pedestrian walkway connects this bustling Market Street area with Roanoke's "Grand Old Lady," the newly restored and reopened 19th-century **Hotel Roanoke**. Back in 1882, when Roanoke was still Big Lick, a hotel was built on this hill overlooking the community. The Hotel Roanoke was developed by railroad magnate Frederick J. Kimball. From the beginning, the hotel's rooms were full. Of course originally, there were less than three dozen rooms; now there are more than 300. But many of the hotel's distinctive touches have remained. The Tudor facade is still striking and the Czech-made chandeliers that once graced the Crystal Ballroom are now part of the new state-of-the-art conference center. A $42 million restoration and new construction project was unveiled when the hotel reopened as a Doubletree hotel in 1995. Even if you don't stay in this delightful property take the time to stroll through the public rooms or enjoy a meal in the Pine Room or Regency Dining Room. For information call (800) 222-TREE or (540) 985-5900.

Directions: From I-95 in the Richmond area, pick up Route 360 west to Burkeville. Then take Route 460 west to Roanoke. In Roanoke Route 460 becomes Orange Avenue which intersects with Route 581 south. Take Route 581 south to the Elm Avenue exit and turn right on Elm. You can also take I-64 west to I-81 south, near Roanoke take Exit 143 to I-581 and then Exit 6. Go right two blocks on Elm Avenue and turn right onto Jefferson Street. Turn right again at Campbell Avenue at Market Square. A parking deck adjoins Center in the Square.

Virginia's Explore Park

Ah, Wilderness!

Virginia's **Explore Park** aptly quotes T.S. Eliot, "We shall not cease from exploration and the end of all our exploring will be to arrive where we started and know the place for the first time." This is indeed what happens when you visit this 1,300-acre frontier living history museum and wilderness park. Many current area resident's great-great-grandparents started in Blue Ridge mountain cabins like those you see at this historic park. Settlers turned the Native American's "Warriors Path" into a wagon road.

Horse-drawn wagons carry visitors around this authentic 1790 to 1860 Blue Ridge settlement. You can also walk the rutted paths and roads stopping at the Hofauger Farm complex of home, barn, shop, garden and orchard. The German-style barn has a huge threshing area as well as horse stables. Samuel Hofauger was of German descent, while his wife, Elizabeth Hays, was English. This farm, where they raised four children, was near Cave Spring in Roanoke County. Old-fashioned breeds of farm animals fill the pens, graze in the fields and roam the yard and include chickens, geese, pigs and sheep. Not far from the farm is the one-room Kemp's Ford Schoolhouse, built around 1860 on the Blackwater River in Franklin County.

THE ROANOKE STAR

WORLDS LARGEST MAN-MADE STAR ERECTED IN 1949
AS A SYMBOL OF THE PROGRESSIVE SPIRIT
OF ROANOKE, STAR CITY OF THE SOUTH.
HEIGHT OF STEEL STRUCTURE — 100 FT.
HEIGHT OF STAR — 88½ FT.
WEIGHT OF STAR — 10,000 LBS.
WEIGHT OF STEEL STRUCTURE — 60,000 LBS.
WEIGHT OF CONCRETE BASE — 500,000 LBS.
DEPTH OF BASE — 6½ FT.
LENGTH OF NEON TUBING — 2,000 FT.
CURRENT CONSUMED — 17,500 WATTS
HEIGHT ABOVE SEA LEVEL — 1,847 FT.
HEIGHT ABOVE CITY — 1,045 FT.
VISIBILITY FROM THE AIR — 60 MILES
SEVERAL POSSIBLE COLOR COMBINATIONS
ILLUMINATED EVERY NIGHT TILL 12.

ROANOKE MERCHANTS ASSOCIATION
ROANOKE CHAMBER OF COMMERCE

The Roanoke Star crowns the top of Mill Mountain. Shendan-doah means "daughter of the stars" so it is appropriate that this 100-foot star illuminates Roanoke's nighttime sky in the Shenan-doah Valley.

Two other public buildings were almost always found in early settlements; they are represented by the 1880 Mountain Union Church, which served as a meeting house for Presbyterians and Lutherans, and the 1790s Brugh Tavern. This German inn, offering lodging, food and drink, was situated on the Great Wagon Road just north of what is now the city of Roanoke. Rounding out this recreated community are a blacksmith and wheelwright shop. Current development plans call for the reconstruction of three additional houses: the 1780 Barnett House; 1840 McClure-Baker House and 1780 Holstine House.

If you take a wagon ride you will get a real feeling for why the first shops established on the frontier were blacksmiths and wheelwrights. The rutted, steep, rocky, muddy roads made travel hazardous. Wagons frequently lost or damaged their wheels, necessitating repairs. The expression, "I'll be there with bells on," derived from the custom of wagons giving their bells to any wagon that stopped and helped them back on the road. Thus, if you arrived with bells on your wagon, that usually meant you arrived without misadventure.

Costumed interpreters are on hand at the Hofauger farm and bring frontier days to life. A Native American, on hand at a Tutelo lodge, and a hunter provide different perspectives on living off the land. Other personalties frequently on hand include a horse-drawn wagon driver and a singing peddler.

Natural history is also part of the story that unfolds here. Six miles of hiking trails encourage you to explore the dense hardwood forest with its abundant wildflowers and wildlife. Trails wind through the scenic Roanoke River Gorge with its striking shale cliffs.

Virginia's Explore Park is open April through October on Saturdays, Sundays and Mondays from 9:00 A.M. to 5:00 P.M. Before starting out into this woodsy setting, an application of bug spray or insect repellant is a wise precaution. Admission is charged. Ongoing special events include blacksmith workshops, wildflower hikes, quilting, Native American craft workshops, historical reenactments, an Appalachian music and craft festival and others; call (540) 427-1800 for details. Currently under construction are a 1750s fort and an Eastern Woodland village. Long term plans call for the addition of a North American Wilderness Park Zoo.

There is already a zoo off the Blue Ridge Parkway—the **Mill Mountain Zoo** just outside Roanoke. Here you'll see 45 species of exotic and native animals on a wooded three-acre park. In addition to wild animals like the Siberian tiger, red pandas and reptiles, there is a children's contact area where youngsters can interact with goats and small mammals. The zoo is open daily from 10:00 A.M. to 5:00 P.M. except Christmas Day. Admission is charged. You also find the **Roanoke Star** on top of Mill Mountain. Shenandoah is an Indian word meaning "daughter of the stars" so it is fitting that this 100-foot-tall star illuminates Roanoke's nighttime sky.

Directions: Take I-81 to Roanoke, Exit 143, and go 12 miles on I-581/US Route 220 to the Blue Ridge Parkway. Take the Parkway north for seven miles. Virginia's Explore Park is at Milepost 115 between Route 220 and Route 24.

Virginia Museum of Transportation

Hop a Freighter

The aptly chosen home for the **Virginia Museum of Transportation** is a restored railway freight station that sits beside the tracks of the Norfolk Southern mainline in downtown Roanoke. While most of the rolling stock evoking railroad's golden age is exhibited outdoors, the complete story of transportation is told inside the station. Exhibited in the galleries are carriages, early autos, freight trucks, fire engines and airplanes.

Much of the action is along Antique Auto Alley, where the oldest vehicle is the 1880 "Doctor's Buggy," an extended roof rockaway. The rockaway was an adaption of a traditional coach first done in Long Island, New York around 1830. Luxury options were available even on the earliest vehicles; this model has windows that open and close all the way around the passenger compartment, as well as window shades for privacy. Another vintage model is the 1885 stick seat square box buggy, meant for speed. It's interesting to learn that when selecting horses for a two-horse team, the important consideration was conformation not color. The horses needed to be roughly the same age and size so that they pulled the carriage in tandem.

The oldest car in the collection is a 1920 Buick touring car. David Dunbar Buick founded his motor company in Detroit in 1902 and in the first year 37 vehicles were sold at $850 each. By 1910, Buick sold 11,000 cars at $1,050 each. The term touring car was derived from the most common use of cars to get to church and then take a Sunday drive. Henry Ford manufactured his first car in 1903. The earliest Ford in the collection is the 1924 Model T Chassis Ford; this was the year the company sold its 10 millionth car. The museum also has a replica of a 1903 Oldsmobile, the first car in the Roanoke Valley. A wide assortment of trucks, buses and fire equipment is included in the outdoor exhibits.

One section of the museum is devoted to the railroad. Exhibits provide nuggets of information like the fact that coal is the commodity most transported by rail across the country. Coal also

The Virginia Museum of Transportation is located in a restored railway station in downtown Roanoke. Trains, automobiles, freight trucks, fire engines and airplanes are exhibited. Young visitors especially enjoy the detailed model of a three-ring circus.

makes up 80% of all goods that are delivered in Virginia. The locomotive and rolling stock are exhibited outdoors. A unique piece is one of the few surviving N&W Dynamometers. Made in 1919 this car could calibrate data connected with locomotive operation and train haul conditions such as drawbar pull, brake pipe pressure and other precise measurements. A system of up to 20 connections provided a precise analysis of locomotive performance. There are 18 locomotives, five switcher cars, and an assortment of diverse equipment like an oil car, derrick car, caboose, boxcar and a passenger observation car. Visitors can climb aboard eight pieces of equipment.

Back inside there's one more discovery to make and it's a doozy—though it doesn't have much to do with transportation. The museum has an incredibly detailed three-ring circus model complete with crowds, performers and wild animals. The link is the railroad, without which the circus would not have been able to travel swiftly from town to town, garnering the reputation as "the greatest show on earth." Between 1872 and 1947, during the heyday of the circus, specially designed railroad cars moved the big top. In 1872 it took 62 cars to move P.T. Barnum's Circus. The circus train peaked in 1947 when Ringling Brothers and Barnum & Bailey used 109 cars to move their extravaganza. This colorful museum exhibit delights young and old with its amazing detail. The Virginia Museum of Transportation is open 10:00 A.M. to 5:00 P.M. Monday through Saturday and NOON to 5:00 P.M. on Sunday. It is closed on Monday in January and February.

Directions: From I-81 take I-581 into Roanoke. At Exit 6, take Wells Avenue, make a left on First Street and a right on Shenandoah Avenue. Take a left onto Fifth Street, then another left onto Norfolk Avenue. The museum is at 303 Norfolk Avenue.

STAUNTON

Andre Viette Farm & Nursery

Perennially Perfect

Andre Viette felt his family and his flowers would thrive more vigorously in the verdant Blue Ridge Mountains than on Long Island. New York was where his 16-year-old Swiss immigrant father, Martin, first started growing perennials while working as an apprentice gardener. Martin established his own nursery in 1929 hybridizing lilacs, phlox and daylilies. In 1976, Andre established a 200-acre farm and nursery in Fisherville, a small community between Charlottesville and Staunton. Operating the nursery and farm with his wife Claire and son, Mark, they grow over a million plants a year and are visited by approximately 15,000 garden lovers annually.

The nursery display gardens feature over 1,000 varieties of daylilies with extensive collections of peonies, oriental poppies and iris. It is a splendid sight to see fields of colorful flowers. Specialty gardens have well-labeled rare and unusual perennials.

Andre Viette, a world-renowned horticulturalist who serves on the board of the American Horticulture Society, has a weekly Saturday morning radio show currently heard on over twenty stations from 8:00 to 11:00 A.M. Listeners can call in with gardening questions for Andre and his co-host, Jim Britt. There are lots of call since, as surveys indicate, about 75% of all households in the country engage in indoor or outdoor gardening.

The garden center is open at no charge April through October on Monday through Saturday from 9:00 A.M. to 5:00 P.M. and Sunday 1:00 to 5:00 P.M. A mail order catalog is available for a nominal fee by calling (540) 943-2315.

Directions: From I-64 (if you are traveling west from the Richmond area), take Exit 91 north. You will turn right onto Route 608, then make a left turn and head west on Route 250. After you go under a train overpass you will turn right onto Route 608 (there was a little jog onto Rte. 250, but this puts you back onto Long Meadow Road). The nursery is $2^{1}/_{2}$ miles on the left. From I-81 traveling south, take Exit 225 and turn left onto Route 275, which will turn into Route 254 East. Then make a right turn on Route 608. The nursery is $2^{1}/_{2}$ miles on the right. Traveling north on I-81, take Exit 221, turn right and go east on I-64, then follow directions above.

Museum of American Frontier Culture

Cultivate America's Roots

Visitors would have a better idea of the breadth and scope of this fascinating 78-acre living history park if it was called "Roots" of America's Frontier Culture. Farmsteads have been rebuilt here in the heart of the Shenandoah Valley with buildings transported from settlers' homelands in Germany, Ireland and England. A fourth farmstead illustrates how these cultures met and merged by the 19th century.

These are not reconstructions or recreations, but actual farms with their original cluster of house and farm buildings and, to the extent possible, appropriate elements of the landscape. Living history brings to life the culture and lifestyle settlers brought to America when they immigrated in the 18th century. Authentically clad interpreters go about their farm work as they would have done in the old country.

After an informative 15-minute video explaining the background of the **Museum of American Frontier Culture**, you'll follow a sandy country lane to the 1688 half-timbered German farmhouse transported from Hördt in the Rhineland-Palatinate. In addition to the main house, there is a barn with a wagon-shed addition and a tobacco barn. The house and barn are both built in the fachwerk style, with a timber frame filled-in with wattle and daub panels. These panels are formed by weaving strips of wood, then covering the strips with a mix of clay, sand, lime and straw. An element of the German barn that was incorporated into the design of frontier farms was the central entry double door with its threshing bay flanked by animal (often pig) pens. Germans introduced pork and smoked meats to the frontier diet as well as sauerkraut. Furnishings in the front parlor, small bed chamber, kitchen and hall reflect the 1750s. The first half of the 18th century was the time of the heaviest German immigration to this part of Virginia. Influences from other countries that made their way to western Germany can be seen, like the curtains of Egyptian cotton and the Roman hearth. Garden plots beside the buildings are enclosed in the traditional wattle and wooden picket fences.

The path to the past next leads visitors to the Scotch-Irish (Ulster) farm, which was originally built in the early 19th century near the village of Drumquin. The house and outbuildings were presented by the Ulster-American Folk Park, whose director, Eric Montgomery, was one of the visionaries who helped found this living history museum. Specialists from Northern Ireland assisted in the reconstruction. Two Irish thatchers competed the roof using a pattern common in County Tyrone. The farm has three buildings: the two-room house with a barn addition, a small outbuilding in front of the house and a long four-room outbuilding at the end of the house. They all have whitewashed sandstone walls. Floors are made of blue clay and flagstone. One part of the longer outbuilding was used as a turf shed to store the peat used in Ireland for fuel. In the kitchen, which also served as the main living area, the parents' bed was located in the "outshot" near the fireplace. Notice the "creepy stools," so called because they were set low to avoid the peat smoke. Those sitting on these low stools would gradually move them closer and closer to the warm stove. The second room was used for spinning, weaving, churning and other household chores as well as providing additional sleeping quarters. Visitors learn that colcannon is virtually the national dish in Northern Ireland—it's made of mashed potatoes, scallions, milk, butter and kale. Hedgerows and stone walls enclose the Scotch-Irish farmstead. The 18th-century blacksmith forge complements the work done by the flax farmers.

Split-rail fences line the footpath that crosses a spring-fed creek delivering visitors at yet another country, this farm reveals our English heritage. Here you'll find a West Sussex farm once situated on the outskirts of Petworth. There is also a farmhouse from the vicinity of Harlebury village in the midland county of Worcestershire. The lifestyle of the 17th-century yeoman farmer is captured at the English farmstead. There are two 17th-century barns, a mid-17th-century house and a late 18th-century cattle shed, all built using the English timber-framed construction. All of these were moved from the Garlands' Sussex farm, but the main house was protected by English preservation laws and was not allowed to be moved out of England. In its place is the Worcestershire house, circa 1630, which was disassembled before the new preservation law became operational and so is likely the last historic dwelling that will be permitted to leave England. The position of the original farmhouse is marked by a stone foundation and partial framework. The Worcestershire house is on a separate site in the English exhibit area. Furnish-

The American farmhouse at the Museum of American Frontier Culture illustrates a blend of ideas brought to the New World by Virginia settlers. Three 18th- and 19th-century working farmsteads represent specifically the English, Irish and German traditions.

ings in the house are accurate reproduction pieces based on original 17th-century probate inventories from this house and neighboring yeoman-class houses. As part of the Foodways Program, authentic English dishes are prepared in the kitchen in brass cookware and on a wooden trestle table. Notice the wagon shed right near the pond. Wagons could be driven into the water to keep the wheels swollen and tight. The design of the English cattle shed and, later, the American smokehouse both incorporated a wooden frame construction with a hip-roof.

The Appalachian farm from Botetourt County southwest of Staunton reveals the synthesis of European building traditions by the early settlers. John Barger settled in Virginia in 1832 and built his farmhouse soon after. He eventually built two barns and enlarged his house as well as additional outbuildings. The oldest buildings use the European-style log construction. Later additions are more varied, like the stone masonry of the springhouse and the wood framing for the square frame smokehouse. A variety of fencing is also seen on this farm: board fencing, picket fencing and split-rail fences. Meal preparation, field work and household chores all remind visitors of a vanished era.

The Museum of American Frontier Culture is open daily 9:00 A.M. to 5:00 P.M. Hours from December through mid-March are 10:00 A.M. to 4:00 P.M. It is closed on Thanksgiving, Christmas and New Year's Day. Be sure to wear walking shoes and remember you will be outside a good portion of the time, so dress appropriately. Many special programs are conducted by museum staff; some are held in the Octagonal Barn Activities Center. This 1915 barn is one of only two octagonal barns in the state. Before leaving be sure to stop at the museum shop and have a look at its wide selection of handcrafted items. For a schedule of special events call (540) 332-7850. The highly popular Holiday Lantern Tours in December require advance reservations.

Directions: From I-81 take Exit 222, Route 250 west; just off the interstate you will see the entrance to the Museum of American Frontier Culture on your left. Turn left on Frontier Drive for the museum parking area. If you come in on Route 64, head north on I-81 for one exit.

The Woodrow Wilson Birthplace and Museum

Family Manse

Thomas Woodrow Wilson was born in Staunton's Presbyterian manse on December 28, 1856 "at $12^3/_4$ o'clock at night," as his proud father recorded in the family Bible. The Bible is on display at his birthplace. When the Reverend Joseph Wilson accepted a call to be minister of the Staunton Presbyterian Church, he and his wife, Jessie Woodrow, and their daughters, Marion and Annie, moved into the manse.

The 12-room Greek Revival style brick house was less than ten years old when the Wilsons arrived in March 1855. The house was built for Mr. Wilson's predecessor, the Reverend Benjamin Mosby Smith. "The congregation has contracted to have a house built for Mr. Smith, " it was recorded, "which it is said will be the best house in Staunton when it is finished. The lot on which it is to be built is one of the most beautiful situations in Staunton. . . ." The total cost of construction was about $4,000. Indicating how little some things have changed over the years, there is a notation in Mr. Smith's diary about his dissatisfaction with the poor work being done by the paperhanger. The Reverend dismissed him and, with his wife's help, finished wallpapering the parlor and dining room himself.

Tommy Wilson, as the future president was called until his law school days, spent no more than a year in Staunton. His father's success led to a call from an even larger, more prosperous church in Augusta, Georgia. The Wilsons left Staunton in late 1857. Even though he spent only a year in Virginia as a child, Woodrow Wilson always considered himself a Virginian and returned to Staunton in 1912 to celebrate his birthday as president-elect.

The Woodrow Wilson Birthplace and Museum has been extensively restored, giving an accurate look at life in a middle-class minister's home in antebellum Virginia. Many of the furnishings belonged to the Wilsons; others are period pieces.

The manse tour includes three floors. The kitchen, workroom, servant's bedroom and family dining room are on the ground floor. On the main floor there is the master bedroom where Thomas Woodrow Wilson was born.

His mother was attended by a physician, an unusual practice for this time and place. This was a measure of the social standing of the minister. The birthroom was identified from a letter that Jesse wrote to her father, in which she tells him that both she and the baby are doing fine. In the front parlor the Wilson family Bible rests on the table. A silver service given to Mr. Wilson by his Augusta congregation and English flatware belonging to Jessie Woodrow's family are displayed in the dining room. You'll also see the pastor's study. The oldest piece in the house is the hall clock, crafted in Staunton in the 1790s. Upstairs there are bedrooms for the children and for guests.

Augmenting the guided tour of the manse is a museum with seven exhibit galleries. They give an in-depth look at the ac-

Thomas Woodrow Wilson, the 28th president of the United States, was born on December 28, 1856 in Staunton's 12-room Greek Revival Presbyterian manse. One year later the Wilsons moved to Georgia but Wilson always considered himself a Virginian.

complishments of Woodrow Wilson as an author, scholar, university president, governor and statesman. Rare artifacts, photographs, family and personal possessions help to narrate the fascinating history of Wilson the man and Wilson the leader in some of the most critical times of our nation and the world. A star attraction is President Wilson's 1919 Pierce-Arrow, used by him during his term and, which he purchased for his retirement. The museum has children's craft activities; call ahead for details and schedule, (540) 885-0897.

The manse gardens, one of the earliest projects of the Garden Club of Virginia, make a delightful add-on to the house tour. They were laid out in 1934 with crescent and bowknot beds and a variety of ornamental trees on the terraced grounds.

The Woodrow Wilson Birthplace and Museum is open daily from 9:00 A.M. to 5:00 P.M. Winter hours are 10:00 A.M. to 4:00 P.M. It is closed on Sundays during January and February and on Thanksgiving, Christmas and New Year's Day. Admission is charged. A gift shop adjoins the garden.

Historic Staunton Foundation offers guided walking tours that begin at the Woodrow Wilson Birthplace Reception House. Staunton has 22 properties included on the National Register of Historic Places. The walk will take you through Gospel Hill Historic District and in to see the Tiffany windows in Trinity Church, built in 1763 and the town's oldest church. Next you'll stroll through the oldest continually-occupied residential area, now the Newtown Historic District. Of interest are an Eastlake-style house at 18 Church Street and the 1854 "Board and Batten" house, the oldest unaltered house in Staunton. From there you'll explore the Wharf Historic District, a significant Confederate supply depot during the Civil War. Tours last approximately an hour; for information call (540) 885-7676.

While you are in the area, consider dining or staying overnight at **The Belle Grae Inn**, just six blocks from the Woodrow Wilson Birthplace & Museum. The inn stands on what was once a 200-acre farm on the edge of Staunton. The Victorian Main House, built in 1873, is now called "The Old Inn" and it is just one of the properties providing overnight lodging. Set behind the 17-room restored inn are an assortment of small houses with a wide array of room arrangements—all individually and creatively decorated. There is fine dining in The Old Inn or in the casual bistro indoor-outdoor cafe. Call (540) 886-5151 for additional information.

Directions: From I-95 in the Richmond area, take I-64 west to I-81. Go north to Staunton, Exit 222, which is Richmond Road, Route 250. Take Route 250 into Staunton and turn right on Route 11; stay in the center lane. Go straight ahead onto Coalter Street. Approaching from the north on I-81, follow the signs from Exit 225. The Woodrow Wilson Birthplace & Museum is at 24 North Coalter Street. To reach The Belle Grae Inn, start from the birthplace and go right on Frederick Street to 515 West Frederick Street.

WINCHESTER

Abram's Delight

Acquired Heiferlessly

In 1682, Valentine Hollingsworth traveled to the New World with William Penn. His family continued to seek new frontiers, sometimes with tragic results. His son, Thomas, was killed by a wounded buffalo while exploring the wilderness. But the third generation established a homestead that is still associated with the Hollingsworths.

When Abram Hollingsworth came upon the Shawnees camped beside a natural spring he declared the site "a delight to behold." He purchased 582 acres from the Native Americans for a cow, a calf and a piece of red cloth. Abram built a log cabin beside the spring and, later, the area's first gristmill. The family prospered and added a flour mill and then a flax seed-oil mill.

In 1754, Abram's son Isaac built a two-story limestone house. It's the oldest now in Winchester, having survived in part because of its 2$^1/_2$-foot thick walls. A wing was added in 1800 by Jonah Hollingsworth, who needed extra room for his 15 children. The house was "modernized" in 1830 in the Federal style. By 1943, when **Abram's Delight** was purchased by the city, it was in ruins. Restoration was undertaken by the Winchester-Frederick County Historical Society and upon completion, it was furnished and opened as a house museum.

Jonah's daughter Mary was the last Hollingsworth to live in the house. It seemed to be filled with more than memories for her. She spoke of hearing people singing and playing the piano in her empty home. Some of the family pieces that augment the 18th-century furnishings are an oil painting done by Mary and several Quaker quilts.

There is an herb garden and a formal boxwood garden outside the house. You'll also see a log cabin on the grounds of the same type Abram first built. You can visit Abram's Delight Monday through Saturday 10:00 A.M. to 4:00 P.M. and on Sunday from NOON to 4:00 P.M. from April through October and by appointment off-season. Admission is charged.

Directions: From I-95 at Fredericksburg take Route 17 west to Marshall and pick up I-66 west to I-81. Proceed north on I-81 to the Winchester exit at Millwood Avenue. Head into Winchester on Millwood Avenue and turn right on Pleasant Valley Road for Abram's Delight which will be on your right.

Belle Grove

The Hite of Fashion

In what turned out to be one of the longest legal battles in United States jurisprudence, Jost Hite retained ownership of 100,000 acres in the lower Shenandoah Valley despite Lord Fairfax's claims on the land. Jost Hite received the land in return for bringing 100 settlers to this part of the Virginia colony.

Jost's grandson, Major Isaac Hite, Jr., who was commissioned by George Washington, built **Belle Grove** in 1794. Isaac married James Madison's sister, Nelly Conway Madison. When his brother-in-law, the future president, married Dolley Paine Todd they honeymooned at Belle Grove. James Madison's friend and neighbor, Thomas Jefferson, provided architectural advice during the building of Belle Grove. His touch can be discerned in the graceful symmetry of the house, in the T-shaped halls and in the top and bottom opening windows. The house is built of native limestone and has a large porticoed porch.

Looking out the windows at the blue haze on the nearby mountains, you don't question how the range got its name, but you do wonder why the house isn't called Belle View. The house is furnished with many pieces made in the valley, but few belonged to the Hite family. The parlor does have Charles Peale Polk portraits, commissioned by Major Hite.

During the Civil War's Valley Campaign, military action occurred in and around Belle Grove. In the fall of 1864 General Philip Sheridan made his headquarters at Belle Grove. At 5:00 A.M. on October 19, Confederate General Jubal Early led a surprise raid on the Union soldiers camped here. Sheridan was in Washington conferring with Secretary of War Stanton. Sheridan heard the gun fire as he returned. Confederate forces were already counting this a victory when Sheridan's timely arrival turned the tide of battle. More than 6,000 men died at what the history books call the Battle of Cedar Creek, the last major battle for control of the Shenandoah Valley.

Confederate General Stephen Dodson Ramseur, a classmate of George Custer's at West Point, was mortally wounded and died at Belle Grove. General Custer visited him before his death.

There was a ladder to a roof-top platform where Sheridan's men sent messages to a lookout at Signal Knob on Massanutton Mountain. Candle smoke graffiti in the attic says, "U.S.A. Signal Corps 1864."

In the cellar you can see the winter kitchen where you will learn the derivation of the expression, "too many irons in the fire." If cooks during the Federal period tried to use more than

311

Thomas Jefferson provided architectural advice when Belle Grove Plantation was built in 1794. This 18th-century plantation is still a working farm and a center for the study of traditional rural crafts.

one cookie press the irons got too hot and burnt the cookie wafers, thus there were too many irons in the fire. Near the kitchen is an extensive herb garden to explore. Before you leave be sure to visit the large regional craft shop that specializes in needlecraft supplies.

Belle Grove is open mid-March through October, Monday through Saturday, with tours from 10:15 A.M. to 3:15 P.M. and Sunday 1:15 to 4:15 P.M. Admission is charged.

Long range plans anticipate the inclusion of a **Virginia Quilt Museum** on the grounds of Belle Grove. Currently the museum is ensconced in the 1854 Warren-Sipe House on Harrisonburg's Main Street. The museum's collection reveals that quilts are far more than bedspreads, they are works of art. Quilts provide insights into the life and times of earlier eras, whether the quilt is an individual effort, a family project or a community endeavor. One exhibit concentrates on quilts made by Virginia children. The museum is open Monday, Thursday, Friday and Saturday from 10:00 A.M. to 4:00 P.M. and 1:00 to 4:00 P.M. on Sunday. Admission is charged. The Shenandoah Agricultural and Transportation Museum is another new museum in Harrisonburg, it is located in the old train station.

Directions: From I-95 in the Richmond area take I-64 west to Route 1-81. Travel north on I-81 to Exit 302, Route 627, and proceed west to Route 11. Then take Route 11 south for to one mile south of Middletown. Turn right onto Belle Grove Road which leads back to the museum. Continue south on Route 11 to Harrisonburg.

Stonewall Jackson's Headquarters and George Washington's Office Museum

Double Duty

In 1854 Dr. William Fuller built a Hudson River Gothic house in Winchester in rural Virginia. His wife, Victorine S. Green, used many continental touches in decorating her new home: diamond-shaped windowpanes, marble fireplaces, hearth tiles and gilt wallpaper. The Fullers soon outgrew their cottage and sold it to Lewis Tilghman Moore, great-grandfather of Mary Tyler Moore, the television and screen actress.

In the fall of 1861 General Stonewall Jackson came to Winchester to plan his Valley Campaign. Lewis Moore, a lieutenant colonel in the Fourth Virginia Infantry Stonewall Brigade, offered his home to Jackson as his headquarters. The general wrote to his wife, "The situation is beautiful. The building is of cottage style and contains six rooms. I have two rooms, one above the other. My lower room, or office, has matting on the floor, a large fine table, six chairs and a piano. The walls are papered with elegant gilt paper. I don't remember to have ever seen more beautiful papering. . . ."

His wife, Mary Anna Morrison Jackson, joined him in Winchester at Christmas time and stayed until March 1862 (see Stonewall Jackson House selection). You'll see the table where they enjoyed Christmas dinner, Jackson's office (just as he described it) and his bedroom.

Stonewall Jackson's Headquarters has photographs and personal memorabilia of Jackson and other Confederate officers on display. The gift shop sells rare first edition books, old hard-to-

313

find books on the Civil War and Confederate money. The house at 415 Braddock Street is open 10:00 A.M. to 4:00 P.M. daily April through October. Admission is charged.

Just down Braddock Street at the intersection with Cork Street is the small log office Colonel George Washington of the Virginia Militia used from September 1755 to December 1756 while he supervised the construction of Fort Loudoun. The museum has a model of this fort that was built to protect part of Virginia's 300-mile frontier from the French.

Washington spent a good deal of time in his early years in the Winchester area, having come here first at the age of 16, in 1748, when Lord Fairfax sent him with a surveying team. His mission was to look at a part of Lord Fairfax's vast five million acres of land. **George Washington's Office Museum** has both surveying and military displays as well as Washington memorabilia. Hours are 10:00 A.M. to 4:00 P.M. daily, April through October. Admission is charged.

Directions: From I-95 at Fredericksburg take Route 17 to Marshall. Pick-up I-66 that will connect with I-81. Proceed north on I-81 to Winchester, Exit 80, Millwood Avenue. Head into Winchester on Millwood Avenue and turn right on Pleasant Valley Road past Abram's Delight (see selection). Turn left on Cork Street and right on Cameron Street. Continue to North Avenue and turn left. Go two blocks to Braddock Street and turn left. Stonewall Jackson's Headquarters is half way down the first block of Braddock Street, on the right. Continue down Braddock to Cork Street for George Washington's Office Museum on the left corner at the light.

Southwest Blue
——Ridge Highlands——

F ollow in the footsteps of Daniel Boone and discover as he did the splendor of the "Grand Canyon of the South" preserved within Breaks Interstate Park and the passage through the Appalachians at Cumberland Gap National Historical Park. You'll feel like a wilderness explorer when you hike these rugged forested parks. In the Guest River Gorge rushing rapids and cascading waterfalls tumble between high cliffs and bluffs. You can hike gorge trails to the 850-foot-long Natural Tunnel William Jennings Bryan called the "Eighth Wonder of the World," or opt for the quick and fun descent by chairlift.

Outdoor theaters in the region tell dramatic stories about life on the frontier, from Mary Draper Ingles's story in *The Long Way Home* to John Fox, Jr.'s *Trail of the Lonesome Pine*. A frontier community has been recreated at Historic Crab Orchard Museum and Pioneer Park. In Abingdon, the oldest town west of the Blue Ridge Mountain, Barter Theatre the country's oldest repertory theater boasts that during the Depression it paid George Barnard Shaw's royalty in spinach and Thornton Wilder's with a Virginia ham. For mountain music you can't beat the fiddlers' convention in Galax.

Abingdon, the Virginia Creeper Trail and Historic White's Mill

Oldest Town West of the Blue Ridge Mountains

Abingdon claims, "Every town has a history, some just seem to have more than others . . ." The town has a lived-in look, one that isn't created for public entertainment but rather has mellowed with age, retaining historic buildings to serve current needs. It is not a town with house museums, but rather a town where homes are redolent of the past. The self-guided walking tour, available at the visitor center at 335 Cummings Street, high-lights interesting spots in the 20-square block historic district.

This part of southwest Virginia was first explored in 1749–1750 by Dr. Thomas Walker, who was given over 6,000 acres by King George II. After obtaining a look at his holding, Walker sold a portion to Joseph Black, who settled it and built a small fort. The settlers and indigenous Native Americans co-existed peacefully during the latter part of the 1760s and early 1770s. But by 1776 the Cherokees were raiding settlements and many pioneers fled to the relative safety of Black's Fort. That same year, when the Assembly of Virginia established Wash-ington County, they designated Black's Fort, now enlarged and strengthened, as the meeting place for the first county court. By 1778 the area around Black's Fort was incorporated as the town of Abingdon.

The first of the 33 points of interest on Main Street is the **1860 Fields-Penn House Museum**. Down the street are two of Abing-don's most well-known sites: the Barter Theatre and the Martha Washington Inn (see selection). The Barter Green adjacent to the inn was at one time the location of Governor John B. Floyd's house. It is now used for the Virginia Highlands Festival Arts and Crafts exhibit held the first two weeks in August. The fes-tival began in 1948 and over the years it has grown and flour-ished—it's one of the top 100 tourist events in North America and one of the top 20 in the southeast. There is a hot air bal-loon event, plenty of entertainment, juried craft shows, regional cooking as well as nationally-known writers, lecturers and vi-sual and performing artists who offer distinctive programs. For details on the festival call (800) 435-3440.

Eleanor Roosevelt's father Elliott was a boarder at 116 East Main Street, the 1847 house of Judge John A. Campbell. One of the houses to survive the three major fires that destroyed so many of Abingdon's old dwellings is the 1798 log section of the Valentine Baugh House at 129 East Main Street. The western sec-tion of the Andrew Russell House, 165–167 Main Street, was built in 1792. The house was used as a Confederate officers' headquarters during the Civil War.

The Tavern, 222 East Main Street, has been serving travelers since it was built around 1779 on the Old Indian Trail and Wilder-ness Road. It is not only one of Abingdon's oldest buildings, it was one of the first built west of the Blue Ridge. Travelers who have stopped here include Henry Clay, French King Louis-Philippe, President Andrew Jackson and capital designer Pierre Charles L'Enfant. One noted visitor passed this way before the tavern was built. Daniel Boone was camped at the base of the hill where the tavern stands. Boone called the area Wolf Hills because during the night his dogs were attacked by wolves. The location of the wolves' den is marked on a barn behind the **Cave House Craft Shop** across the street from the tavern. This excellent shop is the home of the Holston Mountain Arts and Crafts Cooperative whose members produce fine Appalachian craft items.

The first tavern keeper, John Yancey broke the law and enforced it. A month after he applied for a license to operate an ordinary, he was fined for enclosing his sheep in the courthouse, which was across from his tavern. But by the following summer of 1780 the court appointed him Deputy Sheriff of Washington County. Local patriots gathered at the tavern in September 1780 before joining other colonial supporters to fight British Major Patrick Ferguson at the Battle of King's Mountain in South Carolina, a significant British defeat. During the Civil War the tavern was used as a field hospital. On the third floor, charcoaled numbers can still be seen on the plastered wall designating the location of soldiers' beds.

For more than 100 years The Tavern was owned and operated by the Harris family. In 1965 Mary Porterfield, the wife of Barter Theatre founder Robert Porterfield, purchased the establishment. In 1984, The Tavern was restored to its colonial appearance and it is now open for lunch and dinner daily; phone (540) 628-1118.

Another popular dining spot is the **Starving Artist Cafe**, on Depot Square, owned by Kim and Shawn Crookshank. The latter is a noted regional artist whose work, along with many of his contemporaries, often adorns the walls of this small eatery. Most of the tasty dishes are named for noted artists. Across the parking lot is **The Arts Depot**, a cooperative artists association with large airy studios in the 1890 Virginia and Tennessee Railroad's freight station. The artists create and sell their work at this bustling arts center. Classes, workshops and readings are held at The Arts Depot; call (540) 628-9091 for additional information. Art is also exhibited in Abingdon's William King Regional Arts Center.

Many of the regional artists are inspired by Abingdon's splendid natural surroundings. To get out and enjoy the country, take a walk along the **Virginia Creeper National Recreation Trail**. It's a $34^1/_3$-mile hiking, biking, horseback riding and cross-country skiing path from Abingdon to Whitetop. But even an abbreviated hike gives you an appreciation for the area's scenic appeal. The trail follows the route of an old Indian path. It begins at the site of Black's Fort, now marked by a steam engine. Four of Daniel Boone's campsites are documented along this route. The trail is named for the slow-moving steam-powered Virginia-Carolina Railroad that served the area during the 1900s. To reach the in-town trail head turn off Main Street onto Pecan Street and travel two blocks; the trail is well-marked. Another access point that will put you into the forest more rapidly is on Watuga Road. From Abingdon take Route 75 south to Watauga Road and make a left (it will be about three miles past the intersection with I-81); in a few miles you will come to a parking area for the trail.

Another spot of interest on the walking tour guide, is really a drive-to location since it's $3^1/_2$ miles out of town. White's Mill Road is popular with bicyclists although it does not offer any paved berm and cyclists must be alert for traffic. **Historic White's Mill**, tucked away in a picturesque, fertile valley beside a meandering stream, is also popular with photographers. This is one of only a few operational water-powered combination mills in the state. White's Mill is the only one that can be run by the traditional millstone method and by the roller system. Thomas Moffet built a mill on this site in 1790. Some of his foundations were probably incorporated into the new mill Colonel James White built when he acquired the property and surrounding land in 1838.

White's Mill has two stories, plus a full-sized attic and a downslope basement in which stands the original corner fireplace. Be sure to walk out behind the mill for a good perspective on the metal overshot water wheel run by the mill race. The old equipment is still used to grind corn, wheat and buckwheat by traditional methods. You can purchase White's Mill ground flour and cornmeal across the street at White's Mill General Store. The store was built around 1830 and still stocks a wide array of goods. There is an admission to the mill, a Virginia State Historic Landmark and a site on The National Register of Historic Places.

Five miles south of Abingdon on Route 11 is **Dixie Pottery**, whose slogan is "Shop the World!" Like the Williamsburg Pottery, an amazing array of items can be found at Dixie Pottery. It is open daily from 9:30 A.M. to 6:00 P.M.; on Sunday it doesn't open until 1:00 P.M.

Directions: From I-81 take Exit 17, Cummings Street into Abingdon and the visitor center will be on the left. For White's Mill, from Cummings Street make a right on Valley Street and travel east, then make a left and head north on White's Mill Road.

Barter Theatre

A Good Deal

The Barter Theatre wasn't part of Franklin Delano Roosevelt's New Deal, but it did start in the Depression and it certainly was a good deal. Theater for the price of farm produce was the idea of Robert Porterfield, a forward-thinking young actor from southwest Virginia. He left New York with a company of professional actors and on June 10, 1933 Porterfield opened the Barter Theatre in Abingdon. The actors were put up in a nearby house and the patrons paid with vegetables, eggs, milk, fruit and meat—the equivalent of 40 cents. By the end of the first season the company had made $4.35 and collectively gained over 300 pounds!

While Shakespeare was never paid ham for Hamlet, playwrights Noel Coward, Tennessee Williams and Thornton Wilder did accept Virginia hams as royalty payments. George Barnard Shaw, a vegetarian, was paid spinach for the right to stage his play.

Only Philadelphia's Walnut Street Theater is older than the Barter Theatre. The latter was built between 1831 and 1833 to serve the congregation of the Sinking Spring Presbyterian Church. The church used the building for a year. It then became a temperance hall and was converted to a theater. When Porterfield acquired it, he heard that the 1875 Empire Theater in New York was scheduled for demolition. He had one weekend to carry away its interior furnishings and equipment—with the help of volunteers he managed to save $75,000 of theatrical property. His acquisitions included the theater seats, lighting fixtures, carpeting, large gold-framed paintings and red wall tapestries. The Empire lighting, designed and installed by Thomas Edison, was used at the Barter until the mid-1970s. Portraits from the Empire include those of Dennis King, Maude Adams and Katherine Cornell. The large painting of Robert Porterfield was done in 1973 by Hans Clausing.

On the theater's second floor is a collection of photographs of the celebrated actors who have performed at the Barter Theatre. The list of alumni include Gregory Peck, Patricia Neal, Ernest Borgnine, Hume Cronyn, Ned Beatty, Kevin Spacey, Larry Linville and many others. In 1946 Barter was designated the state theater of Virginia. It is the oldest continuously operating theater of its kind in the country.

A variety of theatrical experiences are presented: Barter Theatre does theater in the grand tradition; Barter Stage II offers exploratory theater and Barter's First Light Theatre presents performances for young people. Staged readings of new works take place at Early Stages on selected Monday nights. On the first and last Thursday evening performance of each play, there is an after-theater discussion between the audience and the company. For a current schedule or ticket information call (800) 368-3240 or (540) 628-3991.

Across the street is another venerable institution, **Camberley's Martha Washington Inn**. The inn dates back to 1832, when the center portion was built for Brigadier General Francis Preston, his wife and their nine children. Their living room is now the inn's main lobby. The grand staircase and parlors are remarkably untouched. In 1858, the house became the Martha Wash-

Abingdon's Barter Theatre, the largest and oldest professional theatrical company outside New York, began in 1932 with actors bartering their talents for food and supplies. The theater furnishings were acquired from New York's Empire Theatre when it was torn down in 1935.

ington College for young girls. During the Civil War the students acted as nurses while the grounds served as training barracks for the Washington Mounted Rifles. After one skirmish the college became a makeshift hospital for wounded from both North and South. The college closed in 1932.

For the next 50 years the property served as a hotel under different managements. In 1984 it was acquired by the Virginia-based United Company and underwent an $8 million restoration. Faithfully preserved, the 61 guest rooms retain antique pieces to complement the decor including four-poster canopied beds in many rooms. *Lodging Hospitality* magazine rates this as the 37th most successful resort hotel in the country. In October 1995, the inn became part of the Camberley Hotel Company. Even if you don't stay overnight at this Four-Star, Four-Diamond inn, stop in for a pre-theater cocktail or dine in one of the inn's fine restaurants. One of the most striking pieces of period furniture is the 16-foot-long art deco silver table, discovered in a dusty basement and now in the center of the main dining room. The carved-glass tabletop rests on internally illuminated silver pedestals. For information on lodging, or to make dinner reservations call (800) 555-8000 or (540) 628-3161.

Directions: From I-81 take Exit 17, Cummings Street, into Abington. Follow Cummings Street one-half mile to the intersection of Main Street (first traffic light) and turn right. Camberley's Martha Washington Inn is one-quarter mile on the right and Barter Theatre is across the street on the left.

Breaks Interstate Park

Take a Break

It takes a lifetime of good works to get to heaven. It only takes a few hours of good driving to get to the wilderness paradise of Breaks Interstate Park. For Daniel Boone, who discovered Breaks Gorge in 1767, it was a far more arduous journey. Boone and two companions were searching for a route through the mountains into Kentucky, or Kaintuck as it was called at that time. Following the rivers, the trio headed into the Cumberland Mountain range and began traveling along a northerly flowing stream. Their route is known because Boone carved his name on a tree at a salt lick on Russell Fork just upstream from what is now the town of Haysi. It was downstream from this camp that the travelers came to the rugged, impassable river gorge. The rapids that spilled through the gorge's rock walls made further passage along the river impossible. Giving up their trek west, the men spent the winter camped at the junction of Russell Fork and Levisa River, then returned in the spring to their homes in North Carolina. In 1771, Boone again sought a route west through this region and again left his name carved on a tree.

It wasn't until June 1951 when Virginia-Kentucky Route 80 opened that there was an accessible route though the Breaks. In 1954 Virginia and Kentucky passed joint legislation creating **Breaks Interstate Park** (the only other jointly held state park is Palisades State Park on the New York and New Jersey border). These steps opened an incredible wilderness area for travelers.

The 4,600-acre interstate park encompasses the largest canyon east of the Mississippi River. The five-mile, 1600-foot-deep gorge is called the "Grand Canyon of the South" or, reflecting the lush vegetation, the "Grand Canyon With Clothes On." The brilliant colors of Arizona's canyon walls are more than matched by the brilliant autumn foliage of the Cumberland Mountains.

The gorge was cut by the Russell Fork of the Big Sandy River at the northern end of Pine Mountain. One section of the mountain range was so hard and resistant to the flowing waters that it turned Russell Fork. The fork looped in a giant horseshoe around the mountain. The three-sided pyramid-shaped formation called The Towers is one of the parks most scenic spectacles. Over a half-mile long, one-third mile wide and 600 feet high, The Towers had a railroad tunnel hewn through its solid rock. Local legend holds that Englishman John Swift hid a vast silver fortune somewhere on The Towers. Another striking geological formation is The Chimneys, on the western rim of Breaks Gorge, visible from the eastern rim.

Most of the park facilities are on the one-mile tabletop plateau on the gorge's eastern rim. No highway bridge spans the gorge and the western side is undeveloped and inaccessible. There are 13 miles of trails. Two short trails take roughly 30 minutes: The Tower Tunnel Trail leads to an overlook from which to view the railroad tunnel. In July and August the blueberries bushes along the trail yield a delicious harvest. The Towers Trail also leads to an overlook; this walkway is flanked with rhododendron and mountain laurel. Six trails can be hiked in an hour; of these two—Geological and Ridge trails—have self-guided nature trail booklets that can be picked up at the visitor center. The other short trails lead to a grassy overlook, a cold spring, Laurel Lake, and a connecting loop trail that leads to other trails. It takes about an hour-and-a-half to hike the Grassy Creek Trail; there is a steady uphill grade on this moderate-ranked trail. For those with more time, (and more energy), there are four trails that take two hours or more to walk. The most difficult is the River Trail that takes you down to the base of the gorge; the trail is steep and rugged. The Overlook Trail extends along the edge of the cliffs and offers an array of canyon overlooks. (Children need to be closely monitored on these unprotected promontories.) This is a spectacular trail in the autumn. Laurel Branch Trail leads from the lower end of Laurel Lake to Grassy Creek, and the later part of the trail is steep and treacherous. Prospector's Trail follows the contour of the land about 350 feet beneath the major overlooks, so you can look up at the rock formations and down at the canyon below. There is a three-mile long Mountain Bike Trail.

The physically challenged visitor can view the gorge from the Stateline Overlook, which has a paved walkway connecting the viewing platform with the parking lot. This overlook is 920 feet above Russell Fork, where the river exits the gorge and flows from Virginia into Eastern Kentucky. For those not able to hike, there is a $7/_{10}$ of a mile drive through an undeveloped part of the park that provides an opportunity to spot turkey, deer and other small game. Sports enthusiasts may want to try their luck in the 12-acre Laurel Lake. It is stocked with bass and bluegill (the Russell Fork River is stocked with trout). Pedal boats can be rented near the park's swimming pool. The riding stables are also in the pool area. The best place to learn all about the activities at the park as well as the natural and historical background is at the visitor center, open daily from 9:00 A.M. to 5:00 P.M. Visitor programs are frequently scheduled at the amphitheater.

The park is becoming increasingly popular with white-water enthusiasts who are exhilarated and challenged by the ten-mile course from Bartlick above Breaks Gorge to Elkhorn City below it. Running the river entails a dropping 440 feet in a series of rapids that range in ratings from four to six. There are pull-out points for less-experienced floaters. The level of water depends on releases from the John Flannagan Dam, for information on times of releases call (703) 835-9544.

There are eight rafting companies that run the Russell Fork:

Russell Fork Whitewater Adventures (703) 530-7044

USA Whitewater, Incorporated (800) USA-RAFT

Cherokee Adventures (800) 445-7238

Laurel Highlands River Tours, Inc. (800) 4-RAFTIN

Wahoo's Adventures (800) 444-RAFT

Whitewater Adventures (800) WWA-RAFT

Infiniti Rafting (704) 254-4898

Mountain Streams and Trails (800) 245-4090

Popular as Breaks Interstate Park is with daytrippers, many who visit like to stay for a few days. There are 122 developed camping sites and 30 primitive sites, all on a first-come, first-served basis. Additional accommodations are available at the 34-unit motor lodge (703-865-4414), where each has a balcony overlooking the canyon. Four cottages are nestled in a wooded setting. The Rhododendron Restaurant is open daily from 7:00 A.M. to 9:00 P.M. and it too overlooks the canyon. Picnic shelters and picnic areas are located throughout the park and there are children's playground areas. There is a nominal per car entrance charge. They do rent bicycles in the park.

Directions: From I-81 take I-77 west to Bluefield then Route 19/460 south. At Claypool Hill where the two roads split take Route 460 west. After you pass Grundy you will make a left on Route 609 which will take you into the park.

Cumberland Gap National Historical Park

A Gap Not to Overlook

Cumberland Gap is a pass through the Appalachian highlands near the border of Virginia, Kentucky and Tennessee. The gap was discovered by Thomas Walker in 1750, but it was Daniel

Boone who in 1775 marked the trail the pioneers would follow as they headed west.

Historian Frederick Jackson Turner, whose Turner Thesis explained westward migration, said, "Stand at Cumberland Gap and watch the procession of civilization, marching single file—the buffalo following the trail to the salt springs, the Indian, the fur-trader and hunter, the cattle-raiser, the pioneer farmer—and the frontier has passed by."

Native Americans following paths marked by bison and deer created the Warrior's Path that led south from the Potomac River through the gap and north to Ohio. When European settlers first discovered the trail it was said to be strewn with the bleached bones of the enemies of the raiding parties from the five tribes who fought for control of the area: Cherokee, Miami, Shawnee, Delaware and Wyandot. The first white man through the gap was Dr. Thomas Walker who, after discovering this passage through the Appalachians, named it in honor of the Duke of Cumberland, son of King George II. But it was Daniel Boone, with 30 men, who marked it and created the Wilderness Road in 1775. The narrow winding 208-mile-footpath Boone created took pioneers six to eight months to travel. After crossing through the gap, there were three options: trails led to what would become Boonesboro, Kentucky; Nashville, Tennessee; and Louisville, Kentucky.

During the American Revolution, Great Britain enlisted help from the indigenous tribes to keep pioneers from moving west. But from 1775 through 1796, the gap was crossed by between 200,000 and 300,000 settlers. The westward groups often met farmers driving herds of livestock heading east.

In the 1820s and 1830s new routes to the west supplanted the route through Cumberland Gap. The National Road, a 1796 wagon road that extended north of the Ohio River was an easier route. The Chesapeake and Ohio Canals, the Pennsylvania Main Line and the Erie Canal. Steamboats also plied the Mississippi carrying settlers westward.

During the Civil War, Cumberland Gap was a strategic point dividing North and South—it was called the Gibraltar of America and the Keystone of the Confederacy. Union troops under Brigadier General Robert L. McCook built Fort McCook (earthworks of their fort can be seen from the park's Pinnacle Overlook). It proved too difficult to provision the fort and McCook evacuated his men. The Confederates soon occupied the fort, renaming it Fort Rains. Over three years the fort changed hands four times, with occupying troops never managing to maintain a defensive position due to supplying difficulties. The invasion that both sides feared might come through the gap never materialized.

The 1860s were the military years, while the 1870s heralded the industrial years. In 1875 coal, iron and timber were reported to be abundantly available in the Cumberland Gap area. A railroad was built and the "Industrial Boom" of the early 1880s began. Local fires, bank failures and other unexpected setbacks heralded the end of the economic growth and it wasn't until the early 1900s when roads began to open the gap to traffic that the area began recovering.

The visitor center for this 20,279 acre park, the nation's largest National Historical Park, is on the Kentucky side of the park (just to the south of the park is Tennessee). Exhibits and displays at the center, open daily 8:00 A.M. to 5:00 P.M. (except Christmas, New Year's Day, Martin Luther King's Birthday and President's Day), detail the history of Cumberland Gap. An audio-interpreted diorama reveals Daniel Boone and his crew blazing the Wilderness Road. On his exploration of the gap, Boone said, "I can't say as ever I was lost, but I was bewildered once, for three days." At the center you can view two short videos on the history of the park and on **Hensley Settlement**.

You can hike to the early 20th-century Hensley Settlement by taking the 3.5-mile Chadwell Gap trail up the mountain from Caylor, Va., or during the summer months by park shuttle (reservations can be made up to a week in advance by calling, (606) 248-2817). The Hensleys and their relatives, the Gibbons, moved to Brush Mountain, northeast of the gap, in 1903. They built log houses on their mountaintop and lived without modern conveniences. The last family member left this rural Appalachia community in 1951.

Cumberland Gap National Historical Park has restored three farmsteads at Hensely Settlement. You'll see houses, barns, fences and farm and pasture land. Also restored is a one-room schoolhouse, where all the grades were taught by one teacher. Students had to haul water from the well and bring in coal and wood for the pot-bellied stove. There was no church in the settlement but services were held in the schoolhouse by preachers of various denominations. During the time the Hensleys and Gibbons lived here, there were no roads to the settlement. Access was by foot, horseback or mule-drawn sleds.

The best spot to gain an overview of the park is from the **Pinnacle Overlook**. Getting to this high ground reinforces the concept that pioneers desperately needed a route through the mountains, rather than a trail over them. After parking, you'll see a bronze relief mural of the pioneers trekking through Cumberland Gap. A short walk along the paved Overlook Trail will bring you to the stone overlook platform. A map will indicate Virginia, Kentucky and Tennessee, the town of Cumberland Gap and the city of Middlesboro.

There are more than 50 miles of park trails. The 21-mile Ridge Trail is the longest; it is of medium difficulty and runs the length of the park. A spur off Ridge Trail leads to Sand Cave, located in the White Rocks on top Cumberland Mountain. This is not literally a cave, but rather an enormous opening 150 feet wide and 40 feet high. Sand is deposited in this opening which extends 160 feet into the mountain. The ceiling is of gold, red and green shades of rock. The easy Tri-state Peak Trail lets you stand in three states at the same time.

The park plans restoration work at **Cudjo's Caverns**, located beneath Pinnacle Overlook on the east side of Route 25E. These caverns boast the tallest stalagmite in the world and the many cavern chambers have fascinating formation. When this work is complete the caverns will reopen.

The park has five backcountry campsites and the 160-site Wilderness Road Campground. There is also Martin's Fork Cabin, a one-room primitive cabin with six board bunks and a fireplace, call (606) 248-2817 for reservations.

Directions: Follow I-81 to Morristown, Tennessee. At Morristown take Route 25E north to Cumberland Gap National Historical Park.

Guest River Gorge

Newly Accessible Scenic Splendor

Driving through the rugged mountains of southwest Virginia only hints at the beauty that exists within this forested wilderness. Much of it remains inaccessible, but a new six-mile section of the **Guest River Gorge** can now be explored. Although much of the land in and around the gorge remains in private hands, the Norfolk Southern Railroad donated an abandoned railroad bed along this state scenic river to the Jefferson National Forest in 1991 (see selection).

It is a $5^1/_2$ mile hike from the trailhead through the Guest River Gorge to the confluence of Clinch River. The walk through the scenic hardwood forested gorge fully merits your efforts. Rushing rapids and waterfalls mark the river's passage between the high cliffs and bluffs.

The gorge trail provides access to hikers, fishermen, kayakers and canoeists. The Guest River is rated a challenging Level 5, in terms of difficulty. Frequently caught fish include smallmouth bass, crappie and bluegill. Future development will include wildlife viewing sites along the trail, but those interested in hunting and trapping must do it outside the gorge on National Forest land. While this area is breathtaking year-round, it is particularly splendid in the autumn when the foliage turns and the shape of the rocky cliffs can be more clearly discerned. In early June the mountain laurel blooms, followed by the delicate blossoms of the rhododendrons growing in profusion on the hillsides.

Eventually there will be three locations from which to gain access to the Guest River Gorge Trail; only the northern access point near Coeburn is currently in place. There will also be a southern access point at the trail's end near the Clinch River in Scott County and at Crab Orchard Creek off Route 661. On the drawing boards are visitor facilities at the northern and southern access points with picnic areas, restrooms and an information center where you can obtain a self-guided nature interpretative brochure.

Opening the Guest River Trail, which can be reached from Route 72, is just the first step in the plans to make this area accessible. In addition to the more than 540 acres of private land already acquired, additional property will be obtained to provide alternative trailheads. Long-range plans anticipate a hands-on environmental museum along the Guest River Gorge entrance road.

Nature lovers may also want to hike the **Pinnacle Natural Area Preserve**, a 68-acre preserve along Big Cedar Creek and the Clinch River. This preserve's namesake is a towering rock formation that stands 600 feet above Big Cedar Creek. The lush forested hillsides support a wide variety of wildflowers and ferns, while the two bodies of water, both part of the state scenic rivers system, flow through the preserve to create rapids and breathtaking waterfalls. Visitors are welcome to hike the preserve's trails from dawn to dusk.

Directions: From I-81 take the Abingdon exit and travel west on Route 19/Alt 58 to Coeburn. At Coeburn head south on Route 72 to the sign indicating the Guest River Gorge Road, part of Jefferson National Forest. For Pinnacle Natural Area Preserve, when Route 19 splits, remain on that and travel north to Lebanon. Then bear left on Route 82, right on Route 640 and left again on Route 721 for the start of hiking trails in the preserve.

Historic Crab Orchard Museum and Pioneer Park

Life on the Appalachian Frontier

Europeans occasionally disparage American history because, by their standards, it is all so recent. These critics could not find fault with **Historic Crab Orchard Museum** because history here is interpreted from 570,000,000 years ago to modern times. The museum and Pioneer Park are located on a portion of a 110-acre prehistoric archeological site.

Documented evidence indicates that Native Americans lived here 1,200 years ago; and many archeologists believe it may have been as much as 14,000 years. The museum's exhibits of fossils from this prehistoric period include the leg bone and teeth of a huge mastodon that foraged here millions of years ago. There is also a casting of a 300-million-year-old lepidodendron tree, unearthed as it was showing signs of turning to coal.

The region's first prehistoric inhabitants arrived from Asia by crossing the Bering Straits. The Cherokees, the last of the Native Americans to have settlements in this part of southwest Virginia, were forced out by warring Shawnees and European pioneers. Pottery, hunting, cooking and trade items from the Cherokee period are exhibited in the museum and there is a diorama of their settlement on this site. One fascinating piece is a Woodland Period stone effigy, circa 1550.

The first English explorers crossed the mountains into this part of Virginia in the late 1600s. Diary entries indicate that it rained continually during their passage over the Allegheny range and they mistakingly believed the rivers and fog-shrouded plains they saw west of the mountains were the tidal waters of the Pacific Ocean. The ocean was the original western boundary of Virginia.

Gradually permanent settlers moved into the region from the colonies of Pennsylvania, Maryland and North Carolina and from eastern Virginia. There were formal land surveys and large tracts of land were granted; one recipient was Patrick Henry (see Red Hill selection). The museum has agricultural tools and household items from these early pioneers. But in its **Pioneer Park**, their way of life comes alive. Thirteen historic log and stone buildings bring back the 1830s. The Thompson Valley farmhouse has three buildings connected by a breezeway, or dogtrot. Inside you will see a spinning wheel and spartan furnishings. In addition to the living quarters there is a kitchen and lard house. The latter was used to store salted meats, lard, pickled foods and preserves.

Other buildings include Major David Peery's 1805 log home. It is obvious he was financially secure as his windows have six panes of glass, meaning he was willing to pay the special tax on windows with more than four panes. The park also has a blacksmith shop, smokehouse, hunter's cabin, carpenter and cobbler's shop, apple house, loom house and corncribs. Its largest reconstruction is an 1880 log farmstead.

Fields and gardens typical of the frontier era are planted in season and tended by hand. Of special note are trees replanted

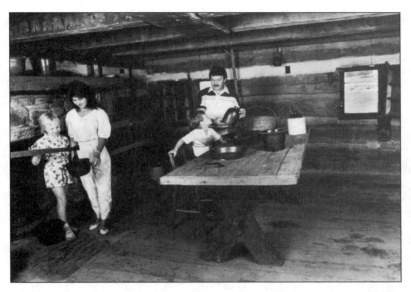

Southwest Virginia's history from prehistoric time to the present is revealed at Historic Crab Orchard Museum. Thirteen historic log and stone buildings recreate the 1830s including a horse-drawn equipment barn with one of only two known original McCormick reapers.

---

from the birthplaces of historic figures: Robert E. Lee, George Washington, Cyrus McCormick and Helen Keller. Near the loom house is a fenced herb garden; a pamphlet lists the early 19th-century varieties you will see growing and gives their medicinal use. Herbs include sage, lemon balm, oregano, lavender, jasmine, thyme, horehound, rue, chives, bee balm, sorrel, lamb's ear, germander, tansy, lovage and comfrey.

There is also a horse-drawn equipment barn that has one of only two known original McCormick reapers made near Staunton (see McCormick Farm selection), along with later, more mechanized models. The barn also has buggies, a flax brake, dog-powered treadmill, pony cart and a wide array of agricultural equipment. A 1917 Model T Ford is a frequent participant in local parades. Near the old Ford is a gravity-operated gasoline "pump."

Agricultural pursuits are explored in Pioneer Park, but the concurrent industrialization of the country is explored in the museum. Exhibits focus on the coal mining that was significant to this region. Finally, the museum is noted for its diverse collection of weapons. Swords, sabers, matchlock rifles, blunderbusses, flintlocks and more up-to-date martial gear are displayed.

Historic Crab Orchard Museum and Pioneer Park are open year-round weekdays and Saturdays 9:00 A.M. to 5:00 P.M. and Sundays 1:00 to 5:00 P.M. They are closed on Thanksgiving, Christmas and New Year's Day plus Sundays and Mondays from November through March. Admission is charged. There is a museum shop with crafts, arts, recordings, books and toys. You can purchase refreshments and there is a picnic shelter on the grounds. For additional information call (540) 988-6755.

Directions: From I-81 at Abingdon take Alt. 58 west, then Route 19 north. Just before Tazewell you will see the museum and park on your right off Route 19/460. An alternative route is to take the I-77 Bluefield exit off I-81 and head west on Route 52, then proceed south on Route 19/460.

Natural Tunnel State Park

Hats Off to Mother Nature

Local enthusiasts claim that "the Natural Bridge is a slice of bread, while the **Natural Tunnel** is the whole loaf." It is likely that Daniel Boone, while blazing the Wilderness Trail, was the first nonindigenous explorer to see the tunnel. It wasn't, however, until 1832, a year after Lt. Col. Stephen H. Long explored the site, that it was publicized. William Jennings Bryan called it the "Eighth Wonder of the World."

This wonder was formed over a million years ago during the early glacial period when carbonic acid in the groundwater flowed through crevices and slowly dissolved the limestone and dolomite bedrock. Then the flowing water, now called Stock Creek, was likely diverted underground where for centuries it continued to carve out the 850-foot-long tunnel. Fossils have been discovered in the creek bed and embedded in the tunnel walls. The tunnel exits in a deep, semicircular basin with walls rising over 400 feet.

During the Civil War, land around the tunnel was mined for saltpeter, an essential ingredient in making gunpowder. Then in 1890, the South Atlantic and Ohio Railroad laid railroad tracks through the tunnel. When the Southern Railroad acquired the tracks in 1906, they opened a passenger line. As many as ten coal and freight trains travel through the tunnel each day.

In 1967, after acquiring the tunnel and 143 acres, the state established Natural Tunnel State Park. Subsequently, Virginia acquired 500 additional acres and the park opened in 1971. Stop at the visitor center when you arrive at the park to see the exhibits that provide additional details on the tunnel's formation and the history of the region. You can also obtain information on the park's seven hiking trails. Trails lead to the tunnel floor, to Lover's Leap, Tunnel Hill and Gorge Ridge. A 500-foot board-walk, accessible for the physically challenged, leads from the visitor center to an observation deck overlooking the gorge.

If you don't have the time or agility to hike to the bottom of the gorge, try the chairlift. The exciting ride is 536 feet long and descends 230 feet. You get a bird's eye view of the mountain slope as you descend into Stock Creek Gorge. Patrons in wheel-chairs can be accommodated on the lift. A short walk leads to the mouth of the tunnel in a natural rock amphitheater that is singularly impressive. Safety considerations prohibit walking into the tunnel.

A myriad of recreational opportunities are available at the park: hiking, swimming in a hilltop pool, camping with electric/water hookups and picnicking. There is even a small butterfly garden visible from the parking lot. Park personnel offer interpretive pro-grams focusing on local folklore, natural history and the local flora and fauna. One of the most frequently told legends is that of Winnanoah, a Cherokee maiden, who was saved from a pan-ther attack by Cochessa, a warrior chieftain. They fell in love but because they were from warring tribes were forbidden to marry. Refusing to live apart, they leapt to their death from one of the gorge's great cliffs; the spot is now called Lover's Leap.

Directions: From I-81 just over the state line in Tennessee take Route 23 to Kingsport, then continue on Route 23/58 to Duffield; signs indicate the park turn-off. The park is located only one mile from Route 23/58.

BIG STONE GAP

John Fox Jr. Museum and
The Trail of the Lonesome Pine

Fox First Million Copy Novelist

John Fox, Jr. wrote his best selling novel *The Trail of the Lone-some Pine* while living in Big Stone Gap. His 1888 house, now a Virginia Historical landmark, is a memorial to the Fox family. Kentucky-born Fox was educated at Harvard and worked as a journalist before settling in southwest Virginia. His father, who ran a prestigious boys' school, purchased the house in Big Stone Gap as a summer home for his large family. He had ten children, three sons by his first wife and five sons and two daughters by his second wife. John, Sr. retired here in 1890 while John, Jr., his oldest son by his second wife, was still in college. After graduating John, Jr. was paid $15 a week as a reporter for the New York Sun. After only a short time ill health brought him to Big Stone Gap, where his brother James was working as an engineer in the coalfields.

John was encouraged to write by his brother and sold his first fictional magazine story, which was about a young mountain girl riding an ox to the mill. Fox later lamented that he had held the story for two years before daring to submit it and the magazine held it for another two before publishing it—though they paid him the princely sum of $262 when they accepted his work. In that four year period, Fox did not write a line. He eventually became quite prolific, writing 14 full-length novels and more than 500 short stories. His most popular novel, *The Trail of the Lonesome Pine*, was set in Big Stone Gap during the boom times when coal and iron were discovered in southwest Virginia. The book tells of the love between a beautiful mountain girl and a mining engineer from the East. His authentic picture of mountain people captured the imagination of the country and gained nationwide fame for Big Stone Gap. The book was filmed three times. The last was a huge box office bonanza—it was the first outdoor Technicolor movie ever made.

The Fox family, all of whom had moved to the area, where badly hurt by the Panic of 1893 since they had invested in coal, timber and land. John's fees from the lecture circuit helped support his family and send his two younger brothers to Harvard and his sister Elizabeth to art school. But John's activities were not all cerebral. He served as a volunteer policeman in Big Stone Gap and in 1898 went to Cuba as a correspondent during the Spanish-American War. He wrote his family, "I don't suppose I shall be in as much danger once, as I was 50 times on the police force." He came under fire while covering the siege of Santiago and contracted typhoid and malaria. These experiences did not prevent him from covering the Russo-Japanese War, though he returned when Japan refused to allow correspondents anywhere near the fighting. In 1908, at age 45, John married Fritzi Scheff, a divorced Broadway operatic star. They spent their summers at Big Stone Gap and she would arrive with 11 trunks— she had the reputation of being one of the best dressed women in the country. The conflicting demands of their lifestyles eventually proved more of an obstacle than they could surmount and they divorced amicably in 1913. Fox spend his last years in Big Stone Gap. During his final illness he had his bed moved out on to the porch so that he could see the mountains he loved. He died on July 8, 1919, when he was 56.

The **John Fox Jr. Museum** is filled with family furnishings and personal touches. Over the mantel in the parlor are portraits of

John Fox Sr. and his wife; their china still fills the cabinets. A large soup tureen on the dining room table was the family's post office; they would all drop notes in the dish. Everyone in the family knew to check the tureen for messages. The children played tennis on the lawn. Seventeen family dogs are buried on the grounds that John Jr.'s wife had landscaped during one of her summer visits. Framed photographs reveal interesting glimpses of the family at various stages of their lives. There is even a framed letter from President Teddy Roosevelt to John Sr. remarking how much he enjoyed a visit by his son. Readers of the Fox oeuvre will appreciate seeing the study where he wrote his stories.

Guided house tours are given Tuesday and Wednesday from 2:00 to 5:00 P.M. and Thursday through Sunday from 2:00 to 6:00 P.M. Admission is charged.

For more than a quarter of a century, the outdoor drama, *The Trail of the Lonesome Pine*,has been presented during the summer months. Haunting folk music, homespun wit and drama make this a popular production. Here you can see how the coal boom brought changes, some welcome and some resisted, to these mountains. The heroine of Fox's story, June Tolliver, was based on a local girl named Elizabeth Morris who lived in the house adjacent to the playhouse. Elizabeth lived here while she attended school in town. Her bedroom and a 19th-century parlor are furnished. Other rooms display mountain crafts. The June Tolliver House & Craft Shop is open without charge Tuesday through Saturday 10:00 A.M. to 5:00 P.M. and Sunday 2:00 to 5:00 P.M.

Performances of the longest running outdoor drama in Virginia are Thursday, Friday and Saturday in July and August at 8:00 P.M. For tickets call (540) 523-1235.

Directions: From I-81 at Abington take Route 19/Alt 58 west. When these split, continue west on Alt. Route 58 to Route 23 into Big Stone Gap. For the John Fox, Jr. Museum make a right on E. First Street and another right on Shawnee Avenue. For the outdoor drama and the June Tolliver House, make a right turn from E. First Street on Clinton Avenue and you will see them both on the right after several blocks.

Southwest Virginia Museum and The Harry W. Meador, Jr. Coal Museum

The Story of Big Stone Gap

Stories about Virginia's rugged southwest mountain region extend back well before it was explored for the Ohio Land Company of Virginia in 1750. The land was a much-sought-after Native American hunting ground with disparate tribes vying for control. Between 1671 and 1685, the Cherokees succeeded in driving out the Xulans before being displaced themselves by the Confederacy of Six-Nations. Warring parties of Cherokees and Shawnees continued to contest the area; this strife deterred European settlement. The high, steep mountain terrain with its deep gorges was not hospitable to agriculture so those settlers who eventually ventured into the area were primarily hunters.

It wasn't until the discovery of bituminous coal in 1879 that the region realized any significant economic prosperity. To haul coal and lumber two railroads, the Louisville and Nashville and the South Atlantic and Ohio railroads, developed lines that extended to Big Stone Gap. One of the most significant towns to grow up along the tracks was Big Stone Gap. The early and boom years of the coal rush are explored in **Southwest Virginia Museum**'s main gallery. Attention is given to what was the crowning moment of the boom years, the visit of the Duke and Duchess of Marlborough, who were considering investing in the region's iron ore. This was the height of the drive to make this community the "Pittsburgh of the South," but the fact that the iron ore was not of the quality needed and the country-wide Panic of 1893 ended the dream. But not before this mining revolution brought hotels, banks, schools, a newspaper and a number of impressive Victorian houses in the section of town called Poplar Hill.

The museum is located in one of these houses, built in the 1880s by Rufus Ayers, who owned iron and coal mines in the area. Ayers served as Attorney General of Virginia from 1886 to 1890. It took seven years to build this limestone and sandstone mansion; no expensive was spared. You'll note that the floor boards were laid thin side up, making an interesting pattern and indicating an availability of lumber unheard of in other areas. The house was eventually purchased by C. Bascom Slemp, VMI graduate, eight times member of the U.S. Congress and the private secretary to President Calvin Coolidge. Slemp wanted a museum in the house that would depict life in southwest Virginia. The collection amassed by Slemp and his sister, Jane, form the nucleus of the museum's exhibits.

The mansion's second floor has galleries that tell the story of Big Stone Gap residents at the turn of the century. One way this mountain region stayed in touch with current fashion was through mail order catalog. The Sears catalog which, as you can see in the exhibit, grew from one page in 1872 to 1,036 pages in 1899, kept residents supplied with the latest merchandise. A selection of these items is displayed: a sewing machine, baby carriage, golf clubs, sled, fan and gramophone as well as clothes and personal memorabilia. There are many items associated with

C. Bascom Slemp, including those he acquired during his travels.

The third floor galleries move back in time to early exploration and settlement. You'll learn about the Wilderness Road that Daniel Boone blazed through the Cumberland Gap (see Cumberland Gap National Historical Park). Less well-known was Dr. Thomas Walker, who explored a passageway through the Western Appalachians. Native American artifacts, hunting rifles, settlers tools, a Conestoga wagon, basic household items, quilt patterns and a multitude of other exhibits tell the story of the early days.

The Southwest Virginia Museum is open Memorial Day to Labor Day, Monday through Thursday 10:00 A.M. to 4:00 P.M., Friday 9:00 A.M. to 4:00 P.M., Saturday 10:00 A.M. to 5:00 P.M. and Sunday 1:00 to 5:00 P.M. At other times of the year, the museum is closed on Monday as well as major holidays. It is closed entirely during January and February. Admission is charged. The museum has a shop with Victorian-era items as well as locally made crafts.

Just a few blocks away you can get more detailed information on the coal boom at **The Harry W. Meador, Jr. Coal Museum**. This industry defines the region, and this museum is the place to find out about the coal industry. Learn about the coal camps where the workers lived (a drive in this area will take you to some of the camps: Imboden, Lower Exeter, Exeter and Keokee) and the tools the miners used. You'll see the office equipment of Westmoreland Coal Company that owns the museum. The museum is named for company vice-president and museum founder Harry W. Meador, Jr. He personally collected, catalogued and arranged the exhibits. Meador believed that the history of the coal mining industry should be preserved and he undertook to see that it was. You'll learn that the miners were paid with script, but if they could manage to wait two weeks they could get cash. The minimum wage in 1950 was 75 cents an hour. You'll see an amazing collection of photographs of the mines and miners, as well as extensive coverage of mine disasters like the 1934 Derby Explosion.

The Henry W. Meador, Jr. Coal Museum is open year-round at no charge Wednesday through Saturday from 10:00 A.M. to 5:00 P.M. and Sunday from 1:00 to 5:00 P.M. It is located on East Third Street and Shawnee Avenue (one block north of Wood Avenue) in Big Stone Gap.

Directions: From I-81 at Abington take Route 19/Alt. 58 west. When these split, continue west on Alt. Route 58 to Route 23 into Big Stone Gap. The Southwest Virginia Museum is at the corner of West First Street and Wood Avenue, which is Business Route 23.

BLACKSBURG

Smithfield Plantation and
The Long Way Home

Mountain Laurels

In their brave hope of extending Virginia's boundaries beyond the Blue Ridge, a band of early settlers carved out homesteads in the Native American-dominated wilderness of what is now southwest Virginia in 1748. On July 30, 1755, the Shawnee Indians, who had heretofore ignored the vanguard of white settlers, attacked and massacred all but a few of the valley families. Two that survived were the Pattons and the Ingles.

Colonel James Patton, who had been given a Crown Grant of 120,000 acres in 1745, headed the valley's militia. A widower, aged 63, he took the responsibility of guarding the valley very seriously. When the French and Indian War began, George Washington stopped in the New River Valley to warn him of the war's potential danger to the settlers. As Washington had foreseen, the war did come to the valley. Colonel Patton died during an attack by indigenous tribes. The Ingles family, who farmed a small homestead on land they had purchased from Colonel Patton, were also grievously affected.

Mary Draper Ingles's mother, Elenor, who years earlier had lost her husband to marauding Braves, was killed in the massacre. Mary Ingles, 23, and her two boys, age two and four, were abducted by the Shawnees (also abducted was her sister-in-law Bettie Draper). They were forced to walk hundreds of miles to the tribal camp near what is now Cincinnati, Ohio. During their trek Mary bore a daughter. After months of captivity Mary escaped with an elderly Dutch woman. Following the Ohio River, they made their way back across 850 miles of uncharted wilderness before Mary Ingles finally rejoined her husband and brother.

This dramatic story is re-created each summer in the outdoor dramatization, *The Long Way Home*. It is performed in an amphitheater beside the Ingles Homestead in Radford, Thursday through Sunday at 8:30 P.M. For many years the role of Elenor Draper was played by her great-great-great-great granddaughter, Mary Ingles Jeffries. Reviewers of outdoor drama give high marks to this stirring production. In addition to seeing the performance visitors can tour the amphitheater and a part of the Wilderness Road. For ticket information call (540) 639-0679 or write The Long Way Home, P.O. Box 711, Radford, VA 24141. The novel,

Follow the River, by James Alexander Thom, also tells the story of Mary's kidnapping and her 42-day walk to freedom.

Despite the adversity, the Ingleses did not abandon the Virginia frontier although they did for a time move to a protective fort before returning to the New River Valley. Neither did the Patton-Preston family. From 1772 to 1774, James Patton's nephew, William Preston, who had been visiting in the New River Valley at the time of the massacre and narrowly escaped death himself, built a story-and-a-half white frame house he called **Smithfield** after his wife, Susanna Smith. Preston represented the area in the Virginia House of Burgesses and was County Surveyor, County Lieutenant, Colonel of the Militia (like his uncle) and a member of the Committee of Safety.

The Smithfield Plantation in Blacksburg is no rough country house; it is furnished in a style William Preston copied from Williamsburg. The drawing room fireplace duplicates the one that can be seen in Raleigh Tavern (see Williamsburg Tavern selection). In this formal room you'll also see a copy of the Gilbert Stuart portrait of James Patton Preston. One of William and Susanna's 12 children became governor of Virginia (1816–1819). Several terms later James's son-in-law, John Floyd, Jr. became governor (1830–1852). Another grandson, James McDowell, also served as governor (1843–1846) but unlike the others he never lived at Smithfield.

Today, only 11 of the original 2,000 acres are still part of the plantation. On these stand the house, outbuildings and interpretive gardens. Four acres are landscaped as they would have been in the 18th century with grazing lawns, shade trees and a kitchen garden of herbs, perennials, fruits and period crops. Costumed docents interpret the five period-furnished rooms: the drawing room, dining room, master chamber, schoolroom abovestairs chamber and below-stairs winter kitchen. One of the few pieces of furniture you see that belonged to the Preston family is the walnut corner cabinet in the dining room. It was made on the plantation and displays Chinese export china. The staircase to the upstairs, carved in the Chinese Chippendale pattern, also reveals the influence of the Far East. The Georgian-style looking glass in the passageway belonged to William Preston's mother. It was carried in the hold of Colonel James Patton's ship with the possessions of the senior Prestons. James Patton was originally a ship's captain from the Ulster area of Northern Ireland who sailed to ports along the "new country." He persuaded his sister and husband to bring their children to the new land. One of those children was William Preston.

Smithfield Plantation is open April to November on Thursday through Sunday from 1:00 to 5:00 P.M. Admission is charged.

Outdoor enthusiasts may want to add a stop at one of the two nearby lakes to their outing. Mountain Lake is just 20 miles north of Smithfield. Claytor Lake State Park and Camping Grounds is 30 miles south.

Directions: From I-81, take Exit 118, U.S. Route 460 By-Pass, around Christiansburg and Blacksburg. Smithfield Plantation is adjacent to the Virginia Tech campus off Route 314. For the Ingles Homestead Amphitheater take Exit 105 off I-81 and go $1/4$ mile on Route 232 toward Radford.

Calendar of Events

JANUARY

Early:
Antique Show, Charlottesville, (804) 296-8018
18th-Century Twelfth Night Celebration, Virginia Beach, (804) 431-4000
Greenberg's Great Train, Dollhouse & Toy Show, Virginia Beach, (804) 437-4774
Mid:
Hunt Country Winter Antiques Fair, Leesburg, (703) 777-3174
Winter in Williamsburg Workshops, Colonial Williamsburg, (800) 204-0571
Stratford Hall Birthday Open House, Stratford Hall, (804) 493-8038
Historic Birthday Parties in Lexington, Lexington, (540) 463-3777
Wildlife Arts Festival, Newport News, (804) 595-1900, ext. 48
Lee Birthday Celebration, Alexandria, (703) 548-1789
Late:
Ghost Watch, Centre Hill Mansion, Petersburg, (804) 733-2404
Virginia Flower & Garden Show, Virginia Beach, (804) 486-0220
Starvation Ball, Centre Hill Mansion, Petersburg, (804) 733-2400

FEBRUARY

Early:
Black History Month, Colonial Williamsburg, (800) HISTORY
African-American History Month, Stratford Hall, (804) 493-8038
Antiques Forum, Colonial Williamsburg, (804) 220-7255
Mid:
Heart of the Winter Wine Tasting Festival, Waterside, Norfolk, (804) 627-3300
African-American Heritage Trolley Tours, Portsmouth, (800) PORTS-VA
Gunston Hall Open Hall, Lorton, (703) 550-9220
Valentine's Day Celebration, Valentine Museum, Richmond, (804) 649-0711
Breakfast with George Washington, Mount Vernon, (703) 780-2000
George Washington Birthday Celebration, Alexandria, (703) 838-5005/4200/4848
Washington in Williamsburg, Colonial Williamsburg, (800) HISTORY
Mid-Atlantic Sports & Boat Show, Virginia Beach, (804) 934-7504
President's Day, Fredericksburg, (540) 373-1569
Washington's Birthday, GW Birthplace National Monument, Northern Neck, (804) 224-1732
Late:
Maymont Flower & Garden Show, Richmond, (804) 358-7166
African-American Heritage Day, Stratford Hall, (804) 493-8038

MARCH

Early:
Mid-Atlantic Wildfowl & Wildlife Festival, Virginia Beach, (804) 490-1876
Southwest Virginia Boat Show, Roanoke, (540) 981-1201
Women's History Month, Colonial Williamsburg, (800) HISTORY
Women's History Month, Stratford Hall, (804) 493-8038
Spring Festival of Crafts, Virginia Beach, (804) 496-6766
Monitor-Merrimack Battle, Newport News, (800) 362-3046
St. Patrick's Day Parade, Alexandria, (703) 838-5005/4200
Monitor-Merrimack Engagement, Norfolk, (804) 625-1720 (weekends), 664-6283 (weekdays)
Mid:
Highland Maple Festival, Highland County, (540) 468-2550
Fine Arts Exhibit, Fredericksburg, (703) 372-1086
Shamrock Sportsfest, Virginia Beach, (804) 481-5090
Spring Arts & Crafts Show, Fairfax, (703) 338-5272
St. Patrick's Day Parade, Roanoke, (540) 981-2889
St. Patrick's Day Parade, Richmond, (804) 672-0158
Knights of Columbus St. Patrick's Day Parade, Norfolk, (804) 587-3548
Military Through the Ages, Jamestown Settlement, (804) 253-4838
Gunston Hall Kite Festival, Mason Neck, (703) 550-9220
Late:
Virginia International Auto Show, Richmond, (800) 345-1487

Mid-Atlantic Home & Garden Show, Virginia Beach, (804) 420-2434
Spring Barrel Tastings & Blendings, Ingleside Plantation Winery, Oak Grove, (804) 224-8687
Kite Day, Stratford Hall, (804) 493-8038

APRIL
Early:
Daffodil Flower Show, Danville, (804) 799-5216
Portsmouth Invitational Tournament, Portsmouth, (800) PORTS-VA
Battle of Lee's Mill Re-Enactment, Endview Plantation, Newport News, (804) 247-8523
Daffodil Festival, Gloucester, (804) 693-2355
Cotswold Olympics, Adam Thoroughgood House, Virginia Beach, (804) 664-6283, 460-0007
Ocean View Spring Egg Hunt, Norfolk, (804) 441-2140
Crab Orchard Museum Open House, Taxewell, (540) 988-6755
Easter Egg Hunt, Stratford Hall, (804) 493-8038
Easter Decoy & Art Festival, Chincoteague, (804) 336-6161
Easter Weekend Celebration, Virginia Beach, (804) 491-SUNN
Easter on Parade, Richmond, (804) 643-2826
Dogwood Festival, Charlottesville, (804) 973-4121
Mid:
Jefferson's Birthday Commemoration, Monticello, Charlottesville, (804) 984-9822
Spring Garden Show, Lynchburg, (804) 847-1499
Strawberry Hill Races, Richmond, (804) 228-3200
Days of Revolution, Virginia's Explore Park, Roanoke, (540) 427-1800
Williamsburg Folk Art Show, William & Mary Hall, Williamsburg, (717) 337-3060
Williamsburg Garden Symposium, Colonial Williamsburg, (804) 220-7255
International Azalea Festival, Norfolk, (804) 622-2312
Virginia Horse Festival, Virginia Horse Center, Lexington, (540) 463-2194
Gunpowder Incident Re-Enactment, Colonial Williamsburg, (800) HISTORY
Late:
Revolutionary War Encampment & Battle Re-Enactment, Petersburg, 733-2404, 734-7490
Civil War Re-Enactment, Oak Ridge Estate, Nelson County, (804) 263-5239
Petersburg Artfest, Petersburg, (804) 733-2400
Earth Day Celebration, Virginia Living Museum, Newport News, (804) 595-1900
Garden Week in Clarke County, Burwell-Morgan Mill, (703) 837-2200
Historic Garden Week in Virginia, Statewide, (804) 644-7776
Gardening Days, Mount Vernon, (703) 780-2000
Garden Day, Centre Hill Mansion, Petersburg, (804) 733-2400
Historic Garden Day, Lynchburg, (804) 384-5315
Garden Day at Point of Honor, Lynchburg, (804) 847-1459
Garden Tour, Lexington, (540) 463-3777
Along Sidewalks & Garden Paths, Fredericksburg, (800) 678-4748
Historic Garden Week, Richmond, (804) 644-7776
Champagne & Candlelight Tour, Ash Lawn-Highland, Charlottesville, (804) 293-9539
Countryside Spring Arts & Crafts Show, Virginia Beach, (804) 486-0220
Mid-Atlantic Art Exhibition, Norfolk, (804) 625-4211
James Monroe Birthday Celebration, Monroe Presidential Center, Fredericksburg, (800) 678-4748
Chippokes Plantation Heritage Handcraft Demonstration, Surry, (804) 786-7950, 294-3439
Garden Week Tour, Alexandria, (703) 838-5005/4200
Leesburg Flower & Garden Show, Leesburg, (703) 777-1262
Virginia Wine Festival, Ash Lawn-Highland, Charlottesville, (804) 293-9539
Vino Concerto Virginia, Gunston Hall, Mason Neck, (703) 550-9220

MAY
Early:
Flying Circus Airshows (thru October), Bealeton, (540) 439-8661
Seafood Festival, Chincoteague, (804) 787-2460
Shenandoah Apple Blossom Festival, Winchester, (540) 662-3863

Greek Festival, Norfolk, (804) 440-0500
Central Virginia Scottish Festival & Games, Scotchtown, Beaverdam,
   (804) 752-6766
Pioneer Days, Covington, (540) 965-1622, 962-2178
Countryside Spring Arts & Crafts Show, Chantilly, (804) 486-0220
Virginia Gold Cup Races, The Plains, (540) 347-2612
Country Festival, Bluebird Gap Farm, Hampton, (804) 727-6739/1102
Native American PowWow, Virginia Beach, (804) 471-5884
James River Wine Festival, Richmond, (804) 359-4645
Arts in the Park, Richmond, (804) 353-8198
Cinco de Mayo, Virginia Beach, (804) 491-SUNN
Blessing of the Fleet, Reedville Harbor, (804) 453-6529
Native American Heritage Festival & PowWow, Occoneechee SP, Clarksville,
   (804) 374-2210
Mid:
Ocean View Beach Festival, Norfolk, (804) 583-0000
Wildflower Symposium, Wintergreen Resort, Nelson County, (804) 325-2200
Jamestown Landing Day, Jamestown Settlement, (804) 253-4838
Heritage Day, Clifton Forge, (540) 862-2000
Goochland Festival Day, Goochland Courthouse, (804) 556-5300
Market Square Fair, Fredericksburg, (540) 371-4504
Court Day, Rice's Hotel/Hughlett's Tavern, Heathsville, (804) 529-6224
Jamestown Weekend Encampment, Jamestown Colonial National Historical Park,
   (804)898-3400
Sheep Dog Trials, Oatlands Plantation, Leesburg, (703) 777-3174
Re-Enactment of Battle of New Market, New Market Battlefield Historical Park,
   (540) 740-3212
Ghent Art Show, Norfolk, (804) 624-1333
Mother's Day at Gunston Hall, Mason Neck, (703) 550-9220
Mother's Day Pageant, Mary Washington House, Fredericksburg,
   (540) 373-1569
New Market Day Ceremony, VMI, Lexington, (540) 464-7207
Prelude to Independence Re-Enactment, Colonial Williamsburg, (800) HISTORY
Cardboard Boat Regatta, Lake Accotink Park, Springfield,
   (703) 569-3464, 321-7081
Legends of the Beach, Francis Land House, Virginia Beach, (804) 340-1732
Town Point Renaissance Faire, Norfolk, (804) 441-2345
Prince William on the Potomac Riverfest, Leesylvania State Park, Woodbridge,
   (703) 670-0372
Appalachian Pioneer Festival, Historic Crab Orchard & Pioneer Park,
   (540) 988-6755
Virginia Mushroom & Wine Festival, Front Royal, (540) 635-3185,
   (800) 338-2576
Mayfest, Luray, (540) 743-3915
Wilderness Civil War Re-Enactment, Orange, (703) 787-9483
American Heritage Festival, Yorktown Victory Center, (804) 253-4838
18th-Century Spring Market Fair, Claude Moore Colonial Farm, (703) 442-7557
Shear Enjoyment, Gunston Hall, Mason Neck, (703) 550-9220
Late:
Highland Blue Grass Festival, Monterey, (540) 468-2550
Olden Days, Historic Smithfield, (800) 365-9339
Sheep Dog Trials, Ligon Farm, Shipman, (804) 263-5239
Sea Wall Art Show, Portsmouth Waterfront, (800) PORTS-VA
Fiesta de Primavera, Mountain Cove Vineyards, Nelson County, (804) 263-5239
Hunt Country Stable Tour, Upperville, (540) 592-3711
Pungo Strawberry Festival, Virginia Beach, (804) 721-6001
Civil War Weekend, Yorktown Colonial National Historical Park, (804) 898-3400
Oakencroft's Spring Fiesta, Oakencroft Vineyard & Winery, Charlottesville,
   (804) 296-4188
Colonial Weekends (through August), Mount Vernon, (703) 780-2000
Memorial Day Ceremonies, Fredericksburg National Cemetery, (800) 678-4748
Delaplane Strawberry Festival, Sky Meadows State Park, Delaplane,
   (540) 592-3556
Memorial Day Horse Fair & Auction, Harrisonburg, (540) 434-4482

JUNE
Early:
Draft Horse Pull, Massie Mill Ruritan Club, Nelson County, (804) 263-5239
Vintage Virginia, The Plains, (540) 253-5001
Fredericksburg Arts Festival, Fredericksburg, (703) 372-1086
Civil War Living History Encampment & Battle Re-Enactment, Stratford Hall, (804) 493-8038
Olde Towne Lantern Tours (thru August), Portsmouth, (800) PORTS-VA
Harborfest, Town Point Park, Norfolk, (804) 627-5329
Seawall Festival, Portsmouth Waterfront, (800) 296-9933, (800) PORTS-VA
Red Cross Waterfront Festival, Alexandria, (703) 838-5005, 549-8300
Boardwalk International Festival & Art Show, Virginia Beach, (804) 425-0000
Chippokes Steam & Gas Engine Show, Chippokes Plantation SP, Surry, (804) 294-3625
Middbeburg Garden Tour, Middleburg, (703) 787-9483
Mid:
Virginia Pork Festival, Emporia, (804) 634-6611
Reedville Bluefish Derby, Buzzard's Point Marina, Reedville, (804) 453-5325
James River Batteau Festival, Lynchburg, (804) 847-1811
Virginia Indian Heritage Festival, Jamestown Settlement, (804) 253-4838
Celtic Festival at Oatlands Plantation, Leesburg, (703) 777-3174
Chautauqua Festival: Arts in the Park, Wytheville, (540) 223-3365
Father's Day at Gunston Hall, Mason Neck, (703) 550-9220
18th-Century Wheat Harvest, Claude Moore Colonial Farm, McLean, (703) 442-7557
Antique Car Show, Sully Historic Site, Chantilly, (703) 437-1794
Late:
Roanoke Valley Horse Show, Salem, (540) 375-3004, (800) 288-2122
Midsummer Night Celebration, Adam Thoroughgood House, Virginia Beach, (804) 664-6283
Hampton Jazz Festival, Hampton, (804) 838-4203, or after 4/1 727-1102
Bayou Boogaloo & Cajun Food Festival, Norfolk, (804) 441-2345
Dairy Days at Mount Vernon, Mount Vernon, (703) 780-2000
Tidewater Scottish Festival & Clan Gathering, Chesapeake City Park, (804) 587-4126
Jazz in the Courtyard, Ingleside Plantation Winery, Oak Grove, (804) 224-8687
Tri-Berry Festival, Westmoreland Berry Farm, Oak Grove, (804) 224-9171
War of 1812 & the Battle of Craney Island Re-Enactment, Norfolk, (804) 664-6283, 625-1720
Fort Days at Explore, Virginia's Explore Park, Roanoke, (540) 427-1800
Ash Lawn-Highland Summer Festival (thru mid-August), Charlottesville, (804) 293-4500
Hanover Tomato Festival, Mechanicsville, (804) 798-1722
British Occupation of Williamsburg Re-Enactment, Colonial Williamsburg, (800) HISTORY
Nelson County Summer Festival, Oak Ridge Estate, (804) 263-5239

JULY
Early:
Monticello Independence Day Celebration, Charlottesville, (804) 984-9822
Fourth at the Fort, Fort Monroe, Hampton, (804) 727-3207/1102
Independence Day Celebration, Yorktown, (804) 890-3300
Fredericksburg Heritage Festival, Fredericksburg, (800) 678-4748
Heritage Festival, Crab Orchard Museum & Pioneer Park, Tazewell, (540) 988-6755
Fourth of July Open House, Stratford Hall, (804) 493-8038
Independence Day Celebration, Colonial Williamsburg, (800) HISTORY
Great American Picnic Town Point Air Show, Norfolk Town Point Park, (804) 441-2345
Independence Day Celebration, Red Hill, Brookneal, (804) 376-2044
Independence Day at Thomas Jefferson's Poplar Forest, Forest, (804) 525-1806
Children's Colonial Days Fair, Yorktown Victory Center, (804) 253-4838
Plantation Days at Highland, Ash Lawn-Highland, Charlottesville, (804) 293-9539
Mid:
Bastille Day Ball, Moses Myers House, Norfolk, (804) 664-6283
Bell'Italia, Airlie Farm, Warrenton, (540) 349-4133

Cock Island Race, Portsmouth, (800) 296-9933, (800) PORTS-VA

Late:

Hungry Mother Arts & Crafts Festival, Hungary Mother SP, Marion, (540) 783-3161

African-American Heritage Day, GW Birthplace National Monument, (804) 224-1732

Pork, Peanut & Pine Festival, Chippokes State Park, Surry, (804) 294-3625

Naval Rendevous & VA Military Muster, Fort Norfolk, (804) 664-6283, 625-1720

18th-Century Summer Market Fair, Claude Moore Colonial Farm, McLean, (703) 442-7557

Pony Swim & Auction, Chincoteague, (804) 336-6161

Seafood Fling at Fort Monroe, Hampton, (804) 727-3151/4248

Virginia Scottish Games, Alexandria, (703) 838-5005/4200

First Assembly Day Commemoration, Jamestown Colonial Nat. Historical Park, (804)898-3400

Mountain Heritage, Skyland, Luray, (540) 743-5108

Virginia Highlands Festival, Abingdon, (800) 435-3440

AUGUST

Early:

Munderly Antiques Show, Virginia Beach, (804) 486-0220

Virginia Mountain Peach Festival, Roanoke, (540) 342-2028

Thomas Jefferson's Tomato Faire, Lynchburg, (804) 847-1499

Civil War Re-Creation, Oatlands Plantation, Leesburg, (703) 777-0519

Old Fiddler's Convention, Galax, (540) 236-2184

Mid:

Street Scene, Covington, (540) 962-2178

Hoover Days, Madison, (540) 948-5121

Civil War Encampment, Evelynton Plantation, Charles City, (800) 473-5075

Carytown Watermelon Festival, Richmond, (804) 359-4645

Virginia Peach Festival, Critz, (540) 694-6012

Lower Potomac Bluefish Tournament, White Point Marina, Kinsale, (804) 472-2977

Vinton Old-Time Bluegrass Festival & Competition, Vinton, (540) 983-0613

Hampton Cup Regatta Summer Nationals, Mill Creek at Fort Monroe, (804) 722-5343, 727-1102

Native American Heritage Day, GW Birthplace National Monument, (804) 224-1732

August Court Days, Leesburg, (703) 777-0519

18th-Century Tobacco Harvest, Claude Moore Colonial Farm, McLean, (703) 442-7557

Late:

Tastes of Smithfield, Old Courthouse, Smithfield, (800) 365-9339

Town Point Jazz Festival, Norfolk, (804) 441-2345

Pasture Party, Somerset, (540) 672-3429/2495

Cabbage Festival, Poor Farmers Farm, Meadows of Dan, (540) 952-2560

Guest River Rally, Coeburn, (540) 395-3323

General Muster/Publick Times, Colonial Williamsburg, (800) HISTORY

Draft Horse & Mule Day, Oatlands Plantation, Leesburg, (703) 777-3174

Oakencroft Harvest Festival, Oakencroft Vineyard, Charlottesville, (804) 296-4188

SEPTEMBER

Early:

Religion Month, Colonial Williamsburg, (800) HISTORY

Kaleidoscope, Lynchburg, (804) 847-1811

Labor Day Celebration, Valentine Museum, Richmond, (804) 649-0711

James River Fishing Jamboree, Scottsville, (804) 286-4800

Blue Ridge Highlands Storytelling Festival, Crab Orchard Museum, Tazewell, (540) 988-6755

Claytor Lake Arts & Crafts Festival, State Park, Dublin, (540) 674-5492

Neptune Festival, Virginia Beach, (804) 498-0215

Washington County Fair & Burley Tobacco Festival, Abingdon, (540) 628-8141

Harvest of Characters at Gunston Hall, Mason Neck, (703) 550-9220

Mid:

Orange Street Festival, Orange, (540) 672-5216

Hampton Bay Days, Hampton, (804) 727-6122/1102

Batteau Day, Appomattox River Park, Petersburg, (804) 733-2400

Northern Neck Seafood Extravaganza, Ingleside Plantation Winery, Oak Grove, (804) 224-8687
Civil War Union Army Garrison Day, Fort Ward Park, Alexandria, (703) 838-4848
Citie of Henricus Publick Day, Henricus Historical Park, (804) 748-1623
Quilt Show, Sully Historic Site, Chantilly, (703) 437-1794
Late:
Edinburg Ole' Time Festival, Edinburg, (540) 984-8521
Virginia Peanut Festival, Emporia, (804) 348-3378
Tour of Historic Alexandria Homes, Alexandria, (703) 838-5005, 751-3391
Fall Hunt Country Antiques Fair, Oatlands Plantation, Leesburg, (703) 777-3174
Festival Cultural Hispano, Valentine Museum, Richmond, (804) 649-0711
State Fair of Virginia, Richmond, (804) 288-3200
A Little Welsh Festival, Monroe Presidential Center, Fredericksburg, (800) 678-4748
Arts & Crafts Festival, Blackstone, (804) 292-1677
Smith Mountain Lake Wine Festival, Moneta, (800) 676-8203
Apple Harvest & Apple Butter Festival, Nelson County, (804) 263-5239

OCTOBER
Early:
Ghosts, Graveyards and Legends Walking Tours, Alexandria, (703) 838-5005, 548-0100
Archeology Month, Stratford Hall, (804) 493-8038
Williamsburg Craft & Folk Art Show, William & Mary Hall, (717) 337-3060
Waterford Homes Tour & Crafts Exhibit, Waterford, (703) 882-3085
North-South Skirmish, Gainesboro, (540) 888-7917
Virginia Children's Festival, Town Point Park, Norfolk, (804) 441-2345
Monticello Baccahanalian Feast, Boar's Head Inn, Charlottesville, (804) 296-4188
Newport News Fall Festival, Newport News Park, (804) 247-8451
Eastern Shore Birding Festival, Kiptopeke State Park, Cape Charles, (804) 331-2267
Fall Fiber Festival & Sheep Dog Trials, Montpelier, (540) 672-2935
Living History at Historic Fort Boykin, Smithfield, (800) 365-9339
Sorghum Festival, Clifford, (804) 946-5168
African-American Life at Gunston Hall, Mason Neck, (703) 550-9220
National Wildlife Refuge Week, Back Bay NWR, Virginia Beach, (804) 721-2412
Mid:
Danville Harvest Jubilee, Danville, (804) 799-5200
Wise Famous Fall Fling, Wise Courthouse Lawn, (540) 679-4461, 328-0128
Stamp Act Crisis Re-Enactment, Colonial Williamsburg, (800) HISTORY
Chincoteague Oyster Festival, Chincoteague, (804) 336-6161
Civil War Day Encampment, Portsmouth, (800) PORTS-VA
Appalachian Celtic Festival, Historic Crab Orchard Museum, Tazewell, (540) 988-6755
Festival of Leaves, Front Royal, (540) 636-1446
Full Moon Hayride & Bonfire, Westmoreland Berry Farm, Oak Grove, (804) 224-9171
Wine & Seafood Festival, GW Boyhood Home at Ferry Farm, Fredericksburg, (540) 659-8681
Historic Appomattox Railroad Festival, Appomattox, (804) 352-2338/2621
National Jousting Championship Tournament, Oatlands Plantation, Leesburg, (301) 371-4924
Halloween at Crab Orchard, Historic Crab Orchard Museum, Tazewell, (540) 988-6755
Late:
Clifton Forge Fall Foliage Festival, Clifton Forge, (540) 862-4969, 863-3181
Oktoberfest, Dominion Winery, Culpeper, (540) 825-4416
Log Homes Tour, Covington, (540) 962-2178
Town Point Virginia Wine Festival, Norfolk, (804) 441-2345
Aldie Harvest Festival, Aldie, (703) 327-6742
Mountain Foliage Weekend, Claypool Hill, (540) 964-7588
Battle of Cedar Creek Re-Enactment, Middletown, (540) 869-2064
Chesapeake Bay Maritime Festival & Classic Boat Show, Norfolk, (804) 441-2345
Yorktown Victory Celebration, Yorktown Victory Center & Battlefield, (804) 898-3400
Farm Color Tour of the Loudoun Valley, Loudoun County, (703) 777-0426

18th-Century Autumn Market Fair, Claude Moore Colonial Farm, (703) 442-7557
Virginia Festival of American Film, Univ. Of Va., Charlottesville, (800) UVA-FEST
Olde Towne Ghost Walk, Portsmouth, (800) PORTS-VA
Needlework Exhibit at Oatlands Plantation, Leesburg, (703) 777-3174
Ghosts of Fort Norfolk, Norfolk, (804) 664-6283 weekdays, 625-1720 weekends
Blue Ridge Octoberfest, Front Royal, (800) 338-2576
Zoo Boo, Mill Mountain Zoo, Roanoke, (540) 343-3241
Virginia Craft & Folk Art Festival, Annandale, (717) 337-3060
Historic Hauntings, A Family Trick or Treat, Alexandria, (703) 838-5005/4200
Ghostly Weekend Candlelight Tours, Petersburg, (804) 733-2402

NOVEMBER
Early:
Urbanna Oyster Festival, Urbanna, (804) 758-0368
Heritage Antiques Show, Purcellville, (703) 338-6381
Holiday in the Valley Craft Show, Salem, (540) 375-3004, (800) 288-2122
Montpelier Hunt Races, Montpelier, Orange County, (540) 672-2728
Autumn Antique Tours & Buggy Rides, Lovingston, Nelson County, (804) 263-5239
Virginia Thanksgiving Festival, Berkeley Plantation, Charles City, (804) 272-3226
Kenmore Needlework Exhibit, Kenmore Plantation, Fredericksburg,
  (540) 373-3381, ext. 3
Black Powder Blast, Bedford, (804) 299-5080
Oyster Festival, Reedville Fishermen's Museum, (804) 453-6529
Mid:
Crafts Show, Fredericksburg, (703) 372-1086
Countryside Christmas Market, Chantilly, (804) 486-0220
Christmas at the Kurtz, Winchester, (540) 722-6367
18th-Century Threshing Day, Claude Moore Colonial Farm, McLean,
  (703) 442-7557
Late:
Grand Illumination Parade, Norfolk, (804) 623-1757
Assateague Island Waterfowl Week, Chincoteague National Wildlife Refuge VC,
  (804) 336-6122
Thanksgiving at Crab Orchard Museum, Tazewell, (540) 988-6755
Holiday Lights at the Beach, Virginia Beach, (804) 463-1940
Celebration in Lights, Newport News, (804) 247-8451
Lighted Boat Parade, Norfolk, (804) 623-1757

DECEMBER
Early:
Christmas at Oatlands Plantation, Leesburg, (703) 777-3174
Holiday House Tour, Winchester, (540) 667-3577
Christmas in Court End, Richmond, (804) 649-0711
Christmas at Point of Honor, Lynchburg, (804) 847-1459
Trains at Christmas Model Train Show, Fredericksburg, (540) 374-5596
Mount Vernon by Moonlight, Mount Vernon, (703) 780-2000
Hampton Holly Days, Hampton, (804) 727-6429/1102
A Yorktown Christmas, Yorktown Victory Center, (804) 253-4838
Christmas Open House at Morven Park, Leesburg, (703) 777-2414
Holiday Open House, Belmont, Fredericksburg, (540) 654-1015
A Pioneer Christmas, Historic Crab Orchard Museum, Tazewell, (540) 988-6755
Old Towne Christmas, Petersburg, (804) 733-2400
A Plantation Christmas at Gunston Hall, Mason Neck, (703) 550-9220
Christmas at Historic Long Branch, Millwood, (540) 837-1856
Abram's Delight Candlelight Tour, Winchester, (540) 662-6550
Yuletide Traditions, Ash Lawn-Highland, Charlottesville, (804) 293-9539
A Victorian Christmas, Fredericksburg, (800) 678-4748
Scottish Christmas Walk, Alexandria, (703) 838-5005, 549-0111
Festival of Lights Parade, Roanoke, (540) 981-2889
Holiday Tour, Orange County, (540) 672-1653
Ye Olde Salem Christmas, Salem, (540) 375-3057
Christmas in Colonial Chatham, Fredericksburg, (804) 432-1640
Holidays with the Monroes, Monroe Presidential Center, Fredericksburg,
  (800) 678-4748
Christmas Candlelight Tour, Fredericksburg, (540) 371-4504

Christmas in Smithfield, Historic Smithfield, (800) 365-9339
Christmas in Historic Abingdon, Abingdon, (800) 435-3440
Operation Decorama, Norfolk Naval Base (804) 444-7637
Grand Illumination, Colonial Williamsburg, (800) HISTORY
Mid:
Civil War Christmas, Fort Ward Park, Alexandria, (703) 838-4848
Holiday Open House, Ingleside Plantation Winery, Oak Grove, (804) 224-8687
Christmas Candlelight Celebration, Stratford Hall, (804) 493-8038
Civil War Christmas in the Field, Endview Plantation, Newport News, (804) 247-8523
Old Town Christmas Candlelight Tour, Alexandria, (703) 838-4200/5005
Christmas Open House at Centre Hill Mansion, Petersburg, (804) 733-2400
Anniversary of the Battle of Fredericksburg, Kirkland Memorial, Sunken Road, (800) 678-4748
18th-Century Christmas Wassail, Claude Moore Colonial Farm, McLean, (703) 442-7557
Gingerbread House Contest & Exhibit, Crowninshield Museum, Fredericksburg, (703) 373-3381
Late:
A Jamestown Christmas, Jamestown Settlement, (804) 253-4838
Appalachian Mountain Christmas, Wintergreen Resort, Nelson County, (804) 325-2200
Yuletide at the Mariners' Museum, Newport News, (804) 596-2222
First Night, Alexandria, (703) 836-1526
First Night Virginia, Charlottesville, (804) 296-8269
First Night, Norfolk, (804) 441-2345
First Night, Leesburg, (703) 771-2707
First Night, Roanoke, (540) 342-2640
First Night, Winchester, (540) 722-6367

INDEX

347

About the Author

Jane Ockershausen, born in Richmond, bred in Maryland and now living in Pittsburgh, has been writing about Virginia for more than two decades. When she returned recently to revise her One-Day Trip Book for its eleventh printing, she explored two regions that were not included in earlier editions: the Southwest Blue Ridge Highlands and the Eastern Shore. She was especially pleased to discover that the legendary Virignia hospitality was as real and warm as ever.

Jane became a best-selling author of nine One-Day Trip Books for the Mid-Atlantic region concentrating on the popular weekend travel market. She was a correspondent for *The National Geographic Traveler* for several years, and her byline appears in *The Washington Post*, *The Chicago Tribune*, *Mid-Atlantic Weekends Magazine*, and numerous other publications.

She serves on the Board of Directors of the Society of American Travel Writers and is a member of the American Society of Journalists and Authors. Active on the lecture circuit, Jane has addressed numerous statewide conferences on travel and tourism and lectured at the Smithsonian Institution in Washington.